HEAVENLY FATHERLAND

German Missionary Culture and Globalization in the Age of Empire

GERMAN AND EUROPEAN STUDIES

General Editor: Jennifer L. Jenkins

Heavenly Fatherland

German Missionary Culture and Globalization in the Age of Empire

JEREMY BEST

UNIVERSITY OF TORONTO PRESS
Toronto Buffalo London

Toronto Buffalo London
utorontopress.com

ISBN 978-1-4875-0563-9 (cloth)
ISBN 978-1-4875-3245-1 (EPUB)
ISBN 978-1-4875-3244-4 (PDF)

German and European Studies

Library and Archives Canada Cataloguing in Publication

Title: Heavenly fatherland: German missionary culture and globalization in the Age of Empire / Jeremy Best.
Names: Best, Jeremy, 1979– author.
Series: German and European studies.
Description: Series statement: German and European studies | Includes bibliographical references and index.
Identifiers: Canadiana (print) 20200377639 | Canadiana (ebook) 20200378309 | ISBN 9781487505639 (hardcover) | ISBN 9781487532451 (EPUB) | ISBN 9781487532444 (PDF)
Subjects: LCSH: Missions, German – Africa – History – 19th century. | LCSH: Missionaries – Germany – History – 19th century. | LCSH: Missionaries – Africa – History – 19th century. | LCSH: Protestant churches – Missions – Germany – History – 19th century. | LCSH: Christianity and politics – Germany – Protestant churches – History – 19th century. | LCSH: Africa – Colonization – History – 19th century. | LCSH: Germany – Colonies – Africa – History – 19th century. | LCSH: Imperialism.
Classification: LCC BV2240.G3 B47 2021 | DDC 266/.0234306–dc23

The German and European Studies series is funded by the DAAD with funds from the German Federal Foreign Office.

Deutscher Akademischer Austauschdienst
German Academic Exchange Service

University of Toronto Press acknowledges the financial assistance to its publishing program of the Canada Council for the Arts and the Ontario Arts Council, an agency of the Government of Ontario.

Canada Council for the Arts Conseil des Arts du Canada

Funded by the Government of Canada Financé par le gouvernement du Canada
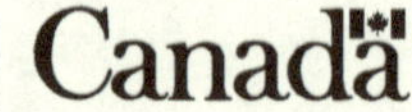

To Mom, who just missed it,

and

For Amy, Ben, and Noah

Contents

Illustrations

Acknowledgments

I didn't know how to do any of this when I started. But, along the way, countless generous people taught me how to do it. I hope these acknowledgments can do justice to those who generously supported me and my work. Any errors that remain in this book are mine, not theirs.

I have studied and worked at several excellent universities during the writing of this book. I owe thanks to the Department of History and the Graduate College of the University of Maryland, College Park, where this book began. At Appalachian State University in Boone, North Carolina, I worked for two years as a contingent faculty member; even so, I always felt welcomed by the faculty in the Department of History there. Later at Iowa State University, my research has received support from the Department of History, the College of Liberal Arts and Sciences, the Center for Excellence in the Arts and Humanities, the Faculty Senate, and the Office of the Vice President for Research. Support for the research and writing of this book also came from the German-American Fulbright Commission and the Institute for International Education, who financed a year of research in Germany at the beginning of the project. Additional support came from the German Historical Institute in Washington, DC, for research conducted in the United States. I could not have completed the work necessary for this book without these institutions' generous support.

Thanks to the generosity of those institutions, I was able to travel to archives and libraries in Germany, Poland, and the United States. In every instance, I encountered accomplished, knowledgeable, and generous professionals whose knowledge of their own collections eased the task of locating hard to find and, occasionally, obscure sources; without the skills of such specialists, academic histories like this would be impossible. In Germany, the staff at the following institutions provided peerless service and advice: the Bundesarchiv, Geheimes Staatsarchiv

Preußischer Kulturbesitz, Staatsbibliothek zu Berlin, and Kirchliches Archivzentrum – Landeskirchliches Archiv der EKBO, all in and around Berlin; the Hauptarchiv Bethel in Bielefeld; the Studienzentrum August Hermann Francke – Archiv und Bibliothek in Halle; and the Unitätsarchiv in Herrnhut. In Poland, I conducted research in the Archiwum Państwowe w Koszalinie oddział w Słupsku in Koszalin; the Archiwum Państwowe w Szczecinie in Szczecin; the Archiwum Państwowe w Wrocławiu in Wrocław; and the Archiwum Państwowe w Zielonej Górze in Zielona Gora; every archivist in Poland accommodated my linguistic limitations with grace and patience. In the United States, I conducted research with the incredible librarians at the Library of Congress in Washington, DC.

I needed a lot of help along the way to make sense of my own research. At Maryland, Jeffrey Herf proved a boundlessly supportive and demanding mentor. His experience and generosity were invaluable. His rigorous standard for research and analysis elevates my expectations for my own work. Andrew Zimmerman at George Washington University graciously agreed to give his time to support my work, and his kind guidance helped keep me working through some of the more difficult phases of the project. Paul Landau, an outstanding historian of southern Africa, provided similar mentorship and support. He never feared to give me a critical push; at the same time his care and concern were never in doubt. Richard Price at Maryland provided invaluable advice based on his experience with missionary sources and the literature of imperial history. Other faculty in Maryland's excellent history department provided invaluable mentorship at other times. It is my pleasure to specifically thank Thomas Zeller and Marsha L. Rozenblit. Finally, after my year of research in Germany, I had the wonderful opportunity to present my work at the Transatlantic Doctoral Seminar in German History hosted by the German Historical Institute and the BMW Center for German and European Studies. One of the faculty advisers at that seminar was Kenneth Ledford. Since we met there, Ken has served as a steady source of kindness and professional guidance, offering a model of mentorship that I cherish.

Transforming idle musings into meaningful scholarship relies as much on peers as it does on mentors. Over a dozen years of attending presentations at seminars, colloquia, conferences, and workshops I have received invaluable commentary and questions from panellists and members of the audience. My thanks go to all of them. A double handful of friends and colleagues deserve special mention for reading some or all of this manuscript as I wrote and revised it. They are Adam Blackler, Kierra Crago-Schneider, Glen Goodman, Amy Rutenberg,

Willeke Sandler, Kevin M. Vander Schel, Sean A. Wempe, Courtney Wilson, and Albert Wu. I would also like to thank the three anonymous readers engaged by University of Toronto Press; their comments and suggestions have improved the book's argument and format. Kate Blackmer designed the maps in this book. The creation of those maps coincided with the first weeks of the COVID-19 pandemic, when I was nearly overwhelmed by the demands of childcare and transition to remote teaching. During that moment, Kate showed me exceptional professional kindness and generosity. Finally, Stephen Shapiro, my editor at Toronto, has supported this manuscript from our first interaction when I cold pitched it to him. His commitment to the book has shown through in his exceptional patience with my many anxious and naïve questions.

Long before this project began, I graduated from a math and science high school. Despite the school's purpose, it was there that I met two amazing educators, Dr Claiborne Skinner and Ms Jackie White. Together they taught me what fun serious study of the humanities could be. I hope they are proud to know that they saved me from what would have been a misspent life as an engineer.

One cannot spend this long on a project and not incur debts to friends. In my life I have been blessed with a number of dear friends whose advice and companionship made completing this project possible. At Maryland, Tony Glocke, Andrew Kellett, Melissa Kravetz, Stefan and Helena Papaiounnou, and Charles V. Reed peopled the seminars and social hours. In Berlin, the seemingly interminable winter and too brief summer were made easier by the company of Yve Andrassy, Lauren Stokes, Kira Thurman, Heidi Tworek, and Uwe Schult. Friends "Up the Mountain" in North Carolina eased the challenges of contingent facultydom; Edward Behrend-Martinez, Kristen and Jason Deathridge, Mary Valante, Benno Weiner, and Jason White were fabulous colleagues and friends. Finally, my colleagues at Iowa State University have cheered me on in the development of this book. Included among those colleagues are the graduate students whose energy infuses the department with life and whose teaching labour empowers our students and supports the production of books like this one. Iowa State's Department of History demonstrates the wonderful potential of a land grant university, with its commitment to scholarship, teaching, and service to the community.

Though these many friends and colleagues have shown faith in my work, the strongest cheerleaders have always been those bound to me by family ties. Before thanking my "official" family, let me first thank the dozens of childcare workers and teachers who enable me to consider myself a working father. Speaking of which, my father, Herbert Best, a retired high school social studies teacher, and my mother, Linda Best, a retired non-profit professional, taught me the values of scholarship, education, and service. They encouraged me throughout my childhood and supported my decision to pursue a PhD, despite the uncertain future that might offer. They deserve infinite praise. My big brother, Chris Best, is also my best friend. Amazingly he has remained what he was to me when we were children: the smartest, funniest, coolest guy I know. His wife, Anna, and daughter, Abigail, are some of the best people on this planet. Halfway through graduate school, my family expanded to include an exceptional set of in-laws. Joel Rutenberg and his wife Virginia Tate have provided and continue to provide respite with many a Sunday brunch. Rebecca Becker Rutenberg is an astoundingly generous woman to whom I owe much more than can be accounted adequately. I consider my brothers-in-law Adam and David Rutenberg my friends; I am proud to know them. Their wives, Julie MacCartee and Marissa Conrad, serve as loyal allies against these Rutenbergs. Imogen and Edith Rutenberg are the most recent additions to this family and I look forward to knowing them as they continue to grow. It has been a blessing to have such an extensive extended family.

Saving the best for last, I turn to the very centre of my world. More than fifteen years ago I met Amy Rutenberg. She is my favourite. Everything she does makes me want to do my own work as well as she does hers. She is an extraordinary scholar, colleague, teacher, and partner. Together we have endured the challenges of a dual-scholar household – professional precarity, geographic relocations, archival separations, committee meetings, and the chaos of young children. Her patience, wisdom, and love have made it *mostly* easy. Ben and Noah, our sons, make this whole thing go 'round. Ben came while I was finishing the dissertation and Noah came while I was finishing this book. On the chance that they one day read the acknowledgments Dad wrote in his book, I want to make sure I write how proud of them I am and how much I look forward to watching them grow into who they want to be. Muh Boys fill my heart to bursting and show me just what joy and love are all about. Along with Amy, they are my Bestenbergs and I love them every minute. This book would never have come to be without the collective commitment of our entire family, I hope they appreciate just how much of them is in these pages.

HEAVENLY FATHERLAND

German Missionary Culture and Globalization in the Age of Empire

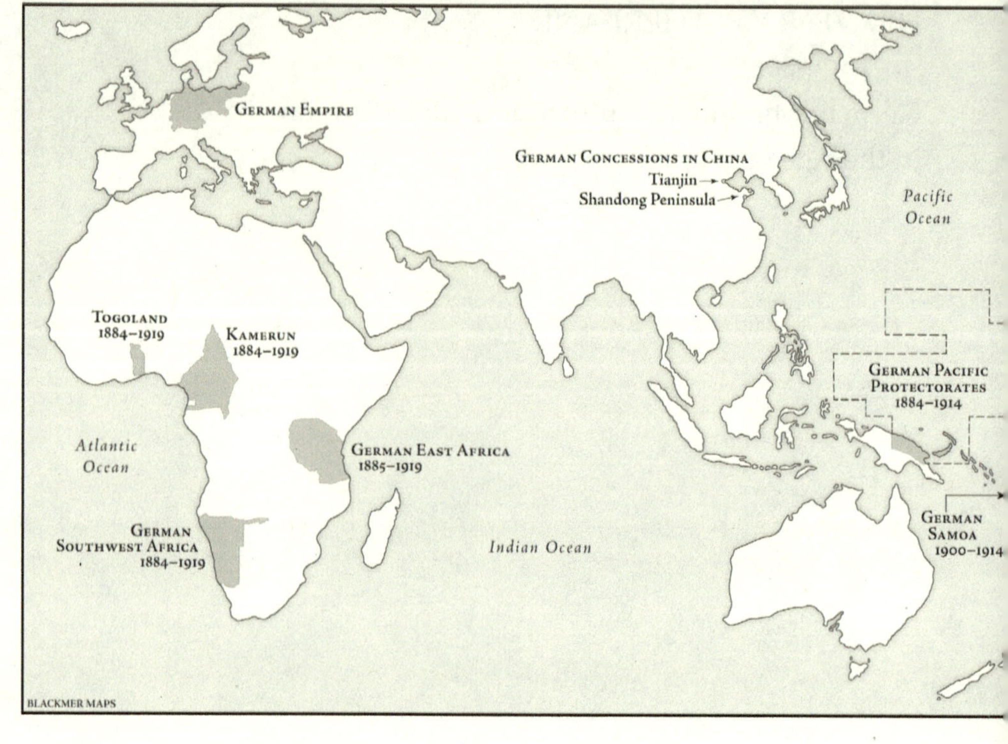

I.1. The German Empire and colonial holdings

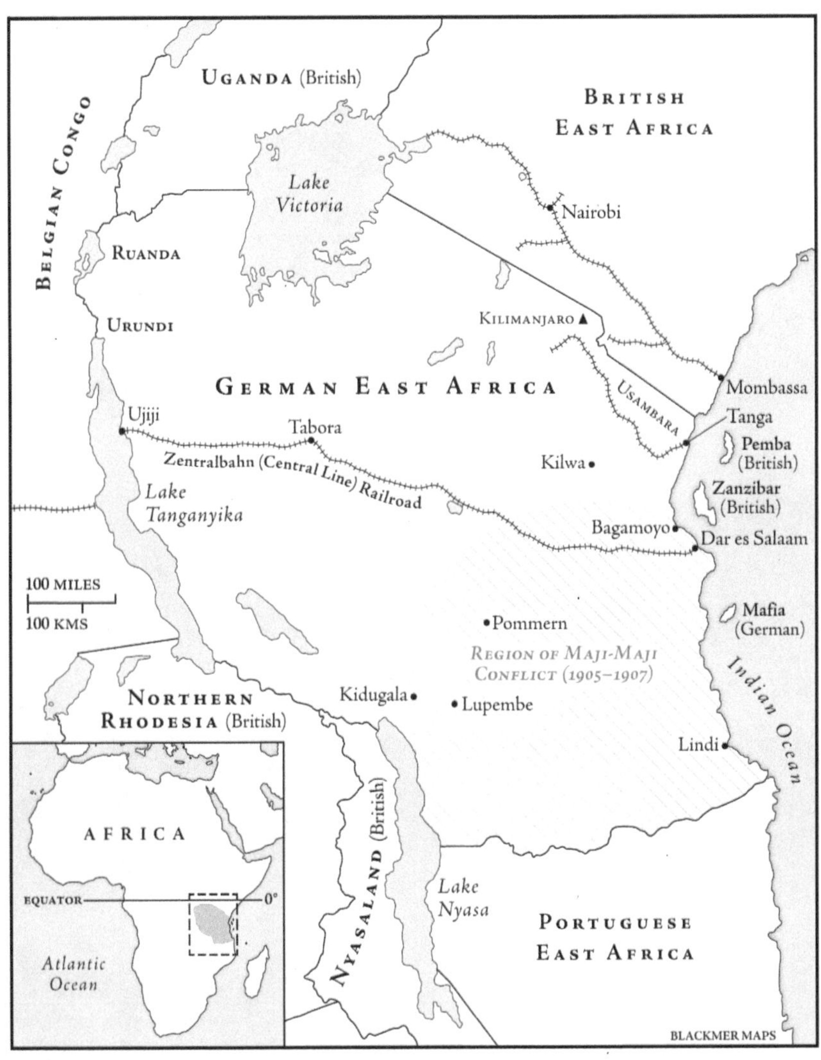

I.2. German East Africa, circa 1914

Introduction

In the beginning were the words. Words said, words written, words read by German Protestants seeking knowledge of God, knowledge of the world, and knowledge of other people. Words that stretched across oceans and empires, that stitched together ideas and communities in new and emerging ways, thanks to globalization. And for Germany's Protestant missionaries during the nineteenth-century age of empires, there were so many words. For the nineteenth century was a remarkably textual age. Technological innovations in printmaking and publication, along with the gradual extension of industrial prosperity into more households, meant that more printed words could rest on the desks and tables of more people. Rising literacy also meant that more people sought out printed matter on a variety of subjects. Private communication expanded as well. In the cities, mail might be delivered several times a day, a clear sign of the expanding personal and business correspondence that demanded regular collection and distribution. Regular train and steamship service meant that distance became less impediment to prompt delivery of messages from abroad. Still quicker communications came at the speed of electricity via telegraph. The ability to transcribe, transmit, receive, and reply made possible the expansion of new empires and the expansion of European imperial power.

The missionaries' outlook and behaviour were extraordinarily textual in an already textual age. And their activities and thoughts matched the colonial and imperial trends of the age. The explosion of text served the interests of the German Protestant mission movement as it added its own fair share of words and pages. Sixteen different mission societies led the way in a nationwide movement that produced dozens of journals and millions of pages of correspondence. The missionaries came by their productivity honestly; Germany's mission movement sprang from the Bible-focused Pietist movement of earlier centuries. Pietists' focus on personal devotion and individual transformation took root in Baden and Württemberg, Saxony, and Prussia first in the seventeenth and again in the early nineteenth century. The movement directed its Christian energies toward small Bible study groups for personal introspection and improvement. In time, the initially insular focus of evangelical and activist energies begat a movement directed toward the improvement of the world. The same forces of industrialization and capitalism that promoted the spread of text also underwrote Western colonial expansion. Especially in Germany in the nineteenth century, Pietism's revivalism spurred a turn to the salvation of the world through Christian mission, a turn facilitated and encouraged by the same period's political and economic drive to build empires.

Born from small circles of Protestants engrossed in scriptural texts, the mission movement in Germany came into its own during the second half of the nineteenth century, when it came under the guidance of a second group of book-obsessed Germans. The creation of a new academic discipline, *Missionswissenschaft* (mission studies or missiology), by a handful of academically trained mission pastors, led to a proliferation of academic texts and the launch of a major academic journal, the *Allgemeine Missions-Zeitschrift*. Imperial circumstances and geographies enabled the expansion of horizons as German missionaries rode the waves of global imperialism into colonial spaces. The work of the missionaries in those spaces provided content for mission society members and missionary academics who came together at regular conferences, conferences which published their proceedings and added still more to the reams of missionary texts. Missionswissenschaftliche texts joined the many periodicals produced by *each* mission society – magazines for families, for children, for women, and for juveniles and young adults. The various mission and religious publishing houses also released hundreds of pamphlets and missionary tracts. Gradually, Germans became inundated with more and more sophisticated texts on mission work. As a result, consumers of missionary writings could read material ranging from academic discourse on global linguistics to indigenous storytelling, transcribed and interpreted by missionaries.[1]

Beyond their deep interest in the production, dissemination, and elaboration of texts for consumption by German audiences, Germany's Protestant missionaries' textual faith shaped their works among "heathens." German missionaries devoted themselves to the study and literalization of indigenous languages. Their projects included the production of grammars and textbooks, religious tracts, and, especially, translations of the Gospels, Epistles, and, ultimately, the full Bible. Missionaries' efforts to create Christian texts in indigenous languages were part of a program to promote literacy in languages that were, in most of Africa and Oceania, preliterate up until the nineteenth century. While producing texts in languages that were new to them, the missionaries documented their observations and activities among colonized and missionized peoples in published and unpublished German texts. With these texts, the missionaries spread knowledge of the world to German-speaking audiences. And, intentionally and unintentionally, they facilitated the traumatic transformation of colonized peoples' worlds.

This book takes the vast corpus of texts produced by the German missionary movement as its source material. Its subject is the political, cultural, and intellectual history of German Protestant missionaries between 1860 and the First World War. It reveals the centrality of these missionaries to Germany's colonial and global history during that period. German Protestant missionaries' use and production of text introduced Christian universalist inclusivity to German culture and produced less particularist and nationalist interpretations of nineteenth-century politics and culture for ordinary Germans to consume. Missionaries brought Protestant believers and their beliefs into contact with the many forces that characterized Germans' confrontation with modernity in the decades before the First World War. And yet, missionaries have received little attention as a political or cultural force in Germany.[2] This work responds by integrating the missionary movement into the wider historical narrative and advocating a revision to prevailing ideas about German colonial history.

Historians of German colonialism have shown that German influence extended beyond its less grand but still immense and relatively short-lived colonial empire. Many of the same historians have also shown that expanding contact with non-Western peoples provoked debates that altered German society.[3] This contact created a specifically German colonial culture that elaborated a contested but cohesive understanding of what it meant for Germany to be a global, imperial power.

Germany's colonial period may have been shorter than those of other nations, but it nonetheless lasted longer than the Third Reich and its predecessor, the Weimar Republic, put together. Research into this important period has, first of all, demonstrated that Germany's colonial history predates the formal annexations of the 1880s. Germans participated in the projects of other colonial powers for centuries and fantasized about their own colonial possibilities for at least a century before German unification.[4] By the end of the nineteenth century, formal colonial empire had become a core feature of German culture and politics. Colonial enthusiasts from the upper classes of Germany, especially the bourgeoisie, promoted an elite vision of colonialism even as they failed to recognize the breadth and enthusiasm of working-class, popular colonialists. Together members of both classes imbricated metropolitan culture with colonial themes of adventure and opportunity.[5] The Germans were enthusiastic colonizers who, even if they had wanted to, could not have avoided a "colonization" of their own culture.

Central to this other colonization project were efforts to educate Germans about the empire, the world, and modernity – whatever that was. Colonial discourse undertook to convey to the German public some sense of the era's burgeoning globality, to enlighten children and adults about the flows of commodities and people that defined a new, modern age. As a result, colonialism became, ultimately, a problem of knowledge and the dissemination of that knowledge. A fascination and commodification of the exotic shaped many Germans' initial contact with their empire.[6] Commercial and popular interest in colonial objects, ideas, and peoples spread, seemingly of its own accord. And so, whenever they could, educators and colonial advocates sought to shape the form that this interest took on.[7] The colonial perspective was normalized in things as diverse as margarine advertisements and children's toys.[8] By the 1890s it was clear that Germans knew very well that the Fatherland was a colonial power. What concerned colonial elites was that the German public understood its relationship with its colonial empire appropriately.

But colonial elites could not control Germany's colonial culture no matter how hard they tried. Nonetheless, the literature on Germany's domestic culture of colonialism paints a fairly clear picture of economically minded interest groups utilizing the colonial empire and its symbols to educate Germans about the modern world. Some of this education came through unintentional avenues in the form of popular culture and mass consumption. And some of it came from commercial actors who wanted to guide Germans into a self-understanding as capitalist, modern consumers.

Other forces, beyond the bourgeoisie's control, acted to shape Germany's colonial culture. Mass culture, communicated through commercial imagery, transformed images of colonial power and racial otherness into a "commercial imaginary" that provided Germans from diverse backgrounds reference points for their relationship to modernity.[9] Commodities and messages from direct and indirect sources informed the colonial relationship as one of modern consumption. Germans learned that colonial modernity involved the consumption of colonial knowledge, colonial goods (rare and prosaic), colonial people, and colonial entertainments.

The motivations of the men who sought to train the German people in these matters were chiefly commercial. The colonial movement, in its institutional forms, housed its brain trusts in academic disciplines and trade groups and carried out its enthusiasms in the venues of those institutions – associations, exhibitions, congresses, and the like. Colonial enthusiasm was, in short, the province of middle-class, bourgeois men. And, as was the norm for bourgeois men's relationship to the masses, their preferred discourse was in the form of "education."[10] They used this discourse as a tool for acclimating ordinary Germans, especially working-class Germans, to their place in a new global economy. These messages were communicated directly, but with less intent in advertising and mass consumer products. But colonial elites in the secular movement very much wanted to communicate them more directly and purposefully to the German masses – especially the lower-middle and working classes. Desire did not always translate into success. Members of the Colonial Society regularly felt frustrated that they could not reach their target audiences in Germany's small towns and working-class districts.[11] They hoped to teach Germans about the empire's commercial promise and Germans' national mission. Instead they were stuck fighting producers in the commercial sphere who focused on the adventurous and exotic elements of empire – though elite colonialists were not above integrating more salacious material in their own propaganda.[12]

Not only did secular colonial culture acclimatize Germans to a modern, commercial, and global present and future, it also offered them lessons about race. Consumer culture perpetuated images of an exoticized other.[13] In particular, the imagery of empire printed in visual advertising taught Germans that they were fundamentally different from Africans. By the First World War advertisers had constructed an imagined generic consumer, one that was taught a construction of race that included Whites and excluded Blacks. Advertisers regularly depicted people of African descent in stereotyped ways that accentuated the Africans' supposed inferiority, immaturity, and bestiality when they sought to sell products with obvious, not-so-obvious, and virtually nonexistent colonial connections. Racialization grew out of a tactical set of choices that created a hegemonic racial uniformity in its representations of Africans.[14] Similarly, the primacy of labour issues in metropolitan politics and economics shaped discussions of colonial economics such that Germans learned to view the empire through hierarchical labour relations in which Whites ruled and Blacks worked.[15]

This secular narrative needs more nuance. It neglects one of the most important groups creating German colonial culture in the metropole – missionaries.[16] In fact, missionaries played an important, but as yet unrealized, role in Germany's colonial culture. At the heart of their role was their devotion to Christian universalist inclusion and a deep-seated ambivalence toward modernity. Germany's Protestant missionaries imagined racial difference differently, and consistently questioned the structures of economic colonialism advocated by Colonial Society members and the like. Furthermore, the missionaries doubted the value of any "civilizing mission" that emphasized economic transformation, as they feared such transformations were only possible at the expense of spiritual transformation. The present study does not dispute the importance of racialized othering or the power of commercial understandings of German colonial modernity, but it does insist that we must recognize that missionaries and their theology led them down a very different path from that of secular colonialists.

Including missionaries in the German colonial story also complicates the work of historians who would place the origins of the Holocaust in Germany's colonial empire. Though Hannah Arendt suggested in 1951 that the origins of totalitarian violence lay in the West's collective history of colonialism, many scholars of German history have located the origins of the Holocaust in Germany's specific colonial history. Despite the fact that this narrows the very scope of Arendt's own argument, researchers have applied her insights and looked to the violent German occupation of German Southwest Africa (modern-day Namibia) to explain the Nazis' racialized program of violent conquest.[17] Between 1904 and 1908 German colonial forces (*Schutztruppen*) in the colony murdered tens of thousands of members of the Herero and Nama ethnic groups as retribution for those groups' resistance to colonial rule. Using the historical facts of genocide in Germany's empire, some scholars have contended that Germany's attempted extermination of Africans indicates a prologue to Auschwitz.[18] Their arguments belong to a tradition that makes a case for continuity between Germany's nineteenth- and twentieth-century histories.

By asserting the centrality of German missionaries, this book disputes the direct lines of continuity presented by those who would argue for a colonial *Sonderweg* (special path) of German history. This focus on missionaries helps demonstrate that German colonial practices had more in common than not with other contemporary empires. Such commonality renders descriptions of a colonial Sonderweg untenable. This work describes a history of German missionaries situated within the wider history of Christian missionary work. German Protestants did not turn away from the National Socialists – in fact many were quite happy to endorse the Nazis' racial exclusionary priorities during the 1930s – but the Protestants (missionaries and their supporters) most engaged with Germany's colonial empire operated through a lens that defined racial difference culturally rather than biologically. Nazi racism was catholic enough to include elements of colonial racism, but the colonies cannot be considered the determinative source for the National Socialists' racial ideology. Colonialism in Germany did not universally sync with racial violence or racist policies.

As a history of missionaries, this book will show that Germans differed in important ways from the prevailing (and Anglocentric) narrative of missionary history. Germans were part of a wider history of Christian foreign mission. Their placement within that wider history demonstrates a more defensible claim about continuity *across* colonial empires *in* time as opposed to continuity *between* German regimes *over* time. Restated, German colonial history during the nineteenth century has more in common with its contemporaneous Western empires than it does with the Third Reich.[19] Furthermore, while historians have little trouble locating evidence that Nazi racial thought had nineteenth-century antecedents, those antecedents did not dominate German culture before the First World War. The missionaries' refusal of racial rhetoric and violence carried over into colonial policy and metropolitan culture.

This is not to say that German missionaries did not bring different prejudices to their work. Colonial history invariably has a certain quality of fantasy about it. Europeans and other colonizers have always projected their own wishes and desires upon the colonized space.[20] "Uncivilized" spaces and people became blank spaces and faces upon which or in spite of which colonizers thought they could design a perfect present and a utopian future. Because German colonial rule was so brief in comparison to the centuries of rule imposed by other powers such as Spain and Portugal, or Britain and France, German colonialism often seems almost entirely composed of the figments of colonialism and its future.

Nevertheless, between 1884 and the First World War, German colonialists played out their fantasies in the real world. At the Berlin West Africa Conference of 1884, Otto von Bismarck, Germany's Chancellor, helped lay the ground rules to formally unleash the European powers' colonization of Africa. Partially compelled by German pressure groups fired by passionate fantasies of colonial power, Bismarck gave government support to the creation of a colonial empire. Between April 1884 and April 1885, Germany created colonies in modern-day Togo, Cameroon, and Namibia, and in mainland Tanzania, Burundi, and Rwanda – administered as Togoland, Kamerun, Deutsch-Südwestafrika (German Southwest Africa), and Deutsch-Ostafrika (German East Africa), respectively. Conquest of these colonies followed European models, mixing together coercive protection treaties, military conquests, and local alliances to create fragile colonial states.

The close of the nineteenth century brought a further expansion to the German Empire as European annexations shifted to Asia and the Pacific. In 1897, two German Catholic missionaries from the Steyler Mission were murdered by Chinese peasant members of the Big Sword Society in Shandong Province.[21] A punitive naval expedition was dispatched to Kiaochow Bay (Jiaozhou) and a formal lease of the surrounding territory was signed in 1898. The addition of New Guinea and Samoa in 1899 came in the wake of the collapse of a concessionary company in New Guinea, the German New Guinea Company, and through an international treaty with the United States that divided the Samoan islands between the countries. The acquisition of these territories and the purchase of the Caroline, northern Marianas, and Marshall Islands from Spain in 1898 extended the indulgence of colonial fantasies into the Pacific.

The history of Germany's colonial empire reflects periodic attempts to shape reality to match the fantasy of a powerful and prosperous German colonialism. Like that of most other colonial powers, Germany's overseas empire was heterogeneous. The social, economic, and political conditions in Togo, East Africa, China, Samoa, and every other colony differed in serious ways. However, it is possible to offer some broad periodization of Germany's colonial era. In the first phase of formal colonization in the 1880s, Germany's overseas territories were organized as "protectorates" managed by colonial companies with imperial charters. These charters guaranteed territorial power and generally rested on the use of destructive violence. By the end of the 1880s, German politicians felt that the conflicts in the colonies between these companies and indigenous populations made the creation of formal colonies necessary. In this second phase of German rule, bureaucratic methods introduced "civilizing" programs that promoted European settlement and plantation economics. Planter agriculture received state support through land seizures and taxation policies that forced indigenous people to seek wage work. Major revolts in German Southwest Africa and German East Africa between 1904 and 1908 in response to this exploitation threatened the entire German colonial project. The third, and final, phase of German colonial rule, sought to correct the apparent errors of the first two phases. A new reform-oriented administration under the leadership of Colonial Secretary Bernhard Dernburg focused on the application of good management policies in order to "develop" the colonies in the years before the First World War.[22]

German colonial plans consistently sought the easiest path to the realization of fantasies about colonial prosperity. Like colonial fantasy, Christian culture rests on dreams for a better tomorrow. Though

Christianity has its share of pessimistic and apocalyptic notions, a core feature of Christianity is the conviction that through God's divine presence the future can be a hopeful place. The promise of salvation and eternal life after death, the eventual or imminent return of the Messiah, and other elements of Christian doctrine encourage a buoyant element within Christian theology and practice.

German Protestant missionaries brought together colonial and Christian fantasies of utopian lands just over the horizon. The same forces that facilitated colonial conquest during the late nineteenth century inspired a Christian, especially Protestant, conviction that the age of globalization would enable a Christian conquest of the world. German missionaries combined the general fantasies of colonial progress with their eschatological dreams for the Christian world and imagined a global Christian community superior to national programs of empire-building. They set aside the German fatherland and directed their desires and energies toward the creation of an international, Christian (Protestant) empire, a heavenly Fatherland. The missionaries envisioned this Fatherland as a universal community of Christians encompassing all the peoples of the earth and devoted to the service of God.

German missionaries imagined internationalism functioned in many of the same ways that secular nationalists imagined political communities operated. While the missionaries did not seek to establish a theocracy – in fact their beliefs judged the future form of government irrelevant – they imagined their ideal community of Christians as limited, sovereign, and autonomous from other mortal powers.[23] German Protestants in the nineteenth century followed a universalist and internationalist ideology that claimed to oppose the nationalism and particularism of many imperialists of the day.

Yet, even as Germany's Protestant missionaries defined themselves as internationalists, they rarely clarified exactly what they meant by that label. In practice, their internationalism rested on a commitment to internationalist practice – to the cultivation and maintenance of international relationships, the use of international solutions, and other such practices that defied or ignored national borders. Missionaries recognized nations as part of the global order, but they gave pre-eminence to other affiliations over and above the national; they elevated Protestant Christianity above every other form of human community. In their most ambitious dreams, German missionaries envisioned a global community of evangelized and spiritually inflamed Protestants who retained some form of national identity. In fact, most agreed that the nations of the world made up some part of God's plan. However, to the missionaries those national identities were meant to fade as the world came under a glorious new regime of Christ. To build an internationalist mission movement, Christendom had to unite and serve "heathendom"; transcending national boundaries required an internationalist movement that resisted any expressions of cultural supremacy.

The missionaries elevated internationalism over nationalism, but they could never fully escape their own national identities or the influence of the national idea. Despite their internationalist loyalties, German missionaries did not deny the meaning and relevance of their own German identities. The theology and Protestant worldview that the missionaries espoused were built upon an understanding of the Reformation as a German movement. Born of awakening movements meant to reinvigorate Christianity in local, regional, and national communities, the German Protestant missionary movement recognized that national identities had meaning in the world. As will be shown later, the missionaries understood national diversity to be a function and a sign of God's intent; the proliferation of Christian and non-Christian (but hopefully soon-to-be Christian) peoples represented the mission of mission work.

While German missionaries laboured to separate their work from German nationalist goals and colonial conquests, they were nonetheless connected to Germany and German culture. That said, the Protestant missionary movement could and did affect broader cultural notions of racial and cultural difference. Though there is a tendency to present German racial thought as existing in an unbroken line from colonial racial science to Nazi racial ideology, missionaries and their ideas about race demonstrate that German cultural perceptions of racial and cultural difference were far from monolithic. Missionaries devoted themselves and their work to a universal Christianity directed toward a global and communal commonweal. This behaviour challenges many narratives of German cultural approaches to nationalism, imperialism, and globalization. The assumption that nationalism dominated all Germans' consumption and experience of imperialism and globalization fails to account for the prevalence and influence of the missionaries' anti-national contributions to German colonial culture. Missionaries insisted that non-White, non-Europeans deserved an equal place at the communion table. And their views challenge our conventional understanding of German Protestantism as predominantly nationalist at its core. The link between Protestantism and German chauvinism is indeed weaker than supposed in most of the literature on the subject, at least when it comes to nineteenth-century colonialism.[24] In point of fact, the universalistic and anti-statist tendencies of the German Protestant mission movement show that the history of German colonialism is more appropriately considered within a larger narrative.

German Protestant missionary history is part of the history of globalization. By 1900 economics, politics, and culture had become highly integrated across borders and oceans. Expanding global trade and production, migration, and cultural exchange all operated in a world shaped by colonial structures, something about which Germans were increasingly aware.[25] Though it was not as invested in its colonial empire as were Britain or France, Germany remained caught up in the same colonial and global forces. Furthermore, the globalizing moment coincided in Germany with a moment of fundamental transformation. "Modernity" in all its forms buffeted, mutated, and disassembled old institutions while forging new ones.[26] As natives of the globalizing and colonial world, German missionaries moved around and within a series of tumultuous events.

German missionaries shared the role of colonial pioneers with missionaries of other nationalities. They intentionally and unintentionally eased the way of the colonial state with their cultural and geographic knowledge of soon-to-be colonized people and polities. Histories of missionaries frequently emphasize this role and contextualize missionary activities and views within the larger history of colonial takeover.[27] This scholarship has emphasized the "pioneering" work that missionaries did for colonial conquest. Missionaries often produced the first useful knowledge of geography, culture, language, and commerce for colonial conquerors and occupiers. Furthermore, missionaries often provided moral cover for conquest with their calls for evangelization and emancipation, their emphases upon the civilizing mission of European and American powers. But the history of Germany's Protestant missionaries muddles that simple narrative. In word and deed, Germans distanced themselves from colonial goals oriented toward economic and political exploitation. At the same time that they pioneered colonial conquest abroad, they turned the process of exchange on its head by acting as pioneers of globalization in Germany as well. In Germany they presented a vision of globalization that encouraged Protestants to embrace a certain cosmopolitanism that might grow from colonial conquest. The missionaries' complicated participation in colonial conquest and cultural imperialism was shaped by their certainty that Christianity, defined as "universal" but certainly German, European, and Western, represented a superior cultural form. They wilfully sought methods for cultural conquest and destruction in their quest to "improve" indigenous morality. Nevertheless, their explicit opposition to nationalist priorities and capitalist expansion came from and created a different set of attitudes toward colonized people. Missionaries were some of Germany's first and most influential agents of globalization; they promoted and built the networks of global interaction that characterized the long nineteenth century.

In the main, Germany's Protestant missionaries favoured globalization. Missionaries' views on the relevance of their own activities, international Christian evangelization, European colonialism, and German state-building were formed through a lens of universalist Christianity that discouraged national loyalty and embraced global cosmopolitanism. As a consequence, Germany's Protestant missionaries influenced ordinary Germans' experience of globalization. They appreciated the interconnections created in the name of global economic and political interests. And they welcomed intercourse with distant cultures as part of the integration of God's heavenly Fatherland. As ambassadors of globalization, missionaries encouraged the dissolution of boundaries (excepting religious ones) and translated globalization for their countrymen across Germany. In the metropole, mission societies and missionary intellectuals built networks of local communities among ordinary Prussians, Pomeranians, Hessians, and so on. German missionaries played an essential part in the construction of a German colonial culture, a collective understanding and experience of German contact with the colonies and participation in the global imperial project in the metropole and the colonies.

Yet Germany's Protestant missionaries could never fully escape their role in German and European colonial structures. They did not renounce their German citizenship nor did they desire to "go native." As missionaries they did not admit to being divided in their loyalties. They elevated Christian identity above all others. And they still had to navigate the contradictions in their Germanness and their desire to transcend that identity. As this work will show, at times the missionaries willingly capitalized on the privileges they might gain as Germans to enact their missionary goals. They did not dismiss national identities or ignore state powers. They thought those distinctions less important than Christian loyalties. They also could not, try as they may, ignore race.

From its beginnings and intensifying in the decades before the First World War, the nineteenth century was a racial century.[28] Although their universalist theology rebuked the most extreme racist descriptions of the world, German Protestant missionaries did not repudiate nineteenth-century ideas about race. As members of the wider European culture, they increasingly came to explain the theoretical and practical aspects of human existence as organized around logics driven by theories of racial difference. But they ended up justifying African inferiority as cultural rather than biological. Missionaries never fully divested themselves of the racial conventions of their age, but they introduced and advocated a different racial understanding into Germany's colonial culture. They rejected essentialized racialized biological categories in their thinking on human difference. If they discussed such distinctions, they did not evaluate them as reflective of cultural, intellectual, or moral capacity. But Missionswissenschaftler and missionaries did view Africans as *culturally* inferior when compared to European Protestant culture at its best. Missionaries ascribed Africans' inferiority to their heathenism and their prolonged isolation from the Gospel. According to the mission view, the cultural backwardness of the African continent had been worsened by the predations of slavers from the West and from the Arab world. Centuries of ignorance and exploitation had deprived Africans of the opportunities to develop the "higher" forms of political, cultural, and social expression, or so missionaries judged. Missionaries' blindness to the evidence of Africans' sophisticated societies deepened their ignorance of Africans' cultural achievements and validated their judgments that the entire African race needed the missionaries' help.

While German Protestant missionaries harboured racial and even racist views, they rejected theories that the African race would die out in the conflicts among the races. Though they judged Africans' "heathenness" the cause of much evil, they did not ascribe that evil to Africans' souls or biology. In fact, many missionaries spoke for the value of many of the cultural products, practices, and perspectives of African communities. Some even argued that African diversity would introduce new truths to Christians' understanding of God. Missionaries' eagerness to bring Africans into their faith encouraged a different racial viewpoint.

The missionaries carried the contradictions of their existence with them wherever they sought to build the heavenly Fatherland. The chapters that follow reconstruct the intellectual, political, and cultural history of the German Protestant mission movement along closely related axes of interpretation of nationalism versus internationalism and of universalism versus particularism. This is primarily a book about German missionaries' influence on the German metropole, where missionaries had much to say *about* Africans and their communities. In the metropole, where most of the conversation about empire, globalization, mission theology, and race took place, German missionaries did not *listen* or even try to listen much to what Africans had to say about those issues.[29] Unfortunately, that means that although this is a book that says a lot about Africans and other colonial subjects, it does not *hear* very much from them. Instead, this book answers questions about the missionaries themselves and the probable impact of arguments between missionaries and other colonialists upon colonial policy and German colonial culture. The missionaries may have seen value in colonized cultures but they did not solicit colonial subjects' input in their debates.

This work brings religious history into the history of German colonialism and places under the jeweller's eye the role of Protestants in German participation in globalization. As a history of Germany's Protestant mission movement during the Kaiserreich, this work takes its analysis to three different geographic spaces: European Germany, colonial German East Africa, and global networks of missionaries. Though the spaces may at times be handled discretely, events were never restricted in their causes or effects to any single space. In Germany, the history of German missionaries takes place in the mission houses, Protestant parishes, and other workspaces of missionaries and mission supporters. Naturally the missionaries applied their ideology to their activities in Germany, but the multiple frames of this analysis allow for an examination of the ideology in practice elsewhere. German East Africa offers a good opportunity to examine the relationship between ideology and practice. Because its history as a site of Protestant mission work largely began with German colonial conquest, mission work and secular colonialism coexisted on a more-or-less equal footing there. Furthermore, German East Africa figured prominently in the imagination of colonialists from its conquest by Carl Peters through the Entente powers' seizure of the colony after the First World War. Finally, the activities of Germans in international networks of Protestants reveals the breadth of the Germans' ambitions and exposes the role they played in creating a global Protestant ecumenicism.

Because of German missionaries' intellectual and textual character, the history of the movement's activities emphasizes the role of Missionswissenschaft in the formation of a cohesive and coherent Protestant mission movement in the German lands. Missionary leaders and intellectuals created an academic discipline that legitimated their work and values in the wider culture of Germany. And because the worldview of these Missionswissenschaftler asserted internationalist values, by the 1870s these values and their practical interpretations prevailed among the individuals and institutions of German mission work. The first chapter of the book details the framework of this ideology and the emergence of major figures and organizations within German missionary internationalism before the First World War.

Missionaries' theoretical interventions had direct effects on the process of colonization in Germany's colonies as well as the colonies of other powers. In particular, the German Protestants' work in the colony of German East Africa offers invaluable perspective on the concrete interactions between the missionaries' internationalist vision and other forces shaping Germany's colonial history. The establishment of schools and the beginning of translation work took precedence over any other work at German mission stations around the world. In East Africa, the missionaries' internationalism and commitment to linguistic diversity led to the promotion of policies that encouraged the preservation of many African cultural practices. These missionary policies clashed with the aspirations of nationalists who wanted missionaries to teach in German. The second chapter explains the ways missionaries defended their internationalism in the face of this threat to their priorities. Preserving indigenous communities as new Protestant *Völker* was part of the construction of a global Protestantism that recognized human difference while binding the "nations" in service to God.

The third chapter continues with the application of missionaries' internationalism to pedagogical challenges in the colony. While German nationalists took exception to the linguistic policies of the missionaries in German East Africa (and elsewhere), secular colonialists more interested in the economic exploitation of the colony expounded a more general critique of missionary teaching. Economic colonialists desired the conversion of Africans in the colony into pliable labourers for plantation work and cared little for the type of conversion that missionaries sought. They complained that missionaries did not fulfil their "German" obligations because the missions would not "educate the Negro to work."[30] Missionaries' religious convictions and pro-African positioning disdained such wholesale capitalistic instrumentalization of African communities. An African proletariat, consumed by capitalism and displaced from its natural communities, could never rise to full membership in the Christian international community. The chapter will focus on the antagonisms that the missionaries confronted because of their desire to create economically autonomous Protestants among the colonized.

The fourth chapter of the book addresses complications to the missionaries' internationalism. Despite the missionaries' aversion to secular colonialism, certain compromises on language and economic policy signalled the undeniable allure of the colonial state's power. And when historic Protestant-Catholic animosity came to the colony, the Protestant missionaries found it even harder to resist the language of nationalism. The chapter also offers a powerful example of the intercourse between the colonial and metropolitan contexts. During the last decade before the First World War, the *Benediktinerstreit* pitted the Protestant Berlin Mission Society against the Catholic Benedictine Brothers of St

Ottilien. Both mission organizations were German, and both operated in the southwestern regions of German East Africa. The clash between the societies concerned the division of mission territory in the colony. During the conflict the Berlin missionaries and their Protestant allies asserted their internationalism while they attacked the Catholics for their supposedly insufficient loyalty to Germany and to Christian evangelism. The chapter details the direct links between German and colonial events while defining some of the limits of the Protestant missionaries' universalism.

While the first four chapters focus on events in the colonies and their resonances in the metropole, the fifth chapter turns its attention exclusively to activities in Germany's European territories. To the missionaries, Germany could be as much a mission field as any other place. Missionaries' message of Christian devotion and global Protestant unity had to be spread to German-speakers in the *Heimat* nearly as much as it did in the "foreign mission field." To do so, missionaries helped organize local associations, *Hilfsvereine*, devoted to spreading the "missionary spirit." In collaboration with these associations, mission societies introduced diverse methods for transmitting the missionaries' message. These methods promoting missionaries' vision of the world reached very large audiences across Germany's provinces. Through these activities, missionaries played a powerful part in the creation of a German colonial culture; they produced, filtered, and synthesized information about the wider world for ordinary Germans. Networks of missionary supporters disseminated missionaries' ideology of universalistic Protestantism to millions of Germans. They promoted an inclusive understanding of the wider Christian world and presented globalization as a positive force.

The final chapter of the book turns to the most explicitly internationalist work of the German Protestant mission movement. At the same time the Germans extended their efforts further and further afield and deeper and deeper into German society, German missionary leaders also expanded the capacities for collaboration between themselves and the international mission community. Driven by confident visions of Christian collaboration, German Protestants used missionary conferences to build ever-wider communities of missionaries. Starting with regional and national conferences in Germany between the 1860s and 1910s, German Missionswissenschaftler and mission society leaders pushed for international conferences of mission leaders. Their efforts culminated in the Edinburgh World Missionary Conference in 1910, a grand cooperative effort with the British and American mission movements. The success of the German Missionswissenschaftler and the wider movement, particularly at the Edinburgh Conference, have been largely ignored by scholars. But this chapter clearly demonstrates a German and international effort by a special interest – missionaries and evangelizing Protestantism – to capitalize on the forces of globalization. The heady successes promised by the Edinburgh Conference exhibit the power and importance of German missionary internationalism.

The men and women who made German missionary culture are dust, but their words and the records of their deeds remain bound in archives and libraries. Between 1860 and 1914 the missionaries' version of Protestantism inspired many Germans to seek a greater engagement with the world. In a time and place more frequently remembered for the perils of intense and even militarized national feeling, devoted German Protestants promoted a different way of viewing the world in a language inspired by the opportunities afforded by globalization. They took the texts of the Bible and elaborated an evangelical understanding of Christianity that encouraged engagement and brotherhood. Because of their internationalist and universalist theology, the missionaries and their supporters became a significant community within German society that did not subscribe to the violently racist dehumanization of non-Western people. Missionaries and their supporters built a substantial movement that told a different story about Germans' place in the world.

1 Preach the Gospel to All Creation

Missionswissenschaft and a German Protestant Mission Movement

Five books of the Christian Bible contain different versions of what is called the Great Commission. In similar but varied phrasing, the authors of these books recorded a command by Jesus for the apostles to journey across the "nations" and preach the teachings of their new faith. The Gospel of Mark, the oldest of the Gospels, captured in its version of the Great Commission a fundamental characteristic of the German Protestant mission movement. In Mark 16:15, Jesus tells his apostles, "Go into all the world and proclaim the good news to the whole creation."[1] Before about 1870, the simple messages of the Great Commission were enough to inspire the creation of mission societies and regional support networks. But after 1870, changes in global economics, politics, societies, and culture animated a broader implementation of the scriptural messages of the Great Commission among German Protestants. Under the leadership of practitioners of the new academic discipline, Missionswissenschaft, German Protestant missions coalesced into a national movement with an internationalist orientation.

During the last third of the nineteenth century, Germany's mission movement grew along with other mission movements in a globalizing wave across the West. In the Germans' eyes, globalization created opportunities as well as hazards for mission work. The synchronous expansion of European (and American) economic and political power that characterized the decades of globalization before the First World War also stimulated an expansion in cultural and, in the specific case of missionaries, religious power.[2] Growing economic and political interest in African, Asian, and Australasian territories made missionaries potential victims of globalization, as economic interests and state power imperilled the autonomy of German mission workers.[3] But at the same time, the networks and technological innovations created by globalization also made missionaries into potential beneficiaries, as globalization suggested the means for building a future global Protestant culture and society.

Somewhat unique among missionary cultures of the time, the German Protestant mission movement was particularly intellectualized and academic in its orientation. This orientation both inspired and was then reinforced by the development of Missionswissenschaft, which applied the rigours and conventions of German academic norms to the theoretical and practical challenges of mission work. And in Germany, Missionswissenschaft was dominated by one man – Gustav Warneck (1834–1910). Other important figures contributed to the formation of the discipline and the articulation of a coherent missionary worldview in Germany, but Warneck was the most influential figure during the decades before the First World War. This chapter will use the framework of Warneck's writings and lectures about German missionary internationalism, supplemented with other important thinkers' work, to reconstruct the worldview that dominated German missionary culture as the Missionswissenschaftler contemplated the possibilities of globalization.

Possessed of a long pre-imperial history and confident of its own independent identity, the German Protestant mission movement comfortably integrated an internationalist ideology into its self-conception. Warneck and others led their missionary followers to keep their activities distinct from other forms of German colonialism. He led a discipline peopled with Missionswissenschaftler who came from all levels of German religious society.[4] Their place and authority within the mission movement increasingly depended upon their ability to prove themselves academically capable. The pages of the discipline's journals were filled with articles by low-ranking missionaries in the field, missionary leaders and administrators, pastors with limited official affiliation with any mission society (a group whose most prominent member was Warneck), Protestant academics interested in applying their studies to missionary issues, and other engaged lay participants. Collectively these men collaborated on the daily workings of mission while also sharing an intellectual life oriented around improving the efficacy of the mission project. The internationalist and independent identity delineated by leading Missionswissenschaftler owed much of its shape to the confidence and clarity that came from its grounding in the professional backgrounds of the pastors and theologians who led the mission movement.

From this collegiality and commonality of purpose, the German Protestant mission movement adopted a shared outlook on the place of its activities in the wider world. The collective identity of missionary leaders and their workers in the field revolved around an intellectualized familiarity with the practical theology of mission work. And the collective worldview produced by the leading Missionswissenschaftler interpreted mission purpose from an internationalist perspective. The analysis in this chapter demonstrates the specific German Protestant missionary stance on the healthiest relationship among governmental colonialist desires, non-governmental secular colonial ambitions, and global missionary aspirations. As will be apparent, missionaries thought hard about mission and about empire.

Between the 1850s and 1870s, German missionaries had little devotion to a German nation. Nonetheless, during the period of German unification and in the early days of the imperialist period, some missionaries hoped to emulate the devotion that they saw British and French mission societies showing to their countries' empires. Friedrich Fabri and others linked mission work with national service. In 1868, the Rhenish Mission Society, under Fabri's leadership at the time, solicited first British and then German annexations of the territory that would become German Southwest Africa. Fabri's heterodox theology believed divine redemption would be spread through direct Western colonial conquest.[5] However, advocacy of direct participation and collaboration with the national government faded alongside Fabri's slide into irrelevance within the mission movement during the late 1870s and 1880s. The cause of this slide was the general ambivalence German missionaries felt about nationalist politics and their commitment to an overriding internationalist ideology.

Germany's missionaries worked internationally. When there was no unified Germany to even contemplate serving, they began developing a new academic discipline that explained the internationalism of their work. As the German Empire emerged in Europe and then as a colonial entity, the missionaries' internationalism informed a view of the emerging globalization as a natural enhancement to their work. At the same time, pressure from intensified colonialism posed a dangerous threat. The consensus these men reached led the wider missionary movement to the conclusion that missionaries had to remain disciplined in order to preserve the internationalist identity of the mission movement. This position meant remaining autonomous in their activities and avoiding any policies that reduced missionaries, mission stations, or mission societies to adjuncts of other colonial actors. The leaders of the mission movement took the Great Commission and applied it to a world in which missionaries, thanks to the railroad, steamship, and telegraph, might actually be able to preach the gospel to all creation – that is, if they could keep anyone else from interfering.

German Mission Societies in German East Africa

German mission societies were active around the world: on the Mosquito Coast in Central America, in India, on the island of New Guinea, in the southern provinces of China, across Africa, and beyond. Their work in the new colony of German East Africa merits special attention for an understanding of the interaction among missionaries working in the metropole, the colony, and international networks. Because the colony had no German missionaries before its conquest by Germany, and missionaries arrived at the same time as the colonial authorities, studying their activities in the colony avoids becoming entangled with precolonial patterns of missionary endeavour. In fact, missionaries in German East Africa pursued their form of colonial intervention at the same time that other interest groups were active there. This simultaneity heightened tensions and encouraged missionaries to articulate their views clearly because of the competitive stakes.

In late 1883, the German adventurer Carl Peters travelled to the region that would become the colony of German East Africa. While there, though lacking any public authority to do so, he signed contracts with local authorities that he hoped would be interpreted as evidence of German authority in the region. He had fantasies that a future colony on the Swahili Coast would be a German "India in Africa." The German government chose to accept Peters's contracts as treaties of protection and granted Peters's Deutsch-Ostafrikanische Gesellschaft (German East Africa Company) an imperial charter to manage a new protectorate. The company's policies provoked constant unrest and, following a major uprising that required imperial intervention, the protectorate became an official colony in 1891. It included the mainland territories of modern-day Tanzania, Rwanda, and Burundi. Its 7.75 million inhabitants participated in an economy that included extensive trade routes to the Omani-Zanzibari Sultanate, and that drew gold, iron, and slaves from as far inland as Lake Tanganyika in return for textiles, porcelain, and spices from the Indian Ocean trade. The colony was Germany's most valuable overseas possession, but it still cost the empire more than it brought in. Cotton, sisal, copra, and peanuts made up the main exports that German plantations sought to control but which were nonetheless dominated by African producers. German power was largely restricted to the coast, though military expeditions into the interior gradually extended colonial authority toward the Rift Valley.

The Maji-Maji War of 1905–8 shook the colonial state to its core and its vicious suppression and a subsequent famine left about 300,000 Africans dead. In the period after the war, Albrecht von Rechenberg, governor from 1906 to 1912, introduced a shift in policy that attempted to transform the economic, social, and even political character of the colony. He tried to remake it as a trading colony that could prosper through the activities of African, Indian, and Arab merchants alongside German plantation owners and traders. With his reforms, he opposed large-scale White-owned plantations and even attempted to bring Africans (very) gradually into the administration of the colony. In these reforms, Rechenberg was viciously opposed by the settler population. Eventually he was forced from his post. Fighting in the colony during the First World War lasted until November 1918 and only ended with the surrender by General Paul von Lettow-Vorbeck.[6]

When the first German missionaries of the Evangelische Missionsgesellschaft für Deutsch-Ostafrika (EMDOA) arrived in the new colony of German East Africa in 1886, the African cultures living within the borders of the colony were largely unknown to the German mission community. These first missionaries arrived at the behest of Peters and the Deutsch-Ostafrikanische Gesellschaft. But the intimate connection between secular and religious interests did not last and was atypical of German Protestant missionary initiatives. Instead, the German Protestant mission movement adhered to an internationalist ideology that kept missionaries' activities distinct from other forms of German colonialism and made them very reluctant to move into the new colony. The history of German Protestant missionary work before this point explains much of the strength of the missionaries' drive for autonomy.

German missionaries were there when modern mission history began. The founding in Britain of the Society for Promoting Christian Knowledge and the Society for the Propagation of the Gospel in Foreign Parts in 1698 and 1701, respectively, encouraged King Frederick IV of Denmark to establish a mission within the small Danish trading enclave at Tranquebar in South India. To do so, he turned to the Pietist communities of Germany to enlist two theology students from Berlin, Bartholomaeus Ziegenbalg and Henry Plütschau, who arrived in India in 1706.[7] A few decades later the Moravians in Herrnhut, Saxony, embarked on mission work, dispatching missionaries to the Danish West Indies and Britain's colonies in the Americas.[8] These mission endeavours predate what is generally regarded as the inaugural moment of the modern evangelical mission movement, the publication of William Carey's *An Enquiry Into the Obligations of Christians*,[9] and the subsequent founding of the Baptist Missionary Society in 1792, the London Missionary Society in 1795, the Scottish and Glasgow Missionary Societies in 1796, and the Society for Missions to Africa and the East in 1799 (after 1812 called the Church Missionary Society).[10] These British mission societies were joined by the German-Swiss Basel Mission in 1815. The Germans even shaped these British activities. From the beginning, the Basel Mission and the many British missions recruited extensively among German-speakers in the Rhine provinces to staff their mission stations abroad.[11]

Though German Protestant missionaries were active around the globe by the 1880s, East Africa's Swahili Coast had not received much attention from them by that time. But by the end of the 1890s, four mission societies had committed to work among the many African groups of the colony.[12] The distinct histories of these four societies show the diversity of the German Protestant mission movement and the successful integration of that diversity into a shared ideology and program. The Moravian Brüdergemeine's Missionsdirektion sent missionaries to the western reaches of the colony near Lakes Nyasa[13] and Tanganyika. The Berliner Missionsgesellschaft – before 1907 called the Gesellschaft zur Beförderung der evangelischen Missionen unter den Heiden zu Berlin (Society for the Promotion of Protestant Missions among the Heathens of Berlin), colloquially called Berlin I to distinguish it from two other Berlin-based mission societies and hereafter simply referred to as the Berlin Mission, also established its mission stations along the shores of Lake Nyasa. The Evangelisch-Lutherische Missionsgesellschaft (Evangelical Lutheran Mission Society or Leipzig Mission, for its home city) took as its mission field the Kilimanjaro region among the Chagga people there. And the Bethel Mission (renamed and reorganized from the aforementioned EMDOA in 1890) operated in the Usambara Mountains in the northeastern reaches of the colony. The Brüdergemeine, founded in 1732, the Berlin Mission, in 1824, and the Leipzig Mission, in 1832, were considered "old missions" because they had been established before the unification of Germany in 1871 and the conquest of Germany's colonies in the mid-1880s. Meanwhile, the Bethel Mission arose directly out of the colonial movement in 1887 and was thus considered in German missionary circles as a "new mission."

The German Protestant mission societies active in German East Africa differed in other significant ways.[14] The diversity among the societies reflected in some cases liturgical and theological differences that stretched back to the Reformation period. In fact, the Moravians of the Brüdergemeine can trace their religious traditions back to early Czech Hussites. In the early eighteenth century the Moravians' forebears fled Habsburg persecution, settling in the Saxon lands of Nikolaus von Zinzendorf, who granted them leave to create a village, Herrnhut, on his lands. Zinzendorf, a Lutheran, had spent his formative years in the Pietist circles of Halle with the renowned theologian and humanitarian August Hermann Francke. Zinzendorf gradually integrated the

Moravians with the local Lutheran congregations around his holdings in the Oberlausitz of southwest Saxony and became a bishop of the Moravians. Eventually the Brüdergemeine formed its own religious community, but one whose simple theology of spiritual renewal allowed it to merge with both Calvinist and Lutheran established churches across Germany and Europe.[15]

The Berlin Mission's founders shared the Pietistic roots of Zinzendorf and carried on a tradition of prayer circles and Bible study whose theology focused on personal faith over high church doctrine. However, in 1817 the king of Prussia, Friedrich Wilhelm III, declared the union of the Lutheran and Calvinist confessions under one Prussian rite, an act that many on both sides of the Lutheran and Reformed divide resisted.[16] Because of its ties to a Pietist circle of nobles close to the Prussian king, the Berlin Mission felt compelled to declare itself a mission within the union. In practice the Berlin Mission's leadership adopted a "mild Lutheranism" and tried to steer clear of difficult theological questions.[17] It operated under the official state church of Prussia but did nothing to enforce doctrinarian purity within its ranks or in its associations.

In fact, the unwillingness of the Berlin Mission to enforce doctrine probably facilitated a schism within its ranks. A number of strong-willed orthodox Lutheran members of the society's missionary training seminar eventually grew uncomfortable with the "unionate" character of the Berlin Mission. These seminarians joined with like-minded congregations in Saxony and founded an independent Leipzig Mission Society dedicated to anti-union Lutheranism in 1832.[18] Still more variance in theology shaped the "East African" missions. After the EMDOA was integrated into the Bethel Institutes and became the Bethel Mission, the theology of the Bethel Institutes came to dominate. In general, Friedrich von Bodelschwingh, leader of the institutes, was theologically conservative and politically nationalist. However, in its work, the Bethel movement's theology had little role in the formation or activities of the mission. The chief goal, and one in harmony with the wider Protestant mission movement, was to integrate foreign mission work with work to resanctify German communities in the metropole.[19]

Institutional structure joined theology to differentiate the mission societies still further. Each of the mission societies had a ruling committee that served as its supervisory power. The Berlin, Leipzig, and Bethel Missions all appointed directors to act as executives – these men interacted with the ruling committees to make the majority of the decisions. In both the Berlin Mission Society and the Bethel Society, directors and ruling committees supervised their missionaries with a high degree of authoritarianism. Mission policies, therefore, originated from the metropolitan centre while an intermediate level of supervision on the regional level attempted to guarantee adherence to the mission societies' standards.

Authoritarianism was an expression of the social makeup of both the Berlin and Bethel supervising committees. The Berlin Mission Society had been founded and continued to be sponsored by a collection of Pietist aristocrats who remained committed to traditional modes of authority, often based on social class.[20] Friedrich von Bodelschwingh, the aristocratic churchman, philanthropist, leader of the Bethel community of religious reformers, and benefactor to whom the EMDOA owed its salvation from institutional and financial ruin in 1890,[21] did not assume the directorship of the Bethel Mission. But following its merger with the Bethel institutions, Bodelschwingh organized the relationship of the mission to the wider Bethel community so that he reigned over the mission as undeclared patriarch.[22]

Meanwhile, the Moravians operated their mission under the supervision of a *Missionsdirektion*, a committee of leaders representing each of the church's provinces in Europe, the United Kingdom, and North America and who reported to the Brüdergemeine's governing body. Furthermore, the diverse geographic origins of Missionsdirektion members weakened any demands the Missionsdirektion might make for uniformity. This structure partially recreated the decentralized structures of the Moravian church. And it prevented any single Moravian from dominating the activities of the mission arm, though certain individuals were able to exert their influence over policy. Whatever their differences, each of the four mission societies took an assertive stance that mission societies and their work must remain independent from the official church hierarchy in the German Empire, maintaining minimal official links with state church leadership.[23]

The ordinary missionaries representing the four East African mission societies also displayed the breadth of experiences that missionary men (and a few women who travelled as missionary wives) brought to their work. The Bethel Mission was the only society of the four that maintained an ongoing commitment to sending university-trained missionaries, all of them drawn from within the wider Bethel movement.[24] In its early years, the Leipzig Mission also committed to sending out only trained ministers, but by the time the society was working in East Africa, that commitment had slipped significantly. Of the sixty missionaries the Leipzig Mission had worldwide in 1903, only twenty-three held theological degrees.[25] The remainder of Leipzig missionaries and every Berlin missionary received his training in a religious seminar run by his mission society.[26] Only gradually did the Moravians institute a form of seminary training like that given by the Leipzig and Berlin Missions.[27] The Missionsdirektion initially sent out lay missionaries who possessed no level of formal religious training and who were frequently drawn from the working classes. The Berlin and Leipzig Mission Societies also recruited many working-class men for their training seminars. Collectively, these four Protestant mission societies and their missionaries came to mission work with a broad range of experiences. And yet, as will be shown, the mission societies held to a shared ethos with regard to their place in the larger sphere of colonial and national life.

The final important marker of diversity among these four mission societies relates to their respective interconnections with other organizations and institutions within Germany and beyond. The Moravian Church had four major provinces by the nineteenth century: Germany, the United Kingdom, and the Northern and Southern Provinces in North America. These four provinces gathered with other, lesser, provinces at decennial synods to decide the direction of the church; the organization's leadership was called the *Unitätsdirektion* (Unified Directorate) and it supervised the Missionsdirektion.[28] The connections of the Leipzig Mission also grew out of international denominational relationships. The Leipzig Mission's rejection of the Prussian Union included a desire to offer a "supra-regional Lutheran alternative" to the existing non-denominational mission societies operating in the 1820s. This meant that the *Generalversammlung* (General Assembly) of the Leipzig Mission included representatives from the Lutheran Churches of Hannover, Schleswig, Thuringia, and elsewhere within Germany; Lutherans in the Russian Empire; and from the Swedish and Danish Lutheran state churches until they each established their own mission societies in the 1830s.[29]

The most intimate connections of the Berlin and Bethel Missions were, on the other hand, internal to Germany. The Berlin Mission enjoyed close connections with the royal house and the Pietist aristocrats of Prussia. For example, King Friedrich Wilhelm III promised a yearly donation to the Berlin Mission Society of 500 thalers in 1833, a donation which the ruling Hohenzollern dynasty continued throughout its reign.[30] Many other important political leaders from the Prussian aristocracy also supported the society; these included Max Berner, the last president of the society's governing *Komitee*, who was also the official within the German Colonial Department charged with managing missionary affairs.[31] In many ways the political connections of the Bethel Mission were even more significant and made the society an extraordinary case. In the first place, the EMDOA was founded expressly to minister to Germany's new colony in East Africa, and its founding executive committee included the adventurer and colonial pioneer Carl Peters.[32] The mission's integration into Bodelschwingh's Bethel movement brought the organization even more closely into conservative circles within Germany. It also meant that the Bethel Mission was tightly bound with the program of inner mission devoted to "re-Christianizing" Germany and institutionalizing Christian welfare through various "colonies" of remediation and vocational uplift.[33]

Despite the surprising diversity of structure, organization, leadership, training, and relationships among the four East African mission societies, the rising forces of political and economic globalization encouraged the German mission societies to embrace a cultural internationalism that integrated the opportunities of globalization into Germany's Protestant mission movement. Though Germany's missionaries comfortably recognized their own Germanness and understood themselves to be clerical descendants of Reformation leaders, they also emphasized and, ultimately, embraced an internationalist logic for their work. The key integrative force for this unity of purpose came from the intellectuals who would dominate the leadership of the Protestant mission movement in Germany. Internationalists overwhelmed and outmanoeuvred nationalist voices in the mission movement during the years of colonialist agitation in Germany. These intellectuals, the Missionswissenschaftler, articulated, promoted, and defended a vision of missionary internationalism that paved over differences among the German Protestant societies and fortified the movement to fight for its vision of a future Christian globe.

Missionswissenschaft and the *Allgemeine Missions-Zeitschrift*

The leadership, membership, and supporters of these four "East African" mission societies participated in the creation of Germany's Protestant mission culture in the same fora as every other Protestant mission society during the German colonial period. Collaboration among the societies arose from circles of mission intellectuals, Missionswissenschaftler, and the conferences that these intellectuals organized in the 1860s, 1870s, and 1880s. After 1886, the sixteen German Protestant mission societies collectivized much of their political activities under the leadership of the Ausschuß der deutschen evangelischen Missionen (Committee of German Protestant Missions). The Ausschuß served as their national representative and lobbying organization. Its leadership was composed of five representatives, three of whom were required to be the executive officers of mission societies. A regular fixture on the Ausschuß was Gustav Warneck, a man whose main employ was as a local pastor in Saxony. Warneck's significance to the mission movement was as the pre-eminent Missionswissenschaftler. Among other leaders of the Ausschuß, Franz Michael Zahn (1833–1900) was prominent as well. Unlike Warneck, he held significant authority as director of the Norddeutsche Missionsgesellschaft (North German Mission Society). Like Warneck, he also contributed regularly to debates within the field of Missionswissenschaft. A second generation of missionary leaders – most prominent of them Karl Axenfeld (1869–1924) and Julius Richter (1862–1940) – reinforced their administrative talents with evidence of intellectual achievement through academic studies and publication. By the middle of the 1890s the Ausschuß had emerged as the main organization of German mission life, acting as the Protestant mission movement's main liaison with the German imperial government and with foreign mission organizations.[34] The leadership, membership, and supporters of all four of the "East African" mission societies subscribed to and contributed to the development of German Missionswissenschaft and German Protestant missionary internationalism.

Before the Ausschuß institutionalized the dominance of intellectual credentials in the German mission movement, much work had already been done to establish the pre-eminence of Missionswissenschaft. During the 1870s, Warneck and his colleagues began drawing together Germany's Protestant mission societies through the activities of their scholarly discipline. In 1874 a new academic journal, *Allgemeine Missions-Zeitschrift*, was founded to serve missionaries, supportive clergymen, and lay supporters. This journal encouraged its readers to identify with German mission work as a collaborative internationalist project. Warneck, its founding editor and chief contributor for the next three decades, created the journal to arouse support in the educated circles of Germany. The journal would bring attention to those "culturally and religiously historical, geographic, ethnological, and similar questions" that could be investigated and answered in order to professionalize, rationalize, and maximize the activities of missionaries. Warneck defined the purpose of the *Allgemeine Missions-Zeitschrift* and Missionswissenschaft as the furtherance of the Christian Gospel, over and above other concerns.[35] The journal and its editor supported an integrationist approach to the relationship between religion and modernity, though not without some reservations about the risks involved in "modernizing" Christianity.[36] A decade later, when overseas empire became a reality for Germany, Warneck argued that the importance of missionary work had grown, because "German colonial policy implie[d] a greater responsibility [for] our mission activities, as well as [made] mission a partner in the civilizing activity of colonial policy."[37] The *Allgemeine*

Missions-Zeitschrift served Warneck and Germany's missionary leadership as a major space for composing their internationalist vision of German Protestant missionary life.[38] Warneck's *Missions-Zeitschrift* served two generations of missionary theorists and practitioners as *the* venue in which Germany's Protestant mission movement debated and declared its positions on the key religious, political, and scientific issues of missionary life.

Missionaries and missionary leaders like Gustav Warneck had a particular definition of politics in these discussions. In general, missionaries insisted that their work was not political, but their denial does not actually mean that they were apolitical. In fact, the missionaries' mere presence in non-Western societies had political causes and political effects on the colonial situation.[39] To German Missionswissenschaftler and missionary leaders, "politics" meant secular affairs, specifically the activities of the state (and almost always the state churches) in the colonies. Though missionaries would willingly admit their role in a larger European, Western, or Christian colonial project, they resisted participating in the "political" activities of any *particular* German or other colonial project.[40] However, of course, their activities in the metropole, namely mission leaders' participation in contests for political, symbolic, intellectual, and spiritual power, all required that missionaries engage in political activities just like everyone else. But in their rhetoric, missionaries used the term "politics" to malign activities they did not view as constitutive of their own activities.

At the heart of German missionaries' aversion to state influence and power was their certainty that their work was divinely sanctified. They interpreted the activities borne of the Great Commission as older and superior to secular forms of colonial activity. Politics in all its forms – interpower rivalry, the false idol of the national state, and the meanness of public policy – was, at least intellectually, seen as a menace that undermined missionaries' work as evangelists. They believed that the globalizing power of both the modern state and modern capitalism threatened Christian values.[41] As a response to this double threat, missionary intellectuals embraced an ideology of missionary internationalism opposed to nationalist pressures at home and strong enough to resist supranational threats like secularism and capitalism. The flexibility of the internationalist position and its theological strength (as compared with more nationalist interpretations of the Great Commission) created a durable and lasting solution to the complex binary of challenges and opportunities created by globalization and colonialism in the late nineteenth century.

Scientific and theological issues had been debated in the ecclesiastical and popular periodicals of the German mission movement before the launch of the *Allgemeine Missions-Zeitschrift*. However, with the journal, Warneck created something new.[42] As editor, he sought to lift the quality and rigour of missionary discourse to achieve two goals: first, to improve the quality and efficacy of Protestant missionary work; and, second, to attract more of the educated middle class to support and participate in the work of the mission societies. The *Allgemeine Missions-Zeitschrift* differed from other missionary periodicals because of its scholarly direction and broad inclusion of material from all Protestant mission societies.[43] The journal had wide circulation. By the end of the 1880s it published 2,600 copies per month with a peak of 3,000 subscribers in 1912.[44] Its scope extended beyond the mission sphere in Germany, and included the colonial director and his aides as regular readers.[45] The *Allgemeine Missions-Zeitschrift* cast a wide net, offering its readers diverse material, ranging from articles on languages of the Himalayan plateau[46] to the history of Christian conversion in the medieval German lands.[47] This broad reach led the journal to become something of a hybrid publication that mixed elements of a news magazine, a scholarly journal, and a digest of mission society news.

The *Allgemeine Missions-Zeitschrift* conveyed German missionary Protestantism's internationalism to its subscribers and readers in a number of ways. First, by presenting articles covering the activities of German mission societies around the world, within and beyond the German colonial empire, the *Allgemeine Missions-Zeitschrift* communicated to its readers the global character of German mission. Missionaries were thus aligned with explorers and scientists as contributors to an international humanitarian project.[48] Second, from this demonstration of German mission's global dimensions, the editors and contributors to the *Allgemeine Missions-Zeitschrift* connected its readers to the broader international missionary movement. This goal was furthered by the frequent inclusion of articles by foreign contributors and about non-German Protestant mission societies. Finally, the *Allgemeine Missions-Zeitschrift*'s focus on presenting the best scientific and scholarly work to its readers helped mark the journal as a sophisticated modern publication, employing the universal languages of the biological and human sciences.[49]

As editor of the *Allgemeine Missions-Zeitschrift*, Warneck exerted considerable influence on the development of German Protestant missionary culture. Born near Halle in 1834, he sought to rise above his father's trade of needle-making and entered the Gymnasium of the Francke Foundation in Halle, where he earned high marks. He went on to study theology at Halle University. In 1858 he passed his theological examination with honours and accepted a position as tutor to a noble family in Elberfeld-Wuppertal. In his early years Warneck thus moved from one centre of German evangelical energy, Halle, to another hotbed of missionary zeal, the Wuppertal of the northern Rhineland. It is thus not surprising that a religious young man like Warneck aspired to become a missionary. But a lifelong lung condition prevented him from achieving that goal. Instead he turned to supporting mission work in the *Heimat*, a term mission societies used to refer to the work of training missionaries, promoting mission goals, and fundraising in Germany. After marrying in 1862, he served as pastor in Roitzsch near Bitterfeld in Saxony (1862–3), where he met his lifelong collaborator on the *Allgemeine Missions-Zeitschrift*, Reinhold Grundemann. He then served as minister in Dommitzsch near Torgau (1863–70), earned his doctorate from the University of Jena (1871), and taught at the seminary of the Rhenish Mission Society in Barmen-Wuppertal, where he collaborated with mission leaders and theologians Theodor Christlieb, Johann Christoph Blumhard, and Friedrich Fabri (1871–4). It was after this period of migration between Saxony and the Rhineland that Warneck settled in Rothenschirmbach, near Eisleben in Prussian Saxony, to serve as pastor for the next twenty-two years.

In Rothenschirmbach, Warneck founded, with many collaborators, Missionswissenschaft as an academic subdiscipline of practical theology – the arm of theology most concerned with the day-to-day work of Christian pastors. And it was during his residency in Rothenschirmbach as pastor of a 700-member congregation that Warneck played a leading role in establishing other pillars of the Protestant mission movement in Germany. The *Allgemeine Missions-Zeitschrift* began publication in 1873. In 1879 he founded the Missionskonferenz der Provinz Sachsen (Mission Conference of Saxony), which served as a model for twenty similar conferences across Germany.[50] Warneck was present in Bremen in 1884 when the assembled leaders of the Protestant mission movement established the Ausschuß and appointed him one of its leaders. From 1892 to 1903, he published a three-volume magnum opus, *Evangelische Missionslehre*, which cemented his position as a leader of the global Protestant mission movement. Warneck's triumphal departure from Rothenschirmbach came after he accepted the first-ever university chair of Missionswissenschaft at the University of Halle in 1896.[51] Warneck's editorship of the *Allgemeine Missions-Zeitschrift*, institutional leadership, and international reputation allowed him to shape Protestant mission ideology in Germany and around the world.

Warneck and his colleagues' internationalism grew from three premises. First, the prevailing majority of Missionswissenschaftler argued, through their interpretation of the Gospels and Epistles, that the only relevant way to sort humankind was into Christians and non-Christians. Thus, no other categorization of humanity was meaningful when compared to missionaries' evangelical criteria. As a consequence, missionary scholars and leaders largely rejected nationalist politics as irrelevant to their activities. Second, "politics," as missionaries in Germany defined them, were seen as corrosive to missionaries' spiritual endeavour. Secular demands for national loyalty and direct service to the secular colonial project, mission leaders argued, led mission away from its higher purpose, demeaned missionary endeavour, and endangered souls by slowing the progress of evangelization. Finally, missionary leaders argued that colonial competition among the powers was disruptive. The free exercise of missionary activities, they claimed, was essential to the success of mission work. Wars and colonial rivalries imperilled missionaries' autonomy and disrupted the transmission of Christ's message. To counter these threats, Warneck and others promoted policies of internationalism in German Protestant mission work. By restraining nationalism, mitigating their own national loyalties, and affiliating with Protestants around the world, missionary leaders argued, missionaries could capitalize on the expansion of global networks to evangelize every corner of the globe.

Despite Warneck's major contributions, Friedrich Fabri is considered the most famous German Protestant missionary. Fabri is frequently credited with launching the German colonial movement with his pamphlet *Bedarf Deutschland der Kolonien?* (*Does Germany Need Colonies?*);[52] he exercised notable influence as an associate of Bismarck's in the early 1880s when Germany seized the bulk of its colonies.[53] But Fabri's importance is more to the colonial movement than to the German Protestant mission movement. In fact, by the time Germany's Protestant mission societies were involved with the German colonial empire, Fabri had been forced out of his position at the head of the Rhenish Mission *because* of the close links he sought between mission work and colonial expansion.[54] The leadership of the Rhenish Mission Society and the actual leaders of the German Protestant mission movement, namely Warneck and Zahn, forced Fabri from his post at the Rhenish Mission in 1884 and from leadership in the various national mission conferences.[55] Given Fabri's marginality by the mid-1880s, this study does not concern itself with his activities.

The views of Warneck, Zahn, and their associates were well established at the founding of the German Empire in 1871 and the conquest of German colonies in the 1880s. Then historical processes of economic, political, cultural, and social change that had begun earlier in the century shifted gears in the last decade of the nineteenth century.[56] After 1890, missionaries had to defend their internationalist ideas and policies during a period of considerable intellectual and cultural tumult in the Kaiserreich. Emerging political institutions and associations, industrialization and urbanization, and real and imagined challenges posed by Germany's multiple fractures in terms of identity and relationship to the nation-state changed the shape of German society in ever-expanding ways.[57] To many cultural critics Germany remained divided along regional, confessional, and political lines. Germany, therefore, required a second founding to eliminate the remaining divisions. Germany's missionary leaders continually participated (willingly and unwillingly) in practical and ideological debates touched by nationalist ideas.[58] In the case of German missionaries, intimately involved in Germany's colonial project and eager to benefit from political opportunities while somehow protecting themselves from the risks, the problem of nationalism and national identity remained of key concern. Missionaries' loyalties to an internationalist worldview only complicated issues; at the end of the day, the missionaries did not care very much about national unification. Their priorities were for a Christian unity that discounted the essential importance of "Germanness" or any other national identity.

The Primacy of Christian Evangelization

The injunction to Christians to spread the Gospel to the whole of creation, the Great Commission, carried such weight that, from missionaries' point of view, no other project could or ought to take precedence. The various examples of the Commission in scripture served as the chief justification for their most basic practice of their faith, the support and promotion of missionary work among Christian and non-Christian communities.[59] The Great Commission provided the biblical basis for German (and other) missionaries' work and evidence that they, acting as direct agents of the divine, had the right and responsibility to give religious concerns priority over any others. The certitude that it provided led missionaries to assume that they held the moral high ground with respect to other colonialists. Morally superior and unsullied by commercial or political goals, missionaries saw themselves as benevolently including all people in their plans.

One of the clearest articulations of this view in the *Allgemeine Missions-Zeitschrift* came from a leader of the oldest German missionary church, Ernst Reichel of the Moravian Brüdergemeine. In 1886, Missionsdirektor

Reichel wrote that missionary leaders must protect their work's "godly, … international, and … [politically] independent character." Otherwise, missionaries in the colonies might easily become an appendage of European colonial immorality.[60] Reichel regarded missions as distinct from colonies. Colonies served profane goals of power and wealth on earth. Missions, in contrast, served to "spread … a kingdom that is not of this world." German missionaries' purpose and goal must be to save "heathen" souls and, through conversions, bring more of humanity into the Christian community.[61] Reichel's clear separation of state-based imperialism and missionary evangelization serves as a productive baseline for recognizing key features of German Protestant missionary positioning during the colonial era. The determination to remain autonomous and international in defence of a religious purpose equipped missionary intellectuals with a consistent starting point for navigating the practical realities of globalization.

In fact, the religious justification for missionary independence continued to equip missionary intellectuals with justification for their positions. In 1891 the *Allgemeine Missions-Zeitschrift* reprinted the text of a lecture given by Warneck at the Saxon Provincial Mission Conference in Halle. In his lecture, Warneck argued that mission work was an "apostolic" project, built upon and drawing inspiration from the traditions of the earliest followers of Jesus. The inspired and human quality of early Christian evangelization, Warneck argued, provided a model for missionary work. Christianity had not spread in antiquity through state action or close collaboration with the state. Instead it had spread through the divinely commanded and spiritually motivated work of dedicated preachers and believers building connections with the pagans and Jews of the Mediterranean world. Historical precedent like this, Warneck's argument ran, proved God's intent and served as evidence of "best practices" that provided guidance for mission work in the modern era. Those who wished to instrumentalize missionaries as servants of an aspirationally technocratic colonial state did not understand mission's history, purpose, or best interests. Warneck wrote that "civilization brings many useful things: trains, the telegraph, gas lighting and the comforts of abundance; but it does not bring Christian faith."[62] According to Warneck, the late nineteenth-century colonial state, with its supposed civilizing mission, did little to advance Christianity.[63]

Perhaps not Warneck's equal as an academic, but certainly his equal in authority in the German mission movement, Franz Michael Zahn, director of the North German Mission Society, produced the most reasoned defence of mission's superiority over nationalism. The North German Mission Society had been founded in 1836 and, after false starts in New Zealand and India, focused its work among the Ewe-speaking groups in territories that would become part of Ghana and Togo. Zahn had been the mission society's leader since 1862. His position threatened the fundamental basis of nationalist arguments for missionary particularism and left little room for compromise. He noted that, since the establishment of German colonies, German nationalists had suddenly become "mission friends" who wished to see German money and lives spent only in German colonies.[64] In his opinion, the ideology these new friends depended on, nationalism, was an intellectual edifice built on unstable ground. In his refutation of nationalism, Zahn offered a defence of human diversity and a clear articulation of tolerance of that diversity as a bedrock principle of German Protestant missionary thought.

To Zahn, biblical tales of human difference and universality demonstrated Christians' "moral imperative to respect" human diversity. Attaching essential characteristics to any group of people, like the Germans or the English, would be an error. He argued that national identity was an ongoing construct shaped by internal and external influences. Furthermore, because of changing borders, the movements of people, and exchanges of ideas across boundaries, there was barely any people of a "world historical significance" that was not a "mixed *Volk*." For both historical and theological reasons, Zahn elevated a Christian multiculturalism above any glorification of national virtues.[65] His elaboration of humanity's mixed origins made the missionaries more prepared to include other groups in the promised Christian future.

Zahn supported the monogenetic argument of Reinhold Grundemann, one of the oldest mission scholars and one of Warneck's founding collaborators on the *Allgemeine Missions-Zeitschrift*, who argued that before there were "peoples" on Earth, humanity had been united. Therefore, the goal of history was to collect humanity, regardless of racial or ethnic origins, into one community of faith and peace. Zahn called any refusal to recognize this truth "immoral patriotism." The Great Commission set the course for human activity, the goal of creating a communal existence without cultural or national distinction. Only a "sickly overemphasis of national feeling" could cause one to move away from this communitarian purpose and ignore the good in another people.[66] The real future of Germany's missionaries, Zahn maintained, required an embrace of the international brotherhood of Protestant Christians, which would help tear down the false barriers of human difference. As Warneck wrote in 1901, "Mission should not make the peoples into Germans, Englishmen, Frenchmen, or Russians; [it] should make them into Christians."[67]

Maintaining that focus on creating Christians and not Germans was a real challenge for German missionaries. They believed the politics of colonial interests threatened to rot everything it touched, especially mission. Nonetheless, in some cases the prosaic concerns of colonial officials and politicians became authentic and troubling threats to mission activities that demanded missionaries involve themselves in political debates. Missionary leaders overwhelmingly agreed that involving missionaries as active participants in the administration of colonial territories threatened to corrupt mission work. The threat was twofold. First, any diversion of missionary energy to support colonial goals was a violation of Christian principles. Second, if missionaries involved themselves in any action by colonial powers it would be even more likely that colonized people would equate missionaries with the colonial regime. Missionaries' supposedly good deeds would be tainted by their affiliation with the irreligious and immoral colonial state. And any turn away from internationalist views would undermine the moral superiority that the missionaries could claim for their works.

On this issue Warneck provided his colleagues with guidance. The correct relationship among national loyalty, the state, and mission work required missionaries to stand against efforts by the colonial state to "misuse religion and mission for political and colonial political purposes." According to Warneck, the colonial state sought to use missionaries as a salve for its conscience, as a justification for conquest. If missionaries allowed the state to use their work in such ways, they would discredit themselves among supporters at home and in the indigenous communities abroad.[68] Warneck's views dominated, but some leaders, like the Moravian Reichel, perceived space for cooperation but still supported Warneck's arguments in order to maintain missionaries' productive autonomy.[69]

Historical circumstances challenged Warneck's positioning. By 1891 he was acknowledging that globalization, particularly its expression through expanding German power and influence, had eliminated the secure isolation from politics that mission societies had enjoyed for most of the century. The expansion of the mission movement had complicated matters. The growing influence of mission, its growth from "child to man," meant that the secular world now sought to channel missionary activities and, as a result, could fundamentally change the mission project.[70] The new proximity (physical and metaphorical) of German state power to mission work required a definition of boundaries, Warneck argued. Economic development for the national interest would only lead missionary work away from service to God. As Warneck put it, missionaries should "build the kingdom which is not of this world."[71]

According to Warneck, secular colonial interests had cynically appropriated humanitarian rhetoric. He contended that secular colonialists took an interest in the lives of the colonized not because they shared missionaries' altruistic concerns for the welfare of indigenous people, but because they wished to extract the most utility out of them for the economic development of the colonies.[72] The threat that German missionaries might be led astray from their divinely appointed task reinforced Warneck's view, and those of his compatriots, that politics was corrosive to the core task of German mission work – the creation of Christians. Education, when left to secular colonialists, did not serve the interests of the student but of the teacher; therefore, missionaries had to preserve their autonomy to avoid the corruption of their work.

The International Question

Even a spiritually pure and universalist mission movement could not avoid every worldly concern. Though a minority of German missionaries saw colonial expansion as a necessary support to missionary activity, the majority responded ambivalently to the expansion of global imperialism in the last quarter of the nineteenth century. This ambivalence arose out of a general understanding among missionary leaders that the increasing competition among the colonial powers fed on and encouraged chauvinistic policies and bald antagonism. The policies that could naturally develop from overt competition were likely to disrupt the morally essential activities of missionaries around the world. Furthermore, a more competitive colonialism could lead to a more assertive and interventionist colonial state that demanded greater loyalty and service from missionaries. In the face of these threats, internationalist ideology became more established.

Evidence of this shift to a more determined internationalism can be seen by comparing reflections on the relationship between missionaries and the colonial state before 1890 and after 1890. In the earlier, calmer period of imperial expansion, Missionsdirektor Reichel of the Moravians argued that his society's experiences in the colonial possessions of Britain, Holland, and Denmark demonstrated that mission and the state could comfortably coexist. In the vast majority of cases, colonial governments did not treat German missionaries appreciably differently from missionaries who shared the colonial powers' nationality; furthermore, the other powers regularly used administrative authority to support the work of German missionaries.[73] Reichel argued that the example set by other Protestant colonial powers – Great Britain, Denmark, and the Netherlands – required that Germany act with the same equanimity.

Even so, he argued that German missionaries must maintain their patriotic agnosticism in order to continue to preserve international comity.[74]

After 1890, German engagement around the world, but especially in East Asia, intensified as a result of *Weltpolitik*, an aggressive foreign policy designed by Kaiser Wilhelm II and his like-minded advisers to solidify Germany's global prestige and power. To them, the industrial, scientific, and economic success of the Kaiserreich confirmed that the global balance of power was shifting and German interests must be recognized as global in scope and import.[75] For those who subscribed to this new turn in German policy, Germany's colonial possessions and ambitions became central to foreign policy. The enlarged colonial empire desired by Wilhelm, Admiral Alfred Tirpitz (the mastermind of the new German fleet), Chancellor Bernhard Bülow, and other *Weltpolitiker* inside and outside the government would offer expanded access to world markets and serve as tangible proof of Germany's strength and diplomatic prestige.[76] Policymakers promoted German intervention in colonial and global affairs designed as much to assert German global privileges as to garner any tangible benefit.[77] This change in policy intensified the threats posed by globalization to missionary activity

The acquisition by the German Imperial Navy of a ninety-nine-year lease to the territories around Jiaozhou Bay (Kiaochow) in 1898, derived as a concession from Qing China, and from the participation of Germany in the Eight-Nation Alliance against the Boxer Rebellion in 1900 marked a new phase of German imperial activity. For decades German Protestant missionaries had been active in China, but the Boxer Rebellion brought fatal attention from Chinese militants and unwanted attention from the European political class to the missionaries' efforts. Many anticolonial and anti-religious critics blamed the activities of German, and especially Protestant, missionaries for inciting the Chinese to violent resistance. Meanwhile, the Ausschuß connected anti-missionary violence in China with anti-missionary rhetoric in Germany. To the Ausschuß, the accusations offered a clear confirmation that global politics threatened to drag missionary work into a dangerous world of profane concerns and agendas.[78]

Warneck took the lead in formulating a rebuttal of missionaries' detractors while promising his missionary readers that the future would promise a "sifting" in China as the European imperial powers asserted new privileges. A new situation in which European and Japanese colonial administrators took greater authority in the Chinese Empire could force missionaries to come to new terms with colonialism. After all, colonial powers might prove more powerful than the Qing emperors and their bureaucrats and use their power to intervene in missionary activities. In general, missionaries conceived of themselves as possessing the upper hand in arguments with the weaker, non-Christian, non-Western Chinese.[79] They might not have the same confidence against German, French, or British colonial officials. Such bald intervention, Warneck suggested, could not be guaranteed to serve Christian missionary interests.[80]

Not only did the crisis spur Warneck's public defence of missionary practices in China, it also goaded him into penning a warning for his colleagues. At the 1901 Saxon Mission Conference and in a reprint of his remarks in the *Allgemeine Missions-Zeitschrift*, Warneck recounted how in the earlier period of colonial conquest missionaries were enjoined to "replace religious missionary work with 'worker education'" and told that they must place themselves in service to the interests of the Fatherland. Missionary experts who defended the religious and universal character of mission "were denounced as 'unpatriotic.'" Accusations of missionary incitement in China and what Warneck (and others) saw as the impending division of China into colonial possessions could portend a new period of secular pressure on missionaries.[81] More mercenary colonial policies could lead to a slackening of missionary momentum and a more intolerant climate for missionary activities in the field.[82] Warneck reminded his compatriots of their international missionary purpose: as he put it, secular imperialism desired a transformation of colonized people into loyal subjects, while missionaries sought to create subjects for the heavenly Fatherland. If expanding imperial rivalry threatened missionaries' internationalist character, it threatened the missionaries' divinely inspired purpose.[83]

That same 1901 lecture also saw the beginnings of a shift in Warneck's ideas about world politics. By 1900 it was impossible for any observer of global politics not to believe that they were witness to important forces of change sweeping the world. European powers had finished the partition of Africa, the Spanish-American War had demonstrated American imperial power and ambitions, and conflicts in China and Central Asia among the imperial powers (now including Japan) made it impossible for any politically active individual to ignore the tense realities of global foreign relations. In the case of Warneck and a few others this meant that other ideologies with international vision might compete with universalist missionary Christianity. The old guard of missionary leaders, like other thinkers and statesmen, recognized the symptoms of globalization. And they noted the new circumstances brought challenges from other social and intellectual movements: global religions (especially Islam), the secular internationalism of socialism, and the culturally and socially integrative effects of global capitalism. In this new reality, the missionaries did not turn away from their old principles but did seek to build a German mission movement that could deal with the challenges offered by competing internationalisms and nationalisms.

Because missionaries felt bound to a higher obligation as advocates of indigenous people, the missionaries could only partially take advantage of the opportunities provided by colonial expansion. "Colonial-political egoism" or ignorance of "native" people's lives endangered the well-being of colonized and missionized people. The ultimate goal, Warneck contended, of mission activity should be an "economically self-sufficient existence" for colonized communities. Missionaries should care for the national identity of the colonized against the frequent tendency of colonial governments to proletarianize indigenous populations, destroying cultural differences and transforming the colonized into creolized labourers.[84] The threats of modern capitalism and the damage it had wrought in Germany's small towns and villages, cities, and neighbourhoods could not be allowed to spread to Africa and Asia.

The dynamic durability of missionaries' internationalist ideology also can be observed in a speech by Carl Mirbt at the 1906 meeting of the Saxon Mission Conference. Mirbt, since 1890 Professor of Church History at the University of Marburg, was one of the pre-eminent academics of Missionswissenschaft. An expert on Catholic Church history, Mirbt also wrote a number of important works on Protestant mission. At the Mission Conference of 1906 he offered an examination of the relative relationships among world religions and an explanation that considered the new global networks of exchange. He cast his lecture as a discussion of the "question of the justice of mission," which ultimately came to the supposition that "[mission was a] granted right … and enjoined duty" of the Christian church.[85] Much of his presentation focused on the calculus of global religious competition; after all, the same expansion of global transportation that facilitated Christian missionaries' work was also available for the propagation of other faiths. Mirbt's ideas neatly capture the duality of missionary attitudes toward globalization – anxious about secular and religious threats and effusive about the advantages of global connectivity.

The new era of globalization portended to Mirbt a heightened conflict among the world's religions. He described growing rivalries among Buddhists, Muslims, and Christians in Asia, Africa, and Europe. Victory in this great conflict would be determined by which faith could mobilize the missionary drive necessary to win new converts. And though Mirbt thought most of the battles would be fought in the colonial sphere, he nonetheless shared the fears of many that globalization threatened to bring dangerous things back to the colonizing states. Specifically, Mirbt warned his listeners about what he perceived as the insidious spread of Buddhist literature and ideas in European and American intellectual circles.[86] Furthermore, Japanese military and economic success also indicated a resurgent energy among non-Christian non-Europeans.[87] The widespread respect for Japanese culture and for Buddhism among certain groups in Europe indicated to Mirbt the weakness of Christian influence among those same groups of European society and not any "inner strength of Buddhism."

Mirbt offered an unusually negative interpretation of the global situation around 1900. While Buddhism apparently threatened to corrupt Christians in their homelands, Islam threatened Christianity in the colonies. Muslims, according to Mirbt, had sought "the subjugation of the world under the crescent" since the seventh century, a campaign waged now by "dervish orders, the elite troops" of Islamic might in Africa and Asia. The Middle East and the Levant already belonged to Islam; millions of Muslims lived in India, China, and the islands off Southeast Asia; North Africa was long ago lost, and in the west and east of the African continent Islam's power was undeniable.[88] Warneck's writings also reflected a growing worry that European secularism threatened to corrupt the *Kulturvölker* of China, Japan, and India. He worried that academic works which undermined Christian belief by spreading "agnosticism, atheism, and materialism," – "modernism" in Warneck's shorthand – might spread to "large half-educated circles of non-Christian Kulturvölker" and lead them astray before Christianity could take hold.[89] Taken together, these two men's ideas show the complicated forces that Missionswissenschaftler struggled to understand and defeat through their work.

Though he agreed with Mirbt, Warneck did not indulge in the same dark fantasies about the expansion of religious conflict in the colonial and globalized world. In his published work he continued to acknowledge that the revolution in transportation and communication and the expansion of wealth that both encouraged and resulted from ongoing globalization had been a boon to the missionary enterprise.[90] Even so, Warneck summarized what he saw as key concerns that world trade raised. He argued that as mission remained uncorrupted, it had become in a sense a "city on a hill" that might still serve as a moral example. Writing in 1908, Warneck pointed out that, in contrast to earlier decades, now very few missionaries in the field preached at isolated mission stations with no contact with the "modern" world. However, mission's position on the hill also put it in an "exposed position" subject to public judgment and at greater risk of secular interference. He concluded that earlier efforts to raise the profile of their activities among the German public had succeeded. Yet, Warneck revealed himself to be uncomfortable with the new scrutiny that success had brought – the criticism after the Boxer Rebellion was only one example. In this period after 1900, German mission societies found themselves embroiled in a series of conflicts with other colonial actors. The growing engagement of other Europeans with mission work because of the growth in global exchange had, in Warneck's opinion, both introduced to missionary enterprise useful advice and subjected it to uninformed and dangerous criticism. Warneck argued that in the same way that a musical understanding was necessary to judge musical works, so was a religious understanding necessary for fair judgment of missionary activities.[91]

Other Europeans in the colonies – merchants, soldiers, officials, and settlers from Europe – might represent fine examples of the "civilizing mission," Warneck allowed. Sadly, such an assumption was "only a beautiful dream." The majority of Europeans in the colonies were "no worthy representation of Christianity"; in fact, their behaviour provided the heathen with manifold examples of Christian depravity. Globalization, as instituted by White Christians who appeared in the colonies, cast "a long, dark shadow."[92] Once again, Warneck's attack on secular colonialists reveals the ambiguity of missionary interpretations of globalization. Missionaries embraced globalization when it expanded the reach and resources of their societies' activities. But, Warneck, representative of other German Protestant missionaries, could not fully embrace globalization's essentially capitalist nature. The response to the "immorality" of economic colonialists was not a rejection of globalization, but an insistence that missionaries needed to adapt to the new global conditions with greater moral purity and ongoing commitment to their godliness, independence, and internationalism.

The competition engendered by world trade and global exchange further imperilled Christian mission in the world. To Warneck, colonialism, world trade, and economic policies had brought overseas people little of worth; the only outcome had been "frequent brutality, violence, and avarice." One only needed, Warneck pointed out, to take note of the countless wars and uprisings led by "native" groups in response to the excesses of colonialism, the opium and spirit trades, appropriation of property and proletarianization of indigenous people, the repression of economic independence, and the cruelty of work contracts to recognize the danger of economic modernization to missionized people. Warneck's interpretation of the effects of imperialism and globalization upon non-Western societies often echoed critics, like Vladimir Lenin and John Hobson, who stood to Warneck's intellectual and political left.

Missionaries shared in the suffering of the people with whom they lived and worked, Warneck argued. He conceded that missionaries lacked the power to stop this global competition for power, but they could, through their "Christian faith and Christian morality," help mitigate its effects. The more that Christian missionaries forced the Christian powers to participate in the competition for markets and trade in a moral fashion, the more non-Christian people would be able to participate in global trade and protect themselves from exploitation.[93]

The Younger Generation

Warneck and Mirbt, both established forces in the German missionary community, agreed that the world was beginning to change in 1900 and the concerns of missionary activity had to expand to deal with mounting challenges. The older generation of thinkers continued to have its adherents, but it was challenged by a younger group who saw mission as only one among many worthy movements which could influence the course of history.[94] The two leading figures of the next class of missionary leaders, Julius Richter and Karl Axenfeld, brought a slightly different view of their German identity and its interaction with missionary internationalism. Their thinking reveals a gradual revision to their predecessors' internationalist ideology in the years leading up to the First World War.

Richter and Axenfeld were both associated with the Berlin Mission Society and both were residents of the cosmopolitan Prussian and imperial capital. By the 1880s Berlin teemed with over one million people and by 1900 it had grown into its role as an international metropolis.[95] The maturation of Berlin and the German Empire had a formative effect on Richter and Axenfeld. Both men, unlike Warneck and his colleagues, had only ever known a unified German state. Their maturation as Missionswissenschaftler had always required them to accept a relationship between missionary activities and German colonial power. After 1900 and as their influence in the mission movement increased, both men continued to wrestle with the threats and promise of globalization. Their comfort with German national and colonial power led them to accommodate a German national identity within their proscriptions for missionary culture. Other pressures in the colonial sphere, particularly colonial wars fought in the first decade of the twentieth century, also contributed to a shift in the wider discourse about Germany's colonial policies and politics.[96] Axenfeld and Richter saw themselves and the mission movement to which they were committed as German and internationalist, as cosmopolitan instead of stateless. But they did not abandon the broad framework that earlier generations had articulated, one which placed German Protestant missionary engagement across borders at the centre of missionary ideology.

The relationship between missionary ideology and the constellation of forces customarily thought of as "modernity" by late nineteenth-century intellectuals was never clear-cut. On the one hand, the roots of the nineteenth-century mission movement in the anti-Enlightenment religious awakening predisposed many missionary theorists to be suspicious of the influence of industrial society upon the world. At the same time a younger generation of missionaries, more comfortable with the mechanized landscape of fin-de-siècle Europe, saw technological developments as a sign of God's providence, evidence of divine intention that Christianity finally spread across the globe. Warneck's work reflected his ambiguous stance toward technology, but Karl Axenfeld provided the best evidence of a younger generation's inclinations – eager to evangelize the world with the tools of the modern age: he exulted that an "express train out of the Christian West" would speed through "the breach in the Chinese wall" created by European technological prowess.[97]

Nonetheless, Axenfeld remained theologically committed to traditional themes of missionary ideology. In one commentary on Matthew 24:14, he predicted that Christian mission's success would arise from religious and spiritual sources, independent of any "political" forces. That verse from Matthew, "And this good news of the kingdom will be proclaimed throughout the world, as a testimony to all the nations; and then the end will come," was one of the many expressions of the Great Commission. Axenfeld's reflection on the Commission in a short article entitled "World Evangelization and Its Conclusion" offers an object lesson that even the most political of missionary animals could see the project of missionary evangelization as spiritually, morally, and practically independent of political considerations. Axenfeld celebrated God as the source of the benefits of globalization. He had placed Christian missionaries in a world with the steamship, telegraph, and railroad, Axenfeld argued, and with this providence had provided to Christians the tools to fulfil his promise of a Christian globe. Axenfeld went on to celebrate that globalization meant the number of people who had never heard the Christian message was shrinking in the current age.[98] Once all men and women were brought by mission to Christianity, every Christian would attend to the teachings of the Bible and hasten the Millennium. The decisive hour for the kingdom of God would be the hour when Christianity had vanquished all other faiths.[99]

Julius Richter, successor to Warneck as editor of the *Allgemeine Missions-Zeitschrift*, wrote the introductory essay of the first 1914 issue. In this essay, Axenfeld's contemporary used an understanding of the world defined by the national idea in order to preserve the internationalist purpose of German Protestant missionary activities. Richter reflected the prevailing missionary understanding that all the world's people were divided by divine purpose into nations. He judged that those nations must be brought together and put into the service of God's internationalist intention, that the nations eventually be made to disappear. World peace and world mission were, to Richter, "vitally connected." And like Axenfeld, he seemed to have firmly embraced globalization in all its forms as essential to his evangelical dreams. The spread of European power across the globe and the awakening of national consciousness in Europe and, in his view, Africa and Asia held great promise for the expansion of Christianity and its message of peace.[100]

The greatest achievement still ahead for European culture was to bring its powerful and important civilization to all the people of the world. Richter, like missionaries before him, turned to moral arguments to guide nationalist energies. He argued that war between Britain and Germany would be a "crime against humanity" because it would constrict the ability of the two great Protestant powers to spread God's humanitarian purpose.[101] If an un-Christian jingoism brought the Christian powers into conflict, then missionaries of every nation would fail in their ultimate goal of spreading Christian peace around the world.[102] It was not necessary for the nations to abandon their national identities in order to serve missionary priorities, but they did have to set aside national rivalries.

Conclusion

Protestant Missionswissenschaft and its authors dominated the leadership of Germany's Protestant missionary culture and movement. A handful of men stood head and shoulders above the rest and their ideas set the tone. Academics and academic responses to globalization shaped approaches to mission work advocated by men like Gustav Warneck and Karl Axenfeld. Their ideas confronted a dualistic understanding of globalization as threat and promise. In their responses the Missionswissenschaftler advocated an autonomous and free mission movement with an internationalist worldview. Globalization offered the opportunity for the Christian message to encircle the globe, but the only way for mission societies to avoid the dangerous aspects of globalization was to remain independent and unencumbered by secular alliances.

For nearly thirty years the dominant view was that mission should hold itself strictly apart from the activities of the colonial state. This position was marked by four characteristics. First, it was spearheaded by Warneck and supported by his fellow members of the older generation of German mission leaders. All had been born before the establishment of a German nation-state and colonial empire, and all judged that mission had been successful before there was a Germany and that it could and should remain successful now that there was an internationally powerful German Empire. Put simply, Germany's mission societies belonged to an international community, a community that served God's design. Second, the imperative of the Great Commission meant that the missionary project superseded all other human ambitions. This meant that German missionaries' work must be by definition international and subject to no secular agenda. Third, beyond missionaries' principled separation of mission and politics there was a vital practical basis for separating missionary activity from colonial political activity. Politics would corrupt mission work if given the chance. Consequently, the older generation of missionary thinkers cited protecting the integrity of missionary endeavour as a further reason to keep mission above and separate from politics. Finally, Warneck and his compatriots agreed that politics in any form was a threat to the resources and attention necessary for missionary success.

Though the second generation of missionary leaders averred that Germanness ought to influence German missionary work, they had no desire to radically remake the consensus view of the older generation. Revisionists but not reformists, Karl Axenfeld, Julius Richter, and others did not abandon the internationalist determination of German missionary culture. And so, for a period of nearly fifty years, German missionary intellectuals and leaders preserved a largely united front in favour of international collaboration. Their ideas would shape Germans' participation in colonial, metropolitan, and international spaces of missionary endeavour.

2 Speaking in Tongues

Language, Education, and Volkskirchen

In our own time, *glossolalia*, or "speaking in tongues," has mostly come to refer to the charismatic expression of religious faith among some Christian denominations – a spontaneous expression of spiritual ecstasy in which the affected, inspired by the Holy Spirit, speaks in an unknown language, in "tongues." A similar phenomenon appears in the Christian New Testament. For example, the Acts of the Apostles recount the descent of the Holy Spirit upon an early gathering of the Apostles and other followers of Jesus. The passage, the story of Pentecost, relates how the gathered men and women came to speak in languages that were not their own.[1] Other passages elsewhere in the Bible reference Christians "speaking in tongues."[2] Scholars of the New Testament and early Christianity hold diverse interpretations of the scriptural and symbolic meanings of these moments. Regardless, the repetitions of biblical narratives which revolve around language and the history of early Christian communities provided scriptural purchase for missionaries to confront their own challenges. Linguistic and cultural diversity across the globe shaped German, and other, missionaries' work.

As German Protestant missionaries spread themselves across the world, the story of Pentecost resonated with them as they encountered men and women who did not speak German and whose languages the missionaries had to learn.[3] In Genesis, the story of the Tower of Babel explained humanity's dissociation into the many languages and cultures of the world. That passage served as literal or metaphorical explanation for the broad diversity of human communities that missionaries encountered.[4] To German missionaries, linguistic facility promised to resolve these divisions of humanity. The stories of Pentecost and the Tower of Babel comforted them as they faced the practical challenge of evangelizing in all the world's languages. The story of Babel helped them to understand that the diversity of humanity was part of God's plan, and the story of Pentecost reassured them that God's message transcended those divisions.[5] While God had divided the "nations" in ancient times, the modern era had equipped missionaries with the tools and skills to reach every human community.

Their respect for the languages of the world and commitment to indigenous languages encouraged German Protestant missionaries to view non-Europeans with a sympathetic mind. To the missionaries, the diversity of human language was but one sign of God's endorsement of human difference. Though Christian unity was meant to bring all the nations together, missionaries still recognized that God meant for his many "nations" to bring different histories and mentalities to the universal Christian faith. Linguistic awareness and inclusivity were entangled and mutually reinforcing. German missionaries understood the Great Commission[6] and rigorous linguistic policy as essential to resolving the dissolution of the globe's cultures and ending humanity's collective spiritual alienation. Missionary movements from other Christian nations also could not ignore indigenous languages. But German Protestants, participating in a movement that was remarkably intellectualized, also inherited German ideas about the relationship between language and community in a way that elevated linguistic plurality among Christians to a higher plane.[7]

When missionaries from the Berlin, Bethel, Leipzig, and Moravian Missions arrived in German East Africa in the late 1880s and 1890s, they had little knowledge of local African communities. But they were neither without experience gained from a century of mission activities, nor without a basic strategy derived from that experience. By the 1860s missionaries' strategizing had settled on two activities that they judged integral to their efforts: linguistic study and school building. Both required slow, arduous work. Mission societies expected that within the first year of founding a mission station, a missionary would establish a school and, if he had not already learned the local language or languages in Germany or at another mission station, that he would commence serious study of the language(s). To a Protestant missionary these strategies were essential. As Gustav Warneck put it, "Man thinks in his native language, it is the mirror of the spirit which enlivens him. And as with the individual it is the same with the nations; the national soul comes to the Word through the national language."[8] Though they knew this work took time, missionaries remained confident that in the long run their hard work would bear fruit. Building schools for teaching in God's name and doing so in indigenous languages brought the work of the missionaries into a parallel practice with that of ancient followers of the Great Commission. After all, in the time of the Apostles, God had blessed his followers with the ability to understand one another.

German missionaries' perspectives on indigenous languages reinforced their internationalism and their internationalism reinforced their commitment to indigenous languages.[9] Their theories as to the primacy of evangelization over any other goal of cultural contact synced with their practical views and shaped their approach to education. Time after time, missionaries prioritized the linguistic preferences of indigenous communities in their pedagogical decisions. Their reverence for indigenous languages encouraged respect for indigenous cultural practices but it also included an endorsement of elements within nationalist theory. Though they committed themselves to internationalist methods, missionaries did not completely abandon their national identity, and, in fact, they built their affirmation of other cultures on German ideas about nationhood and ethnicity. German Protestant missionaries distinguished themselves from most other countries' missionaries by their desire to preserve cultural difference. This basic motivation is probably why the missionaries had little trouble with anti-miscegenation laws because, to their view, racial segregation would help prevent the contamination of African communities with European weaknesses. Nevertheless, this position also placed the missionaries in alliance, at least on this issue, with racial supremacists.[10]

In the 1880s, when German Protestant missionaries were cajoled into taking their work into the communities of German East Africa, they found their commitment to the independence, internationalism, and godly character of mission put to the test. Because language and school policy was central to missionaries' methodology, politics, and identity, the mission societies assertively defended their autonomy in East Africa and in Germany's other colonies. Schools' centrality to the evangelical project made control over educational policy an existential issue for Germany's Protestant missionaries.[11] However, many secular colonialists expected that the missionaries' participation in the colonial project would be explicit participation in a *German* colonial project. As a result, activists from the German Colonial Society and other nationalist, expansionist organizations in Germany interfered as much as they could in the missionaries' linguistic and educational activities. This chapter will examine the global context of the German Protestant missionaries' use of language in their activities. It will do so by examining the German intellectual and cultural origins of the missionaries' "linguistic" conceptions of ethnic and national identity and how German nationalist theories could become a source of missionaries' multiculturalism. In an interesting twist, the strands of the national idea became threads for an interweaving of Christianity and colonialism. Missionaries firmly believed that those elements of indigenous culture that could be retained should be. German Protestants' ideas about the relationship among language, culture, and religion united in a practical aspiration to create indigenous churches (*Volkskirchen*), oriented around cultural and ethnic identities. From this theological viewpoint, German Protestants protected their independent school policy with a strong defence of Christian universalism.

Education occupied such a central role in missionaries' imagined international community that attacks on it from nationalists led intellectuals among them to a profound restatement of their internationalist principles. Whatever slippage the missionaries might allow in their construction of internationalism and nationalism, threats to the missions' autonomy pulled the missionary leadership back to a strong antinational position. Internationalist principles led to the rejection of basic nationalist goals, like the supremacy of the German language in German territories. Missionary leaders defended their indigenous-language instruction by defending indigenous culture. In the process, missionaries described a Christianity that may have had European origins but that could and should change some of its contours in response to local circumstances. Translating Christianity to accommodate human differences extended beyond the challenges of communication; cultural practices also had to be accommodated. One extreme, and difficult, example was the inconsistent and vacillating positions that missionaries took toward polygamy among their followers. On the one hand, missionaries appreciated the dignity that prosperous polygamous men brought to the church when they converted. But, on the other hand, missionaries worried that these men set an example for less prosperous Africans that questioned the Christian missionaries' integrity and commitment to enforcing their faith's stated views of appropriate family life. A key location for these translations and challenges were the schools. And, the schools, key building blocks of missionaries' imagined heavenly Fatherland, had to be defended against efforts by secular groups to control missionaries' religious work, even as the missionaries struggled to convey their message to indigenous communities. The diversity created as punishment at the destruction of the Tower of Babel could be embraced and integrated into a global Protestant Christianity, one whose members spoke many tongues but worshipped the same God.

Global Languages of Faith

As was detailed in the previous chapter, globalization drew attention to the German Protestant missionary organizations. German unification and the growth of cultural, economic, and social pressures shaped this attention. Expansions in global trade, improvements in international transportation, and new ideologies of national expansion developed as cause and consequence of a great wave of globalization in the decades before the First World War. German secular colonialists interpreted the moment as an opportunity for German interests to assert themselves on every continent. Colonial advocates and activists among the secular colonial movement assumed that missionaries would join in the German national colonial project. They insisted that German mission societies prioritize their efforts in the German colonies. Though German Protestant missionaries did not share the same interest in extending German political power during the period, the same forces of global expansion encouraged them to imagine greater possibilities for extending Protestantism around the globe. This pressure bore some fruit as the four Protestant mission societies began working in German East Africa during the last two decades of the nineteenth century.

German missionaries seized opportunities afforded by faster and more frequent steamship schedules, greater material wealth, and more and better information about the world. Missionaries already had networks and resources on many colonial frontiers, and their elevation of language as metaphor and method for understanding the world's human diversity provided a theoretical framework for adapting to the nearly infinite contexts in which they might find themselves.

The attention that globalization and colonial energies brought to missionaries and their work provoked conflict. Before 1884 German missionaries' theology and policies had been largely invisible to secular authorities. But with the creation of a German colonial empire and the growing engagement among secular mercantile and national interests with the forces of globalization, the German mission movement quickly found its activities under greater scrutiny from outside the movement. In supporting the use of indigenous languages, German mission societies aggravated secular colonialists. German Protestant missionaries took pride in their own cultural inheritance but did not share in claims by expansionists and colonialists in Germany who argued that Germans everywhere should be ensuring German cultural pre-eminence. While British missionaries largely worked in the tradition of David Livingstone, promoting British culture and commerce in train with Christianity,[12] and French Catholic missionary orders partnered closely with French republican colonial authorities,[13] German Protestant mission societies resisted attempts to make them carriers of German language and promoters of capitalist transformation in the colonies.

Missionaries from the German societies recognized the essentiality of language to their faith. The Gospel of John opens, "In the beginning was the Word, and the Word was with God, and the Word was God."[14] To a nineteenth-century German missionary the identification of God with language was elemental. During the Reformation Martin Luther translated the Christian Bible directly from ancient Greek and Hebrew into German, which had encouraged the emergence of a standardized written German tongue. German missionaries of the late nineteenth century drew strength from Pietist energies reawakened in the late eighteenth and early nineteenth centuries. Pietists gathered in small prayer and Bible study circles. In these circles, resolute Christians faced hostility from the rationalist clergy of the time, but they drew personal and spiritual meaning from Christian scripture in a manner reminiscent of that of Romantic poets and scholars.[15] And around 1800, German nationalists (subject to the same cultural energies as the Pietists and the Romantics) increasingly fixed their nationalism to the language of the people living between the Rhine and Oder (or Vistula or Nieman) Rivers. Advocates of the "German Nation" felt they had no other object of loyalty in the absence of a unified and unifying German state. Though the missionary theology composed by Warneck and his associates in the 1860s and 1870s rejected nationalism in preference to a structure that ignored national particularities, and missionaries from Germany divided humans into Christians (Protestants) and heathens, when they subdivided those two groups they turned to language to do so. Even beyond this lineage, missionaries claimed practical and moral reasons for the commitment to language.

German Protestant missionaries' educational agenda rested on the principle that a man or woman is more likely to receive the grace of the Gospels in his or her native language. In addition, most missionaries regarded indigenous culture as a valuable conduit for Christianity. Some German Protestant missionaries' theology even suggested that indigenous cultures might possess special insight into scripture and could help enrich global Christianity.[16] Protestant mission societies from Germany therefore encouraged their representatives to learn the local vernaculars and to teach in local languages. Protestant missionaries in Germany's colonies instructed their students in many different languages, all of them derived from local communal contexts. The missionaries' insistence on indigenous instruction and their devotion to internationalism led the secular colonial groups of Germany and, at times, the German colonial government to attack missionary independence and pedagogical practice. To missionaries, this amounted to an effort to subvert the entire Christian project of evangelization. The growing archive of Missionswissenschaft provided the mission movement with a rich internationalism that could inform the missions' rhetorical defences.

German Linguistic Nationalism

German Protestant missionaries were predisposed to link group identity with linguistic identity. Contemporary understandings of German national identity emphasized the importance of language and missionaries followed along. Though German Protestant missionaries generally de-emphasized their national identity and loyalties, their understanding of the ties that bound people together into a community focused on the importance of language and culture above political or geographical confines. As a result, German Protestant missionaries emphasized language as an essential element in organizing their work.

Missionaries categorized the nonliterate cultures of sub-Saharan Africa and the Pacific Islands as *Naturvölker* – using the same label ethnographers used – to distinguish them from the literate *Kulturvölker* in regions like South and East Asia. German ethnographers and missionaries recognized the differences in approach that working with non-literate societies required.[17] Mission work among Kulturvölker required different methods; in some cases it could even be "short cut" by appealing to the cultural leaders of literate societies. Meanwhile, the pre-literate Naturvölker required the creation of a literate culture, a process that also meant evangelization could operate across social divisions. The sorting of missionized people only began with definitions based on literacy. Linguistic work by the missionaries further sorted African and Pacific Islander communities into language groups and then into "nations" or "tribes" based on the missionaries' and linguists' taxonomical criteria.

This tendency to sort people based on their linguistic affinities had deep roots among the educated middle classes of Germany. The process of constructing German national identity on linguistic elements dates back to humanist discourses of the Renaissance.[18] Protestant Germans developed a particularly strong connection to the linguistic roots of their nation; Martin Luther's translation of the Bible into German acted as a major milestone. Protestants' elevation of scripture as the core determinant of their faith carried over to Protestant missionaries and underlined the importance of language and literacy. To many German Protestants, German national identity was intimately built on the Reformation and the "national" struggle against Catholicism and the pope.[19] And the Protestant mission societies within the German Empire thought of themselves as *German* in certain basic ways. For example, the official name for the Ausschuß was the Committee of German Protestant Missions, even as it included the Basel Mission Society from the German-speaking regions of northern

Switzerland. To the leaders of the Ausschuß, "Germanness" could be defined linguistically.

During the late eighteenth and early nineteenth century, German proponents of the "national idea" began explicitly arguing that the German nation could only be defined by cultural markers, especially the German language. Johann Gottfried Herder, Ernst Moritz Arndt, and others argued that Germans' strongest bond was through their shared language. The absence of any true German national state and the lack of a strong political movement for unity among German-speakers reinforced the definition of *Deutschtum* (Germanness) as an essentially cultural phenomenon.[20] Germans were bound by their language and the cultural production in that language. Herder's cultural nationalism, like most other contemporary nationalisms, was pluralistic and egalitarian. Every nation had a right and obligation to fulfil its national genius, and the Germans, by fulfilling their cultural mission, could contribute to the ennoblement of the entire world. And every national language, as part of a national character, had a role to play in the ultimate perfection of mankind.[21]

During the first half of the nineteenth century, the German language, continually being regularized by projects like the Brothers Grimm's dictionary, remained essential to projects designed to preserve Deutschtum wherever it could be found in Europe, the Americas, or beyond.[22] In the Vormärz period and at the Frankfurt Parliament, German nationalists associated language with national identity but did not insist on the latter as being essential to participation in a state defined as German.[23] In this same time period, German philology rose to pre-eminence and shaped much of scholarly work in this period. As a natural consequence, when German missionaries sought to reinforce their work with scholarly credentials, they also validated the centrality of language to their work. Philologists' quest in the nineteenth century to find the primordial language of humankind spoke to missionaries' quest to unify the globe through Protestant conversions.[24]

The intersection between Herder's ideas about culture and nation on the one hand and those of German Protestant missionaries on the other has not gone unremarked by scholars.[25] "On the ground" their views could be used to impose control upon colonized people. Birgit Meyer has argued that missionaries from the North German Mission Society used their notions of culture and nationality to control the Ewe people of modern-day Ghana and Togo. The missionaries of the North German Mission applied their linguistic tools to create their own literate version of the Ewe language to bind the various communities in the region into one nation. Meyer emphasizes that missionaries theoretically saw all languages, and thus all nations, as equal, but, in practice, the North German Mission Society crafted a version of Ewe nationhood that subordinated the Ewe people to colonialism and encouraged only a Protestant religious expression of Ewe identity.[26]

Meyer's account of Protestant missionaries' activities among the Ewe shows one manner in which language could be used as a weapon for domination. Yet German Protestant missionaries' prioritization of indigenous language often benefited and empowered local communities. Many Germans interpreted a positive correlation between language and national identity, between language and collective personhood. German Protestant missionaries' emphasis on language grew out of German scholars' collective interest in communities bound together by a shared culture and language.

Volkskirche

German Protestant missionaries' understanding of how the vast diversity of humanity was organized came from their own educational and cultural context. Nationalism had never been monolithic in its flavours and proclivities.[27] But in Germany for a century or more by 1880, the grouping of human beings into "nations" emphasized linguistic and cultural markers of community affiliation. At the time these ideas began to come into use among intellectuals, in the mid-eighteenth century, enthusiasts for a German nation compared the political conditions of the various principalities and kingdoms of Germany unfavourably with the centralizing states of Britain and France. These nationalists emphasized the cultural unity of their people, highlighting supposed unity in language and other cultural characteristics as evidence of the genius of the German people. Some scholars have stressed the chauvinistic tendencies of this cultural emphasis – celebrating the culture (and by implication the spirit and talent) as superior could be used to justify expansionism, especially when the territory of "German" culture outsized whatever German state or states may have existed at the time.[28]

Germany's Protestant missionaries had by 1900 integrated their linguistic understandings of nationhood with their mission work and embraced the practical theological principle of the Volkskirche.[29] The concept arose in the theology of Friedrich Schleiermacher nearly a century earlier. Schleiermacher's concept dominated Missionswissenschaft as both the natural conclusion of Protestant missionary theology in Germany and as a practical solution to the challenges of managing and financing the growing communities of indigenous Christians which began to form around mission stations by the end of the nineteenth century.[30] It meant, simply, that each identifiable *Volk*, in a categorization process impeded from the beginning by colonialists' flawed understandings of indigenous social organization, would organize itself into its own church, as the Danes, Frisians, Saxons, Prussians, Dutch, and other "nations" had in Europe.[31]

On the one hand, missionaries expected that Christian communities built around the Protestant tenets would govern themselves, naturally with continuing advice and counsel from the missionaries, and be formally independent. The Basel Mission Director Otto Schott emphasized the aim of mission in the "Three Self." He and others advocated churches develop independently through self-financing, self-administration, and self-propagation of the Gospel.[32] On the other hand, missionaries also wished to shift the economic burden of running these churches onto indigenous congregations. If pastors, teachers, and deacons could be found among the local Christian communities, then White missionaries could move to new areas and evangelize new groups of heathens.[33] In Warneck's view, the transformation of a mission field into a Volkskirche was the ultimate purpose of all mission decisions and education. He and other Missionswissenschaftler encouraged missionaries to work to develop the *völkisch* identities of their congregants so that those new Christians could become the core of a new "national" faith. The project meant the eradication of "superstitions" and "sins" like slavery, polygamy, sorcery, blood feuds, ordeal by poison, or consultation of oracles.[34] In practice this meant the identification and cultivation of an indigenous *Volkssprache*, or national language, cultivation of "natural" communal forms within the missionized community, the establishment of schools to reach the youth, and enticements to keep Christians concentrated in communities – in sum, this was a campaign of "ethnicization" but not a concerted campaign of Europeanization.

This campaign of ethnicization could and did have racial overtones. Control over the identification and definition of any given African *Volk* rested almost entirely in the hands of the missionaries. And these definitions could just as easily be made for the sake of European convenience as for African community-building. The history of African ethnicization is a long one; it certainly includes examples of African agency, and, while this moment must have included indigenous input, missionaries kept close control over the Volkskirche concept.[35] Furthermore, before the First World War the missionaries were reluctant to fully endow Africans with positions of authority within the churches ostensibly being built for their communities.

German Protestant missionaries' resistance to the Westernization of indigenous colonial populations distinguished them from other missionary movements. German missionaries, like the British, were an important force for the "colonization of consciousness," as Jean and John L. Comaroff described missionaries' impact upon the Tswana.[36] German Protestant missionaries may have imagined that they could eradicate "superstition" and replace it with Christianity, making little alteration to indigenous culture; but this prospect was clearly impossible. Missionaries' choices about which cultural practices entailed "superstition," and which were appropriate representations of indigenous difference and values, deeply involved missionaries in a process of colonization that included the contested and collaborative creation of African ethnicities.[37] The embrace by missionaries of African "customary communities" had important implications for African communities.[38] But the evidence of German missionaries' understanding of the Volkskirche and indigenous language forces a re-evaluation of the general assumptions that German missionaries, like their British colleagues, desired the total dissolution of indigenous cultures.

In 1895, Franz Michael Zahn of the North German Mission Society, proponent of a free and international mission movement, offered a defence of missionaries' use of indigenous languages that stressed not only the practical benefits but also a theology that embraced human diversity. The main thrust of Zahn's argument was that God had intended the world to be a diverse place. This diversity provided Christians with a multitude of cultural perspectives and revelations which collectively allowed for a more complete Christianity to develop. The imposition of German or any other universal language would therefore lead to the destruction of indigenous cultures and violate Christian dogma. Zahn's influence on this point remained strong among missionary intellectuals. Even as the cultural force of nationalism grew in Germany, the linguist and mission scholar Carl Meinhof, himself a German patriot, argued in 1906 that when a people gives up its language it gives up its "fundamental character and the form of its peculiar mentality."[39]

The study of language, to Zahn, allowed for believers to publish in every language the "great deeds of God"; the use of indigenous language for evangelization "opened the door to the most expansive philosophical, philological, historical, [and] theological considerations." Language was, after all, the means by which a person expressed his or her spiritual being; it was only through language that a man or woman could fully participate in a personal and collective spiritual life.[40] Meinhof agreed, writing that "the thousands of languages glorify the great deeds of God … with their own rhythms, their own melodies." The European understanding of Christianity was not universal, and "every non-European [finds] beauty in the Gospel that we [Europeans] do not

2.1. Interior view of the Rungwe Church (n.d.). The Rungwe Mission Station was established by the Moravians in 1891. The two signboards beside the altar demonstrate the missionaries' engagement with indigenous languages. They read "Mbamba ari ku bupipi" on the left, "Kimpare Kiara ikisu kiosa" on the right. Written in a local dialect of Nyakyusa-Ngonde and translated by the photographer, the missionary Paul Theoldor Meyer (who also retouched the image), the translations read "The Lord is coming" and "Praise the Lord all ye lands," respectively.

Source: Unitätsarchiv.

see."[41] Like Warneck before him, Zahn argued that the only correct way to develop a person's faith was through his or her mother language, and the worldwide linguistic babble reflected God's intentions.[42] The many and strange cultures of the world, Zahn felt, reflected the scattering of the nations as told in the story of the Tower of Babel. But these different "nations" all possessed a spark of God's message; missionaries discovered everywhere people who "[spoke] differently and at the same time [thought] differently of God."[43] Zahn defended indigenous language use in that it aided in the spread of the Gospels, the multiplicity of languages on Earth sprang from a divine plan, and the challenge of reconciling human difference served to strengthen the global Christian faith.

Zahn imagined mission schools as the key support for communities of Christians joined together in Volkskirchen. He wrote that "only a true national education, that is to say one conveyed in the national language, is healthy." Foreign language instruction should be limited. The establishment of European languages as languages of instruction created an "educational construct [*Bildungsbau*] without a healthy national foundation and [bore] radical fruit." If language were detached from cultural roots, Zahn argued, people might learn a language but not retain an appreciation for their inherited cultural values. Another risk was that by not using the indigenous language for instruction the European colonial state would only create subjects able to "parrot" English, French, or German. It would be far better to integrate the moral education offered by the missionaries into indigenous culture.[44]

Zahn concluded that "[i]t is possible and it is necessary to missionize in native language[s]." After all, the "goal of human history and of mission history [was] not the earthly kingdom"; it was "one great people, whose numbers no one can count, out of all the peoples and tribes and nations and tongues."[45] The message of revelation gave the ultimate basis to Zahn's view that it was God's intention that there be human difference and that the dissolution of that difference through Christian faith could only be aided by Christian missionaries. But first all people would have to be made Christian, and only after that great achievement could the unification of humanity become possible. Because of this precondition to earthly salvation, Zahn contended that the first step should be making Christians, and the appropriate way to do so, according to the scriptures and principled reasoning, was to evangelize in indigenous languages. Zahn's argument neatly fused indigenous language instruction and German Protestant missionary cultural attitudes into a defence of missionary independence and internationalism.

The Language of Instruction

German missionaries viewed schools as the foundation of the Christian communities they hoped to create. Children were seen as ripe for conversion because "heathen superstition" had yet to fully take root. A school also allowed the missionaries some contact with the children's parents. Schools had the additional virtue of providing indigenous leaders with an incentive to allow missionaries to remain in local communities.[46] In those African regions where a clear central authority existed, missionaries were frequently welcomed with the expectation that they establish a school. Through a school, indigenous leaders could begin to gain access to the knowledge of the colonizing states. Missionaries cited examples in their many publications of the versatility of schools as *entrepôt* to indigenous societies. For example, the ruler of Bali in modern-day Cameroon "knew nothing" about the Basel missionaries who came to create a mission station among his people in 1902 except that they were teachers and this "was enough for him."[47] Schools also provided the training grounds for indigenous catechists and teachers. These educators could help spread the Christian Gospel; for instance they could go to small villages among the Batak people of north Sumatra and prove to resistant communities that one could be a "true Batak[48] and also a Christian."[49] As missionaries developed their fluency in indigenous languages, their pupils and local assistants provided invaluable language practice and assistance. In short, there was little, the missionaries believed, that a school could not help the mission societies achieve.

Missionaries designed their schools to create the basic skills needed for one to be a good Protestant: basic literacy, numeracy, and the foundations of Protestant religious life. The schools were also intended to instil in the students the basic "Christian" values of sobriety, discipline, and industry. As one leading missionary put it, "the best apology for the education of the native is that through education mission can promote [the native to] lead in his own affairs."[50] Protestant missionaries hoped to create autonomous Protestant individuals, each of whom would be a building block for a new and vital Volkskirche. This meant the care and development of African religious communities and churches built around Africans' "natural" communities and languages. The needs of the colonial state and mission societies could be met by providing advanced students with "basic German instruction" in upper grades.[51] The successful Christian community could also serve as a beacon in a sea of heathen resistance. The "new" Christians would live in an upright, moral, and prosperous community, speaking and worshipping in their own language and continuing as many local practices as the missionaries believed could be reconciled with Christian life. The success of this new community would encourage further integration of the larger Volk into its Volkskirche.

The mission societies' confidence in their methods created a curriculum that did not differ radically from the curricula of late nineteenth-century grammar schools in Germany.[52] In 1897 the Ausschuß sent the German Colonial Office a memorandum emphasizing schools' main goal as that of "plant[ing] and advanc[ing] the Holy Scripture." The schools' prerequisites included strict missionary autonomy and instruction in indigenous languages.[53] Students received instruction in the elements of literacy (reading and writing) and basic mathematics; they also received some basic instruction in the social and natural sciences and in the arts. According to one missionary leader, education in the schools should be confined to the simplest skills and in the "native tongue"; only older students should be given German-language instruction.[54] The Ausschuß defined mission schools as "Christian primary schools,"[55] and Julius Richter argued that the project of cultural elevation, adherence to pedagogical principles, and fulfilment of the missionaries' goal to create a "solid native community" required instruction remain in indigenous vernaculars.[56]

The schools created by the missionaries were fundamentally Eurocentric. The celebration of Christian civilization and the emphasis on Western forms of knowledge left little room for African agency. Student attendance was, at times, compulsory through colonial authority. At other times, missionaries enticed students to attend with material rewards in the form of textiles or other manufactured goods. Families who wished to live on mission land or near mission stations usually had to bring their children to the schools. As discussed earlier in this section, schools were considered by a wide swath of the population to be a path to success in the new colonial context. That the German missionaries defined that path as something other than full subservience to the colonial economic and political order is an essential piece of context. The missionaries chose a curriculum that served their needs. Nonetheless, their commitment to indigenous-language instruction and Volkskirche theology was more than just pragmatism. The missionaries understood human diversity as an intentional creation of God, and they understood the Word – in language, in the text of the Bible – to be inherent to the human self and to the soul. Their understanding of diversity might have been limited but it involved more than lip service.

Kultur and Indigenous Cultures

German Protestant missionaries substantiated their defence of autonomous mission schools with arguments for indigenous people's fundamental humanity. Missionaries' discussions about Africans' educability turned on the term *Kultur*. Translated simply, *Kultur* means "culture," but in the missionaries' lexicon it came to also represent technologies, social mores, and every other supposed marker of "civilization." Missionaries did not automatically judge Africans as lacking Kultur.[57] They argued that Africans were educable and, if superstition could be eradicated through good Christian teachings, capable of the same spiritual achievements as Europeans.[58] The key argument made by missionary leaders was that Africa was fertile ground for the spread of Christianity. Africans could learn, but the process demanded patience and the application of the correct methods. Missionaries' approach to African cultures, therefore, while undeniably paternalistic, reflected a surprising level of cultural understanding. Though from a twenty-first-century perspective we can recognize that the goal of replacing "native superstition" with the "truth of Christianity" denied any true possibility of a non-intrusive cultural exchange, it is remarkable how seriously the missionaries cautioned themselves and their readers to avoid unnecessarily interfering with African culture. As Warneck put it, "Christianity comes to the peoples as a foreign religion, and this foreign religion can only become indigenous to [these peoples] ... if they [can] grasp it in their mother tongue."[59]

Warneck's ideas appeared in the *Allgemeine Missions-Zeitschrift* for an educated readership. Many other examples of missionary views about Kultur could be found in the publications of individual mission societies. For example, embedded within a typical piece of reportage about a Herrnhut mission station on Lake Nyasa in German East Africa, missionary Theodor Bechler demolished the idea that prior to European contact the Konde of Nyasa lacked any culture whatsoever. As he put it, if their skills as weavers and ironworkers were not sufficient, he could "speak of their huts, astoundingly clean and with four-cornered or round construction; of farming and cattle-raising; of boat- and bridge-building, of drums and pipes, of cuisine [*Kochkunst*] and medicines." Since the arrival of the Moravian Church, the culture of the Konde, according to Bechler, had taken on a more "refined character." The missionaries had introduced a written form of the local dialects and had begun training teachers and catechists to work in their mission and form the core of a future, independent Konde church. In Bechler's presentation Kultur was an important element of the missionary project;

he wrote, "Truly, mission is a culture-bearer of the first echelon! Work and cultured behaviour [*Gesittung*], education, and ultimate fortune are brought to those who not only have an equal right to *Kultur* as the White race, but also show themselves to be just as worthy."[60] Richter agreed that mission "[tried] to bridge the abyss between our cultural affluence and the [Africans'] lack of culture [*Unkultur*]."[61] The Kultur of an African community could be improved by contact with Europeans and refined by missionaries' efforts to build a Volkskirche.

In the missionaries' eyes, these positions emphasized their benevolent relationship to African communities. Their worldview created something of a virtuous circle. Missionaries followed the true teachings of God regarding mission work and the nations; they embraced indigenous cultural practices that conformed with their understanding of Godly life; they avoided affiliations with and service to secular colonial interests. Missionaries' avoidance of secular temptations made them virtuous actors in the colonies; thus their work was proven to reflect God's intention that people live as Völker but within a global and international community of Christians.

Carl Buchner, a leader of the Moravians, defended Africans against claims of cultural decline in an April 1904 lecture to the Brandenburg Mission Conference, one of a number of regional conventions of German mission societies. According to Buchner, the evidence of the recent past showed that, unlike other "uncivilized" groups like the Eskimos and the people of New Guinea, who had declined after contact with Whites and their "celebrated and notorious" culture, people of African descent had prospered. He claimed that where the "influence of civilization" had ended civil strife and slave raids, people of African descent flourished more than did people of European descent.[62] The great success of colonized Africans meant they had boundless capacity for improving their cultural achievements. His chief evidence: the condition of African Americans. He cited W.E.B. Du Bois's *The Souls of Black Folk* favourably and quoted at length a passage in which Du Bois laid out the technical, economic, and cultural accomplishments of African Americans. Buchner commented that they "prove[d] nothing less than that the black race in America in every area of culture, science, and technic [has begun] to distinguish itself" and these successes undermined the accepted belief in the "spiritual inferiority of the Negro."[63]

The apparent positive response of Africans to "civilization" was a result of education, Buchner continued. Western civilization, in general, had failed to make an "earnest effort through education" to develop African people's "psychic" and "intellectual" strengths. Missions had addressed some of this shortfall and, according to Buchner, "Wherever the formation and development of a mission station" had been permitted, one "[saw] how the primitive people [*Naturkinder*] first in garments, then in their housing, then in conventional labour, [and] gradually in language and spiritual views, as well, emulate[d] Whites." Buchner's description seems to violate the principle of leaving African cultures as untainted by "civilization" as possible, and this reflects the diversity of mission thought on the specifics of Africans' potential. However, Buchner's main point of the promise in Africans remains representative of the general position of missionaries in Germany with respect to African communities. With the good example of Christian missionaries and the training that they offered to Africans, Buchner argued, the "African" could be converted into a good "Christian."[64]

Other leaders of the Protestant mission movement also argued for the educative capacity of Africans. Alexander Merensky's pamphlet *Deutschlands Pflicht gegenüber den Heiden und dem Heidentum in seinen Kolonien* (Germany's Responsibility with Respect to the Heathens and Heathendom in her Colonies) argued forcefully that the solution to the "native question," as in "what to do about the natives," laid in improving the material and spiritual conditions of indigenous people with effective and moral policies. Merensky's pamphlet was intended for a broad audience and it conveyed the German missionaries' viewpoint of African societies. He called for Germany's colonial policies to be defined and determined "by the fact that natives are men [*Menschen*]." Non-Western people were in need of education because "these so-called primitive peoples [*Naturvölker*] [were] nothing other than members of a great human family who have lagged behind in their development."[65] He wrote that it was the responsibility of Germany to see to the moral improvement of its subject people but "[t]heir language, customs, morals, and legal views must be treated with care." Only those practices which he called "pagan atrocities" could be forbidden.[66]

By the first decade of the twentieth century Germany's Protestant mission movement had developed a theology and anthropology that confirmed African communities as culturally relevant. Theodor Öhler, the head of the Basel Mission, summed up this view in the Basel Mission's *Evangelisches Missions-Magazin* in 1908. His article appeared during a period of heightened efforts by secular colonialists to force a change in missionaries' pedagogical practices. Öhler reminded readers that there were no "cultureless" people, only those whose culture was "undeveloped," who were nonetheless "capable of development.[67] The key to encouraging this development was education. Schools provided valuable literacy that helped deliver to "primitive" groups a greater understanding of the "civilized" world. He wrote, "Schools destroy superstition with their lessons in history, geography, natural science, [and] contribute to the destruction of heathendom." These lessons in the cultural products of Westerners showed the entangled vines of mission and Kultur; to Öhler "Nothing shows us more convincingly the close and indivisible connection between mission and cultural work than the area of mission schools."[68]

Missionaries' program to "destroy superstition" and replace it with lessons in Western knowledge promised inclusion in a Westernized Protestant world, or at least the missionaries hoped it could. But it also stripped away aspects of African culture that the missionaries did not view as Christian, either because they did not understand them or did not care to understand them. As the Comaroffs' work shows, this cultural transformation could be profound. While the missionaries believed themselves to be in a project of cultural restoration, resurrection, or preservation against the forces of heathendom and capitalism, they were also the authors of much damage.

During the late nineteenth century, missionaries argued that Africans possessed the facility to join the cultured "nations" of the Earth. This view not only validated their work as Christian missionaries seeking converts, it also argued for the value of missionaries' educational and social welfare activities. Missionaries likely held these beliefs for much of the nineteenth century but felt little need to justify themselves before 1900. The intensification of national feeling in Germany after 1900, the growing challenges to missionary capabilities in the colonies, and direct attempts by secular colonialists to force a change in missionary school language policy caused missionary intellectuals to produce defences of their work, defences that obscured the missionaries' own complicated relationship to their national heritage. Their arguments for the cultural potential and value of indigenous people (suitably purified of "superstition") served to substantiate missionaries' claims for the moral value of their educational activities. Missionized people's cultural value supplied missionaries with justifications for maintaining indigenous language instruction and reasserting missionary internationalism. German mission scholars justified their activities as legitimated by the "truth" of human cultural equality. Missionaries deployed their pluralistic vision of humanity as a defence of indigenous language instruction.

Unwanted Attention and Pressure

German Protestant missionaries' commitment to indigenous language, and that position's related affirmations of local cultures in German East Africa and elsewhere, encouraged conflict between the mission societies and secular colonial associations. Many liberals viewed Germany's empire as just as fundamental to the nation's modernization as a parliament, railroads, and free markets. To such men and women, a German and Germanized empire had universal benefits. This concept within liberal imperialism could trace its roots back to before the Revolutions of 1848 and an understanding of the colonies as sites for the construction of German nationalism, capitalism, and expansionism, rather than for the "improvement" of indigenous people.[69] Such views threatened German missionaries' orientation toward indigenous cultures and people. The threat from liberal imperialists was soon joined, and then supplanted, by threats from more conservative "patriotic associations." These associations emerged in Germany in the late nineteenth century to encompass a number of movements oriented toward Germany's foreign, military, and colonial policy. These groups joined with mercantile, industrial, and political actors interested in Germany's affairs abroad to form a wide coalition of secular colonialists. And they expected that the missionaries would join their project.[70]

Ideology like that of the liberal imperialists put pressure on missionaries. The coalition for a colonial empire in Germany included liberals from both the progressive and national wings of the German liberal movement. But support for a German colonial empire stretched from the liberals all the way through to the populist and ultra-nationalist right in Wilhelmine Germany; even some Social Democrats developed a certain affinity for colonialism in the years before the First World War.[71] Many of these secular colonialists demanded that missionaries make German the *lingua franca* of Germany's colonial empire, yet missionaries insisted that their evangelical goals demanded that mission policy respond to indigenous needs and demands.[72] Missionary intellectuals ridiculed chauvinist cultural views and defended indigenous cultures as positive sources of identity for missionized people. Schools helped build indigenous Christian cultures, missionary leaders argued, and therefore, for pedagogical and religious reasons, instruction had to continue in indigenous languages. Mission societies refused to adulterate their spiritual purpose for nationalist reasons and insisted that missionary schools continue instructing in whatever language the missionaries thought most suitable. They interpreted the attacks by the nationalists and the apparent support the nationalists received from the German colonial state as a mortal threat to the evangelical project, and when national "political" pressure threatened, the German Protestant mission movement returned to its basic principles, in this case the primacy of a universal Gospel over secular political concerns.

Secular colonialists less inclined to support a liberal political program also posed a threat to Protestant missionaries. Conservative nationalists and ultra-nationalists eventually came to understand the seizure and control of overseas territories as evidence of Germany's national strength. While liberal imperialists established the general parameters of German colonial power – based on evidence of national health – it would be more conservative imperialists and nationalists who would raise the most prominent challenges to missionaries' linguistic principles.

The chief opposition to the missionaries' position came from the collection of nationalist and right-wing political associations that grew in size and strength during the last three decades of the Kaiserreich.[73] These groups joined other economic and political interests bent on capitalizing on the opportunities created by German colonialism.[74] To the secular colonial organizations, indigenous-language instruction was an affront to German prestige and power. Occasionally the colonial government joined with secular colonialists to criticize mission school policies, though the interests of the colonial governors were usually narrowly designed to promote the training of clerks, translators, and the occasional craftsmen to support the colonial state. Disagreement among these various interests was common at all levels of colonial politics.[75]

The secular organizations that challenged missionaries' autonomy were a product of a general associational growth that took place over the course of the nineteenth century.[76] But between 1880 and 1900 a new classification of "national associations" emerged. These self-styled patriotic societies represented a populist challenge to traditional conservativism and elite-led nationalism.[77] They cultivated access to government, endorsing aggressive policies on military and colonial issues and making use of public opinion to advance their goals.[78] In many instances their plans for Germany's future matched the general framework of Weltpolitik pursued by Chancellor Bülow and his allies. The national associations had practical and ideological objections to missionaries' insistence on indigenous-language instruction. Practically, they argued that the exploitation of the colonies and the Germanization of the populations would progress more satisfactorily if missionaries collaborated and institutionalized German-language instruction in their schools. Ideologically, these societies and their allies argued that a German colonial empire must be a German-speaking empire to prove Germany's global cultural prominence.

Though each of these groups oriented its policies around a specific program, in every case their programs were designed to preserve, promote, and expand German culture and power in Germany and abroad. Some advocated German military armament, for instance the Deutscher Flottenverein (Navy League) and the Deutscher Wehrverein (Army League). Others groups concerned themselves with Germans abroad, including the Verein für das Deutschtum im Ausland (Association for Germans Abroad), the Hakatisten or Deutscher Ostmarkenverein (German Eastern Marches Society), which focused on the "Polish Question" in Prussia's eastern provinces, and the Alldeutscher Verband (Pan-German League), which focused on all these issues and more. The Deutscher Kolonial Gesellschaft (German Colonial Society) can also be considered part of the movement of patriotic associations. No doubt many local and national members of the Colonial Society were also paying dues to other national associations.

The Colonial Society supported colonial expansion and, like the other patriotic associations, called for colonial policies that supported a broad nationalistic ideology. It was founded in 1882 to "support the colonial endeavours of the German nation" by pressuring the imperial government to expand German trading posts to encompass new colonies and to promote the creation of new colonies. Its leadership included high-ranking government officials, retired military leaders, and well-known politicians.[79] Local branches undertook the work of promoting the society's vision of colonial policy in their communities. The rank and file of the society came from the middle classes employed in commerce (merchants, manufacturers, and businessmen), and also included government bureaucrats and naval officers.[80] These men (women were eligible but their membership was negligible) and their organization would emerge as a major adversary of the mission societies. Starting in the 1890s the Colonial Society, with support from other patriotic associations, economic colonialists, and settlers, took up the baton and attempted to force mission schools to adopt German as their primary language of instruction. Missionaries' resistance to German-language instruction drew accusations of disloyalty and "unpatrioticness" from the Colonial Society and its allies.

An example of interference by the secular colonial movement began in 1896 at a meeting of the colonial director's Kolonialrat (Colonial Council). The Kolonialrat had begun meeting in 1890 as an advisory council to the colonial minister. Its membership included commercial and financial interests, manufacturers, colonial scholars, and, importantly, representatives from the Colonial Society and the Catholic and Protestant mission movements. At the October 1896 meeting of the Kolonialrat the head of the German Colonial Society, Duke Johann Albrecht zu Mecklenburg, proposed that it should be obligatory that European-language instruction be delivered solely in German. Mecklenburg cited "patriotic reasons" for his proposal and argued that if mission societies wished to work in German territories then they should teach in German.[81] Though Mecklenburg and his allies were chiefly annoyed by the teaching of English in the North German Mission Society's schools in Togoland, this attack was interpreted by missionaries on the Kolonialrat and across Germany as a generalized effort to interfere with missionaries' pedagogical work. Mecklenburg's attack did not amount to much at that meeting because the Catholic missionary representative, Franz Hespers, and the Protestant missionary representative, Karl Jacobi, prevented any official pronouncement in support of Mecklenburg's proposal.

Mecklenburg did not surrender on this issue. Two years later a memorandum was presented to the Kolonialrat "concerning the taking up of the German language in the curriculum of the schools in the protectorates." In the view of the head of the German Colonial Society, "we must act as the French and English; ...we must show the natives that we Germans are the masters. Therefore it [is] undeniably necessary that German must be promoted ... in the schools of the colonies." The colonial director, Paul Kayser, agreed with Mecklenburg's assertion that it was Germany's "national responsibility" to teach German in the colonies. The Catholic Hespers deflected this attack upon missionaries' autonomy by suggesting Mecklenburg's proposal be voluntary for mission societies, with the incentive of government subsidies for those schools that taught German. Hespers's proposal was adopted unanimously and the meeting moved on to other matters.[82]

The assault by nationalist colonialists on missionaries' language policies was not confined to Togo and German East Africa. In the German colony of Kamerun, missionaries from the Basel Mission prioritized Duala, a local language spoken by the dominant ethnic group on the colony's coast, and other indigenous languages as they moved their operations inland. American Baptist missionaries in the south of the colony also preferred to use indigenous languages in their activities.[83] From the establishment of the colony until around 1900, this policy presented few problems. However, starting after 1900 members of the Colonial Society and colonial officers began pressing for a wider program of German education. Motivated by economic interests and long-standing policies meant to undermine the power of the Duala people on the coast, the administrators pressed the Basel Mission to reform its curriculum in the colony. As in Togo and East Africa, the same pressures from secular sources contested missionary priorities. And as in those other colonies, the missionaries resisted this interference in their activities, until the outbreak of the First World War, made continuing the argument pointless.[84]

Over time Germany's Protestant mission societies' financial condition grew more dire and government subsidies became increasingly critical to missionary schools. The expansion of the German Protestant mission societies after 1890 stretched their resources. Damage suffered at the Berlin and Moravian Missions' stations in South Africa during the Boer War (1899–1902) aggravated both societies' financial problems. In the colonies, the colonial state paid subsidies to support the training of a small number of clerks and translators to aid the administration of the colonies. Another intrusive attempt to control the mission schools in 1904 provoked Warneck to admit that financial support for the schools gave the state a claim to a say in the schools' operations. But the aging Missionswissenschaftler argued that the governors' power to interfere in curriculum should be limited, "especially in the content of religious instruction."[85]

From the missionaries' perspective, the 1904 intrusion, with roots in Togoland, featured a worrying alliance between colonial governor Julius von Zech, nationalists, and economic interests.[86] On the Kolonialrat, Karl Jacobi defended the North German Mission Society's right to teach as it wished. The society offered English in its schools because that was what the local people wanted. The Basel Mission Society also taught in English in its missions in the region. English had emerged as the dominant language of the coastal trade, and fluency in it equipped African students to compete for desirable opportunities, an important recruitment tool of the schools.[87] Jacobi supported missionary internationalism by arguing that if the German government sought to enforce language policy in its colonies then the work of German missionaries might be impeded in a similar manner by other colonial powers. By favouring independence in language instruction, Jacobi endorsed missionary autonomy and internationalism against nationalistic patriotism.

Mission scholars recognized that surrendering power over the schools carried with it the threat of surrendering control over their most significant contact with the people the missionaries hoped to evangelize. Once again, the Ausschuß defended the primacy of Christian evangelization and the obligatory use of indigenous languages in instruction to the new colonial secretary, Bernhard Dernburg, in the summer of 1907. However, this time the Ausschuß acknowledged the interest of the state in German-language courses. The association of mission leaders informed Dernburg of their "preparedness to implement German instruction in [our] schools" following elementary instruction of students in "local languages."[88] In exchange the Ausschuß expected the Colonial Department to recognize the independence of missionary activities and respect the missionaries' autonomy in the design of curricula. Missionaries' willingness to compromise reveals some of the limits of their theology of diversity. When faced with a threat to the spread of Christianity in the form of a state power, missionaries sought compromises.

The fight over missionary language instruction continued through the first years of the twentieth century. Secular colonialists manoeuvred in the Kolonialrat and the Reichstag to force mission schools to change their language policies. Attacks in 1904 sought to create government schools as a direct challenge to missionaries' schools, expressly for the purpose of spreading German in the colonies.[89] In 1913, when the imperial governor of the German colony of Kamerun tried to force German instruction on the Basel Mission's schools in the colony, the missionaries appealed to the colonial minister. They argued that for "pedagogical reasons and general consideration" German instruction should not be elevated above the educational interests of the mission schools. In the missionaries' view, a system of education "adapted to the cultural level of the peoples" did the colony greater service than a "rash and an inevitably superficial Germanization."[90] Some of their resistance to German-language instruction came from a fear of cultural imitation by Africans, "ill-equipped" to do anything more than emulate without understanding. Comfortable with difference, but uncomfortable with hybridity, the missionaries chose whatever path would allow them the best chances of continuing their work.[91] Friends of the missionary societies fought to protect missionaries' autonomy in the Reichstag as well. Reichstag member Reinhold Mumm of the Christian Social Party spoke in the early spring of 1913 against legislation designed to bring the mission schools under a "more exacting oversight."[92] Throughout this period missionaries held to a strong defence of their educational prerogatives.

Missionary intellectuals devoted considerable time and energy to explaining the importance of language in their work. The use of English in schools in Togo demonstrated the missionaries' determination to choose the language for instruction that made the most sense in a given mission context. On the Bight of Benin, English dominated as the language of commerce; missionaries, responding to pressure from the local African communities, used it alongside indigenous languages. In German East Africa, another language, Swahili, mirrored some of the commercial dominance of English in West Africa. As in Togoland, the missionaries made concessions to serve their greater purpose, but at the expense of local indigenous languages. The decision drew on four rationales. First, missionaries adhered to the overriding principle that Africans be instructed in an African language to help stimulate the development of Volkskirchen and Christian communities. Second, missionaries hoped that adopting Swahili as the language of their work would arrest the spread of Islam in the colony.[93] Third, Africans on the coast and inland seemed to desire instruction in Swahili and, by obliging, missionaries could bring more Africans into contact with missionary institutions.[94] Last, the colonial state's adoption of Swahili as a key language of administration would allow missionaries to collaborate with the colonial state.[95] The adoption of Swahili could aid missionaries in their fight against the secular colonialists who wanted German-language schools. A compromise with the East African colonial administration allowed missionaries to preserve their internationalist vision and to resist nationalist pressure.[96]

Karl Axenfeld helped develop the missionaries' policy of Swahili instruction in German East Africa. His more nuanced understanding of missionary internationalism likely inspired his development of this compromise. Axenfeld's 1908 essay entitled "The Language Question in East Africa from the Standpoint of Mission" proposed a closer link between the missions and the colonial government on language policy. Axenfeld counted more than 600 different languages in East Africa, though most, he claimed, were spoken only by "a handful of people." This linguistic diversity – if missionaries sought to instruct all Africans in their mother tongues – threatened to fracture the evangelical project into ever smaller pieces. At the same time, Axenfeld reminded his readers of missionaries' basic principle that "every nation should be presented the Gospel in its native language" and that the "displacement of native languages by European [languages]" was a "pedagogical mistake." Axenfeld sought a solution that maximized the possibilities for creating "healthy Volkskirchen" in the colony.[97]

Further complications for the missionaries, Axenfeld felt, came from the agents of governmental and economic power. He declared that mission's powerful evangelical message, system of schools, development of indigenous-language literature, and training of catechists made mission a "great language-forming and language-preserving power; but the government and the tendency of commerce are stronger yet."[98] For this reason, Axenfeld argued, the most rational choice of a language for East African missionary instruction was Swahili.[99] Swahili was the language of East African coastal traders and the peoples of the caravan routes of the colony, a group Axenfeld and contemporaries called "Arabs." Swahili was already favoured by the indigenous elites as well as by the colonial administrative and economic representatives; it was all but inevitable that European missionaries also adopt the language for practical, political, and religious reasons.[100]

Realistically speaking, Swahili was, in Axenfeld's perspective, already the dominant language of the region. The language served in East Africa as the language of trade and Axenfeld suggested that the German government was likely to adopt it for administration as well.[101] In fact, in July of the previous year the Ausschuß had agreed to Colonial Secretary Dernburg's request that the Protestant and Catholic missions in East Africa work together and standardize a Latinized orthography for Swahili.[102] So some of the work had already begun. Furthermore, Swahili had political advantages, ones that missionaries could use to help increase the prestige of Christianity. As Axenfeld described it, to the "uneducated backcountry African [*Buschneger*]," whoever spoke even "broken Swahili" appeared "an educated man."[103] If missionaries and their Christianized students came to be perceived as fluent in Swahili, then, the reasoning followed, Christianity would come to be seen as a path to upward mobility.

Axenfeld's final argument for mission schools to adopt Swahili as their instructional language revolved around the change in policy as an attack on Islam. The long-standing opposition to Swahili by older missionary leaders rested on the view that Swahili, as the language of the "Arabs," was a carrier of Islam. Axenfeld countered, "The victory of Swahili [in the colony] is long since decided, but it need not necessarily be a harbinger of Islam." Furthermore, Swahili was superior to German as a daily language because German, Axenfeld wrote, was too difficult for most speakers of Bantu languages. The adoption of Swahili would not be a concession to Islam; Axenfeld saw it as an opportunity to win a great victory against that religion's spread. The key step was to convert Swahili from a written language which used the Arabic alphabet to one which utilized the Latin alphabet. Such a transformation would allow missionaries to appropriate the language of the Muslims for their own evangelical purposes.[104] Hostility to Islam among Protestant missionaries had grown over the decades and, as is seen here, Islamophobia could serve as a powerful motivator for collective action.[105]

As Axenfeld put it, "The land and the time needs a unifying language, and no one can prevent it from developing ... One can lament the victory of Swahili for linguistic, cultural, or religious reasons but one must make the best of the matter. Not only the government but also the natives wish ... for instruction in Swahili." Mission could either take advantage of the situation or miss an opportunity to make itself indispensable to Africans and German colonial administrators alike. Axenfeld concluded with this proposal: in general, missionaries should continue to seek to learn and utilize the "higher-impact" local languages in order to communicate with the Africans in their mission fields. Major dialects within the various languages should be elevated as the most promising general pastoral and school languages. On top of this local program, Axenfeld proposed that Swahili become an integral part of curricula; as either a secondary language or, wherever appropriate, as the primary language of instruction. In this way "the day [would] come when [the printed word in Swahili] [would] serve a greater Christian [purpose] in East Africa."[106] The long-term consequences of Axenfeld's proposed policy was that the work of missionaries and the German colonial administration helped spread a standardized Swahili from the East African coast into the interior of the colony over the next decade.[107]

The success of government schools that taught Swahili, and the clear preference for that language, proved that Africans across the colony influenced decisions related to the forms of education that were offered. The example from Togo of the Ewe people, in their preference for English over German instruction and in securing the missionaries' prioritization of Ewe-language instruction, gives some insight into the role that African agency likely played in the making of linguistic policy in East Africa.[108] Missionaries' orientation toward indigenous languages for missionization gave them an obvious advantage over those who advocated the teaching of German.

Irregular Vocabulary

Missionaries were undeniably part of the worldwide process of colonization that established and reinforced the Western hegemony that characterized the late nineteenth century. Meyer's argument that the Basel missionaries utilized linguistic nationalism to control the political and cultural development of the Ewe people illuminates the necessity of recognizing the irregularities in German Protestants' behaviour. Missionaries in German East Africa decided, in consultation with indigenous collaborators, what constituted a *Volkssprache* – a national or tribal language. They then imposed a particular dialect of local languages on their students and the Volkskirche that they sought to create. Indigenous catechists and local leaders were often stifled in their attempts to assert agency in these churches, even as the Germans claimed to aspire to create autonomous communities of Christians.[109]

Furthermore, missionaries' authoritative descriptions of "authentic" indigenous cultures were themselves political declarations of authority in a contested German colonial space where, as George Steinmetz has shown, ethnographic knowledge translated directly into authority.[110] With their work to define indigenous cultures and *Völker*, missionaries participated in a process that mirrored efforts by colonial administrators and scholars to define African traditions, customs, and polities – a process that, in the end, served to essentialize indigenous cultures based on an imagined past fashioned by colonizers and colonized alike.[111] Missionaries pioneered German studies of African languages, and key linguists from the missionary movement – Carl Büttner, Carl Meinhof, and Dietrich Westermann are the most prominent – founded the study of colonial languages at the Seminar für Orientalische Sprachen (Seminar for Oriental Languages) in Berlin and the Kolonial Institut (Colonial Institute) in Hamburg. Both organizations trained colonial officials and merchants in the various languages of Germany's colonies starting in the late nineteenth and early twentieth centuries.[112] At the same time, German missionaries belonged to an intellectual tradition that included German Orientalists.[113] And any time German thought turned to the *Volk* and *völkisch* theory, it is not difficult to find troublesome links to Nazi ideology.[114] Nazis and their intellectual forebears used the same arguments regarding the spiritual and "natural" character of ethnicity to build their notion of the *Volksgemeinschaft*.[115] The contests between missionaries and Africans of all social strata who saw Christianity as a tool for political and social advantage constituted the fundamental genetic material of mission Christianity. In these negotiations, Christian missionaries' understandings of African Christianity stretched and morphed as an outcome of missionary and African behaviour.[116]

Missionaries' have been identified in many other places as leading agents of colonization. They were often the first Westerners to arrive and remain in a region, and their work to learn the language and culture of indigenous cultures could easily serve the interests of other colonizers. In addition, missionaries frequently called on the state to defend the mission societies and their work over the objections of recalcitrant indigenous rulers. Indeed, the colonization of indigenous cultures with Western Christianity was a form of cultural violence. Missionaries could overtly or covertly use their access to Western knowledge as a cudgel with which to compel indigenous cooperation or acquiescence. Often missionaries' benevolence was imperfect or absent. For example, indigenous informants and linguists played a prominent role in the innovative studies by Meinhof, Westermann, and the rest. But their valuable contributions were almost never acknowledged.

The relationships between missionaries and the missionized could not be equitable. The evidence is that German Protestant missionaries were, like their British counterparts, entangled with European empires. Nonetheless, the British regularly assumed that conversion to Christianity required conversion to Western social and cultural norms. German missionaries diverged from this normative assumption about missionary work. Their maintenance of indigenous language instruction and theoretical prioritization of eventual autonomy shows one of the major ways that the Germans' Protestant universalism could lead to autonomy.[117]

Conclusion

German Protestant missionaries' understanding of the religious self, the religious community, and the national community rested in linguistic definitions. From the scriptural tales of *glossolalia* and the Tower of Babel to nineteenth-century German philosophy and history, missionaries understood their own identity and the identity of the people to whom they missionized as defined by the tongues in which a faith might be built. The centrality of linguistics to their choices meant that the attendance by Africans of missionaries' schools was of inherent importance to missionary strategies. Missionaries sought to learn and develop indigenous written languages and then to build Volkskirchen around these linguistic communities. Their focus on linguistic sovereignty when it came to identifying cultures reinforced a general sensitivity to indigenous cultures. The "cultural inclusivity" this indicated was mutually and reciprocally constitutive of missionaries' internationalism. Yet, it was also reflective of the undeniable relationship between national thinking and the missionaries' international imagination. Missionaries' religious commitment to human universality allowed them to avoid a potentially dangerous consequence of an emphasis on linguistic and cultural diversity. They never translated their preference for "national" or "völkisch" languages into a direct support for segregation and "native" reservations. In South Africa, linguists, anthropologists, and missiologists used linguistic categorizations to justify racial and ethnic segregation in the lead up to and during the apartheid era.[118] Such outcomes demonstrate the slippery slope over which internationalist missionaries walked when they merged elements of völkisch ideologies with their universalist Christian message.

Debates between missionaries and secular colonialists over the language of instruction and the purpose of schools excluded African students, families, polities, and indigenous instructors from deliberations. The present study does not attempt to trace the influence of African stakeholders upon the development of a missionary school policy. Missionaries may have engaged in debates with their own missionized communities but the influence of these probable contests over control are hidden from the intellectual and political literature of the mission leadership and the colonial administrations. Without direct evidence it is impossible to determine with whom African families would stand, but the evidence is there to demonstrate that missionaries did not build their schools to satisfy German nationalist designs on the colonies.

And when German nationalists targeted missionaries' schools as representative of their founders' insincere devotion to the German nation, missionaries responded with a spirited and principled defence of their methods. To missionaries, indigenous-language instruction was spiritually, pedagogically, and practically adaptive to the realities of mission work on the ground. The defence that missionaries formulated emphasized the appropriateness of indigenous-language instruction based on evidence from scripture and contemporary ethnology. Missionaries argued for the basic dignity of indigenous culture and defended their commitment to learn and teach in indigenous languages as essential to the successful spread of Christianity. In this area, education, missionaries held to their internationalist principles and fiercely resisted efforts to integrate their ideology with more nationalist views. However, missionary policies did make concessions to outside influences. The compromise with the East African colonial administration on the use of Swahili as a language of instruction represented a tactical manoeuvre that helped bring together the missionaries and the state during the period of the Dernburg Reforms, when the colonial state and missionaries shared a general economic plan for the colony as well. Schools and indigenous-language development represented missionaries' most valuable tool, and missionaries' historic internationalism, cultural sensitivity to indigenous people, and local political circumstances in German East Africa all came together to hold off challengers to their cultural authority in the colony.

3 Give … to God the Things That Are God's

Labour and Capital in the Mission Field

German nationalists called on the missionaries to teach German to the people of the colonies. In their desire to validate German prestige and honour by globalizing German culture, nationalists frequently came into conflict with missionaries because of the latter's refusal to adopt a nationalist program of education. The missionaries' internationalism gave them the confidence to resist such secular interference. That confidence would become necessary once again as another challenge to mission schools' curricula arose from among the secular colonialists. This time the secular activists challenged the functional purpose of education. Economically focused imperialists attacked missionaries' pedagogy because they wanted colonial schools to create labourers for colonial development. The missionaries refused and insisted that their principal goal was the creation of Protestants. The battle over the idealized mission school graduate required another definition of the missionaries' internationalism.

The title of this chapter abridges the well-known verse from the Gospel of Matthew, "Give therefore to the emperor the things that are the emperor's, and to God the things that are God's."[1] The passage has often served as justification for obedience to the state, but to the missionaries it also justified their autonomy. The Great Commission sanctified their work, and the words of the Gospels and Epistles embroidered their loyalty to the mission project with numerous sources of moral certitude. The message of Matthew in this verse, from Jesus' confrontation with the Pharisees in the Temple, explained to Christians how to manage their dual loyalties. And the German Protestant mission movement used the lesson to manage relationships with the colonial state. When they worked in the territories of other states, German Protestant missionaries understood their submission to earthly authority as necessary in order to carry on their spiritual work. In colonies like German East

Africa, the message of the verse explained how missionaries could live under their own government but maintain their commitment to international mission.

Mission Christianity – as many believed at the time and many continue to believe – reinforced and justified colonialism.[2] Missionaries, like other imperialists, constructed the colonial world. But it is overly simplistic to lump missionaries together with other colonizers for the sake of narrative convenience. The intentions of German Protestant missionaries ran counter to one of the most commonly interpreted thrusts of colonialism – economic subjugation and exploitation. In general, the relationship between the missionaries and the colonial state in East Africa and between the mission societies and the metropolitan state in Germany was congenial.[3] The missionaries had much more fraught relationships with the other major secular force in the colonies: capitalist economic actors, including plantation owners and large-scale trading companies. In this respect the missionaries drew on another useful passage from the Gospels. As Gustav Warneck put it, missionaries should "build the kingdom which is not of this world."[4] Efforts for "[t]echnical worker education, plantation construction, agricultural testing stations, commodity marketing – these are all matters of colonial interests, not of mission ... No [man] can serve two masters, [and] neither can mission."[5] Warneck's closing line would have immediately reminded readers of another verse in Matthew: "No one can serve two masters; for a slave will either hate the one and love the other, or be devoted to the one and despise the other. You cannot serve God and wealth."[6] Most literate Christians would have recognized Warneck's indictment of capitalist greed and the clear implication that a German colonialism aimed at wealth could only lead to bitterness.

Missionaries' main field of conflict with the state and economic interests came, unsurprisingly, in more squabbles over colonial education. Those representing economic interests promoted school policies that would transform the African population of German East Africa into a capitalist labour pool, and they wanted missionary schools to train young people in the required skills. And, if necessary, the economic colonialists wanted the state to enforce such a policy. For their part, missionaries favoured educational policy designed to create economically autonomous Protestant communities and individuals. Along with the conflicts about the languages of instruction in mission schools, discourse about the "Erziehung des Negers zur Arbeit" (education of the Negro to work) sat at the centre of missionaries' conflict with secular colonial interests. As this chapter will show, the missionaries' theology and internationalist worldview provided the rhetorical ammunition for them to resist the form of vocational education demanded by those who advocated corporate capitalist exploitation in the colonies. And it gave the missionaries the spiritual commitment to guide a program of African economics and community that stood in contrast to the intentions of business interests.

"Erziehung des Negers zur Arbeit"

It did not take long for European colonizers, including missionaries, to recognize the essentiality of possessing "wealth in people" as the main currency of power in Africa.[7] In this determination they joined a long tradition of African rulers whose state-building focused on exerting power over people rather than territory because of the relative scarcity of the former. Public and economic policy in German East Africa required the effective control of people. For the plantations and other European ventures, the process of capitalistic development and exploitation required the conversion of the African population into a labour pool that responded to European labour needs and had the necessary skills and knowledge to fulfil European workplace expectations. In the interim, employers were more than happy to utilize *corvée* systems and the lash to meet their needs. German economic stakeholders in the colonies, and their allies, called for a broad policy program designed to "educate the Negro to work." They argued that appropriately conditioned African wage labour promised the means to transform Germany's colonies into a source of raw materials for its massive industrial sector and a market for its consumer goods.

During the early decades of the colony, economic development and exploitation consisted largely of ventures by concessionary companies, first among which was the Deutsch-Ostafrikanische Gesellschaft, founded by the adventurer Carl Peters and a consortium of banking and commercial interests. The company, after losing all official administrative duties in 1889, focused on the establishment of cash crop plantations and the export and import trade. Later, other advocates of colonial development became involved in the economy and, by extension, grew interested in the labour pool situation. A second major proponent of colonial development was the Kolonial-Wirtschaftliches Komitee (Colonial Economic Committee, or KWK), an affiliate of the German Colonial Society. The KWK became the major advocate of economic colonialism within the secular colonial movement. Funded by the Colonial Society and mercantilist supporters, the KWK funded research into colonial development schemes and helped organize and promote the Tuskegee cotton-growing expedition to Togo in 1901–9 as well as agricultural research in German East Africa.[8] Colonial development schemes like those promoted by the KWK sought to maximize colonial production and consumption. The schemes usually entailed the operations of concessionary and large plantation companies, entities with which German Protestant mission companies had already clashed by 1904.[9] These large capitalist enterprises demanded a source of docile and reliable labour. As early as the 1890s, economic colonialists began to insist that Protestant and Catholic mission schools join in the training of that sort of work force.[10]

A leader among the intellectuals who advocated training Africans to labour for the global capitalist economy was Paul Rohrbach.[11] He was born to German-speaking parents living in Russian Courland (modern-day Latvia). His family's cultural Germanness grew through his attendance at the German-language university at Dorpat (Tartu) and then through ongoing economic and theological studies at the University of Berlin. He continued his theological studies in another German borderland, at Strasbourg in Alsace. Rohrbach blended progressively liberal politics and German nationalism with a Protestant chauvinism that supported German imperial aggressiveness. Rohrbach travelled extensively, visiting Russia's Central Asian and Caucasian provinces, the Ottoman Empire, and Persia. He developed theories that advocated the expansion of a "Greater Germany" in the interests of promoting an "ethical imperialism."[12] Rohrbach's publications on German colonialism and foreign policy, paired with his biographical and professional profile as an international German, eventually led to his employment from 1903 to 1906 in German Southwest Africa as a settlement commissioner and economic expert. He was unquestionably a liberal imperialist.

Rohrbach provided important ideological support for economic colonialists who sought to create an "ethical imperialism" independent of missionary input. Others with more economic and political power would take up the project of promoting a particular form of economic colonialism, but Rohrbach typified a new ideology of German colonialism that has wrongly been identified with the missionaries because of his claims to promoting "cultural Protestantism" around the world. Rohrbach's training as a theologian and his role in colonial administration are the basis for a historical argument that he was typical of the collusion between German missionaries and the colonial state.[13] However, in his work *Die Kolonie* (1909) Rohrbach is in fact quite hostile to missionaries.[14] Furthermore, in the aftermath of the Maji-Maji War in German East Africa and the Herero-Nama War and Genocide in German Southwest Africa, Rohrbach and others grew more determined to orient colonial administration to the interests of Whites to the exclusion of

African dignity or prosperity. Advocacy of settler interests necessarily meant opposition to indigenous autonomy and property rights, placing Rohrbach's ideas in opposition to the German Protestant mission movement.

The general state of scholarship on missions and colonialism has led to erroneous assumptions linking German missionaries and economic development. As mentioned earlier in this work, while German missionaries cannot be acquitted of a role in colonization, their actions and collaborations with colonized and colonizing individuals and groups transcended economic motivations. And the connections between missionaries' educational efforts and European economic interests in other colonial empires reveal the ambiguous relationship between missionaries and secular colonists.[15] In most cases, historians have judged missionaries as willing participants in empire-building. In particular, historians of the British colonial empire and of British missionaries have focused on the role that missionaries played in preparing Africans for participation in the capitalist agricultural and mining enterprises of European settler regimes. For example, in Southern Rhodesia missionaries were far more concerned with the desires of the settler population than they were with their own ideas of Christian equality. When pressed, they constantly hedged their answers about the possibilities of African uplift. For missionaries in Southern Rhodesia, settlers were a constituency of mission education equally important to the Africans actually being educated.[16] Europeans interested in maintaining the "aristocracy of colour" in Britain's colonies prevented African participation in European working-class traditions and assisted the formation of a racialized African peasantry. Missionaries, in this interpretation, encouraged Africans' subordinate role in the colonial cultural system.[17]

Historians of Britain's empire argue for a convergence of economic and missionary interests. David Livingstone, Wiliam Carey, and their compatriots closely linked the spread of "legitimate trade" as a replacement for the slave trade and the proliferation of European commerce with the positive spread of Christianity.[18] But this close linkage does not hold up as well in the German case. Missionaries wholeheartedly included the abolition of slavery within their "civilizing mission," but the leap to "legitimate trade" did not prevail.[19] As has been detailed earlier in this work and will be elaborated below, even as they could not avoid a role in colonial transformations, German missionaries were sceptical of the modern capitalist world and sought to insulate their converts from the worst excesses of global trade and its purveyors.[20] Nonetheless, the missionaries maintained a perception of Africans as the Other, perhaps not permanently so, but as definitively "different."

Africans and African culture seemed unsophisticated to missionaries. Though missionaries defended the richness of these cultures in many instances, they still frequently judged unconverted Africans as spiritually deficient.

Other German colonialists moralized their conquests with claims to abolitionism, and missionaries endorsed this reasoning for European intervention. To the missionaries, the presence of slavery offered evidence of Africans' need for spiritual uplift. However, German administrations did little to formally abolish slavery in their colonies. The suppression of the slave trade in German East Africa did contribute to an end to slavery in the colony through social forces, but that was further facilitated by the emergence of a wage market that created opportunities for self-emancipation and was less a result of direct action by the regime.[21] The anti-slavery campaign provided one natural area of alliance between the missions and colonial state, an alliance that pitted the Germans against African slave traders.[22] An anti-slavery lottery in 1891 raised two million Marks.[23] For a short time anti-slavery activism fed the campaign to colonize East Africa, but the links between German mission societies and the German abolition movement were far less profound than those of their British counterparts.[24] It is dangerous to overestimate the strength of these bonds, as the administration's campaign against slavery in German East Africa was intentionally protracted, even plodding, in its pace. Missions of both confessions spent the 1890s, 1900s, and 1910s repeatedly pressing the colonial government in Berlin and East Africa to further suppress the slave trade and abolish slaveholding among Africans.[25]

The Economic Argument

In the German colonies, advocates for economic development joined in with nationalists who demanded German-language instruction. Though certainly some of them shared the nationalists' principles that sought to extend the German cultural sphere as far as possible – Paul Rohrbach, for example, would have been deeply sympathetic. But more importantly, economically minded actors argued for German-language instruction as key to economic development of the colonies. The KWK, along with the nationalistic elements leading the Colonial Society, supported German-language instruction as essential to managing the colonies' labour pools. Together the two groups favoured a form of economic colonialism that demanded Africans be trained to work on plantations and in other economic enterprises.[26] They judged it more efficacious to develop a source of German-speaking employees than to train their White managers in African languages. Leaders within these organizations and their supporters thought that Africans should be taught the minimum skills necessary to create a viable labour force for market-oriented activities. This strain of thought hoped to convert the German colonies into miniature replicas of British India, to create a store of consumers and producers whose production and consumption could feed the economic expansion of Germany.

Along with focusing on basic fluency in German, representatives of economic interests in German East Africa thought some basic education in arithmetic and in obedience constituted an effective program of education for the African population. Plantation managers and trading agents cared little for the indigenous cultures of the colony and showed little commitment to the "civilizing" mission of colonialism. They wanted to convert the millions living in the German colonies into consumers and workers. Both goals encouraged or required Africans to remake their economic and social systems, to physically uproot themselves from their homes, in order to participate in the new colonial economy. The colonial administration aided these goals by introducing and circulating an official currency, the German East African Rupee, and requiring tax obligations be met by Africans in cash rather than in kind. The acceleration of economic transformation encouraged by these policies represented the leading edge of an aggressive program of economic and cultural transformation to further colonial economic interests. Missionaries' focus on indigenous-language instruction, resistance to wholesale cultural transformation of mission communities, and antipathy toward capitalism put the mission movement squarely in opposition to economic colonialists' efforts to shape education in the colony.

As will be shown, school curricula from mission schools communicated clearly that the goals of mission education did not coincide with the goals of economic colonialism. One example can show the secular colonialists' interest in controlling missionary education. In 1904, at the height of the Herero-Nama War and at the urging of the secular colonial movement, a law was proposed in the Kolonialrat that would grant colonial governors extensive control over the placement of mission stations and "the right to supervise teaching activities" in mission schools.[27] The law capitalized on missionaries' dubious public standing at that moment. Settlers in German Southwest Africa and their allies had used the fact that missionaries had been spared by the Herero as support for a specious argument that missionaries were to blame for the uprising in the colony.[28] The economic development argument behind the change is obvious, but missionaries also divined a deeper philosophical difference. According to Warneck, secular critics of missionaries were motivated by missionaries' insistence that "Blacks are just as beloved by God as Whites." He accused the advocates of the law of having only evil designs upon the colonies' indigenous inhabitants. Their goal was the transformation of indigenous people into serfs of trading concessions, plantations, and mining companies.[29] The emancipatory qualities ascribed by Warneck to mission schools challenged the secular colonialists' plans, and this fact, according to Warneck, provided the basis for the campaign against Christian missionaries. Thankfully for the missions, the law was not enacted, but it displayed the potential for conflict.

Schools and Missions

The largely unified opposition to economic colonialists' intentions among German Protestant mission societies sprang from the missionaries' shared ideological position. Nearly every German Protestant missionary believed Africans gained little from any project designed to "educate the Negro to work." What really mattered in the missionaries' eyes was an educational program designed to create autonomous (Protestant) Christians living in an economically healthy, self-sustaining community of Christians within a wider Volkskirche. When the missionaries thought about the values they wanted to emphasize in their education they might use words like "obedience" and "diligence," but they meant those to be individual values directed toward service to community and to God, not as touchstones for functioning on a plantation or railroad construction site. The distinction is very clear in Karl Axenfeld's comparison of Protestant and Catholic educational achievements. He claimed, "The Berlin Mission [has] achieved pleasing results in the promotion of native culture and … the education to work … which is much more valuable, in my opinion, than the Catholic attempts [to make] the natives dependent upon plantations."[30] Confessional boosterism aside, Axenfeld's comment shows his ideal pedagogical policy.

The missionaries believed that schools should not only develop certain "modern" skills needed to support a future independent church, and to mediate between Christian ethics and European scientific and technological achievements, but also strive to avoid wholesale transformations of cultural practices.[31] As discussed in chapter 2, missionaries wished to nurture the development of an African class of independent farmers that would form the social foundation for a healthy and vital Volkskirche.[32] This methodology had mixed results, but it did represent strong evidence of missionaries' belief in a universal Christianity and an educational program geared toward indigenizing Christianity while denying mission education as a tool for creating a pliant capitalist labour supply.[33]

Missionary leaders called for full autonomy on the part of missionary schools and minimized any goal of educating Africans to create a tractable workforce. Schools that "educated the Negro to work" would ruin the missionary project in the colonies. Labour practices on the plantations included the use of corporal punishment and the alienation of a worker from his or her home community. Missionaries were not always the most vocal opponents of corporal punishment but they did not want to be associated with the exploitative and abusive elements of colonial systems of labour.[34] Furthermore, because missionaries' theology depended upon the preservation of indigenous communities, they would never endorse educational goals that encouraged the dispersal of communities or the dilution of ethnic groups through migrant labour. The missionaries argued that, for these reasons, their schools should remain independent and unburdened by economic goals. Those missionaries willing to participate in a colonial project to "educate the Negro to work" and serve the colonial state remained a small minority.

Most missionaries refused to tailor their educational programs to practical economic demands. When the mission societies designed their educational programs, they focused on the skills that they judged essential to the life of a good Protestant. Missionaries did wish to inculcate Africans with a Protestant vision of industriousness, a quality Africans supposedly lacked, according to the prevailing European view, but for missionaries "educating to work" was directed toward individual productivity and not wage labour.[35] Most missions included some vocational training but the types of trades taught could never be considered industrial. The missions encouraged students to acquire the skills to become tailors and cabinetmakers or to farm their own land.[36] Leading missionaries emphasized an educational goal of individual and community independence.[37] Missionaries' defence of their schools included the development of a rhetoric that asserted the cultural worth of indigenous, in particular African, ways of life. By defending the cultures of missionized people, missionaries took their internationalist worldview to its logical extent – arguing that Africans did not need to be transformed completely to become full Christians.

Unintended Translations

We must, of course, take this presentation of German Protestant missionaries as culturally enlightened vis-à-vis other European colonialists with a grain of salt. No matter what missionaries' intentions, the extension of Western Christian culture through mission education could not help but facilitate the integration of African cultures into the global economy.[38] While most Germans did not encourage David Livingstone's union of "civilization, commerce, and Christianity," they did seek to bring African cultures into community with Western Christendom. This goal, as discussed in the previous chapter, required African societies to transform their cultures, a process that missionaries facilitated. African cultures did not require wholesale Westernization, but German missionaries nonetheless understood the cultures as something other than what the missionaries judged to be Christian. Even as they sought to embed new cultural practices, the missionaries did so with an eye toward preserving some aspect of African groups' uniqueness, and in service of that same preservation they refused to serve the colonial economic order.

Major economic changes the missionaries did cause generally belonged to the category of unintended consequences. As best they could, German Protestant missionaries isolated their work from the economic transformations wrought by colonialism even as their activities forced certain translations of economic life in East Africa. When the missionaries of the four Protestant mission societies first arrived in German East Africa, most of them set out for the hinterlands of the colony – seeking "virgin" territories and communities. Such communities "needed" missionaries the most because natural exchange and settlement by Christians would take too long to reach them otherwise, and the (erroneously) perceived isolation of these communities also promised that missionaries could work without the distortions propagated by Europeans' secular world. However, many mission stations developed economic features that implicated missionaries in the economic transformation of missionized groups such as the Nyakyusa near Lake Nyasa.

In early periods, missionaries from the Moravian and Berlin Missions followed common practice and distributed certain trade goods to entice children to attend school lessons and to entice adults to attend church services. The distribution of these goods enhanced demand for materials like calico cloth. Trade goods could also be acquired through cash purchases. When the mission stations also began employing indigenous labourers in the construction of mission buildings and cultivation of mission fields, the missionaries introduced more trade goods and, eventually, wage labour to the region.[39] As a result, for the period before 1900 the mission stations in the southwest of German East Africa provided the bulk of European goods to Africans and employed the great bulk of wage labourers. However, over time the expansion of the colony's economy soon reached the region via caravan and labour migration routes; this expansion drew Nyakyusa in large numbers to the coast and railroad construction sites hundreds of miles distant.[40] In German East Africa, the missionaries played a direct role in the creation of a market for European products. The missionaries' role as cultural explorers for colonialism, as the first source of knowledge about the geography and people of inland colonial spaces, is well known. Their role as pioneers for certain economic transformations is also important, unintentional as it was.

Another basis for arguing that German missionaries favoured economic initiatives in the colonies has arisen from analogies with British missionary ideologies. British missionaries embraced their role in transforming African societies, with a general adoption of the civilizing project: supplanting Africans' precolonial communal identities with a society based on individualism; instilling some basic affiliation among Africans with European culture through the English language, literacy, and Christianity; and integration of Africans into the capitalist marketplace as labourers and consumers. British missionaries also sought to separate the African Christian from his non-Christian community. This British mission policy dominated at precisely the time German mission societies were embracing the creation of the Volkskirche, which sought to create a core of Christians among non-Christians to encourage the spread of the faith by example.[41] Though German missionaries shared in the colonializing effects of European Christianity, their interest in the economic colonial project was weak. Instead, German missionaries followed a practical theology of Christian evangelization that prioritized cultural difference and economic autonomy.

For a time, David Livingstone's argument for the unity of civilization, free commerce, and Christianity inspired certain mission societies to organize trading companies to support their work. Such commercial ventures were not common among the German mission societies, though Friedrich Fabri argued in their favour for all mission societies and created one for the Rhenish Mission Society in 1869.[42] Fabri's ideas were inspired by the model of the Basel Mission, one that set the goal of developing commercial elements of its work to provide employment and vocational training to new converts and to finance the expensive work of foreign missions in India and Africa. While this "industrial mission" dominated the character of the Basel Mission, it also supported a cultural chauvinism that measured African achievements against the standard of German-Swabian civilization as lived by the missionaries in their home region. These views did not persist in the 1880s or after, but they do show the imperfect segregation of economics and mission work.[43]

Among the German Protestant mission societies active in German East Africa, the Bethel Mission deviated most consistently from the mission movement's consensus. In particular, around the "education of the Negro to work" the mission's membership could not escape its metropolitan connections. As Sebastian Conrad has shown, the Bethel Mission Society happily collaborated with economic demands for a reliable African work force.[44] In nineteenth-century Germany, globalization and nationalism were interdependent products of the expanding "interlinkages" of the period. These interlinkages resulted in a highly mobile labour force. This mobility raised the anxieties of certain segments of German society who feared for the country's long-term social coherence. As a jingoistic nationalism expanded its influence around and after 1900 (shown, in part, in the expansions of patriotic associations like the Colonial Society), efforts to define the members of the German national community intensified in order to compensate for the rapidly declining relevance of economic and political boundaries.[45]

Certain politicians and academics scrambled to develop techniques and technologies like border controls, immigration laws and regulations, work passes, and racializing technologies designed to identify and regulate Germanness. In Germany, activists in and out of government became more and more concerned with disciplining Germany's labour force and controlling immigrant labourers. German politicians acted to regulate and control a workforce which was continually shifting to include migrating Poles, Belgians, Dutch, Italians, and even Chinese.[46] As part of the general attempt to shore up physical and intellectual boundaries, a project of defining "work" and "labour" as either German or foreign emerged. Within this project, Germans who were indigent or unemployed became targets for rehabilitation and remedial "education [back] to work." Migrant labour forces also required control and regulation so that they provided labour satisfactory to German standards.

The link between labour ideology in Germany and among the Bethel missionaries in German East Africa hinges upon the work of Friedrich von Bodelschwingh and his Bethel community in the realm of "inner mission." Inner mission was a wide-ranging and important social movement that aimed to recover and restore Christian community life and individual faith across Germany. Similar to the Salvation Army and settlement houses in Britain and the United States, German inner mission activities extended from "Bahnhof Missions" in the major train stations of German cities (volunteers stationed themselves in the waiting halls and on the platforms of the stations to intercept migrants to the city and prevent their falling into "White slavery" or the hands of unscrupulous agents of other kinds),[47] to social welfare activities aimed at improving the material and spiritual condition of the urban poor,[48] to the care of the disabled at hospitals and sanitaria like those of Bodelschwingh's Bethel Institutes. In the 1860s Bodelschwingh organized workers' colonies in Germany for the vocational education of mentally handicapped individuals. A little over a decade later these institutions expanded to include training for "vagabonds" and the "work-shy."[49] Ultimately, work became a central value of the Bethel movement. The Bodelschwingh workers' colonies all taught a curriculum of manual labour designed to aid the individual in his or her daily life. When Bodelschwingh expanded his philanthropy to the German colony of East Africa, this habit of inculcating the inexperienced, inept, ignorant, and indolent with the virtues of hard work was extended to the African, who was, by turns, labelled all those things. The link between training poor Germans and Africans to work was not coincidental. Conrad has argued that German missionaries had a history of collaboration with secular colonialism similar to that of British missionaries.[50] By this interpretation, German missionaries were, in fact, trying to serve two masters, and were not preserving their precious autonomy.

The views of Friedrich von Bodelschwingh and his missionaries did not extend beyond the halls and stations of the Bethel Mission Society. The connection between works of inner mission – efforts to save Christians at home – and foreign mission – efforts to create Christians abroad – have been thoroughly covered in the British context, and Conrad's addition of a German case corroborates a general pattern of close linkages.[51] The Bethel Mission Society provides the best example of this connection in Germany, but connections also existed within the Herrnhut Mission of the Moravian Brotherhood and in the work of the North German Mission Society.[52] However, neither of the other mission societies made the same universal claims about the value of labour as a moral corrective. The thread linking all of German Protestant mission to a program of national labour control via the Bethel Mission is too thin by any measure. While the Bethel Mission Society was undoubtedly interested in educating Africans to work and was not opposed to working closely with the colonial government, other mission societies and their leaders were less eager to cooperate in an economically motivated program of "educating the Negro to work."

The Bethel Mission belonged to the German Protestant mission movement. But it certainly deviated on the issue of "education to work." The causes lie in the specific character of the mission society. First, the Bethel Mission Society and its leader, Friedrich von Bodelschwingh, were the most politically conservative and nationalist of the German mission societies working in Africa.[53] Second, though many missionary intellectuals spoke of "educating the Negro to work," their meaning deviated greatly from Conrad's description of church policy. Finally, the Bethel Mission Society joined the ranks of the foreign missions in the 1880s, making it one of the "new missions." Missionaries from the Bethel Society viewed themselves as part of a communal project to "elevate" colonized people and needed the work of "government schools and mission schools" and "planters, administrators, teachers, and missionaries" for success.[54] The other mission societies operating in German East Africa had much longer histories, stretching back into the era before there was a German Empire in Europe, let alone one in Africa, and their view of "educating Africans to work" differed drastically as a result. Furthermore, their independent history made them far less likely to align themselves with other colonialist groups. The sources of the extraordinary character of the Bethel Mission emphasize the near unanimity among the other mission societies at the time.

Across the German mission fields, individual missionaries expanded the teachings of the Missionswissenschaftler. They pursued projects deeply hostile to the economic transformation of indigenous cultures. In German East Africa, the Leipzig missionary Bruno Gutmann refrained from imposing European civilization for the sake of Christian conversions. Gutmann and his colleagues are more representative of the shape of German Protestant missionary ideas about education and labour than Bodelschwingh's Bethel missionaries. To Gutmann, cultural transformation, like that advocated by the Bethel Society and by other "missionary nationalists" such as Friedrich Fabri,[55] failed to respect the divinely crafted receptacles for Christian witness – the primeval bonds of family, neighbourhood, peer groups, and language. Tearing apart historical links among missionized people and replacing them with European cultural impositions would make Christianity more alien to those the missions hoped to reach.[56] The preservation of "primeval bonds" epitomized how the missionaries could simultaneously favour African culture while imposing Western judgments. The missionaries' emphasis on their priorities – Christian evangelization and education – meant they developed little awareness or appreciation for the complexity of African social systems. Instead, they assumed that because they, the missionaries, were the Christians, their social forms were the forms intended by God. So, they favoured families built around monogamous patriarchy and the creation of single-family economic units. What distinguished them from other colonialists was that they thought about these issues and oriented their priorities to include considerations of African welfare.

3.1. Leipzig mission at the Kilimandjaro (n.d.). The Leipzig missionaries arrived in the Kilimanjaro area and around Moshi in 1893.

Source: Basel Mission Archives.

Like the Leipzig Missionaries in East Africa, German Protestants operating with the small Neuendettelsau Mission in Papua New Guinea crafted a similar methodology. Christian Keysser, one of the Neuendettelsau missionaries, decided that the cultural practices of the people among whom he worked on the island of New Guinea provided a foundation for Christian belief and insisted that local Christian congregations should lead the spread of the faith.[57] Like Gutmann and others, Keysser argued that existing cultural practices and social structures could become the foundation for Christian communities. Christianity had to adapt to local cultural impulses if it would ever have success. Views like Gutmann's and Keysser's were not always held as strongly or as firmly by every German Protestant missionary, but they were far more typical than the views of Bodelschwingh, Friedrich Fabri, or other nationalist missionaries.[58] The presence of "missionary nationalists" is undeniable, and they could give some moral heft to the secular colonialists when they endorsed nationalist goals. But within the missionary movement their presence was generally marginal. When most German missionaries gave thought to the relationship among evangelization, the social relationships among Africans, and the Africans' labour, they set out to train Africans to the satisfactions of individual industriousness.

Why Not "Educate the Negro to Work"?

The historical record clearly demonstrates that there is good cause to set aside "nationalist" missionaries as exceptions. It shows that German Protestant missionaries, from the beginnings of the colonial period, viewed education as their own proprietary tool for the purpose of evangelization and for little else. This certainty fed antipathy toward the "education of the Negro to work."[59] Just a few years after the creation of the German colonial empire, attentive supporters of the mission movement, colonialist advocates, and, most importantly, the staff and clergy within the mission societies witnessed three prominent missionary leaders in Germany renounce economic goals. The *Allgemeine Missions-Zeitschrift* reprinted the discussion between veteran missionary Alexander Merensky and Basel Mission leader Theodor Öhler. Merensky and Öhler's thoughts originated at the 1887 meeting of the Saxon Mission Conference, a regular meeting of Missionswissenschaftler and mission society leaders. Warneck added an editorial afterword when he published the texts of their presentations in his journal. Collectively these men's views provided a clear ideological position that mission schools were for mission purposes.[60]

Merensky opened the discussion by observing that missionaries could not avoid the issue of indigenous labour. Their mere presence in the colonies demanded they take some role in the "education of the primitives to work."[61] However, Merensky's use of the phrasing "Erziehung … zur Arbeit [educating … to work]" was not the same as its use by economic colonialists. To Merensky the duty to educate arose from the need to speed the decline of "heathen traditional belief" and "plant the Holy Ghost" in indigenous people's hearts. Christian missionaries, Merensky wrote, had always kept the moral "improvement" of uncivilized people at the forefront of their minds.[62] Theodor Bechler's celebration of the Konde's skills as weavers and ironworkers, the quality of their home construction, and their agricultural knowledge demonstrates the admiration that missionaries had, and hoped to spread, for Africans' productive talents.[63] Training indigenous people to the standards of the colonial state and its economic actors too often led to abuses of indigenous labourers, and to a negative association by colonized people of productive labour with violence and slavery. The mission station ought to provide guidance in order to promote "industriousness, constancy, endurance, [and] wisdom" among the evangelized. African people could be kept from becoming a "proletariat" through self-sufficiency, while educational programs remained "grounded in the character of Christianity."[64] Merensky and Bechler may have refused to endorse the proletarianization of African cultures, but they still described the cultures which they served as those of a different sort of human. Merensky's use of the term "primitives" reveals a lot about his particular viewpoint. Furthermore, the belief that Africans needed protection and guidance away from colonial exploitation through missionary ideology is one that continues to restrict colonized people's agency.

Theodor Öhler of the Basel Mission went further than Merensky to indict the abuse of non-Westerners as plantation labourers. He agreed with Merensky that the priority of mission education should be to serve the students, not Europeans or their colonial goals. Educating Africans to work on plantations was un-Christian; it helped the "rich become richer" while devaluing hard work. Labour for the sake of an employer lacked the moral value of independent toil. When it came to "educating the Negro to work," Öhler defended Africans against contemporary accusations of laziness. The "Negro" was not by his nature lazy but simply appeared to be so as a result of circumstance, Öhler argued. First,

> There are among us [Europeans] many rich people who do not work very much because they are rich. Rich people believe it is not necessary to work. The Negroes, one can say, are rich people … they have a truly rich countryside which delivers that which they require and more to them in copious abundance with little effort. In this way are Negroes rich people as they have in excess what they require, or [what they need] can be easily acquired in abundance.[65]

And besides, Öhler pointed out, accusations of laziness rested on observations of Africans working for White settlers and plantation owners who garnered all the benefit while the labouring African was left poor. Enslaved Africans in the Americas had suffered similar accusations of indolence. Öhler discounted these accusations and argued for the character of Africans. Mission education would reinforce the natural abilities of the "Negro" through moral education. In Africa, according to Öhler, polygyny and slavery had led to the cultural valuation of a man as tied to his ability to avoid labour – the prevailing opinion was "that work [was] for wives and slaves and unworthy of a free man."[66] Öhler's critique of "sinful" polygyny and slavery should not be any surprise as it wove middle-class Protestant morality into the debate around African labour.

Warneck's editorial comment translated the conference discussion into a political position for the mission movement. He reminded his readers that the utilization of indigenous labour had become "the main question on the agenda for colonial political discussion." The mission movement's disregard for "training the Negro to work" placed the mission in clear opposition to the abusers of colonial power. Work, and by this Warneck meant, like his colleagues, the hard work and industriousness of an independent individual, could serve to civilize and educate people in "the spiritual ethic" of Christianity. This work ethic could help root out negative cultural qualities like polygyny and slavery by showing African men the "dignity of work."[67] Warneck and his colleagues agreed that "work" could help spread the Gospel and build churches and schools, but capitalist labour could not.

The Protestant missionaries' opinions of "Erziehung des Negers zur Arbeit" and the outcomes they foresaw of such training were supported by their rival Catholic missionaries' views on education. In an 1897 debate the Catholic mission representative on the Kolonialrat, Franz Hespers, agreed that training Africans to the dignity of labour would establish the first step to "cultural competence."[68] Ten years later, Norbert Weber, Abbot of the Benedictines of St Ottilien, told a meeting of colonial enthusiasts in Strasbourg that Africans did not need to be educated to take part in the global economy. In fact, paying Africans wages was not necessary to induce Africans to purchase Western goods. Like Öhler twenty years before, Weber argued that Africans were not lazy. Rather, so long as the "African," Weber wrote, believed the surplus of his labour would be taken from him by "brigands" (whom he implied included European merchants and colonial tax collectors), the "African" would be unwilling to work as the European wished. Colonialism required a government strong enough to protect its subjects from exploitation, and only then could African people, learn "work, because work ennobles men," and the newly industrious Africans would then be ready to advance further in their cultural development.[69] The agreement between bitter confessional opponents on this issue further highlights the peculiarity of the Bethel Mission and its missionaries' attitudes toward labour.

The discussion of Merensky and Öhler at the 1887 Saxon Mission Conference, and Warneck's commentary after the fact, showed that missionaries did not devalue labour in all its forms. They did, however, oppose using Christian missions to develop colonial economies for European interests. All three shared the view that Africans' educational, economic, and moral conditions required a concerted strategy for improvement. They also agreed that missionaries should see the "improvement" of African culture as an essentially moral project. The Catholic missionaries' supportive position might even demonstrate a broader Christian consensus against "educating the Negro to work." As special experts in "native affairs" and defenders of African culture, the missionary leaders pointed out, Germany's missionaries were not in Africa to promote capitalist development. Their project remained one focused on instilling the social and cultural markers of Christianity. Mission schools were tools for making Christians, not for making a proletariat.[70] To the missionaries, proletarianization threatened to bring social democracy, and social democracy brought atheism. Because the missionaries felt themselves to be morally secure and to be true advocates of indigenous people's interests, their opposition to capitalist labour forms became as important as their commitment to indigenous-language instruction.

The German Protestant missionary movement's deep suspicion of secularism and industrialization emerged from the movement's broad connections to the Pietist movement. It extended beyond through certain connections with inner mission activism in Germany that fed a sceptical view of many of the supposed benefits of laissez-faire capitalism. As a consequence, German missionaries were generally anti-capitalist. In particular, they resented the creation of a massive working class in Germany, one whose treatment by capitalism and industry seemed to ignore the basic principles of Christian charity. The regular conflict between employers and employees threatened missionaries' conservative communitarianism. It was doubly threatening because capitalist transformations encouraged the creation of a vast sea of working-class families in which Germany's influential and dynamic socialist organizers and activists swam with ease. These ministers and missionaries were also Christian. And in most of the industrializing world of the nineteenth century, that also meant they were anti-socialist.

This cultural context in Germany reinforced the Protestant missionaries' opposition to economically motivated education. Advocates of cultural transformation in Africa favoured the creation of a loyal labouring class in the colonies. Some of them argued that such a total transformation of indigenous people was the surest path to achieving the "civilizing mission." But Warneck disputed this interpretation. He argued that it was natural that missionaries, as Christians among the "uncivilized peoples," provide medical help; build hospitals; care for the hungry, orphaned, and widowed; and support the oppressed against their oppressors. But he also argued that missionaries must remain focused on their main work – the salvation of the sinner and the planting of the Gospels in the hearts of heathens. As a consequence, Warneck came out against efforts by colonial administrators, traders, and concessionary corporations to instrumentalize mission stations and schools as training grounds for African labour. He cautioned that Jesus did not send out his apostles with the instruction to "teach them to work" but with the instruction to "make them my followers."[71] Any secular colonialist who hoped for a more pliable workforce should accept that it would come only as a secondary effect of Christian mission.[72] He reminded missionaries that the expansion of secular colonial power and the proletarianization of colonized people would transfer the ills of European industrial society to newly Christianized places and destroy the hard work of the mission societies. The creation of a proletariat might serve capitalists but it also threatened to recreate the conditions that had, in Europe, led to the socialistic radicalization of the masses. He counselled, "Just like happiness, contentment, and virtue ... belief in the Gospels is not dependent upon a particular degree of civilization." Missionary enterprise and Christian evangelization were not dependent upon the advancement of "modernity."[73] And, thus, Warneck argued, Christian mission did not need to submit to the pressures of colonial and economic powers because mission's goals were not dependent upon the benevolence of those powers.[74] Attachment to the economic project would destroy this independence and violated the missionaries' principles.

Giving to the Emperor

Over time missionaries' resistance to economic colonialists' goals drew greater and greater attention. Secular colonialists wished to see Germany's colonies and, more directly, their inhabitants put to work to serve Germany's international economic and political interests. As a result, missionaries frequently locked horns with the secular colonial movement; the source of this conflict arose, in large measure, from German Protestant missionaries' resistance to settlers', plantation owners', and concessionary companies' often violent exploitation of workers. Missionaries regularly stood with colonized Africans against abuses by employers and the colonial state and criticized the "immoral" behaviour of colonial administrators.[75] The bureaucratic attacks detailed earlier in this chapter and in chapter 2 reveal the determined antagonism of secular colonial organizations toward the missionaries. Yet the mission societies proved savvy operators, taking advantage of a shift in colonial policy under Colonial Secretary Bernhard Dernburg and Governor Albrecht von Rechenberg to interdict attacks by economic interests.[76] In the last decade of German colonial rule, the missionaries and German East African administration worked together to promote African "peasant agriculture." The promotion of Swahili by Karl Axenfeld represented one outcome of this new comity. A second feature of the alliance was the regularization of German-language training for advanced students. In return for a state subsidy to the mission schools, the colonial state could count on the development of indigenous translators and clerks for its purposes. However, the secular colonial movement found its own allies among the several thousand White settlers in the colony and turned to political allies back in Berlin.[77] The period before the First World War in German East Africa saw an intensification of conflict among Whites over the economic future of the colony.

The intensification of the conflict during the first decade of the twentieth century led Julius Richter to formulate a new defence of mission schools. It is no coincidence that the two authors of compromise with the colonial state during this period were Richter and Axenfeld. Their leadership at this time indicated their ascent to a more general position of leadership among Germany's Protestant missionaries. Defending the mission schools, Richter acknowledged the shared interests of the missions and the colonial administration in schools. He wrote that in matters like education policy, in which missionaries and administrators had the same goals, both sides should be governed by the slogan "march separately and attack in unison."[78] Shared goals provided a workable basis for cooperation. The colonial state needed schools because the indigenous people of Germany's colonies needed to be "elevated" in their cultural achievements so that they could support themselves and the administration of the colony. Schools, as has been detailed, were necessary to the mission societies because Protestant faith required literacy and community.[79] Missionaries already had the schools. The colonial administration had the power and money to support and protect those schools. By working together, the missionaries and colonial officers could achieve more.

The compromise on language instruction between missionaries and the colonial state required a shift in missionary principles. Though internationalism and independence remained core features of missionary ideology up to the First World War, some bend can be perceived after the turn of the twentieth century in the ideology's previous inflexibility. A useful comparison to understand how this happened can be the shift among anthropologists in Germany during the same period. Many scholars have observed that the German anthropologists grew gradually *more* racial and racist in their thinking after 1900. While there is no evidence that the missionaries' views of Kultur and race changed at the same time and with the same results as anthropologists' views, similar forces explain the gradual shift in missionaries' views of nationalism and internationalism. In particular, one source of the change may have been generational. In Missionswissenschaft the accession of Axenfeld and Richter, following the deaths of stalwart internationalists like Warneck and Franz Michael Zahn, coincided with a shift to a more accommodationist view of the state.[80] Axenfeld and Richter had come of age in a period when nationalism and colonial ambitions suffused the political culture of the German Empire.[81] Protestantism's close link with the state in Prussia and the German Empire meant that missionaries who rose to prominence after 1880 frequently held more favourable views of German nationalism and the German imperial state. Finally, the increasing belligerence of the Great Powers after 1900 gave credence to right-wing nationalists' depiction of a world divided into competing nations.[82] As a result, a moderate nationalism developed some inroads among missionaries, facilitating a series of compromises with the colonial state in German East Africa. In addition, starting during the Herero and Nama War and Genocide in German Southwest Africa, the racialization of Germany's colonial empire intensified.[83] This intensification of racial thinking may have raised anxiety among the missionaries that they could lose their autonomy in the face of increased state control over the movements and activities of colonized Africans.

The Dernburg-Rechenberg Regime

Bernhard Dernburg became colonial director in 1906 and colonial secretary in 1907, when the Colonial Department of the German Empire became independent from its previous superiors in the Foreign Office. The new secretary came from the very height of Germany's capitalist class.[84] Before taking his position as colonial secretary, he had prospered personally and professionally with the Deutsche and Darmstädter Banks, becoming a member of thirty-nine corporate boards. Chancellor Bernhard von Bülow elevated the Colonial Department and gave his new colonial secretary expanded powers as part of a gambit to secure nationalist and liberal support for his government in the "Hottentot Elections" of January 1907.

Long-running shortfalls in colonial budgets, the cost of two colonial wars, and the weight of successive scandals from the German protectorates in Africa provided the reform wing of the Catholic Centre Party and the Social Democrats with the ammunition to confront the government of Chancellor Bernhard von Bülow and force a new election. Opponents of von Bülow's conservative regime pointed to the cost of the colonial empire, especially the millions of Marks spent on violently crushing the Maji-Maji in German East Africa and the Herero and Nama in German Southwest Africa, as evidence of the need for greater parliamentary supervision.[85] The criticism reached its apex in 1906 and revealed that Bülow could no longer rely upon an effective coalition in the Reichstag. However, the imperial chancellor saw an opportunity to turn his political weakness into advantage. With a bold if brittle strategy, Bülow leaned into the colonial wind and used colonialist and nationalist rhetoric to build an electoral victory by promising a proactive and assertive colonial policy. The chancellor dissolved the Reichstag and called new elections. He then set about making the elections a referendum on Germany's colonial empire – an empire he presented as essential to Germany's future and which he promised to reform.[86] He enlisted support from the patriotic associations in the campaign with promises of a new expanded imperial investment. Dernburg became colonial secretary with considerable political capital to reorganize the Colonial Office and to remake Germany's colonial policy. Pre-eminent among the goals was that the colonial empire become financially secure. Each colony was to implement policies designed to make it self-sufficient. Ironically, the victory by the government's parties led to the implementation of many of the policies the advocates of reform had demanded.[87]

On an imperial level, Dernburg's program of reforms did much to reduce the influence of colonial interest groups. It abolished the Kolonialrat, which had long allowed commercial and political interests to influence policy directly. Dernburg regularized systems of professional training, promotion, and authority for colonial officials and devoted resources to recruiting talented men to work in his administration. By raising the prestige of colonial administrators, Dernburg better equipped them to act independently of the colonial lobbies. His goal was to make the empire's management operate within certain liberal values – to emphasize rational, economical, and humane principles in colonial policy.

In German East Africa, Dernburg found a willing ally, Albrecht von Rechenberg. In the same year Dernburg became colonial secretary, Rechenberg became governor of the colony. Neither man had a lengthy prior attachment to Germany's colonial project. Rechenberg had served as consul in British Zanzibar for several years, but his main career had been in European consulates. Dernburg's service as colonial secretary came after a career in high finance with no direct connection to colonial business. Furthermore, Rechenberg, as a Catholic, and Dernburg, as a Jew who had converted to Protestantism, stood somewhat apart from the traditional social and economic elites of imperial Germany.

Rechenberg oversaw the final suppression of Maji-Maji forces in the south of the colony; he concluded that the conflict showed the precariousness of German rule without African collaboration. Governing seven to eight million Africans and only several thousand Europeans, Rechenberg concluded that administrative resources and priorities should focus on the needs of the colony's African population. Rechenberg recognized that African production of export crops like cotton would generate far more revenue than settlers' plantation production, and that such a policy promised the added benefit of encouraging a prosperous African integration into the colony's economy.[88] With Dernburg's support, Rechenberg began instituting policies designed to economically develop indigenous communities. He eliminated the worst forms of corporal punishment, intensified interdictions against slavery and slave-trading, and limited his administration's use of forced labour.[89] In addition, as part of a program to make the colony more self-sufficient (for Germany's colonial administration), Rechenberg used a visit to the colony by Dernburg to advocate for investment in the Zentralbahn, a railroad line across the waist of the colony and linking the regions of densest African population with the coastal ports. Dernburg's financial connections helped complete the Zentralbahn over the settler-favoured Nordbahn, which would have taken a northern route to the main area of White settler plantations.[90] Rechenberg's "native" policy carried out Dernburg's determination to use the indigenous populations, like the colonies' other resources, with the assistance of "the missionary, the physician, the railroad, the machine, … the advanced theoretical and applied sciences in all areas" to remake the colonial empire.[91]

The new *Eingeborenenpolitik* (native policy) of the Dernburg and Rechenberg era in German East Africa coincided remarkably with the sort of economic policy that the German Protestant missionaries favoured. Rechenberg's economic policy aimed to stimulate African agriculture and chose to invest in indigenous communities rather than in settler communities. African agricultural productivity would support a broader-based and more prosperous cash-crop export economy and provide more stability in terms of finances and African subsistence. While Rechenberg's motivation was not exclusively humanitarian, his administration's overall goal of reducing the colonial burden placed on Africans in order to strengthen the colony coincided closely with missionary priorities.

The settlers, as vanguard of the diverse economic interests that sought to capitalize on African labour for White-owned enterprises, demanded that colonial policy serve their interests. In their newspapers, settlers in German East Africa proclaimed the "irreversible … superiority" of Europeans over Africans that forbade a "moral equality of Black and White."[92] This rhetoric stands in stark contrast to that of the German missionaries. And it contradicts the Eingeborenenpolitik of Rechenberg in the colony. Every European in German East Africa believed that the Europeans in the colony had a duty to transform the territory. Everyone argued for his or her position with the confidence that he or she spoke for the truest application of the "civilizing mission." To most settlers, "civilization" would come to the colony through White hegemony and a colonial policy that supported European prosperity. From 1906 to 1914, German Protestant missionaries and German colonial administrators agreed that "civilization" would be built through the material and cultural uplift of African populations. To the missionaries, material uplift seemed to be a fundamental step in the direction of cultural uplift. The familial and community prosperity that Rechenberg and the missionaries sought focused on creating indigenous smallholders whose productivity would, most importantly to Rechenberg, support the administration of the colony. Rechenberg and the missionaries agreed that an economy oriented toward African production would bring stability to African communities. And the missionaries believed that the creation of a solid class of African small-scale producers would support the creation of healthy Völker who could support the emergence of their respective Volkskirche.

At times terminological discipline was imperfect among the missionaries as they reflected on their work. When the "Mission Pastor [Missionsprediger]" H. Kurz explained to readers of the Basel Mission Society journal the difference between missionaries' work and colonial work, he substituted the term *Kultur* for "civilization" and set it carefully in contrast to "mission." At the very moment that the missionaries and colonial administration were building their compromise, he presented the two terms as a choice: "Mission or *Kultur*?" *Kultur* as a concept had two components; the subjective: "the labour, care, and formation of our spiritual constructions and physical capabilities"; and the objective: "the contest with the environment which surrounds us, its commodities and power, in order that we might make them useful."[93] Kurz largely denied the imperative to emphasize *Kultur* and rejected the material elements of the "civilizing mission." Like Bechler, Kurz argued no "cultureless people" existed; differences in material culture grew mainly from environmental differences. For example, people of the equatorial regions had little use for warm clothing or housing and so they had not developed an extensive sartorial or architectural heritage. Though there were no "cultureless" people, Kurz did identify "culture-poor" people. The great difference between those people and "culture-rich" people (i.e., Europeans) grew out of the idea of "work which leads to the concept of property, and out of heterogeneity of the same trade and commerce."[94] But clearly the concept of property could be learned, so no culture was excluded from the ranks of "culture-rich" people.

To Kurz, *Kultur* represented a dangerous threat to missionaries. The people who were rich in *Kultur* were driven by their nature to conquer; their presence seemed to bring benefits – conquest brought "spiritual and material culture in its wake."[95] So far, Kurz would concede, *Kultur* sounded a suitable partner for mission. After all, Whites stood "in scientific-intellectual, aesthetic-cultural, and practical-industrial activities" above all other people. And yet, these *Kulturmensch* – the bearers of *Kultur* – frequently lacked religious elevation. Missionaries had to maintain a sceptical stance when it came to the "advancements" of European culture; the material benefits of colonialism were not reliable partners for the evangelist. Like other missionaries, he recognized that colonialism and capitalism threatened the communal spiritual health of communities in Europe and the colonies. Mission should focus on a clear moral uplift, not the promotion of European *Kultur*.[96]

Missionary leadership in the metropole reminded missionaries to keep "civilization," now labelled as *Kultur*, at a distance. For example, Öhler acknowledged the impossibility of separating mission from "civilization," but he did not surrender the independence of mission. He recounted contemporary opinions that missions should act as "cultural pioneers," promote the development of the colonies for the sake of the Fatherland, "train the Negro to work," enrich scientific knowledge, and, "in the interests of the ruling nation[,] spread the language." But with this aspect of "civilization," Öhler contended, mission had nothing in common. If mission followed these calls then it became faithless toward its true calling. In his opinion, "Mission [was] not in service of *Kultur*, but of the kingdom of God" and should contribute to the spread of "civilization" only for the good of bringing the world's "nations" to Christianity.[97] Öhler's article expressed in another way the general principle that missionaries should remain aloof from the contemporary project of "civilizing" the African, since to many this project of "civilizing" meant subjugating Africans to European culture. However, in Kurz and Öhler we can still see room for the compromise with the Rechenberg agenda.

Indeed, in the years between 1906 and 1914, the missionaries' work as evangelists moved in harmony with much of colonial policy. Rechenberg ultimately lost out in his fight against the settler interests and eventually more exploitative "native" policies were restored, but for a time his policies allowed for congenial coexistence with the mission societies in the colony.[98] Missionaries had rejected secular affiliations in their training for economic interests. But as pressure mounted in the decades after 1900, and through the new leadership of younger men like Axenfeld and Richter, the missionaries found common ground with the secular forces of the state. In German East Africa this compromise led to the increasing favour shown to Swahili in instruction and a willingness to accept government subsidies and supervision of schools.

Conclusion

Missionaries' theology of Christian universalism led them to focus on the Christian future of African communities *as* African Christian communities. And that theology influenced their determination that the future economic life of Africans should not and could not be as a proletariat toiling for European colonialists. A Volkskirche required a discrete and contiguous Volk around whom to build a Kirche. So, the missionaries stood strong against pressure to change their language of instruction and attacked calls for them to train Africans in the skills and temperament of wage labourers. The ultimate compromises that the missionaries made with state policy over and against non-state economic interests demonstrate the flexibility the missionaries could deploy to preserve their ultimate commitment to God. They followed the apostolic rule to obey God rather than men.[99] They would "give to the emperor" when they had to, but only in order to continue "giving to God."

Together secular colonialists who prioritized the national or economic mission of imperialism found themselves unable to intimidate the German Protestant missionary movement into compliance. Missionswissenschaftliche internationalism stiffened the backbone of the missionaries, held off attempts to force German-language instruction, and rebuked calls for plantation-oriented education schemes. Instead, the missionaries retained their autonomy. Because the missionaries' ideology allowed them to argue for the morality of their position, the missionaries' anti-capitalism and "pro-African" policies persisted. Once again, missionaries believed themselves to be inclusive because their theology was largely so. Furthermore, when they compared what they wanted for African communities, the missionaries had little trouble arguing that an African world transformed by the Gospels would be morally and materially superior to one transformed by colonial capitalism. Finally, collaboration with the colonial state could be explained as a matter of expediency in dealing with powerful opposition even as it was eased by the missionaries' mixed feelings about their own national obligations.

4 Go In and Take Possession of the Land

Anti-Catholicism and the Limits of Protestant Missionary Internationalism

Albrecht von Rechenberg, governor of German East Africa from 1906 to 1912, presided over a colonial regime that, like every other colonial regime, operated through implied and overt violence; he enabled and encouraged a system of colonial oppression and exploitation. Prior to his appointment as governor, the Catholic nobleman Rechenberg had built a career in the German diplomatic corps, serving in the consular services to Moscow and Warsaw. Before that he had served as an administrator in Tanga in East Africa and then consul in Zanzibar between 1893 and 1896. Rechenberg returned as governor of the colony in time to oversee the completion of the "counterinsurgency" campaign against the Maji-Maji forces, who had shaken German control over the southern half of the colony for nearly a year. In the end, nearly 300,000 Africans died in the fighting and the famine that resulted from the German Schutztruppen's strategies. Rechenberg then undertook the reorganization and reconstruction of the colony under the supervision of the new colonial secretary, Bernhard Dernburg. Rechenberg and Dernburg's Eingeborenenpolitik favoured indigenous agriculture over White-owned plantations and sought to counterbalance the various ethnic and racial groups of the colony.[1] As a result, Rechenberg faced increasing opposition from the colony's settler population and its allies in the German metropole. Ultimately, Rechenberg would be forced to resign his post as governor after his patron Dernburg left office. Unprotected by Dernburg's successors, colonial secretaries Friedrich Lindequist and Wilhelm Solf, Rechenberg withdrew in scandal amid accusations by the settlers' journalistic allies that he had engaged in homosexual liaisons with African subjects.

Such a turbulent term of office might be enough, but Rechenberg (and his successor Heinrich Schnee) had to contend with a conflict of religious dimensions as well. The so-called *Benediktinerstreit* lasted for half a decade; it jeopardized the fragile coalition that undergirded colonial stability in the aftermath of the Maji-Maji War and threatened to reignite confessional rivalries between Catholics and Protestants in the metropole. A conflict over mission territories in German East Africa, the Benediktinerstreit called into question the very possibility of Protestant-Catholic coexistence. The territorial disagreement between the Catholics and Protestants had the potential to send shockwaves across German society. The Berlin Mission Society accused the Catholic Benedictines of St Ottilien of illegally building mission stations in territory that "belonged" to the Protestants. To win this fight the Berliners appealed to the colonial government in German East Africa, the Colonial Department in Berlin, and Protestant politicians in the Reichstag, all while engaging in a war of recriminations with the Benedictines and Catholic politicians in Germany.

To the Protestant missionaries of the Berlin Mission Society, the conflict over land was an existential threat to their ability to operate in the colony. The reaction of the leaders of the Berlin Mission to the actions of the Benedictines indicates, in the first place, that Protestant missionaries' internationalist ideology did not preclude nationalistic outbursts. Second, it shows German Protestant missionary internationalism was not always a force for reconciliation and peace. And, in fact, the German Protestant missionary movement proved, at times, to be more concerned with the conflict between Protestantism and Catholicism than with its internationalist or nationalist credentials. This raises the third point, the challenge that national culture posed to missionary internationalism. The border conflict with the Benedictines tapped into a long history of anti-Catholicism in Germany.[2] The ease with which the leaders of the Berlin Mission utilized old traditions of confessionally coded nationalism demonstrated the strength of national culture and how difficult it could be to transcend national particularity.

The German Protestant mission movement at the time of the Benediktinerstreit found itself under a significant amount of stress. The reaction of the Berlin Mission Society to the Catholic "invasion" of its territory betrayed the pressure that the mission felt in German East Africa, and also highlighted the increasingly uncertain identities of German Protestant missionaries during this period. The tendentious Benediktinerstreit brought the many tensions of mission work in the colony around 1910 into clear focus. A localized conflict between the two confessions threatened to overflow into metropolitan political and social arenas. The expanding attention in Germany on colonial matters and on mission at the turn of the century also raised the anxiety levels of German Protestant missionaries, no doubt adding to the threat they felt from the Catholics. For that reason, the Benediktinerstreit demonstrates the importance of missionary ideology and politics beyond the narrow sphere of mission history.

In East Africa, German mission societies needed direct and lasting contact with settled communities of Africans to do the work they thought had been divinely prescribed. The directive that a missionary establish educational and religious facilities as soon as practicable in the mission field demanded the acquisition of land. As a result of European conquest missionaries had access to more land upon which to establish mission stations. Missionaries, whatever their denomination and nationality, wanted a place, hopefully salubrious to White constitutions, to build their churches, schools, missionary residences, and outbuildings. Beyond the relatively small acreage needed for the mission station, missionaries made other demands related to land and geographic territory. They aimed to go further, because control over land meant sustained and persistent access to African individuals and communities. They felt justified by the Great Commission, with its echo of God's message to the ancient Hebrews that they "[g]o in and take possession of the land" to serve their Lord.[3]

Conflicts between Protestants and Catholics in Germany revealed weaknesses in the strong internationalist position that most missionary leaders took during the nineteenth century. In fact, the Benediktinerstreit threatened to dispel the utility of internationalism for Germany's Protestant missionaries. The vibrating strand of anti-Catholicism in German Protestant missionary discourse carried an obsession with international and national loyalty that missionaries transcribed from the pre-imperial period into their own particular fixations.[4] For much of their history Protestant missionaries had repressed their anti-Catholic urges and concentrated on their own work. Nevertheless, Protestant missionaries' virulent criticism of the Catholic establishment stretched from before the establishment of the Kaiserreich to the First World War. It varied in intensity at different times, but was strongest during the Benediktinerstreit.[5]

The Benediktinerstreit brings German Protestant (and Catholic) mission history into direct dialogue with a number of other histories that demand some contextualization. This chapter will open with a discussion of the history of anti-Catholicism in Germany in order to clarify the broader historical themes to which the Protestant mission societies contributed with their campaign against the St Ottilien brothers. However, the metropolitan history of anti-Catholicism is not sufficient to explain the heat with which the Berlin missionaries responded to the Benedictine "assault." In order to provide context for missionary concerns over territory, this chapter will also provide additional background from the history of the East African colony and especially the Maji-Maji War. Sufficiently prefaced, the story of the Benediktinerstreit proper will then take centre stage, starting with a brief discussion of general differences between the Protestant and Catholic mission methodologies before continuing with the conflict proper.

In the end the Benediktinerstreit had no resolution; the conflict disappeared along with so much else at the opening of the First World War. But it demonstrates the Protestant missionaries' determination to lead a successful international mission movement against all foes. And it adds necessary layers to our understanding of the internationalism underpinning the missionaries' methods. The Protestants' anti-Catholic anxiety opened the movement to nationalist influences – especially considering the missionaries themselves turned to nationalist arguments to attack the Catholics. Though the missionaries' internationalism did not disappear, the episode illustrates some of the limits of the heavenly Fatherland. The missionaries made a panicked turn to nationalist arguments in the hopes they would protect their evangelical project. For Rechenberg, the Benediktinerstreit was a kettle of discontent that never boiled over. But he, like the other political leaders of Germany, was forced to recognize the importance of missionary affairs in colonial governance by the Protestants' (and Catholics') determination to go into the colony's interior and follow the biblical instruction to "take possession of the land."

Anti-Catholicism in Germany

Understanding the Benediktinerstreit and the virulent anti-Catholicism of the Protestant missionaries necessitates a grasp of anti-Catholicism in Germany writ large. At various periods in German history harsh explosions of anti-Catholicism arose from a simmering cauldron of confessional hostility. From its origins in the Reformation and Thirty Years' War, through the Enlightenment, into state-led hostility in the 1870s, and continuing among Protestant missionaries, the polemics against Catholics and the Catholic Church had recurrent themes. The nineteenth-century period of state-based anti-Catholicism, known as the *Kulturkampf*, sought to break the power of the Catholic Church in Germany and simplify Catholic Germans' loyalties. Priests and bishops were jailed, church property was seized, and the Jesuit order was exiled from the country.[6] The anti-Catholic language of German Protestant missionaries reproduced many of the themes that defined Catholics and their faith as irrational, feminine, and archaic.

Paradoxically, Kulturkampf legislation, designed to unite the new German Empire culturally, worsened the dissonance among Protestant and Catholic communities in Germany.[7] David Blackbourn has even argued that by the 1880s there were two Germanys within the Kaiserreich, one for each confession.[8] Even after the end of the Kulturkampf, Catholics felt themselves the victims of an ongoing "silent" or "creeping" Kulturkampf. Laws across the German states continued to discriminate against Catholics and though one-third of the German population was Catholic, Catholics trailed in the highest ranks of the Prussian and imperial civil services, were underrepresented in academia, and generally lagged behind Protestants in educational achievements.[9]

The experience of repression brought Catholics together into social and political organizations across class and occupational divisions.[10] Foremost among these organizations was the Catholic Centre Party, which quickly emerged as the focus of political Catholicism and the primary advocate of Catholic interests.[11] Though the party was a coalition of economic, social, and regional constituencies, it displayed remarkable durability with support second only to the Social Democrats among the German political parties.[12] From 1890 to 1914 it possessed one-quarter of the seats in the Reichstag. Together with the parliamentary decline of the National Liberals and Conservatives, traditional allies of imperial chancellors, and the ascent of the permanently anti-government Social Democrats, the Centre Party's parliamentary strength made it the only possible means for the chancellors to construct any parliamentary majority.[13] The Centre Party, therefore, wielded disproportionate power within the Reichstag as a sometime friend and sometime opponent of the government.[14]

Relations between Protestants and Catholics during the second half of the nineteenth century were suffused with a historical memory of the conflicts of the Reformation and the decades of religious warfare that had followed. The dominant religious identity among German Protestants committed the heirs of Luther and Calvin to completing the Reformation. And nationalist currents within that identity joined with religious certainty that Catholics' anti-Protestantism constituted a concerted campaign to deny German national unity and strength.[15] German liberal nationalists and conservative Protestants joined together behind a program of integrative nationalism focused on a shared anti-Catholicism, one that defined the German nation as Protestant.[16]

During the early nineteenth century, Protestants and the liberal national state adopted a view that fostered suspicion that the Catholic Church, which was undergoing revitalization in the period, was conspiring to destroy German national life.[17] Conservative Protestant and

Liberal suspicion of Catholics provided the basis for the rhetoric and mindset of German anti-Catholicism. German Protestants, missionaries among them, viewed Catholics as intrinsically unable to fully join the German national polity.[18] The Liberals' attack on the Catholics during the period of the Kulturkampf labelled Catholics and their clergy as "stupid, medieval, superstitious, feminine, and un-German." Catholicism, in their view, was the antithesis of the German values of "rationalism, bourgeois individualism, high industrialization, free-market capitalism, the unified nation-state, and gender-specific public and private spheres."[19] Protestant missionary leaders adapted many of these accusations to their own needs. They too associated Catholics with hierarchy, absolutism, and censorship;[20] qualities that were anathema to Protestant missionary ideals of individual and independent pursuit of personal salvation and a mission program dependent upon the protection of freedom of conscience in the colonies. Ironically, the Protestant campaign during the Benediktinerstreit applied the arguments of German Protestant nationalism and subverted the very ideals of religious freedom and missionary internationalism that Protestant missionaries treasured.

The Reichstag held significant influence in colonial affairs, and the Centre Party had proven its influence in these matters in the past.[21] In spite of these facts, the missionaries believed that a strong campaign of nationalist anti-Catholicism could be the solution to their territorial conflict in German East Africa. Protestant leaders believed that if the conflict in East Africa could be depicted as a battle against anti-nationalist Catholics, then perhaps the Centre Party could be isolated and the missionaries' allies could join with pro-government Conservatives and pro-colonial National Liberals. By appealing to a long tradition of anti-Catholic rhetoric from the Conservatives and Liberals in Germany, the Protestant missionaries sought to compel the Colonial Department to enforce a system of territorial division that favoured Protestants' long- and short-term interests.[22] Recent history may have also made it appear that the Centre Party was out of favour and therefore politically vulnerable. Unlike previous chancellors, Bernhard von Bülow had not forged any coalition with the Centre Party, particularly in the wake of the "Hottentot Election" of 1907, which had pitted the government against the Centre Party and the Social Democrats.[23] The successful electoral campaign waged by the government and its political allies against the Centre Party had demonstrated the residual strength of anti-Catholicism in German politics and revived attacks from the Kulturkampf, as the Kaiser gave public voice to his usually suppressed anti-Catholicism.[24] Protestant missionaries clearly had reason to believe that the application of familiar anti-Catholic methods from the recent and distant past might lead to success.

Methodological Conflict

By the turn of the twentieth century the Protestant mission movement had a well- developed and suspicious view of the Catholic mission movement. German Protestants took pride in their long experience as missionaries in the "modern era." In contrast, they judged Catholics as backward and out of touch. Catholics lacked the tools of "scientific" mission work that distinguished Protestant and especially German Protestant mission.[25] In addition, German Protestant missionaries claimed that political Catholicism, the German Centre Party specifically, existed solely to manipulate the politics of the Kaiserreich for Catholic ends, with no regard for the nation's broader welfare. Protestant missionaries' journals and pamphlets frequently levied attacks upon the Catholics for their supposed political corruption and mendacity.

Catholics' close relationship to the colonial state frustrated Protestant missionaries from a very early date. In particular, the Protestants felt the Catholics had done little to earn other colonialists' respect. Franz Michael Zahn observed that, after all, Catholicism had had 450 years to "conquer Africa." And yet, the Catholics remained more concerned with the "dressings of institutional life" than creating new Christians. Protestant missionary methods required more time than Catholic methods because of the ease with which Catholics baptized converts.[26] Nevertheless, time had proven that Protestant mission methods surpassed Catholic mission methods; according to Zahn, Protestant missionaries had needed just one century to match the achievements of the Catholic Church.[27] What Christianity the Roman Catholic converts had, one Missionswissenschaftler argued, was "Roman" rather than an independent "national" indigenous church. Protestants believed the goal of the Catholic Church was not individual or national salvation but rather the expansion of the Catholic Church's earthly influence.[28] The civilizing mission that justified the entire colonial project did not mean perpetual tutelage, Protestants felt, and yet that was what Catholic mission promised to the Africans.

As early as 1901, several years before the Benediktinerstreit, some in the Protestant movement called for a public campaign against Rome and the Catholic mission because of its supposed ultramontanist and anti-Protestant agenda.[29] Catholic mission organizations were accused by German Protestant missionaries of service to a Catholic political agenda of world domination.[30] In fact, Carl Mirbt, a prominent scholar of Catholic Church history and Protestant Missionswissenschaft, proposed that the growing strength of Rome within the Catholic Church was a direct result and further impetus for the expanding power of Catholic mission in the late nineteenth century.[31] Gustav Warneck accused Catholics of taking up an anachronistic "medieval mission of the sword" by declaring their activities a "crusade."[32] The work undertaken by the Catholic mission orders to serve the colonial state, Protestant missionary intellectuals declared, concealed the real agenda of the Catholic Church, one which sought temporal power for the pope. Newly converted Catholics would become slaves of the Roman church and their bondage would prevent them from becoming true Christians.

Protestant missionaries argued that their work was not only methodologically superior but also morally superior because, unlike the Catholic mission, it sought to create an indigenous Christian community. The Protestant mission societies, the argument went, worked for Africans as opposed to exploitative economic interests.[33] Protestants argued the Catholic mission societies worked to satisfy the needs of trading companies, plantation owners, and other European economic enterprises as part of a determined strategy to displace the Protestant missions.[34] Alexander Merensky of the Berlin Mission argued that Catholics "educate[d] the Negro to work" in service to secular colonial interests because they could not succeed by spiritual persuasion.[35] Infuriatingly, the colonial state still preferred Catholics' determination to acclimate Africans to labour in the new economy of the colony. The administration's preference for this approach, according to Julius Richter, threatened to undermine the strength of the German Empire. The Catholic missions, he cautioned, cared more for the "glorification of Rome" than either Christian evangelization or the German nation.[36] Catholics were also willing to compromise with indigenous customs more, at least according to Protestant missionaries. One scholar described the Catholics as more willing to "sweeten" their ministrations with "song and dance."[37] The Protestants argued that because they operated independently of the state and refused to serve economic colonialists, unlike the Catholics, they were the true Christians in the colonies.

Though Protestant missionaries did worry over the doctrinaire differences they had with the Catholics, their truest concerns were focused on more concrete differences. They mainly objected to the political success that Catholics had achieved in Germany. To them, Protestant mission was morally and methodologically superior to the Catholic variety of mission work and therefore more legitimate than the Catholic mission project. Moral and methodological superiority validated Protestant attacks upon the Catholic Church and provided fuel for Protestant missionaries' anti-Catholicism. The main, usually unacknowledged, source of hostility was Catholic success relative to Protestant efforts. As the Protestants' animosity smouldered, long traditions of anti-Catholicism in Germany provided a steady source of fuel for the Protestants' well-tended fires of acrimony.

The Kulturkampf had been the most direct form of anti-Catholic activity in the Kaiserreich. Though the official assaults ended by the mid and late 1870s, legal discrimination continued to afflict German Catholics. As state-sponsored attacks on Catholics faded and the Centre Party became a political ally of Bismarck in the 1880s, the most aggressive attacks came from anti-Catholic groups like the Evangelischer Bund (Protestant League), founded 1886.[38] The Evangelischer Bund drew support from many prominent missionaries; in fact, Warneck and Mirbt were both members, as was Paul Wurm, contributor to the *Allgemeine Missions-Zeitschrift*.[39] The Kulturkampf and Protestant League attacked Catholics with centuries-old indictments refined by Enlightenment critics. To those rationalist arguments they added the nationalist flavouring of nineteenth-century German liberals. Catholics were depicted as anti-intellectual, anachronistic, superstitious, feminine, and generally without the supposedly fundamental German qualities of sobriety, industriousness, and rationality. Protestant activists argued the Catholics in Germany blindly followed the pope and could only offer insincere protestations of national loyalty.[40]

Even before 1900, Protestant missionaries attacked German Catholic mission life in order to advance their own agenda.[41] After all, Catholics, in the Protestant missionary narrative, lacked any spiritual motivation for their work. The Protestant attacks argued that when Catholics brought their institutions to the German colonies, they sought to promote the interests of the Catholic Church above the German nation. As one Protestant saw it, "[t]he Catholic Church of today does not promote Christianity; [the Church] seeks only to erect papal hegemony across the globe."[42]

Roman Catholic missionaries, in the words of Protestant missionary leaders, served only to promote the political ambitions of the pope and had no true religious purpose. The Catholic Church cared nothing for Germany's interests, and true Germans had no interest in supporting the anti-German ambitions of the Roman church. After all, Protestant missionaries pointed out, the bulk of support for Germany's Catholic mission orders came from outside Germany.[43] These attacks by Warneck and his associates created the image of a distinctly anti-Protestant and anti-German program of Catholic aggression emanating from Rome in the late nineteenth century.

Protestant missionaries were able to neatly undermine Catholic defences that cited humanitarian achievements by arguing that Catholic work in the colonies served a papal conspiracy. Warneck suggested the Catholic Church fought slavery only as part of an attempt to garner prestige for itself. He charged that the mission orders of the Catholics sought only "ad majorem gloriam," striving solely for the greater glory of the Roman church and the papacy. According to Warneck, Catholics had done nothing about slavery for centuries, and their new anti-slavery agenda was thoroughly cynical.[44] "Ad majorem Dei gloriam" was the motto of the Society of Jesus, the Jesuits, which had been banished from Germany during the Kulturkampf and whose members had gained a healthy reputation as Counter-Reformation zealots and anti-Enlightenment crusaders. According to another mission scholar, the Jesuits dictated the path of Catholic mission work and used their power to continue their battle against the Reformation.[45] Both references to the Jesuits were clearly designed to draw upon historic German Protestant prejudices.

At the 1901 Continental Mission Conference in Bremen, one speaker argued that Catholic missionaries used the Centre Party's power in the Reichstag to promote their interests in Germany and called upon the support of the French state abroad. All the while, German Protestant missionaries watched helplessly as their interests were neglected.[46] France was the centre of nineteenth-century Catholic mission work, and Germany's historic antagonism with France added another damning association. Furthermore, the missionaries' latent suspicion of the centralizing forces of ultramontanism within the Catholic Church provided further evidence that Catholic missionaries could not serve German interests. Taken together, all these attacks on Catholics allowed Protestant missionaries to adopt nationalist discourses in their confessional fight. The turn to political argument allowed the Protestants to attack the Catholics' success in the mission field as the result of political machinations and not from any spiritual superiority. After all, the Roman Congregation for the Propagation of the Faith, the Propaganda Fide, directed all Catholic mission work and did so at the command of a pope supposedly bent on Catholic world conquest. Even the relatively pacific journal of the Basel Mission observed that "the Roman mission is predominantly French, its resources and its missionaries are mostly recruited from France."[47] According to Protestant commentators, German Protestantism's two great enemies, the Catholic Church and France, had allied themselves to bring the home of the Reformation to its knees. Mirbt described France's metropolitan politics as "thoroughly un-clerical," but in the French colonies it was a different story. There, the state was a "patron of the Roman Church."[48] Protestant missionaries described Catholic missionaries' political and religious connections as part of a vast plot designed to serve the pope and expand the secular and religious power of Rome.

Before the Benediktinerstreit began in 1908, Protestant missionaries had already begun to hone their anti-Catholic message. They convinced themselves that the Catholic mission orders served the political ambitions of French Jesuits and the Roman curia. According to the Protestants, the Catholic orders did not serve the truest propagation of Christian faith but instead worked to increase Catholic political power at the expense of both Protestant mission societies and Germany's national interests. German Protestant mission leaders peppered these anti-Catholic attacks with nationalist themes. These themes, developed from German Protestant cultural prejudices, would be readily available when missionary leaders entered into their most vicious conflict with the Catholic mission orders. In a desperate fight for confessional dominance, Protestant missionaries opportunistically set aside their internationalism to defeat the Catholic menace.

Marking the Missionary Battlefield

German missionaries in East Africa, like missionaries in European colonies around the world, had intimate dealings with the colonial state. In the case of German East Africa, both Catholic and Protestant mission societies had entered the colony either in collaboration with or at the urging of secular colonial groups within a decade of the establishment of the colony. This meant that both the Catholic and the Protestant missions in the colony passed through similar stages at roughly the same time.[49] Missions of both confessions emerged from this early, challenging phase around 1900 and entered a period of expansion. In particular, the Berlin Mission and the Catholic Benedictines' simultaneous growth and close proximity in the southwest of the colony contributed to their eventual clash.

As has been discussed already, the relationship between missionaries and colonialism in Germany was, on an ideological level, ambivalent at best. Missionary leaders generally viewed the colonial state with scepticism. However, on the ground in the colonies, missionaries still looked to the colonial state for protection and support, and some institutions in the metropole brought missionaries and the colonizing state together. In particular, the compromise between the colonial administration in East Africa and Protestants on linguistic policy and the common purpose they would find on "native policy" indicate the comfortable accord possible between missionaries and the colonial state.[50] The most direct link between missionaries and the colonial administration in Europe was the Kolonialrat. An appointed council of "colonial experts" and constituencies, the Kolonialrat was seen by contemporaries as a check on the colonial administration that, nonetheless, generally supported the government's efforts.[51] The Protestant representative, Karl von Jacobi, his Catholic colleague, Franz Hespers, and their successors served as intermediaries between the mission societies and the metropolitan colonial administration. Unfortunately, the Kolonialrat's useful position as an intermediary between colonial interests and the colonial secretary was left vacant after the council's dissolution during the Dernburg Reforms of 1907–8.[52]

Missionaries' complicated relationship with the colonial state did not prevent Berlin missionaries in the south of the colony from viewing the colonial administration as an ally, even flying the flag of the administration and displaying portraits of the Kaiser and his wife, the Kaiserin.[53] Similarly, Catholics in the colony showed their loyalty by close adherence to the administration's educational directives.[54] In return for their loyalty the missionaries of both confessions were able to enforce compulsory school attendance with state assistance.[55] Colonial tax policy also helped incentivize mission and school attendance with tax dispensations for Africans resident at mission stations.[56] Mission schools and other ventures also received funding from the colonial administration, integrating them into the colonial state.[57] However, missionaries still frequently viewed the colonial state as a rival, seeking to protect "their" Africans from the violence of the state and other interest groups like settlers and corporate enterprises.[58] Clearly, the relationship between missionaries and the colonial state was complex.

Since German society harboured systemic prejudices against the Catholic population of the empire, the Protestant missionaries also could see the possibilities of alliance with the state. As seen in their strategy against the Catholics, the Protestant missionaries thought an appeal to patriotic loyalty could win the state to their side. Internationalism as the missionaries understood it included an acknowledgment of certain national differences. In fact, it was in their argument with the Catholics that the Protestant missionaries made their greatest concession to their national identity and sympathies. And because the Catholics with whom they quarrelled in German East Africa were ostensibly German in origin, the Protestants' attacks challenged the Catholic missions' national loyalties. The missionaries' anti-Catholicism was also deeply embedded in Protestant German identity. As a result, it drew the missionaries into a familiar script of anti-cosmopolitanism, or even anti-internationalism, when it came to the drafting of their polemics against the Catholics.

The actions of the government could, at times, provoke the concern of the Protestant mission societies. In 1892 the colonial government of German East Africa opened its first school in coastal Tanga, and by 1902 about 4,000 pupils attended secular schools in the colony. The government's schools trained translators, clerks, and skilled artisans for the needs of the colonial administration.[59] From the start, these non-confessional schools were the focus of missionary hostility.[60] Because these schools had been built in the coastal regions and catered to the Muslim elite of the colony, missionaries worried that the schools might feature Muslim religious instruction.[61] The growth of Islam in general in the region, combined with the perception by missionaries that the colonial government favoured its Muslim subjects, intensified missionaries' apprehensions.[62] Missionaries increasingly felt that the growth in non-confessional schools, particularly with their largely Muslim student bodies, signalled that the government was cutting mission schools out of the supply line for colonial administrators.[63] Despite Catholic and Protestant missions' opposition to the government schools, they remained in operation, contributing to fear of an expanding Islam. Efforts to change the policy in Berlin failed, as did missionary hopes to use the German administration's codification of African "common law" to suppress Islam.[64] Taken together, the situation in Germany and East Africa led the Protestant missionaries to feel deeply anxious about their position, even as a major crisis was about to strike the colony.

The Dernburg Reforms in the colony came as a direct response to the crisis of the Maji-Maji War. The Maji-Maji War was a seminal event in the history of German East Africa and in the history of modern Tanzania. Historians of the conflict argue that the defeat of African military resistance to colonial rule led to a turn on the part of Africans to educational and political paths of resistance.[65] The remarkable events of the war challenged and transformed colonial administration and indigenous life across the colony. Furthermore, the near total destruction of African polities that had resisted, and the depopulation of the region as a result of insurgent and anti-insurgent warfare, transformed the region. In late July 1905 a multilingual and multicultural coalition of African polities from across the southern portion of the colony, inspired by the prophecies of Kinjikitile Ngwale, joined together in resistance against German rule. Fired by opposition to forced labour and certain in the power of the *maji* medicine propagated by Ngwale and his followers, Africans attacked the colonial state, including many mission stations. For several years, regional African groups organized a quasi-national rejection of imperialism that unified diverse African communities.[66] The symbolic value of *maji* brought unity and purified African societies as they entered the conflict. The acceptance of the *maji* medicine by local African leaders followed "established patterns of statecraft and authority" that validated their claims to sovereignty.[67]

Maji-Maji warriors represented twenty-five different languages, and their unified opposition to colonialism targeted whatever symbol of German rule they could find. Attacks on Zanzibari Arab, Indian, and German traders on the coast and inland, raids on Protestant and Catholic mission stations, and the killing of the Benedictine bishop on 14 August 1905 marked the beginnings of a resistance that stretched from the southeastern coast of the colony all the way to the shores of Lake Nyasa, the southwestern border of the colony.[68] For a few weeks German colonial rule looked to be collapsing in the territory. But in late September German forces began to reassert control. The suppression of *maji* forces lasted into 1906 and the pursuit of the leaders of various rebel groups continued into 1907, and was characterized by horrific violence and extrajudicial killings.[69]

The suppression of Maji-Maji, particularly after the last pitched battles in November 1905, became a task of German-led patrols of African troops whose main purpose was the seizure of food and the destruction of crops in order to force African resisters to submit. In response, rebels seized food from pro-German communities and sought to create safe regions in which they could cultivate crops. The last two years of the Maji-Maji War were devoted to a guerrilla campaign that created a widespread famine in the southern areas of German East Africa. Along with the massive death toll, the defeat of *maji* medicine may have delegitimized indigenous faiths. In the decades that followed, Islam and Christianity grew significantly in the regions most affected by the fighting.[70]

Traumatized by a horrible war and seemingly beset by secular and Muslim threats, Protestant missionaries in East Africa were primed to react strongly to a new threat from the Catholic missions. That perceived threat came in the form of a conflict over land. Missionaries' preoccupation with land rights reflected their existential need for access to indigenous people. In this pursuit of African soil and souls, missionaries did not readily tolerate competition. Mission societies thus sought monopolistic access to indigenous groups and sought to preserve exclusivity through territorial agreements with the colonial state and other mission societies. Part of this process involved contentious discussions for and in defence of missions' land ownership rights.

Land ownership made visible to indigenous people the missionaries' political and economic authority and entailed fights against land concession companies and other competitors to validate the missions' strength.[71] Between 1904 and 1907, the Berlin Mission successfully secured control over extensive lands in the west and south of the colony, as a direct consequence of the Maji-Maji War and the destruction of African communities.[72] In apparent contradiction to Rechenberg's reforms, the Berlin Mission's policy included the destruction of indigenous land rights through a process of appropriation by the colonial state in a paternalistic plan to protect Africans from economic exploitation. In general, however, the colonial administration sought to prevent Europeans from monopolizing land in the colony and expanded the program after 1907,[73] and, since Protestant missionaries generally distributed land to Africans as an incentive for cooperation, missionaries' use of land generally complemented the East African colonial administration's intentions. So, the missionaries participated in a convoluted process of expropriation and redistribution that allowed the mission societies to claim an important position within the colony's economy, politics, and culture.

The different uses to which each confession put its lands further alienated Catholics and Protestants from one another. The Catholic orders had a stronger hunger for land than the Protestant missionaries, who demonstrated, according to one scholar, "relative abstinence." Protestant missionaries emphasized their plans to distribute the land to create an independent farming class of African Christians. In the period of the Dernburg-Rechenberg Reforms, the Protestants' prioritization of African farmers made them allies of the colonial administration.[74] The Protestant missions probably truly believed that they sought land for the sake of their African neighbours and subjects, but this meant that the mission often ended up taking on the political authority of a large landowner. Frequently, this resulted in the mission becoming ever more interested in land for its own interests rather than for the interests of Africans. To the Protestant missionaries, as one scholar has described it, the construction of a Christian agrarian community represented a geographical expression of the evangelical project.[75] The symbolic, economic, and political value of land explained Protestant missionaries' tetchiness about their territorial rights.

Missionaries, targeted by Africans during the Maji-Maji War, had fought on the side of the colonial administration and their mission communities had suffered significantly. Clearly many Africans recognized the missionaries as representatives of colonial rule but, nonetheless, the mission leadership insisted their position vis-à-vis the Africans was distinct from that of the colonial state. The violent suppression of the African population during the later years of the war left both confessions' mission territories depopulated by the colonial forces' scorched-earth methods, exacerbating challenges in an already unevenly populated territory.[76] At the same time, the general insecurity and shortages of food in the region led to phenomenal expansion of the missionized communities, as desperate people sought safety around the mission stations. These swelling populations strained missionaries' land resources.[77] A rise in the actual cash value of the land further heightened the Berlin missionaries' anxieties about acreage under their control.[78] In spite of the broad and deep impact of the conflict in the colony, the Protestant Missionswissenschaftler made almost no direct observations about the conflict in their public or private works. Such a blind spot is surprising because the dislocation of indigenous groups due to the rebellion made control of territory, and therefore of African populations, even more crucial to Protestant leaders.

Political manoeuvres in Berlin supported Protestant missionaries' interpretation of contemporary conditions. The political crisis in the Reichstag precipitated by Centre Party and Social Democratic opposition to the government's conduct as a result of colonial scandals including, but not limited to, the Herero-Nama and Maji-Maji Wars led Chancellor Bülow to turn the tables and win a coalition for colonial reform.[79] The standard-bearer for this new program of colonial reform was a banker with a reputation for resurrecting moribund businesses: Bernhard Dernburg. The election of January 1907 rewarded Bülow and Dernburg with a resounding victory. Dernburg and the government actively participated in the election, a first in German history, as the government did not represent any party and was not responsible to the representatives of the Reichstag. The victory cemented a program of development and, where possible, expansion of the German colonial empire.[80] In this moment, expertise and knowledge became the focus of colonial rule.[81]

The impact of this turn to "rational" colonialism depended upon the support of each colony's governor. With Dernburg's blessing, Rechenberg, eager to reform the colony, promoted a form of economic colonialism (as opposed to settlement colonialism) that focused on African development.[82] Rechenberg's program in East Africa was designed to develop indigenous cash-crop production.[83] Its marquee project was the construction of the Zentralbahn (Central Line) railroad from the coast to the densely populated areas in the west of the colony.[84] The Zentralbahn served African agricultural production, and not European settlement, by connecting large areas of African cultivation with the export market. The program of African agriculture bore fruit for the colony, and quickly out-produced settler-controlled plantation schemes.[85] In light of these events, colonial economic policy seemed to be falling in line with Protestant missionaries' goals, in particular, their support for the promotion of an independent African agrarian population.[86] Dernburg's new program of colonial development stimulated the Protestant missionaries' concerns over land. Rechenberg's pro-African development program made missionaries' land all the more valuable as African producers sought to increase their cultivated acres. The use of colonial pressure groups and nationalist organizations by the government in the 1907 election accentuated colonial development as a national project. This reality put additional pressure on the missionaries as they resisted political pressure from the patriotic associations.

Protestants, with their worries over land and their cultural and political prejudices carried over from Germany, needed little encouragement to come in conflict with Catholics. There were also circumstances in German East Africa that further aggravated Protestant sensitivities. Since the German state had taken control of the colony as a result of Carl Peters's Deutsch-Ostafrikanische Gesellschaft in 1891, the Catholic missions had developed superior credentials within the colonial state and the secular colonial movement in Germany.[87] Catholics more eagerly accepted the role that colonialists prescribed for them and pursued a policy of education designed to prepare Africans to serve the colonial economy and state.[88] This left the Protestant missionaries jealous and suspicious of Catholic activities. Second, given their mission methods, Catholic territories had the potential to grow faster than Protestant territories. Protestants enforced stricter criteria before baptizing applicants than the Catholics and therefore lagged behind the Catholics in numbers of converts.[89] Furthermore, the Protestants took longer to create ethnically focused churches in their territories than the Catholics, who baptized applicants more readily and expected them to develop orthodox belief over the longer term.[90] If territorial boundaries became meaningless and Catholics and Protestants were left to compete for African parishioners in a religious free market, the Protestants had no hope of success. So, in order to prevent a Catholic "victory," the Protestants sought fixed, monopolistic territorial divisions and, when pressed, chose to fight for their demands.

The Fight over Territory

It is no coincidence that the Benediktinerstreit broke out over the division of territory in German East Africa. While the actual ownership of land was important to missionaries, what the Protestant missionaries sought are more appropriately understood as exclusive spheres of influence. Territorial control was only valuable because of the communities that lived on a given swath of land. Desire for exclusive access to African communities generated conflict over territory in East Africa between the Catholics and Protestants.[91] Mission societies argued for exclusive privileges of Christian evangelization within territories they

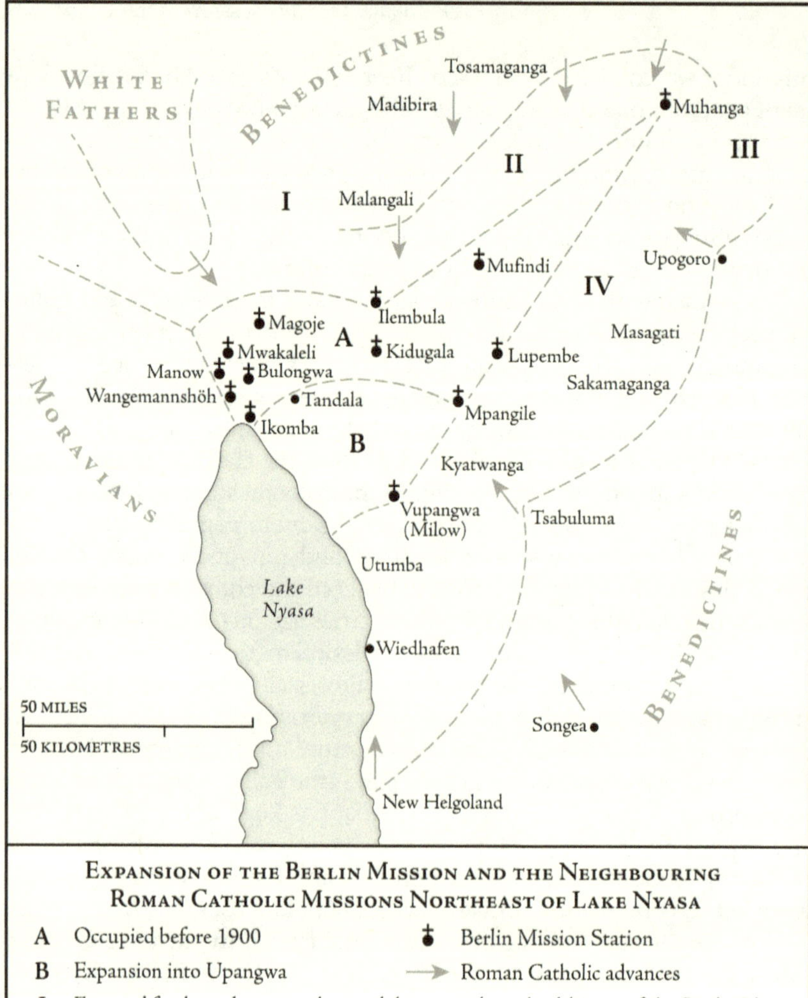

4.1. Reconstructed strategy map, attributed to Martin Klamroth (1902), showing expansion of Protestant and Catholic missions in the area of the Benediktinerstreit.[92]

defined as "theirs." This conflict threatened to become a matter of national and colonial policy in the decade before the First World War. The Benediktinerstreit grew out of Protestant interpretations of Catholic activities and eventually developed into a political dispute between the Berlin Mission Society and the Benedictines of St Ottilien.

In 1902 Martin Klamroth, the Berlin Mission's chief missionary in German East Africa, produced a map of the region around Lake Nyasa that demonstrated how he and the Berlin Mission perceived the situation in the region (see image 4.1). On his map the Berlin Mission stations are encircled by Catholic mission societies and arrows reveal the offensive intentions of Catholic expansion. Klamroth's version of the situation matched the understanding of the mission society's leaders in Berlin. Territorial competition, real and imagined, became a central concern of the Protestants.

For more than a decade before the Benediktinerstreit, the leadership of the German Protestant mission movement saw the territorial rivalry with the Catholics as indicative of Catholic deviousness. The Catholics' behaviour challenged Protestants' control of their territories, control that the Protestants saw as essential. Warneck described the stakes of the conflict:

> Missions are the outermost outposts of a church and simultaneously the [means of their] territorial expansion. The destruction of one such outpost means the destruction of the foundation of a new church colony. Rome has attacked [our missions] and we should ultimately attack the [Catholics].[93]

To Protestant leaders like Warneck, the Catholic Church had already shown that it was hostile to every aspect of Protestant mission work.[94] The Catholics' political motives and extreme anti-Reformation intentions explained their brazen willingness to flout existing border agreements crafted by colonial administrations.[95] The centrality of land, Protestants' dependence on exclusive privileges within a territory, and Catholics' apparent disdain for territorial boundaries made the Benediktinerstreit a fundamental threat to the Protestant missionaries' work in East Africa.

Missionaries from the Protestant mission societies were able to point to apparently damning evidence of Catholic intentions in the pages of one of the Catholics' most bellicose publications, *Gott will es!*, the organ of the Afrika-Verein deutscher Katholiken (African Union of German Catholics). The Afrika-Verein supported Catholic mission operations and took a militant stance for other Catholic causes. As early as 1893, the magazine was arguing that the balance of Protestants and Catholics in the German colonies would impact the balance of power between the confessions in Germany. A growth in Catholic power in the colonies would lead to a growth of Catholic power in the metropole.[96] According to Protestant commentators, this position sparked a dangerous expansion of Catholic mission organizations in Germany. One speaker at the Bremen Mission Conference of 1901 declared that "next to every Protestant mission church and school" now stood a competing Catholic mission.[97] The Catholics had waged a very direct and very effective campaign and now threatened to overtake the Protestants.

Protestants, moved by what they perceived to be a Catholic assault, proposed radical action in 1897. At the Bremen Conference that year, Carl Buchner outlined a vigorous program of confrontation. Protestant missions should ignore the territorial divisions and show no regard for the activities of Catholic mission orders when establishing their stations and schools. Protestant missions should also consider bringing their grievances into the public sphere and reigniting old prejudices. Buchner cautioned his audience in Bremen that "sadly ... the aggression of the Catholic Church [would] not lessen, but instead [would] expand and that more and more ... our Protestant mission [would] be forced ... to resist these attacks more energetically than before."[98] This strategy was not implemented, but it demonstrated the danger many Protestant missionaries felt.

Still later, as the Catholic threat apparently continued unabated, Warneck proposed a more complete strategy for defending Protestant mission interests. He reminded his readers that Germany's Protestants were direct heirs to the leaders of the Reformation. Mission societies should remind Germany's Protestant congregations of this inheritance and the obligations that came with it. In the process, Warneck reasoned, missionaries could transform support for Protestant mission work and missionaries into a defence of German Protestant "honour." Warneck's nationalist strategy aggressively ignored his stated aversion to such politics.[99] By referencing the Protestant Reformation as a special German legacy, Warneck directly linked nationalism and anti-Catholicism. To him, the Catholic threat was an attack on the spiritual character of Germany. The activities of Catholic missions in German East Africa and elsewhere represented to Warneck and his colleagues yet another battle in the centuries-long campaign by the Catholic Church to reverse the Reformation. These strategies would become the core of Karl Axenfeld's activities when the actual Benediktinerstreit broke out.

The Benediktinerstreit

The Berlin Mission set up mission stations among the Ngonde and Bena peoples on the shores of Lake Nyasa in the southern highlands of modern Tanzania in 1891. By 1902, the Berliners had thirteen mission stations in the region. At the same time, Catholic mission orders, specifically the White Fathers and the Benedictines, established mission territories to the north, northwest, and south of the Berliners' operating area.[100] Conflict arose in late 1908 when the Berlin missionaries built a new "outpost" at Isofi, near one of their stations at Lupembe, at the eastern "frontier" of their territory. According to the Berlin Mission, the outpost at Isofi had become necessary as a response to Benedictine school construction in the region. Catholic expansion threatened the Berliners' work and the missionaries accused the Catholics of thus violating a 1906 territorial agreement. From this initial disagreement, a years-long conflict expanded to the metropole as Catholic and Protestant missionaries drew their allies into what became known as the Benediktinerstreit.

The Benediktinerstreit lasted five years. The length of the disagreement owed a good deal to delays in communication: messages had to travel from Berlin to St Ottilien in Bavaria; Berlin to the unofficial government expert on Catholic mission in Cologne, Franz Hespers; Berlin or St Ottilien to Rome; and, longest of all, Berlin or St Ottilien to the mission stations several weeks' travel away. However, even had the communication been near instantaneous, the conflict would have lingered. Protestant mission leaders perceived their work in East Africa to be seriously at risk and therefore the Berlin Mission had little interest in surrender or compromise. In any event, the Catholic Benedictines had no power to agree to the Protestants' demands. The Propaganda Fide forbade any lasting agreement with Protestants over territory. In November 1908, just at the beginning of the Benediktinerstreit, Governor Rechenberg and Colonial Secretary Dernburg were both willing to put civil peace over confessional freedom and establish territorial boundaries, only the Catholics refused to agree to any legal divisions.[101] In 1912 the head of the Benedictines in German East Africa, Bishop Thomas Spreiter, made very clear the position of the Catholic Church. In a letter to Axenfeld he explained that the Propaganda Fide wished for "peaceful coexistence" with Protestant missionaries but would not permit any border agreements.[102] There was, in fact, no possible Protestant-Catholic resolution to the Benediktinerstreit. Any reconciliation would have required the government in Berlin or Dar-es-Salaam in German East Africa to force a solution.

Protestant missionaries distrusted the expansion of the Benedictines, particularly as it seemed designed to squeeze the Berlin Mission's Nyasa territories from two sides, the north and the south. Because the Protestants depended on physical territory, their anxieties rose, especially as they felt their position threatened by more than just the Benedictines.

In the first place, the depopulation of the colony during the Maji-Maji War meant that resources were even more scarce. Secondly, colonial development allowed Islam to spread more rapidly among the colony's communities. Furthermore, in German East Africa, missionaries worried that government schools favoured Muslims living in the colony and threatened the mission schools' status as entrepôt to lucrative clerkships for African students. Finally, the Protestant missionaries feared that influence of the Centre Party in Germany and the rapid expansion of the Catholic mission movement, with its tide of Catholic mission friars and eagerly baptized parishioners, would result in Protestant communities in the colony being overwhelmed. Supporters of the Berlin Mission in Silesian Bunzlau (Bolesławiec) observed this persistent anxiety, reporting that German Protestant missions were growing fast where "Islam and Roman mission" had not seized the "rich soil" of Africa.[103]

In the communications of the missionaries during the Benediktinerstreit, the Berliners depicted the Catholic mission orders and their church as aggressively anti-Protestant. Naturally, in this version the entire conflict was the responsibility of the Benedictines. The presence of a Berlin Mission Society Komitee member, Max Berner, as a key adviser to the colonial secretary provided influential support to the Protestants' position that they bore very little blame in this "border conflict."[104] Theodor Öhler, of the Basel Mission Society and chairman of the Ausschuß, declared that recent history proved the willingness of the Protestant missions to "make great sacrifices in the interest of peace."[105] The Ausschuß's support of the Berlin Mission Society demonstrates the unity of the Protestant mission movement and the breadth of the movement's anti-Catholicism.

At the same time, Protestant missionaries, predisposed to expect antagonism from their Catholic rivals, hoped that they might be able to turn to the colonial administration for a solution to their problems. Yet, those administrators ultimately hoped to avoid religious conflict. In Dernburg and Berner's first correspondence on the matter, both men took the position that the government's prime responsibility was to maintain peace and order in the colony. They feared a religious dispute could lead to indigenous unrest.[106] An assertive response by the colonial government might have foreshortened the conflict, but Berner's earliest attempts to facilitate negotiations came to little effect. The Catholics seemed amenable to discussion. But Ausschuß leaders could not forge a consensus among their member societies.[107] Instead, the Berlin Mission's main tack with colonial officials was to insist the pre-1908 territorial agreements be enforced. In the face of this impasse, Dernburg, his successors, and their subordinates took no direct action between 1908 and 1912; instead they continued working on a negotiated settlement. The tendency of both Catholics and Protestants to misrepresent their positions further complicated matters. For example, in 1913, after the Benediktinerstreit had stretched for over four years, Öhler of the Ausschuß "reminded" the colonial secretary that Protestants had always sought a peaceful resolution. And that they had done so in spite of their distrust of the Catholics. Regardless, Öhler insisted that any agreement reached by the mission societies would require the government's backing.[108]

Late efforts by Colonial Secretary Wilhelm Solf in 1912 to mediate a solution came to naught. Solf, like Dernburg, sought an informal agreement without any direct government participation. In order to pursue an informal solution, Solf invited Alois zu Löwenstein, the Centre Party's Reichstag expert on colonial issues, to join efforts to resolve the dispute.[109] Solf counselled Berner that to ensure the peaceful coexistence of Catholic and Protestant missions "no method" should be left unused, but, despite his own words, he excluded unilateral government action from the methods available.[110] Prior accommodations between the Catholic missions and the colonial state encouraged the Colonial Department to believe the Catholics could be trusted to avoid bringing scandal to Germany.[111]

In the last year before the First World War, a final push to resolve the Benediktinerstreit took place among Berner, Löwenstein, and the battling mission societies. In retrospect, the Colonial Department's unwillingness to take a strong position undermined the likelihood of a permanent resolution. Clearly, no one of any import in the German administration wanted anything to do with what was a politically toxic situation. The new colonial governor, Heinrich Schnee, echoed the refrain that inter-confessional strife threatened colonial peace. But he failed to offer a strong or original solution. His January 1913 proposal of a return to pre-1908 conditions was too little too late.[112] In fact, as we shall see, by then Axenfeld and the other leaders of the Berlin Mission had decided to pursue a more aggressive stance. Meanwhile, Löwenstein's commitment to the Catholic mission movement meant that he was just as willing to battle as Axenfeld.

The Benediktinerstreit confirmed to Protestant missionaries in the Berlin Mission and its allies that the Catholic Church was pursuing a new Counter-Reformation. However, the utilization of anti-Catholic critiques premised upon a Protestant definition of the German nation also demonstrated the growing engagement of Protestant missionaries with nationalist ideologies. To the Protestant missionary leadership, the weak response by the government to what was clearly an anti-Protestant campaign by the Catholics demanded that the mission societies make their struggle an issue of popular politics. Protestants began to expand upon earlier arguments that hinted at anti-German behaviour by the Catholics. In the early years of the Benediktinerstreit the Berlin Mission's Komitee only reminded Governor Rechenberg, who they distrusted because he was a Catholic and "declared protector of the Benedictines,"[113] that negative restrictions on the Protestant missions would contradict the good will Protestants had supposedly earned with their cooperation during the Maji-Maji War.[114] They made no stronger or more public threats. But around 1912 the strategy of the Protestant missionaries became more blatantly populist.

The Protestant missionary leaders decided to make the Benediktinerstreit a battle in the public eye by enlisting allies in the Reichstag and the press. Political circumstances around 1912 boosted their confidence. An apparently vulnerable Centre Party, a threatened Protestant mission movement, and a new national mission ideology converged to encourage missionaries to utilize the rhetoric of nation and Protestant unity. Bishop Spreiter's letter of September 1912, in which he had finally clarified that the Benedictines could not and would not sign any territorial agreement with the Protestants, marked the immediate cause of the Protestants' nationalist strategy. The letter came just as Axenfeld had begun preparing for a more overt campaign against the Catholic mission movement in Germany. Shortly after Spreiter's letter arrived, Axenfeld began gathering information from the other Protestant missions active in the German East African colony to document Catholic "aggression." He and his colleagues spread articles about these Catholic "invasions" in sympathetic nationalist and ecclesiastical newspapers across Germany.[115] For the Protestants, the Catholics' construction of schools and mission stations within what the Protestants perceived to be their territories "demonstrate[d] that the hindrance of Protestant mission [was] more important [to the Catholics] than the conversion" of Africans. Catholics had become, as Klamroth, the Berlin Mission's leader in East Africa, put it, "enemies of the Gospel."[116] The Ausschuß believed Catholic actions were intended to impede Protestant evangelization.[117] And, in response, Axenfeld and the Berlin Mission enacted a new strategy. They began trying to activate historic confessional animosities in a bid to defeat the Benedictines outright. Specifically, the Protestant mission movement began promoting an explicit narrative that the Catholic missionaries' activities in German East Africa were part of a broader campaign by the Catholic Church to finally drown the Reformation churches in a wave of mission converts.[118] This view was already widely held among the Protestant missionaries, but it had not been widely disseminated before this moment.

The institutional anti-Catholicism of Germany favoured the Protestants' strategy. Max Berner's dual role as Colonial Department official and head of the Berlin Mission Society Komitee made him a valuable ally for Axenfeld's strategy. In December 1912, Berner dispatched a letter to the leadership of the Protestant mission societies in which he stressed earlier efforts by the Berliners to reach a peaceful solution. Then he declared that recent Catholic actions had, in the eyes of the government and "public perception," made peaceful coexistence impossible. The Catholic Centre Party's political strength required that the Protestants mobilize every ally they could in the public sphere. The press, Colonial Department, and Protestant missionaries' Reichstag allies were all notified of the change in purpose.[119] Part of this change included the full investment of Axenfeld by the Komitee with the freedom to deal with the "invasion of the Benedictines into our territory."[120] Axenfeld described the new situation in the *Allgemeine Missions-Zeitschrift*. According to him, the Catholics had knowingly defied the legal representative of the Kaiser by breaking a border "treaty" agreed upon in 1906. In addition, the Catholics had abandoned racial and religious solidarity by working to undermine established relations between the Berlin missionaries and Black African leaders.[121] A similar article appeared in the Berlin Mission Society's journal, the *Berliner Missionsberichte*. This second article outlined Axenfeld's goal. By increasing public pressure on the Benedictines, Axenfeld and the other leaders hoped to force the imperial government to take assertive action and to order the Catholics to surrender. The *Missionsberichte*'s summary of the Benediktinerstreit set up the lines of attack that would be used in the new campaign: the Catholics had no loyalty to German authority and, rather than focus on an earnest program to spread the Gospels, they sought only to increase Catholic political power.[122]

In addition to exerting its influence in the missionary press, the Berlin Mission Society began organizing its allies in the Reichstag. Chief among these allies were the Conservative Kuno von Westarp and Christian Socialist Reinhold Mumm.[123] Mumm had succeeded his father-in-law Adolf Stöcker as leader of the Christian Social Party, a populist Protestant confessional party that had a history of religious agitation, most notably anti-Semitic attacks. In January of 1913, Axenfeld's successor as supervisor of East African mission work, Wilhelm Gründler, contacted Mumm with materials on the conflict with the Benedictines. Gründler counselled Mumm that the Berlin Society was not interested in "fuelling the confessional quarrel" in Germany. However, he hoped that Mumm and his associates in the Reichstag might prepare to take up the matter. In this interest, Gründler informed Mumm that Berner had also contacted von Westarp to prepare the Protestant missionaries' other parliamentary allies.[124] Gründler, Axenfeld, and the rest of the Berlin Mission were not so naïve as to think a parliamentary debate on Protestant and Catholic missions in conflict could possibly not "fuel the confessional quarrel." Despite their claimed aversion, it is likely that the possibility was exactly what they desired.

By the spring of 1913, Axenfeld and his associates had made significant moves to bring their disagreement with the Benedictines into the public eye. Any reader of the articles in the *Allgemeine Missions-Zeitschrift* or the *Berliner Missionsberichte* would have believed the Benediktinerstreit was the result of a broad anti-German, anti-Protestant campaign by the Catholic Church. The Komitee and Gründler had marshalled members of the bureaucracy and the Reichstag for the coming conflict. Axenfeld took it one step further and began making contacts with the Evangelischer Bund. The Bund, determined anti-Catholic crusaders who identified Catholics as internal enemies of the nation, had a long history of inflammatory, demagogic anti-Catholic work.[125] At the Bund's 1913 national gathering Axenfeld enumerated the Berlin Society's complaints against the St Ottilien Mission.[126]

In his speech before Bund members, Axenfeld made the first attack on the Catholic mission movement outside Protestant missionary circles. Axenfeld's speech infuriated his Catholic opposition. To make peace between Axenfeld and the father superior of the Benedictines, Norbert Weber, the Colonial Department enlisted Franz Hespers, former member of the Kolonialrat and Catholic priest from Cologne. Berner assumed that Hespers would bring word from the Catholics that the Benedictines were ready to make concessions, that they would "seek the means to lessen the sharpness" of the attacks.[127] Berner was mistaken. To Hespers, the actions of the Protestants were less a marker of strength than a marker of weakness. He warned Colonial Secretary Solf that the Catholics intended to call the Protestants' bluff.[128]

Axenfeld's public attack on the Benedictines with the Evangelischer Bund in the spring of 1913 drew an even stronger response from Löwenstein. Löwenstein warned Axenfeld away from his belligerent course. He wrote that the Berlin Mission would not appreciate what Axenfeld's efforts and the "Catholics might reveal to a broader public" about the Protestants' work. Furthermore, Löwenstein acknowledged the dangerous state of confessional issues in the metropole. He warned Axenfeld that "should the current clash take on the poisonous form of a public incitement of the confessions, [it would] shatter the peace" and destroy any hope for calm, "neighbourly" work in German East Africa. The Centre Party leader wrote Axenfeld that when the Catholics had "discovered that you used a gathering of the Evangelischer Bund, our hated enemies, to publicize the conflict in East Africa," they realized how deeply hostile his position had become. Löwenstein felt both sides were lucky that the Catholic press had thus far ignored the conflict, but informed Axenfeld that he must restrain the Protestant press in order to "hold back a public fight."[129] Such attacks were likely to lead to a public confrontation between both confessions. Löwenstein seems to have missed or ignored that this was exactly Axenfeld's intent, to put public pressure upon the Catholic mission orders. The Berliner took Löwenstein to task, questioning his characterization of the Evangelischer Bund and arguing that whatever turmoil arose from the Benediktinerstreit in Germany was the fault of the Catholics.[130] Axenfeld's strategy had become an appeal to public opinion in order to circumvent the strength of the Centre Party.

A letter from Axenfeld to one of his leading missionaries in East Africa, Christian Schumann, captures the depth of the Protestants' animosity by this point. He wrote that his "battle" against the Catholics had moved into the open. According to Axenfeld, Norbert Weber hoped that by closing two offending schools (a concession the Benedictines had offered) he could force Axenfeld to "declare himself satisfied and silence" the fight in the press. Despite Weber's requests in the name of "religious consideration," Axenfeld intended that the Berlin Society immediately occupy the stations vacated by the Catholics. This "defeat" should be immediately communicated to the "natives" as a victory of Protestantism over Catholicism. By the end of May, Axenfeld saw the conflict with the Benedictines not as a misunderstanding but as an open confessional conflict which demanded that the Protestants give no ground. He ended his letter to Schumann, "God lead you justly in every responsibility and effort and in the battle [forced] upon us!" He signed, "Your true companion and spear-carrier."[131] While Axenfeld's position in the late spring was clear, the Komitee began to appeal to the Colonial Department for assistance. For his part, the colonial secretary remained concerned only with protecting public order in the colonies and unwilling to take on any position that might anger either the Protestant or Catholic camps.[132]

The nearly intractable hostility between the Protestants and Catholics forced Colonial Secretary Solf to act in December 1913. He felt the conflict was beginning to spill over to both missions' African congregants, so he forced a meeting between the two mission societies and forged a compromise. The substance of the compromise was a formal dissolution of all previous territorial agreements. The Catholics and Protestants agreed to avoid interfering with each other's work. Solf also declared that both sides would cease promoting the conflict in public, especially in the press. Furthermore, the Berlin Society would publicize through its organs that an agreement had been reached (the Benedictines had no such requirement because, as Solf stated, "they had made nothing public"). Solf offered these points as a basis for further negotiations toward a more lasting understanding. The colonial secretary bid the Berlin Mission appoint a delegate to work with Hespers in pursuing a more permanent peace.[133]

Negotiations on a permanent solution never came to much and, though the temporary solution to the conflict in East Africa held, the Protestants continued their campaign against the Catholics. They had won a partial victory and seemed determined to fight for a final victory, especially since it seemed to them that Catholic resistance might be waning. Already in April of 1914 the Komitee decided to end the ongoing negotiations, and informed the Colonial Department that the Berlin Mission "[was] no longer prepared to take part in negotiations with the Benedictine Mission and [could] no longer avoid" further expanding its public campaign.[134] The Berlin Mission's Komitee continued its attacks on the Catholics through the spring and summer of 1914 because, as Axenfeld put it, "Löwenstein knew for a long time of the pending conflict and could have prevented the public denunciations [of the Catholics], had he proposed timely solutions." Consequently, the campaign against the Catholic missionaries continued.[135] Though the Berlin Mission worried that the balance of political power in Germany favoured the Catholics,[136] on the eve of the First World War the Komitee again informed the Colonial Secretary that reconciliation was completely impossible and that full guilt lay upon the Catholics and their unwillingness to compromise.[137] The Komitee defended itself in writing, "We hope that you will agree completely with our even-tempered, factual presentation of our relations with the Benedictines … May this piece help bring final clarity to these tangled relations."[138]

Conclusion

Germany's Protestant missionaries valued land out of proportion to their stated spiritual goals. Land in the colonies afforded the mission societies local authority, local economic opportunity, and local access to potential converts. In colonial German East Africa, wealth in people depended on significant wealth in real estate. The advantages of territorial control encouraged the missionaries to approach colonial territories as lands into which they could go and take possession. The presence of and competition from Catholics in the colonies further strained the limits of Protestant missionaries' anti-political and anti-national stance. Anti-Catholic sentiment was common among German Protestants. The Benediktinerstreit draws out for us the imperfect values of Protestant missionaries' ideology. In addition, it serves as an ugly example of how political realities in the metropole could and did interact with religious activities in the colonies.

At the end of four years of correspondence, conflict, and rancour neither the Benedictines nor the Berlin missionaries had retreated from their antagonistic rhetorical and territorial positions. However, the actions of Karl Axenfeld and his allies indicated much about the state of the German Protestant mission movement in the five years before the First World War. These last years of the German Protestant mission movement were filled with opportunity and risk. The language of the nation and of German nationalist Protestantism offered a tool for the mission societies that might be employed to address some of the challenges they faced.

The strategies utilized by the Berlin Mission during this final phase of the Benediktinerstreit indicate a number of things. First, the strategies demonstrate emerging cracks in the absolute internationalism of the mission movement by 1912. The entire missionary strategy was suffused with the "politics" and nationalism condemned by earlier mission intellectuals. Second, the efforts by the Protestants revealed how powerful confessional differences remained in German political and social life. Finally, Axenfeld and his associates' efforts demonstrate that the Protestant missionaries believed these tactics would work. The examples of German political life from the 1870s and from 1907 must have seemed like proof that the aversion missionaries felt toward "politics" might have denied the mission societies a tool that they could have used to build their position within Germany. The Benediktinerstreit was one example of a historical opportunity that the Protestant mission societies discovered and attempted to capitalize upon to advance their interests.

Interreligious conflict like the Benediktinerstreit activated German Protestant missionaries' historic antipathy toward the Roman Catholic Church. Religious and social conflict in Germany could regularly play out according to a shared store of memories, one that provided a script for dramatic revivals of past trauma.[139] So it is unsurprising that anti-Catholicism was always present within the German Protestant mission movement. It had old roots, and internationalists like Warneck and Zahn did not lack ugly opinions of the Catholics and their church. However, the older generations' focus on internationalism and aversion to "politics" prevented anti-Catholic prejudice from forging a link between nationalism and Protestant mission work. However, a world that was seeing greater forces for interconnection and global collaboration also witnessed efforts by communities and polities to define their membership more stringently. After a half decade of insecurity in German East Africa, the Berlin missionaries found themselves under serious stress and that stress challenged their commitment to internationalism. The "Roman Church" became an enemy of Protestant missionaries, one that tempted the missionaries to adopt nationalist positions as part of their response to a multitude of threats brought about, in part, by globalization.

5 Tending the Flock

Bringing Mission to the Heimat

By the summer of 1914, the Berlin Mission Society had dozens of mission stations in South Africa, China, and German East Africa. In those places, missionaries worked together with indigenous assistants to proselytize to tens of thousands of locals. The Berlin Mission Society and its sister associations' existed to work among the "non-Christian" people of the world, but from their foundation, missionaries, mission society leaders, and mission supporters all conceived of their Christian work abroad as part of a dual commitment to maintaining the spiritual health of Christians in the West. While the Great Commission justified through faith the existence of the mission societies, mission work in Germany also fulfilled the Petrine injunction that Christian leaders "tend the flock of God that is in your charge."[1] Protestant mission societies in Germany (and elsewhere) not only measured the success of the work in counts of missionaries, mission stations, indigenous schools, and new Christians. They also soberly and seriously calculated the strength of their support from German Protestants; they estimated the depth and fervour of *Missionsgeist* (mission spirit) and devoted themselves to developing networks of supporters across Germany, all while reinforcing deep connections among Protestant communities across the globe.[2]

As a result, mission societies spent time, talent, and treasure managing their respective networks of *Missionshilfsvereine*, mission aid associations made up of local mission "friends." In many ways mission societies treated their work among the residents of Germany's cities, towns, and villages as another form of evangelism. In Africa, missionaries hoped they could inspire the Chagga or Nyamwezi people to match their lives to missionary notions of Christian living; in Germany, missionaries hoped to inspire Pomeranians or Silesians to live as active members of a mission church. In both places the leadership of the mission society worked through intermediaries to achieve its goals. And in both places the German Protestant missionaries' internationalist and cosmopolitan theology shaped the methods and messages.

The Berlin Mission and every other mission society in Germany devoted itself to and relied upon local communities of Protestants; and at the centre of these local relationships were the Missionshilfsvereine. As voluntary organizations, mission societies needed local networks of mission friends to nourish the global activities of the missions. Local mission support networks could be relied upon to provide the needed funds to pay for missionary work abroad, to sponsor individual missionary candidates from their own or neighbouring communities, and to maintain the excitement and devotion upon which mission societies depended in times of hardship. The vitality and efficacy of these local organizations reinforced the necessity of tending to the flock in Germany. Alongside its ambitious activities in mission fields across Africa and East Asia, the Berlin Mission Society had a broad philanthropic and voluntary presence in its home country. By the summer of 1914 the Berlin Mission Society had over one hundred local Missionshilfsvereine across Germany. When combined with the Hilfsvereine of the other Protestant mission societies, the local presence of the German Protestant mission movement matched, if not outstripped, that of the German Colonial Society.[3]

The Missionshilfsvereine, in partnership with the mission societies and Missionswissenschaftler, produced German missionary culture. This culture emerged against a backdrop of proliferating literary and material representations of colonial and global spaces in Germany around the turn of the twentieth century. In this period, German missionary activity blossomed and expanded, fed by many of the same social and economic changes propelled by globalization. German mission societies took advantage of expansions in infrastructure and productivity to expand their presence in the lives of religious Germans. Travelling preachers and missionaries home on leave took part in a decades-long evangelical tradition, taking advantage of Germany's extensive rail network to reach distant and previously isolated Protestant communities.[4] In areas of dense Protestant residence, Missionshilfsvereine could be found in every town and many villages. For example, two Missionshilfsvereine served a population of 47,000 Germans in the Landkreis around Belgard (Białogard). Through these associations and their extensive publishing efforts, German Protestant mission societies made their contribution to Germany's colonial culture. Missionaries promoted a different image of Africa, one still interested in control but much more aware of Africans' cultural achievements and respectful of their shared humanity. Broad-based in support and geographically distributed in communities of every size, missionary culture in Germany competed with other representations of Germany's place in the world.

Programs and activities by the Missionshilfsvereine were a key element in the creation of a German colonial culture. The colonial project, especially when joined with the disruptive and disorienting waves of change driven by globalization, created broad feelings of anxiety in the Western world.[5] The economic, cultural, and demographic changes that globalization had already wrought, and the further transformations that it portended, took a more tangible form in the colonized person and colonized space. Germans were exposed to a number of stereotypes about their own and other nations' imperial possessions in a variety of media.[6] Most historiographical analyses of the penetration of colonial knowledge and the nature of Germans' colonial prejudices have focused on commercial or literary methods of production. In general, these descriptions stress that the images of Africans and other non-Europeans came to the average Johann through advertising, mass market and colonial consumer goods, and through popular and high literature like the works of Karl May and Frieda von Bülow. These sources impressed upon German minds an image of Africans that was essentialized. Advertising images reduced Africans to caricatures. Novelist Karl May's Kara Ben Nemsi manfully outwitted and outperformed the people of North Africa. Toys trained children in colonial rule. Taken together, these representations domesticated the world for German consumption.[7] German Protestant missionary culture offered an alternative image, one which reached masses of Germans through the work of mission societies and Missionshilfsvereine.

The missionaries' version of global cultures and the colonized other avoided the stark racialization apparent in forms of colonial representation like advertising and secular literature. Missionaries' penetration of rural and smaller towns was far greater than that of the Colonial Society, which regarded these areas as largely terra incognita.[8] While colonial products had a wide distribution and trends in advertising spread as far as commerce did in the German Empire, missionaries offered a more sustained and rich depiction of Africans and other colonized subjects of Germany. The networks created by the German Protestant mission societies offered a clear challenge to these other sources of information about the world. Missionaries leaned into their role as experts and interpreters while using many of the same techniques of popular representation in order to transmit their message of Christian universalism. They took that message to places and people less exposed to such messages;

beyond Germany's major and mid-sized cities, missionaries were the main creators of Germany's colonial culture.

The collective network of German Protestant mission societies and their connected Missionshilfsvereine would provide enough material to merit a book of its own.[9] In this chapter I will instead draw on data gathered on one specific mission society – the Berlin Mission Society. The Berlin Mission Society provides a useful case study for a number of reasons. First, it was one of the larger German Protestant mission societies and therefore had a wide enough network of its own to make study useful. Second, though the Berlin Mission Society was one of the larger mission societies, it was not so large as to be distinct or idiosyncratic in its behaviour. Third, the Berlin Mission Society was one of the four societies with a presence of consequence in German East Africa, providing easy connections with other analyses in this work of missionaries' theological worldviews and activities. Fourth, since the Berlin Mission Society's network of supporters was distributed fairly widely across the kingdom of Prussia, a sampling of its local activities can be drawn from Missionshilfsvereine in cities, towns, and villages in three different provinces of the kingdom.[10]

The work of the Berlin Mission Society and its supporters brought a new perspective to German communities as those communities came to recognize the complexities of colonial rule. German missionaries differed significantly from other colonial actors and agents. In their words and actions, the German mission societies presented a more cosmopolitan vision of German culture's place in the world and a less racialized vision of colonized people. The missionaries' view was brought to ordinary Germans in a program of mission work in the Heimat that reached many communities. The message of the missionaries must have had a deep effect on German views of non-Western people and their communities.

Missionshilfsvereine and Missionsgeist

Missionary leaders described their goal in the *Heimat*, the term they used to refer to the missionary home front in Germany,[11] as the conscious and devoted promotion of Missionsgeist. Missionsgeist fostered a more spiritually healthy life for ordinary Germans, they argued. Stimulating spiritual support for mission work extended the command to tend to one's spiritual flock beyond the clergy and to the lay congregation.[12] Care for the flock of God would bring the "crown of glory" when Jesus returned.[13] A greater service to God in this manner would then influence a general moral improvement in the country, helping

5.1. The Prussian provinces of Brandenburg, Pomerania, and Silesia, including Missionshilfsvereine mentioned in the text

eradicate evils as diverse as infidelity, alcoholism, pauperism, and labour unionism[14] – collectively the evils of industrialization and statist governance.[15] Placing mission at the centre of Christian life, according to the Missionswissenschaftler Gustav Warneck, rejuvenated the tools of Christian religious revival, strengthened Christians' inner lives, advanced Christian community life, stimulated Christian generosity, spread Christian love, and positively influenced Christian theology.[16]

Official and unofficial advocates of the Berlin Mission approached the challenge of promoting mission spirit from two directions. From Berlin, the *Missionsdirektor* and his associates produced instructions and facilitated contact between local Missionshilfsvereine and other arms of the mission society like *Missionsprediger* (mission preachers) and missionaries in Germany on leave or still at their stations abroad. At the same time, local Missionshilfsverein committees in villages and cities like Mützenow (Możdżanowo) and Belgard in Pomerania initiated a wide array of locally sourced programs to promote local "mission spirit."[17] In every case, the leadership in Berlin provided strong guidance on language and message. This leadership meant that attendees at German mission events in Friesack or Reppen in Brandenburg were exposed to the general internationalism and cultural "relativism" espoused in the academic and bureaucratic materials of missionary intellectuals and leaders. But local networks and local preferences certainly influenced Missionshilfsvereine's activities as well – it mattered what a local pastor or Gymnasium instructor on the board of the local Hilfsverein thought.

The interrelations between the leaders of the Berlin Mission Society at the mission house in Berlin and the local councils of mission supporters in the provinces provide the central framework for understanding the effectiveness of missionary culture in penetrating the wider German public. Much of the evidence of how the mission society operated in the Heimat comes through the correspondence between the mission directors and their subordinates in Berlin and the pastors and other local notables who led the local Missionshilfsvereine. The penetration of missionaries' global consciousness can be reconstructed by discussing the networks of missionary contact with the wider public.

As long as there have been mission societies in Germany there have been Missionshilfsvereine. In fact, the Basel Mission Society began as one providing support to the English Church Mission Society before sending its own missionaries abroad in the 1820s. As metropolitan and colonial politics encouraged the expansion of German Protestant missionary institutions starting in the 1870s it also increased the quantity and diversity of mission work carried out by local support organizations in Germany. New opportunities and challenges spurred the Berlin

Mission Society to focus more effort on planting, nurturing, and cultivating local missions across Germany. The shape of local mission culture and the robustness of local participation provide important indicators of the success mission activists and supporters had winning ordinary German Protestants over to the mission cause. Drawing from examples of activities in communities in Berlin and the Prussian provinces of Brandenburg, Pomerania, and Silesia, a commonality of methods for the formation of local cultures of mission support becomes apparent.

German social life in the nineteenth century revolved around associational life.[18] At its most successful, local mission culture activated these instincts for associational participation in order to provide leadership and organizational support for the promotion of missionary spirit. One important measure of the vitality of local mission life was the success that a given Hilfsverein had recruiting local notables to participate in its activities. A few examples will demonstrate that the combination of Protestant piety, global engagement, and philanthropic service afforded by membership in the local Missionshilfsverein could attract an impressive collection of local dignitaries.

The local Hilfsverein of Ratzebuhr (Okonek) in western Pomerania served a local population of 15,000.[19] A small industrial city, the local noble family and industrialists alike took an active role in the Hilfsverein. Ernst von Hertzberg, of a family with aristocratic roots dating to the fourteenth century and distinguished service to the Prussian royal Hohenzollerns since the reign of Frederick the Great, served on the local committee from 1902 until the First World War. His participation in the Hilfsverein conformed to his wider local service. Hertzberg served as chairman of the regional branch of the Pomeranian land bank; in the Prussian upper assembly, the Herrenhaus; and as an *Ehrenritter* of the chivalric and philanthropic Johanniterorden (German branch of the Knights Hospitaler). Another local notable, the landowner and businessman Johannes Ostermann, served on the committee for most of the first decade of the twentieth century. He was the managing director of the Brennerei-Verein Bahrenbusch, a distillery with a capitalization of 20,000 Marks in 1898.[20]

In the small city of Angermünde, north of Berlin, the eminent Dietlof von Arnim-Boitzenburg served on the board of the Angermünde Hilfsverein. Von Arnim-Boitzenburg ended a thirty-one-year career in the Herrenhaus as that body's last president in 1918. He also served in the Brandenburg provincial assembly and on the Brandenburg Synod of the Prussian state church. Arnim's impressive resume was typical of his noble family, which had served the Prussian royal family as civil servants and military officers since the sixteenth century.[21] Hertzberg and Arnim's participation, and to a lesser but important extent Ostermann's, lent a significant social, political, and economic presence to the activities of local Hilfsvereine. In small communities where aristocratic influence still predominated, leadership by these men could bring significant prestige to the Hilfsvereine's programs. Their participation also demonstrates the local importance of mission society work to associational and charitable life and the long legacy of aristocratic support of Protestant mission work.[22] By securing the participation of local notables like these, the Berlin Mission demonstrated the social desirability and cultural value of supporting mission work.

In other places, the organizing energy behind local Hilfsvereine came from Protestant clergymen. In Angermünde, Arnim sat on the association's board, with pastors drawn from churches across the surrounding Uckermark region.[23] Pastors also dominated the leadership of the Bunzlau Missionshilfsverein in Silesia. In that increasingly industrialized centre of ceramics manufacturing, twenty-four local clergymen dominated the circle of mission friends. But in Bunzlau, secular notables also participated; five government officials served alongside the clergymen.[24] At St Elisabeth's in the Oranienburger Vorstadt district of Berlin, the pastor and leader of the St Elisabeth Missionshilfsverein represented both the social elite and ecclesiastical leadership. Otto von Ranke, the pastor at St Elisabeth, was the son of the eminent historian Leopold von Ranke. Otto also built a distinguished career of his own as a pastor and theologian, one that included close work with the Berlin Mission Society.

In Pomeranian Belgard, a growing city of 9,000 as of 1913, leadership of the local mission community also belonged in the hands of the local pastorate. Belgard also illustrated the richness of personal connections that could sustain mission support. Before he became director of the Berlin Mission Society in 1895, Martin Gensichen had been head pastor of Belgard's main church, the Marienkirche, and superintendent of the Belgard church district. He maintained close contact with the Belgard Hilfsverein through his friend and former colleague Friedrich Büttner, who guided the association's work with the mission society.[25]

The personal connections and direct recruitment shown in the Belgard Hilfsverein can also be discerned from a package of correspondence between the mission house in Berlin and individuals in the large town of Sprottau (Szprotawa) in Lower Silesia. In January 1912, Siegfried Knak, the Berlin Mission Society's director of Heimat operations since 1910, exchanged a series of letters with a woman from Sprottau, Henriette Werner, who had complained about the absence of missionary knowledge in her community. Knak requested that Werner suggest local men whom Knak could attempt to recruit.[26] Before the end of the month, Knak received a reply from Wilhelm Papst, pastor in the village of Gießmannsdorf, a few miles northeast of Sprottau. Fortuitously, Papst had been born to a Rhenish missionary father in German Southwest Africa. Papst claimed to fully appreciate the link between the Great Commission and Peter's injunction to congregational ministry. He promised to collect for the mission society, to win new supporters, and to "call forth a lively interest" in the Berlin Mission because, to him, mission support and awareness was a "touchstone of [a congregation's] spiritual life."[27] Knak soon invited Papst to travel to the Silesian capital of Breslau (Wrocław) for the upcoming grand missionary festival there and to join in the pastoral course the regional mission supporters would offer in April of that year to augment ministers' mission knowledge.[28] By 1912 the Berlin Mission had developed an extensive set of tools for recruiting and cultivating supporters and Knak mobilized them to build mission culture in and around Sprottau.[29]

The pursuit of Papst revealed the importance of cultivating individual clergy for the mission society.[30] Local pastors, trained in missionary knowledge and the mission society's theology and ideology, could be appointed by the Berlin Mission to supervise and organize mission activities in the various provinces of Prussia. These men were called *Missionssekretär* (mission secretaries) and expected to make a higher commitment to serving the mission's interests. The Missionssekretär played an integral role in the sustenance of Missionsgeist in the provinces. One of their chief tasks was to stimulate local mission feeling by helping establish new Hilfsvereine; they were also called on to resuscitate or restore stagnant organizations and to help form other types of mission support organizations, like *Nähvereine* (knitting associations), alongside the mission aid associations.[31] These men were carefully selected for their connections with the mission society; they were trained by mission professionals in Berlin and given access to mission society resources and ongoing education. They were expected to be conduits of the mission leadership's worldview to the local organizations.

Across Prussia, the Berlin Mission also developed a network of Nähvereine in order to draw women and their social circles into providing material and spiritual support for overseas mission work. This initiative was extraordinarily successful. A report in 1901 tallied 360 knitting associations with approximately 8,400 members. In Berlin one circle had 129 members and another in Silesia had 140 members. Many of these circles sold their products in local markets with the proceeds given to the mission society, while others sent their output directly to the mission field.[32] In Angermünde, the Missionshilfsverein organized Nähvereine in the city and in six nearby villages.[33] The town of Ratzebuhr hosted a knitting circle specifically for young, presumably unmarried, women to provide opportunities for moral sociability.[34] The Belgard Nähverein, led by Martin Gensichen's sister, Elisa Gensichen, dispatched regular shipments of clothing and partially finished raw materials to mission stations. For example, an 1899 shipment included ten large work aprons, five pairs of men's wool stockings, five small aprons, and four wool kerchiefs.[35] The creation of such physical totems of spiritual support was effective at connecting groups of women and girls to missionary work.[36]

Filling Pews, Filling Coffers

It is possible to measure the success that the Berlin Mission Society's network of supporters had recruiting the devotion and the contributions of ordinary Germans. Each Hilfsverein produced annual reports of its activities and tabulated its financial collections for the mission society. These numbers provide evidence that in the decades before the First World War, the Berlin Mission Society developed a significant cultural and social presence across Prussia's towns and cities. Furthermore, as the examples below will demonstrate, the mission society and its Hilfsvereine accessed and maintained supporters from a broad cross-section of the social strata. Across the board, local communities marshalled significant financial support from ordinary Germans, frequently lower-class Protestants. For example, the Hilfsverein in the small village of Parchwitz (Prochowice) in Lower Silesia recorded in 1884 that the overwhelming majority of its donors were *Freigärtner* and *Freihäusler*, labels used for rural residents who owned little land and lived largely off of their labour. Other donors in Parchwitz came from the local *Mittelstand* of tavernkeepers and small-time merchants.[37] Though it was a small town, its mission friends organized an affiliate organization for young women, a *Jungfrauensverein*, to expand the influence of the mission's message to new groups within the community.[38]

While the collection of donations defined one share of mission societies' Heimat purpose, mission society leaders had other goals for their work in Germany. Small cities and villages provide some of the most impressive records of participation and contribution. In 1913, the population of Bunzlau was 16,125 people, over 80 per cent of whom were Protestant.[39] Operating among ceramics manufacturing workshops and factories in that city and its environs, the Bunzlau Missionshilfsverein collected annual contributions in 1911 from 1,441 individuals or families.[40] The records show that those who contributed were overwhelmingly craftsmen and women from the workshops in the area.[41] Similarly, Sprottau's population of 7,700 had a Hilfsverein supported by between 400 and 500 individuals and families; they made their donations at mission study nights (*Missionsstunden*), mission festivals, and special church services for children and adults across five parishes in the area.[42] And the small village of Mützenow, operating around the city of Stolp (Słupsk) in Pomerania, distributed 1,400 copies of its annual report in 1906.[43] Local enthusiasm for the activities of the Hilfsvereine could and did draw large crowds. For example, in 1897 a mission festival at the ruined medieval cloister in Chorin, near Angermünde, drew 600 people on a Sunday afternoon in August despite thunderstorms.[44]

From these communities the Berlin Mission Society received considerable sums to support its work. By the first decade of the 1900s, the Hilfsverein for Ratzebuhr was raising over 1,000 Marks for the Berlin Mission and by 1912 contributions had surpassed 2,000 Marks.[45] In 1900, Sprottau mission supporters gave 1,843.50 Marks, the Angermünders in the same year gave 972 Marks, and the Belgard Missionshilfsverein contributed 2,971.51 Marks.[46] In 1913, the Angermünde circle more than tripled its 1890 contribution – dispatching 2,024.38 Marks to the central office of the mission society.[47] Mission supporters in Germany's colonial metropolis also proved quite generous. One day's events held by the St Jacobi Hilfsverein in Berlin highlights the expanded opportunities afforded by a city with a wider array of social offerings and millions of possible donors. On 20 February 1910, the Hilfsverein organized a morning service, followed with a "Mission Tea Evening" featuring a presentation by the missionary Otto Maaß about a typical day's work at his station in Kidugala, German East Africa. Tickets for the evening's event were sold for 40 Pfennig and in total generated 225.25 Marks.[48] Events like this, spread across an entire year, give a sense of the fundraising possibilities.

Local Programming

The impressive network of missionary support that the Berlin Mission Society was able to develop and sustain during the last decades of the Kaiserreich demonstrates the impact that mission ideas had on Germans' perceptions of the world. Every year hundreds of thousands, and likely millions, of Germans enjoyed programming promoted by the Protestant mission societies of Germany. This programming came in many forms and displayed the profound dynamism of German religious life and religious Germans' engagement with mission works.

And that programming carried within it a strong missionary message of cosmopolitanism and internationalism.

Leaders in Berlin and their collaborators at the local level across Germany recognized that attracting and inspiring local Protestants to join in the spiritual and practical work of mission required sustained effort. In response, the mission society and Hilfsvereine collaborated to bring a robust schedule of mission programming throughout the year. These activities originated in early prayer circles during the first half of the nineteenth century, only to mature and proliferate into more complex activities.[49] By the 1880s, programming ranged from monthly or semimonthly "mission study" evenings, visits by travelling preachers deputized by the mission society to spread its message at multi-day festivals and revival-style meetings, appearances by missionaries and converted individuals from the mission field, and "magic lantern" shows with examples of indigenous material culture from every continent save Antarctica. Missionary leaders, in particular at the Berlin Mission Society, devoted themselves to filling local calendars with events focused on delivering mission education and spiritual elevation. And though the collection of Marks was an important motivation, the programs put on by Hilfsvereine with society assistance were also intended to connect German Protestant communities with the work of missionaries all around the world.

The centrepiece of the Berlin missionaries' strategy for work in the Heimat was the local mission festival. Hilfsvereine organized celebrations of their local communities' engagement with the missionary enterprise by mobilizing local resources to host representatives of the wider project. Some communities hosted only one festival per year, but, in larger or more energetic areas, several mission festivals might be held during the warmer months. The Berlin Mission Society itself reported that between Pentecost (26 May) and the end of September 1901, local Hilfsvereine held 322 mission festivals, an average of more than two per Hilfsverein over just four months.[50]

The small village of Parchwitz provides substantial proof of the frequency and energy that local Hilfsvereine mustered every year to support the Berlin Mission Society. Every mission festival there drew in many of the local common folk. On 4 July 1893, for example, the festival began at 3 p.m. in the church and churchyard at Jenkau (Jenków), a small village south of Parchwitz. The festival was a joyous combination of sermons, hymns, and bell-ringing, all graced with a presentation by a missionary from the Berlin Mission's field in the Transvaal.[51] In many years the Parchwitz circle organized two such festivals.[52] Starting in 1904, the Hilfsverein started renting a magic lantern apparatus and presentation slides from the Berlin Mission Society for its activities.[53] The Parchwitz festivals are just some examples among dozens. The Belgard Hilfsverein scheduled its 1908 mission festival to coincide with the local harvest festival so that a "spiritual harvest for mission" could be collected as well.[54] These events would have been meaningful experiences and educational opportunities for many men, women, and children to learn more about people in distant and very different lands. Such regular and energetic celebrations made mission support a part of the yearly calendar for local communities.

The Hilfsverein at St Elizabeth's in Berlin organized the usual mission festivals with attendant missionary speakers and celebratory sermons.[55] Like other communities, the leadership organized special children's services and the Elisabethkirche hosted mission study hours, which took advantage of its close proximity to the mission house, and organized guest appearances by missionaries and officials.[56] Beyond the suburbs of Berlin, other Hilfsvereine had to be content with such illustrious and exciting visitors only as a dividend of the festivities surrounding a mission festival. For example, in 1904 the mission preacher Ernst Moldt travelled to Belgard and visited with the students at the city's Gymnasium, recruiting the director of the school to include instruction on the mission movement and its work in the school's curriculum.[57]

The most impressively extravagant example of a mission festival was organized by the collective Hilfsvereine of the Berlin region, including St Elisabeth's and St Jacobi's. They came together to organize a steamship excursion to a suburban location for a "grand mission festival" in June 1910. This festival on the River Spree in Niederschöneweide drew hundreds of Berliners for the event. For 50 Pfennige and 25 Pfennige apiece, an adult and child could enjoy the one-hour steamship journey to the Neptunshain restaurant. There attendees were treated to speeches by Berlin Mission officials and foreign missionaries, performances by a large choir that had been assembled from the mission house and other boys' choirs, and the pleasant wooded environs of the restaurant.[58] One year later, the Berlin Mission supporters in the metropole held another "Steam Ship Mission Festival" at the same price and with the same promised activities.[59] And two weeks later, on 26 June 1910, they gathered for another excursion in the Zinnow Forest, in the suburb of Zehlendorf, for a festival featuring speeches by Alexander Merensky and other luminaries.[60] By combining their religious and educational purpose with recreation and the chance to escape the heat of Berlin, the Hilfsvereine drew in many ordinary people.

Mission festivals offered the opportunity for still greater contact with the mission field. At these festivals, mission preachers, mission officials, and missionaries home on leave could mix and mingle with local Germans. Surprisingly elaborate events would be staged to amplify the experience. An example of the extensive effort put forth to make mission life part of local life can be seen by exploring the work of the Silesian mission secretary M.W. Mahler.[61] In November and December 1903, Mahler joined with the Hilfsverein of Bunzlau to organize visits to the local orphanage, boys' primary school, Gymnasium, and teachers' college. While there, Mahler assisted the chairwoman of the Bunzlau Nähverein as she planned the upcoming annual festival.

Along with mission festivals and mission preaching tours, events that required less investment also became regularized. For example, every three months the Angermünde Hilfsverein hosted "Mission Hours" for children, alongside more regular gatherings for adult education. Most other parishes also hosted similar sessions of mission study for their parishioners.[62] Regular reporting in the *Angermünder Zeitung und Kreisblatt*, the local bulletin and newspaper, covered the activities of the Hilfsverein closely and further expanded its community footprint.[63] Coverage informed possible attendees of the opportunity and provided readers with short summaries of the meetings' content.

Flashier and more novel events also brought news of the mission movement to Angermünde as well. Otto Hagena of Stolpe-an-der-Oder, a mission preacher, worked with the Angermünde Hilfsverein to organize and lead programs. In March 1904 he used slides borrowed from the Berlin Mission Society to present a magic lantern show. The local newspaper reported that the lectures by Hagena and the missionary Friedrich Sack "warmed hearts for mission" and refuted "unjustified" attacks on its work.[64] According to Hagena, his vigorous use of the magic lantern shows had convinced many of "his farmers" that mission work should be taken more seriously.[65] That year collections topped 2,000 Marks for the first time in Angermünde.[66]

Magic lanterns were integrated, at least in Angermünde, into local mission festivals with great effect. In August 1906, the Hilfsvereine organized a regional *Missionsfest* which featured a morning service with a celebratory sermon by the missionary Adolf Kunze, on leave from Kiaochow. In the afternoon Merensky, visiting from Berlin for the festival, delivered a lecture entitled "Germany's Responsibility to the Natives in Her Colonies."[67] Earlier, in February a mission preaching tour visited eight churches and eight schools in the region. The tour culminated with an event at a local festival hall, the Kaisergarten. The hall was "so full of participants that ... hardly a place could be found" to hear a lecture and view a magic lantern show that left an "awesome, unforgettable impression."[68] In fact, some years later, the Kaisergarten expanded on this sort of activity to become one of the earliest cinemas in Angermünde.[69] Like the Kaisergarten, the Berlin Mission saw great potential in a leap from magic lantern slideshows to motion pictures. In 1911, Karl Axenfeld returned from a trip to England impressed with the effectiveness of the "Kinematograph." He soon began working to win support for the purchase of the necessary machinery, the production of inspirational films, and widespread presentations of those films, as had been done in America and England, to extend the influence of mission work into more people's lives.[70] The use of motion pictures never grew to real prominence in the Berlin Mission Society's work, but nevertheless demonstrates its serious investment in its work in Germany.[71]

Regional Resources

Mission supporters in Parchwitz and elsewhere worked diligently to elevate the quality of "mission spirit" in their corner of Silesia. Their labours were eased by direct assistance from regional and national operations organized by the Berlin Mission Society. For example, in 1902 Mission Secretary Mahler travelled to Parchwitz to assist in the Hilfsverein's operations.[72] He returned to Parchwitz one year later, on Sunday, 20 September 1903 and gave a festival sermon that insisted it was congregants' duty to behave like the Good Samaritan and lend their aid to the world. That evening the festival continued with a celebration in a local banquet hall. There Mahler shared a collection of artefacts of "heathen" life and mission work from Africa and China. The *Jahresbericht* reports the artefacts were "received with great interest by the attendees."[73] In its support of Mahler and other regional mission secretaries, the Berlin Mission ensured that local mission programming was guided by a professional and devoted agent of the society. The policy ensured greater continuity between the mission society's goals and the messages delivered on the ground.

In the same year of his visit to Parchwitz, the Berlin Mission Society designated Mahler, the pastor of a congregation of approximately 450, mission secretary for Silesia.[74] Mahler's official association with the mission in Silesia had begun in 1893, when he attended a training session put on by the Berlin Mission.[75] Maintaining contact with the mission through the next decade, he helped his wife Ella organize a Nähverein in his parish.[76] He inaugurated his first year as mission secretary by taking a magic lantern presentation on a tour through eight congregations in the Bunzlau district between 1 February and 18 February. After each stop, he reported his presentation and supplementary events as "well-visited" family evenings with good sales of pamphlets and postcards.

On that same tour he visited eight schools with large-format posters to display the work of the missions in German East Africa. On 2 March he also visited with a "youthful, and very lively" Nähverein.[77] Mahler's activities in Parchwitz and around Bunzlau were one example of how the Berlin Mission promoted local mission support by planting new associations and by continuously supporting their work with activities and resources.

During this period, Mahler's work as mission secretary extended to public apologist for the mission society. He supplied local newspapers with articles and clippings on mission work for publication. Mahler mixed his mission advocacy with general colonial advocacy; he had joined the board of the local Colonial Society in 1900. On a national level and in the colonies, the German Colonial Society and German mission societies were more frequently adversaries than allies. But his position on the board of the Bunzlau branch of the Colonial Society allowed him to defend the mission in its meetings as well. At one meeting, Mahler claimed to have turned back attacks on the mission with the help of articles from the *Allgemeine Missions-Zeitschrift*.[78]

One month after his February tour of Bunzlau, Mahler returned to the boys' primary school there and spoke for ninety minutes to 300 students.[79] As part of his presentation he utilized a large-scale poster to illustrate the Berlin Mission's work in East Africa. According to Mahler, the students "marvelled" at the examples of "mission things," examples of "ethnology, natural products, school notebooks and textbooks from the mission schools." After a closing prayer and hymn, Mahler distributed donation books and 100 copies of a children's mission magazine.[80] Mahler's two months of activities in Bunzlau offered locals opportunities to interact with images and artefacts that brought the mission field into their churches and classroom.[81] Other mission preachers worked in ways similar to Mahler's. For example, Pastor Ernst Moldt of Pomerania led a children's service in the Stolp Marienkirche for 2,000 children in August 1904, and followed up that service with a "forest mission festival."[82]

Mahler's work in Silesia exemplified a structure set up by the Berlin Mission Society in 1903 to support local Hilfsvereine. Starting in that year, the mission society inaugurated its program of recruiting and training mission secretaries. These men provided a layer of organizational and local expertise between the Berlin Mission and pastors in their regions. Their activity did not interrupt direct contact between mission officials and mission friends on the local level, but men like Otto Hagena of Stolp and M.W. Mahler provided regional leadership.[83] They organized and took part in preaching tours and related mission programming.[84] Along with the mission secretaries, another form of support for local mission groups came from the *Missions-Lehrkurse* (mission training courses) regularly staged by the Berlin Mission. A committee of Berlin Mission officials described the purpose of the Lehrkurse as outfitting attendees with scientific and practical knowledge for their service to the mission and their congregations.[85] The courses directly competed with efforts by the German Colonial Society and other secular colonialist educators to supply teachers with material for colonial education.[86] The curriculum at one week-long Lehrkursus in 1895 included sessions on mission preaching, mission study sessions, mission methodologies, informational sessions on the various mission fields, and a visit to Berlin's ethnological museum, guided by Merensky.[87]

The Lehrkurse served local mission supporters, especially pastors and teachers, and was frequently the first place that a more ambitious missionary supporter might go to. The Berlin Mission Society also organized mission preaching tours, which they staffed with missionaries home on leave, mission society staff, and pastors who had been recruited from a pool of enthusiastic or knowledgeable supporters. After 1903, planning these tours fell to the provincial mission secretaries, but the Berlin Mission Society continued to provide specific guidance to the secretaries. According to the society, the best time of the year for tours was between the hay and corn harvests at the beginning of the summer and the final harvest at the end of the fall. The best times for events were early mornings, evenings, and Sunday afternoons. Once timing of a preaching event had been chosen, the church was to be decorated to convey to parishioners the joy and extraordinariness of the event and thus encourage greater attendance. All of this was designed to satisfy the primary goal of a mission preacher's visit; Siegfried Knak emphasized the goal was to provide local Hilfsvereine with new energy, a "strong push." To achieve this, mission-speaking tours had to be planned with "increased energy and greater orderliness" to enhance and sustain the missionary spirit of a community.[88] Local organizations were encouraged to publicize their events in local newspapers and organize meetings between local notables and visiting speakers in order to recruit new missionary disciples in the community.[89] A 1912 guide clarified that instruction and explicitly encouraged recruiting supporters from among local educators, who could arrange lectures in Gymnasia, teaching seminars, and other educational settings.Thus the mission could draw local educated elites into mission circles. Primary school teachers could also help bring missionary speakers into contact with children, who in their excitement would bring their parents to mission events in town.[90] Adult participation was further encouraged by holding celebrations at local beer gardens and taverns.[91]

Representing the World and Its People

The extensive network and varied programming that Hilfsvereine of the Berlin Mission Society created in the decades before the First World War expanded the influence of the mission society. When hundreds of Berliners gathered at a mission festival, the Berlin Mission naturally wanted to fill its collection boxes. But the mission society also wanted attendees to understand the shape and purpose of the mission's work. So, when ordinary Germans were called together to learn about the holy work of the Berlin missionaries, they were provided with representations of the global mission movement and, most important, the colonized and missionized people of the world.

The mission society wanted parishioners to understand that the Berlin Mission Society was part of a global Protestant mission movement, and that the movement worked in every corner of the Earth to bring all the people of the world into one Christian communion. To do so, they devoted much of their resources to spreading knowledge of what the missions did abroad *and* dispensing the knowledge that they produced about the lands in which they worked. Examples of both could be found in the mission societies' publications and in the visual and verbal material covered at in-person presentations by mission representatives. One Hilfsverein described how visiting missionaries "smartly describe[d] the black and brown, the copper red and yellow children in heathendom" and the missionaries' "travels and labours, joys and sorrows, successes and failures."[92] In their teachings, visiting missionaries and Hilfsvereine stressed to ordinary Protestants the bonds of their shared humanity with colonized people. Missionaries' unifying representation of the people of the colonies as part of Germans' Protestant community differed in intent and humanistic goals from secular projects that sought to integrate figuratively depopulated colonial spaces.[93]

The mission society and its supporters linked local contexts with global purposes through presentations on colonized places and people. While these presentations inscribed racial difference, they did so with an approach that still fundamentally reinforced the shared humanity of Europeans and non-Europeans. German Protestant missionaries' worldview resisted nationalist or reductively racist ideas. Their programming on the local level repeated the messages about racial difference, missionary purpose, and cultural transformation that missionary ideology and practice revealed. Through their work among local German Protestant congregations, the mission societies delivered the same message to ordinary Germans. The humanity of non-Europeans came through in presentations by the mission movement's advocates that insisted on the equality of all people before God – all Christians were equal in God's eyes and God's message was not linked to race.

The intersection of German Protestantism and African or Chinese Protestantism encouraged Hilfsvereine to connect their community's cultural expressions of Protestant tradition with those of missionized people. According to the Mützenow Hilfsverein, a new missionary would arrive in the field to the same sort of reception a new pastor would in Germany, greeted by indigenous equivalents of "honorary arches and garlanded parsonages, choruses of schoolchildren, celebratory welcome speeches, and the like."[94] This normalization of mission practices with the familiar rituals of provincial Lutheran communal celebrations would have helped German Protestants recognize the missionized people of the colonial world as fellow Christians. The missionaries' message competed with other messages Germans received about the colonized space and people. It contested the hierarchies present in commercial imagery and in Colonial Society educational endeavours. The missionaries could not completely overturn the explicit hierarchies, particularly given their own role as cultural overseers toward African communities. The missionaries viewed the relationship as necessary to the current state of Christian practice in the mission fields but thought the hierarchy to be only temporarily necessary.

In practice, German Protestant missionaries used diverse methods to propagate their vision among ordinary German Protestants. The Protestant universalism of German missionaries can be loosely collected into presentations and representations by White missionaries of non-Westerners, in this sampling especially Africans, and different ways in which ordinary Germans were brought into more intimate contact with colonized and missionized people; examples include direct correspondence and philanthropic linkages between a Hilfsverein and the mission field, artefacts brought from colonized spaces, visits by missionaries from the field, and, most intriguing and complex, sponsored visits by African or East Asian Christians to the towns and villages of Germany.

The connection that the Berlin Mission Society sought to create among its German parishes and mission stations thrived as ordinary philanthropy, often in a form more intimate than a donation of Marks. For instance, the Mission Society encouraged local Nähvereine to have specific mission stations in mind as they did their work. Even before the modern expansion of Heimat mission work, the Berlin Mission was encouraging women to gather and use their sewing and knitting skills to create materials for the mission. For example, in Belgard in December 1862, the Nähverein sent six shirts, one skirt, one dress, one "covering," one apron, thirty-five "Mittel" (presumably pieces of unfinished knit cloth to be used for making specific items), sixteen pairs of stockings, and one bodice to their African "brothers and sisters" in the Transvaal.[95] These activities could subsequently expand into closer contact with the mission field. In 1910 the Bunzlau Nähverein moved from textile donations to sponsoring a missionary visit to their city. The visit garnered an additional donation of 220 Marks; local mission supporters embraced the connection between their work in the Heimat and work in the mission field in the person of a missionary.[96]

The most ambitious and impressive attempt by the Berlin Mission to disperse knowledge of their work among ordinary Germans came in the form of a travelling exhibition. Drawing from the example of the Basel Mission Society, the Berliners began planning and gathering materials in 1910 for their own exhibits to highlight the activities of the mission and the cultures of missionized people.[97] Working with a budget of 10,000 Marks from the Berlin Mission Society Committee, Axenfeld described an exhibition plan that would lead a visitor through the prehistory of mission (the "original, heathen condition"), recent history of mission work, and the contemporary cultural life of people "converted" by missionaries.[98] In this ambitious form, the exhibition brought together news of mission work and missionary knowledge about the mission field. However, there is evidence that the focus of the exhibition was more on knowledge of the lands in which the missionaries worked than on the finer details of mission practice. Unfortunately, no records of the exhibition's final form exist so an assessment of its content is only possible from planning documents and descriptions from other sources.

The Berlin missionaries planned to emphasize the cultures of German East Africa over those of South Africa in the exhibition's Africa section. Organizers sought this emphasis because South African indigenous culture had "lost much of its original character." Widespread and long-term White settlement, along with the capitalistic transformation of South Africa by the British, meant that African groups in that region were unsuitable for the presentation that the missionaries hoped to craft. In this prioritization, we can see once again the missionaries' certainty that capitalism damaged African cultures. Their stated preference for "unspoiled" examples from East Africa shows the missionaries' preference for a certain kind of transformed African culture: not changed for economic purposes, but changed for missionary purposes. Additionally, an East African focus allowed the planners to avoid complications caused by dealing with a foreign colonial administration.[99] The "East African" plan for the display focused on the concretization of indigenous lifeways, with significant attention paid to the design of "authentic" replicas of dwellings in the style of the Nyakyusa ("Konde"), Bena, and "Bwanjigra" (a name used in reference to Chewa-speaking people from around Lake Nyasa). Other dwellings described as "Bawenda" and "Basuto" were also sought, despite these groups' communities lying in the mission society's South African territories, contrary to the organizers' previously outlined preferences.[100]

The Berlin Mission planners hoped to display, along with those dwellings, examples of Africans' lived world in the form of objects of everyday life.[101] Wilhelm Gründler, an official in the Berlin offices of the mission, explained that the exhibition wanted material goods that "illustrate[d] Negro life" without emphasizing the "ethnographic" over the "missionary" viewpoint. Gründler's choice of words is important and intriguing. His phrasing suggests a desire to position the travelling exhibition as something different from those of existing ethnographic museums. Though German ethnologists of the nineteenth century supported cultural pluralism, over time the interaction of their scientific project with colonial expansion led them to abandon their inclusive and internationalist approach for more reductive efforts.[102] By framing missionized people as part of a process of Christianization, missionaries' theology agreed with German ethnological theories that insisted on the historical and geographical contingency of human development.[103] Deeply problematic as it was – missionaries represented Africans' past as decadent and debased – the Protestant missionaries' rejection of representations of African culture as *ex nihilo* is more evidence that missionaries diverged from other groups representing the culture of colonized people for mass consumption. In order to realize his vision of "missionary" representation, Gründler asked the missionary Fritz Reuter to send examples of skilled handicrafts produced by *Christians* and examples of schoolwork from the mission's schools.[104] Nonetheless, organizers sought material goods "like mattocks, spears, machetes, musical instruments, kettles, and so on." With this emphasis on indigenous homes and hand tools, exhibition planners clearly meant to emphasize the simple, un-mechanized, and artisanal (rather than mass-produced) elements of indigenous cultures. To add a sinister representation of pre-Christian African culture, the missionaries also proposed a display on "witchcraft" featuring a "sacrificial" hut.[105] Missionaries' commitment to creating an exhibition that was legible and pleasing to visitors reproduced trends in ethnographic display around 1910 as well, as museums were transforming themselves more and more into didactic and pedagogical spaces.[106] German missionaries' intellectualized movement and its connections to other academics likely played a role in this parallel.

The "after mission" stages of the exhibition emphasized missionary tracts in local languages, school workbooks, knitting, and examples from the mission's furniture-building workshop.[107] These physical manifestations of the work of mission existed in the same visual and corporal frame as the examples of pre-evangelization life. More robust examples of the Christian life that missionized people were creating did not appear on the list of desired objects for this area of the exhibition. An exception might be noted in the case of the schoolwork that the missionaries in Berlin requested. In fact, at the March 1912 meeting of the travelling exhibition's planning committee, it was noted that it was not essential that the schoolwork sent be flawless. A work with "red corrections" could be used to help illustrate the "developmental path" of a student before the "very eyes" of a visitor.[108]

The curation of the exhibition betrays the blind spots of the missionary leadership, but it also provides evidence of missionaries' caution when it came to representing African life in its real contours. The German public was used to an anthropologized vision of Africans; missionaries were compelled to operate with the same visual vocabulary. Visitors expected to see the *things* of other cultures. But the missionaries included examples that encouraged a Christian humanization of colonized Africans. A catalogue of items from the exhibition included school workbooks from children in the mission schools; furnishings; examples of locally cultivated corn and wheat; jewellery from the "Sotho, Gwamba, Matevele [sic], [and] Wenda" peoples; examples of stonework and ironwork; the tools of "sorcery"; and, remarkably, phonographic recordings of hymns performed by catechists-in-training, schoolchildren, and a mission congregation.[109]

The representation of Africans that comes through in these artefacts and the planned exhibition layout is complicated. As was often the case with exhibitions on foreign, especially non-Western, cultures, the people of the Berlin Mission's stations became transformed into the physical elements of their lives. The focus on "authentic" dwellings and material goods dehumanized Africans and other communities. However, the intentional design to narrate cultural change and progress, albeit in a narrative lacking in African or any other non-Western agency, encouraged visitors to recognize the missionized people as people of the present and as people with some history, attenuated as it may have been by the missionaries' presentation. Quotidian examples of Africans in the process of participation in and adaptation to the mission project through student workbooks would have also encouraged an engagement with mission school students. Many Germans, especially children, might have recognized their own challenges with grammar in the work of a Konde or Bena child. Gründler described the impact of "indigenous works" at the exhibition as "fixing the impression" upon the visitor so that he or she left with a "lasting reminder of [his or her] mission responsibility."[110] Recordings of Africans singing Christian hymns literally gave voice to the exhibition's subjects. By presenting missionized people as in the midst of a historical process with contemporarily historical significance, visitors were encouraged to place themselves within the same process and Christian community as the missionized.

Like many other pieces of missionary programming, the Berlin Mission's travelling exhibition garnered surprising successes. Its opening in Dessau, where it ran for three weeks in April 1913, and its following visit to Halle both relied on local individual volunteers to serve as trained tour guides. In this process we see, once again, the mission society exerted itself to ensure that its message about mission work and missionized people was conveyed as accurately as possible.[111] Tour guides could help ensure that the exhibition brought "foreign peoples closer and the worth of the mission's work" to the visitors' attention.[112] At the Dessau opening, the mission society promised a "glimpse into the life and labour of the natives" of Africa and China, and the opportunity to witness the "works and successes of the Protestant mission" in those lands.[113]

The Berlin Mission Society's records indicate that 9,789 visitors passed through the exhibition in Dessau, a city of approximately 55,000. Of those visitors over 5,000 were children. Entrance fees totalled 2,309.79 Marks, and the sale of souvenirs and merchandise raised an additional 1,985 Marks.[114] After Halle, the travelling exhibition went to Naumburg, where, for a time, the exhibits were "packed up in a furniture wagon on the street."[115] A stop in Lissa on the outskirts of Delitzsch, north of Leipzig, brought in a much-reduced visitorship. In February 1914, the organizing committee began discussing dismantling and selling off the pieces of the exhibition, but then in June 1914 it opened at the Baltic Sea resort of Kolberg (Kołobrzeg).[116] No reference to its fate after this and through the First World War is present in the Berlin Mission Society's archives.

Missionaries were essential to the collection of material for the Berlin Mission Society's travelling exhibition. They assumed a central role as interpreters and mediators of African (and other non-Western) people for German Protestants, seen regularly in their participation in local Hilfsvereine events. The Berlin Mission Society and other societies maximized the advantages of globalization to bring their missionaries home at regular intervals. Missionaries regularly returned to Germany from their mission fields to recover from their exertions, visit with family, and reconnect with the mission society. During these visits they were expected to travel to designated locations and preach the message of mission work. Joined in this endeavour by retired missionaries, the visiting missionary brought the mission field even closer to German Protestants. Face-to-face contact between missionaries and their supporters in the Heimat was another opportunity for the mission movement made possible by the processes of globalization. In earlier eras, missionaries rarely returned to their home countries until the end of their careers, assuming they survived the travails of mission work. Regular steamship traffic between the colonies and European ports made the cost and exertion of returning to the metropole much more manageable. These new opportunities linked local German congregations to the global Protestant mission movement and to the mission fields.

Just a sample from Angermünde will help convey the impact of these missionary visits. In 1894 Carl Johannes Voskamp visited Angermünde with twelve members of the Berlin Mission House's mixed vocal and brass choir.[117] That same year Carl Nauhaus led festivities at Greiffenberg in the countryside outside Angermünde, presenting details of his experiences in East Africa. In 1901, the missionary Johannes Wedepohl from Mashonaland in modern-day Zimbabwe promoted the missionary cause while travelling among the villages surrounding Angermünde.[118] The following year, the Angermünde Missionshilfsverein enjoyed a season of "bountifully visited" mission festivals in Angermünde and the smaller communities of Chorin, Crussow, Lunow, Pinnow, and Stolpe. August Prozesky, home from British South Africa, preached at three of these festivals and Otto Reiniger, home from China, preached at two.[119]

Short of journeying to Africa or China, a local German was unlikely to meet an African or Chinese Christian. But the records of the Berlin Mission Society indicate that it was far more common for an articulate representative of Germany's Protestant mission work abroad to appear in a local German community than might be assumed – another opportunity provided to the mission movement by globalization. These visits gave Germans an opportunity to "consume" the colonial empire, but in contrast to colonial products or touring colonial explorers, the consumption was filtered through Christian universalist messages.[120] Such meetings reinforce the notion that human interactions among geographically disparate communities were typical of globalization, and Protestantism could provide a shared language to ease the interaction.[121]

Again, we can look to the example of Angermünde to understand something about these interactions. In 1902, the missionary Friedrich (Fritz) Reuter, a local farmer's son, returned home to describe his spiritual and professional development as a missionary working in Africa. Reuter brought to a mission festival in Lunow near Angermünde a "real Black," Joseph Mokitimi. With Reuter's assistance as translator, Mokitimi bore Christian witness in his native Sessuto and sang the hymn, "Lobe den Herren, den mächtigen König der Ehren" (Praise to the Lord, the Almighty). Mokitimi's visit must have been striking, though his communication through a translator would have maintained a barrier between the Germans and Mokitimi. He was hardly the only person of African descent to find himself in the German provinces, educational migrants occasionally provided a visible link to the colonial project in some of Germany's smaller communities, but they typically led highly sheltered lives while in the metropole.[122] The description of the remarkable festival closed with the comment, "It is a truly beautiful thing, when one can see the living fruit of mission, a Black whom one can love as a brother."[123]

The circumstances of Mokitimi's visit are quite extraordinary. The missionary Reuter had brought Mokitimi and one of his assistant teachers among the Lobedu of the northern Transvaal, along with sixty-five other members of his congregation, to Germany in 1897 as part of an attempt to raise money for his mission station and to finance the formation of a brass choir.[124] Reuter hired out the Lobedu to appear in a *Völkerschau* (plural *Völkerschauen*), a "people's show" or "human zoo," in Berlin that year – the Berlin Transvaal Exhibition. A Völkerschau was a typical way for people of African descent to appear before ordinary Germans during the colonial period. However, Reuter's utilization of the Lobedu in that way was atypical of presentations of Africans by the Berlin Mission Society. Völkerschauen physicalized the commercial consumption of Africans and their culture for Germans; they represented the fullest expression of "commoditized racism."[125] Such exhibitions were common across Europe; one of the most famous organizers of such shows was the entrepreneur Carl Hagenbeck, who combined menageries and Völkerschauen into a lucrative business.[126] These exhibitions were yet another way in which colonial culture came into the lives of ordinary people beyond the control of colonialist elites. Human zoos, or "ethnographic shows" as they were sometimes categorized, intermingled with the longer tradition of the annual fair and freak shows that had nearly always included occasional representatives from far-away places.[127]

Reuter also brought Mokitimi, without the rest of the Lobedu, on a tour of various congregations outside of Berlin.[128] In support of Reuter's campaign to raise funds for his idiosyncratic plan (the formation of a brass choir in the Transvaal), Mokitimi sang and spoke to the people of Angermünde. Reuter's willingness to participate in the peopling of a Völkerschau reveals the imperfections of any hard division between missionary and secular representations of African people. However, the preferred and normalized place of an African mission teacher in the Berlin Mission Society's representation of their work and the mission's congregants in Africa is very different from that at a Völkerschau. Mokitimi sang a hymn to the gathered Germans and spoke of his faith. Though some of his appeal was certainly as a curiosity, he was not presented as a scientific example of primitive cultures and races or as a commercial spectacle for low entertainment. At the Transvaal Exhibition, the Lobedu offered visitors a contrast between the modern exhibition halls and the reconstructed "huts" meant to recreate the Lobedus' "natural" habitat.[129] In Angermünde there was no such contrast offered; instead Mokitimi came as an example of shared Christian humanity. It is unfortunate that we do not know more of Mokitimi's own impressions of Angermünde. But we do know that Reuter's brass choir was formed thanks to a donation from a German parishioner in another village. A short time thereafter, Mokitimi wrote back to the congregation at Gartz-an-der-Oder, near Angermünde, to express his gratitude for its support of the brass choir.[130]

In 1908, Moses Chiu travelled to Angermünde from Berlin, where he was studying for his doctorate of theology at the Friedrich Wilhelm University. Chiu would become an important professor at the first Western-style university in China, the University of Peking. He gave a lecture, "Christianity as an Absolute Truth in Light of the Chinese Religions," in Angermünde.[131] Three years later Dr Chiu returned and gave a second lecture on the work of Christian missionaries, "The Spiritual Fight in China."[132] Such encounters no doubt fed the international spirit of the Angermünde Missionshilfsverein. Their thirty-eighth annual report included the avowal that "[h]eathen mission work is global mission work … With rapid strides the promulgation of the Gospels spreads among all the nations; sadly participation in this work does not grow at the same rate among Christians in the home country."[133] The opportunities available to these two men in terms of education and authority reflect very clearly the stark difference in the South African and Chinese contexts. The impressions they made upon the Germans would have been similarly different. Nonetheless, from the mission's perspective, visits by men like Joseph Mokitimi and Moses Chiu brought home to German Protestants the reach of their mission support, and both men's honoured presence as preachers and lecturers at their respective events would have sent a clear message of each man's respected place as a fellow Christian.

Missionary Messages

Between 1880 and 1914, and in collaboration with local and regional partners across Prussia, the Berlin Mission Society created an extensive network of Hilfsvereine. Together they established a diverse and robust program of cultural activities for local Protestant congregations. It is impossible to know what ordinary Germans thought about the program of mission work promoted by the Berlin Mission Society, or what their opinions were about the colonial project or globalization. Likewise it is impossible to know what average parishioners felt toward colonized and missionized people or how sophisticated their thinking was about race. However, by going deeper into the Heimat work of the Berlin Mission Society it becomes possible to reproduce one major set of ideas presented to ordinary Germans about these issues. By making careful use of local Hilfsvereine and supporting those organizations closely, the Berlin Mission Society transmitted a consistent message of international universalism. They argued that because their work fell under the Great Commission, and because they maintained the freedom and autonomy of their activities and made the church a communion table for all, international approaches to mission work must remain dominant. They translated internationalism into a primitive and imperfect multiculturalism. Guided by Missionswissenschaftler and mission society leaders, the Heimat programming created a broader base for German Protestant mission culture.

Hilfsvereine's financial support for mission societies like the Berlin Mission netted local groups subscriptions to mission periodicals. Many local groups received complimentary subscriptions for their donations; many also subscribed to more general mission society publications. For example, the Bunzlau Hilfsverein received, among other periodicals, the society journal of the Berlin Mission Society, the *Berliner Missionsberichte*; the *Missions-Freund*, edited by Alexander Merensky; the *Basler Missions-Magazin*, from the Basel Mission Society; Julius Richter's popular illustrated family magazine, *Die evangelischen Missionen*; the *Allgemeine Missions-Zeitschrift*; and the Moravian Brotherhood's mission society journal. These journals, along with a lending library of mission-related books, circulated at no cost among members – they could be picked up from the schoolmaster at the Bunzlau orphanage.[134] Lending libraries like the one in Bunzlau show that the simple circulation numbers of missionary periodicals do not accurately convey their reach. Prayer and Bible study circles were an established form of religious observance among many devout German Protestants; such circles would have been a ready pool of candidates for the sharing of copies of missionary periodicals.[135] As has been shown elsewhere in this book, missionary periodicals contained the richest evidence of missionaries' universalist Christian message about empire, globalization, and the races of the world.

Mission periodicals were the most basic way that mission leaders encouraged local mission supporters to learn about the goals and vision of mission organizations. But more direct, interpersonal connections were a preferred way to encourage local engagement. Karl Axenfeld described how "personal connections" with the mission headquarters and missionaries in the field eased the engendering of "mission affection" among supporters. By cultivating organizational connections, local support for foreign mission could be maintained through "shared labours."[136] Nearly two decades before, Reinhold Grundemann had detailed the challenge of Heimat mission work; he claimed mission spirit could be left to the inspired circles of mission advocates, fired by their Pietistic enthusiasm. But in the 1890s, the demands of mission work and shifts in social relations required that "care for mission life had to become embedded" in church life so that every parishioner might connect Christian practice with support for missions.[137] The recruitment of Wilhelm Papst of Sprottau, detailed earlier in this chapter, illustrates the seriousness with which new "converts" to the mission movement were pursued.

The more hands-on approach encouraged by Grundemann and Axenfeld, when it came to "message management" in provincial work, can be seen in the many ways that the Berlin Mission created tools for guiding provincial and local preachers and planners. In addition to the organizational and promotional work carried out by its mission secretaries, the Berlin Mission offered direct instruction to local mission supporters. The leadership in Berlin provided to pastors guidance for the composition of a mission sermon. In it the mission cautioned against "developing large, heavy thoughts" in the opening section of any sermon. Instead, the preacher should start with a short "striking" story or parable. In the body of the sermon, the preacher should "develop the mission ideas" in the scriptural source material and illustrate the revealed mission ideas through "well-chosen stories from mission in the present." The stories must be "concrete, vernacular" and, if possible, include "names and numbers and accurate descriptions of the [mission] environs." The practical goal of the sermon was to "stand in organic relationship" to the scriptural text, provide tangible inspiration for prayers and donations, and act as an authentic and positive stimulation of Missionsgeist.[138] Beyond its general suggestions for the writing of mission sermons, the Berlin Mission supplied preachers with a collection of anecdotes and parables to flesh out the message from the pulpit. The collection was organized around themes such as school, church life, "spread of Christianity among the heathens," "witnesses to noteworthy mission feeling in the Heimat," and African concepts of death and the afterlife.[139]

In the same vein, the mission society supplied Lehrkurse attendees with circulars that included anecdotes and exemplary stories from the mission field. The mission leadership designed the mission training seminars to provide friendly pastors and teachers with a fundamental knowledge of mission history and to inculcate them with the spiritual view of the mission movement. A record entitled "Means for the Illustration of Featured Material of the Training Course" provides insight into how the mission society's insiders represented the mission field, its residents, and the everyday interactions between missionaries and the missionized population in the field. The twenty-page compendium appears to have been produced for consultation by instructors at the 1909 or 1910 Lehrerkurse offered to school teachers (distinct from the Lehrkurse offered to pastors). By and large the missionized are presented in a positive light. In the section on school, children give "very appropriate answers" to inquiries about the place of Jesus in the Trinity; one youth recited Luther's evening blessing "from the heart and with feeling," while another offered an extemporaneous prayer for forgiveness. In these passages, the missionaries demonstrated the spiritual capacity and perspicacity of children, their "educability," in the mission schools of Africa.[140] In many instances, the missionary instructors who compiled the stories praised the singing of their African converts. According to the missionaries, the Africans sang hymns in multi-part harmonies with ease; in one story a church choir delivered a hallelujah chorus in eight-part harmony. While these sorts of praise essentialize certain qualities, they also represent a celebration of Africans' possible contribution to the cultural attainments of Christianity and a nascent appreciation of diversity. When paired with praise of the devotion of converts and the support the missionaries received from elders in the missionized communities, the stories contained in the "Means for the Illustration of Featured Material of the Training Course" convey a growing presence of Africans in the Protestant community. Using the text would have helped connect mission-preachers-in-training and their future audiences to a multiracial faith community beyond the borders of Germany.[141]

The actual words used by travelling mission preachers, missionaries, and local preachers during mission services are largely unrecorded. But through various reports we can reconstruct, to some extent, how they translated the mission message for their listeners. For example, Mahler reported that in a June 1906 mission festival sermon in Bunzlau, he called on his listeners to transcend the provincialism of their lives and make space for all the "nations" of the earth at their grand communion table.[142] Others used the theme of biblical sustenance to emphasize the ongoing relevance of mission work to Christian morality and ethics. At the 1908 mission festival, Missionary Superintendent Krause offered the celebratory sermon. He argued that the feeding of the multitudes with loaves and fishes proved that so long as needy people dwelled upon the Earth, Christians could not stop proclaiming their message of salvation.[143]

We can also reconstruct some of the message of Christian universalism as promoted by the Berlin Mission in the reports of the various Hilfsvereine. In 1892, the Angermünde annual report reminded its members that their contributions to the Berlin Mission Society's work would help make Africans, especially in Germany's new East African colony, into "free people" as Christians. Two years later, the Angermünde Hilfsverein reminded readers they owed love to the "spiritual empire of Jesus."[144] German Protestants' duty to the kingdom of God was also a theme in the Belgard congregations. Like the Angermünders, the Belgarders used the occasion of the Berlin Mission Society entering German East Africa to remind local supporters of the special duty that missionaries in the new colony had taken on in the name of Germany's Protestants. It promised that in time, "Every Negro tribe of German East Africa will have burned its fetishes of its own accord, and joined itself to Europeans with questions about the true God and the immortality of the soul."[145]

The Belgard *Jahresbericht* then pivoted to a standard explanation of the purpose of mission, "We should and will not forget" that we do this work not to "break a path for Germandom in the world … not to open up new territories for trade and industry." Our purpose is to "make heathens into children of Jesus … Only faith can win souls for the kingdom of God."[146] As the same body wrote in 1907, "We have reason to weep over many hardships … about every emergency of our households, congregations, and state. But deeper sadness than all that" comes from Christian sin; and by implication, failure to support God's mission.[147] The local Bunzlau mission supporters echoed the sanctity of mission work's autonomy from "worldly" influences that many Missionswissenschaftler expressed. The Bunzlau *Jahresbericht* stated that the "harvest work in God's field demands more than flesh and hard work, [it requires] abstinence and deprivation."[148]

The Bunzlauers and others shared the hostility that missionary leaders felt toward secular colonialists who made the work of missionaries and mission societies increasingly difficult.[149] In Parchwitz, the pastors on the Hilfsverein explained that secular colonialists could not be relied upon to concern themselves with the "heathens." If the colonized people were left in the hands of "unbelieving" mariners and merchants, then the colonized would become "children of the devil."[150] Contemporary conditions required unity and support from Germany's Christian communities so that mission could fight the battle "between belief and un-belief." Through participation in the work of mission, ordinary Christians' lives and communities could be brought into closer communion with God.[151] As a whole, the sentiments expressed by the various Hilfsvereine serve as a clear summary of the mission society's goal for its work in the Heimat and the successful integration of the missionaries' worldview into local understandings of mission work.

Mission in the Heimat and in the Field

If the Berlin Mission Society wanted to send the message that mission work was an essential element of Christian life because it brought heathen people into the Christian community, and if the message was founded on a certainty that all humans were equally welcome in that community, then it should not be surprising that significant tools for the transmission of these messages and certainties were the activities and communications that brought local German communities into affinitive relationships with mission communities abroad. Local mission supporters in Germany hungrily sought bilateral contact with mission communities, and the Berlin Mission responded to that hunger by facilitating those connections wherever and whenever it could.

Many local Hilfsvereine had direct funding relationships with mission stations abroad. For example, the Ratzebuhr Hilfsverein had a direct affiliation with the Pommern mission station in German East Africa.[152] Such a direct affiliation meant that monies collected in Ratzebuhr went directly to supporting the work of Berlin missionaries at the station, a commitment that concretely connected donations at mission programs around Ratzebuhr with support for African Christians. Starting in 1864, the Belgard Hilfsverein built its own relationship with the South African mission station at Amalienstein, in the Western Cape.[153] In addition to contributing direct financial support, the Belgard community kept up a regular correspondence with the missionaries stationed

5.2. "I am presenting the 'mission Negro' to my class" (n.d., [1913/14]). Photograph likely of Leipzig Missionary Georg Rother (r). Hans Rother, his son born in German East Africa, appears centre. Georg holds in his hands a "Nickneger"; for an example, see image 5.3.

Source: Leipzig Mission.

at Amalienstein. And when the long-resident missionary Daniel Heese returned to Germany in 1880 from Amalienstein, it was completely natural that he would further certify the links between the two mission spaces by visiting Belgard.[154]

Such bilateral connections were common for Missionshilfsverein. In 1907 the Angermünder Hilfsverein carried out a normal program of mission festivals, mission study evenings, and magic lantern shows. But it also facilitated what would grow to be a close connection between one of its subsidiary Nähvereine, in the village of Stolpe, and the mission station at Kidugala in German East Africa.[155] Three years later, the energetic support by the knitters of Stolpe led to a visit by the missionary Otto Maaß from Kidugala. In visits like this, the mission society and its missionaries could bring home to ordinary Germans the reality of their work. All of this was made possible by regular steamship and railway service that allowed the Berlin Mission Society to bring its missionaries home to recuperate and reconnect with their metropolitan countrymen and -women.[156]

Often the concrete connection that the Berlin Mission Society sought to create between villagers in Prussia and in German East Africa through correspondence was also forged through donations in kind. The Hilfsverein at St Jacobi's in Berlin donated a bell to a mission in East Africa in 1892.[157] Many years later, in 1909, a children's mission service raised

5.3. Missionsspardose "Nickneger." Mission collection box from Württemberg, circa 1900. Collection boxes like these were used in Germany and other nations to raise funds for mission societies in congregations, Sunday schools, and the like. Coins inserted through a slot (in this case the bowl in the figure's lap), caused the figure to bow its head in "thanks."

Source: Landesmuseum Württemberg, Stuttgart; Photo: Dirk Kittelberger.

funds for the future purchase of a second church bell, also destined for an African mission station.[158] In January 1911, Karl Axenfeld recommended the bell be given to the mission station at Brandt, to give the church there a "voice of God to call the heathens to their Redeemer."[159] A second children's service at St Jacobi completed the raising of funds for the new bell in July 1911.[160] The missionary zeal of the children of Berlin was matched in spirit by that of parishioners elsewhere in Pomerania. In 1904, a single service led by Mission Secretary Moldt in the Pomeranian city of Stolp delivered 120 Marks, a baptismal basin for a congregation in Mashonaland (in modern Zimbabwe), and altar and pulpit cloths for a mission station in German East Africa.[161]

In 1907, Jeremia Moloisi, the indigenous "helper" at Dikgale, a subsidiary congregation of Gottfried Beyer's mission station at Mphome-Kratzenstein in British South Africa, asked the Belgard Protestants to help his congregation with the acquisition of a new church bell. "Helpers" like Moloisi did essential mission work across the world in this period; indigenous catechists, preachers, and teachers expanded the reach of White missionaries far beyond the missionaries' capabilities. According to Moloisi, the original bell had cracked, leaving its tones "dull and barely audible." Without a functional bell, local congregants could not hear the call to services at the church and, as a consequence, their Christian community could not thrive. As Beyer put it, the people in Moloisi's community had built a church and school with their own resources and therefore deserved as much support against "heathen influence" as possible.[162]

About a month later, Moloisi's call for aid received an answer. In October 1907, Friedrich Büttner of Belgard's Hilfsverein wrote asking if Director Gensichen of the Berlin Mission knew of any uses for a 100-Mark surplus.[163] Gensichen immediately suggested that the Marks could be used to address Moloisi's request.[164] Büttner took the suggestion back to his community and, two weeks later, the Belgard Hilfsverein approved the purchase of a new bell for the congregation at Dikgale.[165] It took time for the bell to be cast and delivered, but one year later a note of thanks and a photograph of the congregation at Dikgale arrived in Belgard.[166] The connection between the congregations of Belgard and Dikgale initiated by the bell purchase grew in the following few years.

In the spring of 1908 Büttner, at the urging of the Missionshilfsverein, inquired into the possibility of transforming Belgard's general support for the Berlin Mission to a direct sponsorship of a mission. He learned that the estimated cost for such a sponsorship was approximately 4,000 Marks per year. At that time, Belgard mission support did not reach that goal. But Büttner confidently anticipated that the community would embrace the commitment and new donations would flow into the Hilfsverein.[167] Unfortunately, local disagreement about which mission station to support delayed the initiative, and over time inflation raised the cost of sponsorship beyond the capacity of Belgard's mission philanthropy.[168]

The Hilfsverein at Ratzebuhr joined in the exciting work of supporting its own local mission using funds raised with lantern shows and other methods.[169] The group increasingly defined its work through its support for the station "Pommern" in German East Africa as a "defence against the Islamic danger," betraying a growing sentiment among missionaries of all societies and nationalities that the gravest threat to Protestantism in Africa and elsewhere was the rapid spread of Islam.[170] Remarkably, a pastor on the Hilfsverein's committee even journeyed to the station in 1913. Heinrich Julius Oelke, missionary at Pommern, remembered the visit by Pastor Haegeholz from Zamborst, near Ratzebuhr. According to Oelke, Haegeholz came to observe the progress of the work in East Africa and expand his own "mission awareness." He remained for several days to observe the building of the station before departing.[171] The Ratzebuhr Hilfsverein does not record or report on Haegeholz's trip and no record exists elsewhere, so it is not clear if the main focus of Haegeholz's visit to East Africa was to visit the Pommern station or was part of some other plan. But it does illustrate the expanding possibilities for connections between the Heimat and the mission field by 1913.

The project that the mission society took upon itself – to bring ordinary Germans into Christian communion with the people of the mission field – had notable side-effects. In Belgard the authors of the *Jahresbericht* proved to be keen observers of global events. Manifestations of resistance against the spread of Western colonial power around the turn of the twentieth century drew comment, perhaps stimulated by the community's expanded global awareness. To the Hilfsvereine, violent expressions of anti-European and anti-colonial sentiment around the world served as turning points in a narrative of Christian progress. Events such as the Mahdist War, "disturbances in Uganda,"[172] the Boxer Rebellion, the Herero rebellion, the "unrest" in Heheland (a reference to the initial stages of the Maji-Maji War), and indigenous restiveness in Cameroon were described as "the death throes of a dying heathenism."[173] In some cases, local mission supporters connected Germany's new global power to a German cultural obligation; the 1911 report from Mützenow's Hilfsverein commented, "Germany, the land of the Reformation, cannot hold back in the conquest of the world for Christ."[174] These messages about colonial and international conflict ran in clear parallel with the usual militant language of spiritual war produced by mission societies and adopted by local Hilfsvereine. In 1894, the *Jahresbericht* in Bunzlau urged readers to join "our warlord, the sovereign of our host, Jesus Christ, [who] holds his banner in his hand and once again storms the fortress of heathendom. Our brothers attack with him; and we would remain at home with cold, slumbering hearts?"[175]

Through their connection to the mission societies, ordinary German Protestants processed global events with the assistance of missionary methods and language. The Bunzlau Hilfsverein explained to its members that "Christendom bears a global vocation ... to teach and proselytize ... [with] no fixation for certain circles, instead a fixedly fundamental work for God."[176] A smaller mission festival in Bunzlau, on 17 August 1880 concentrated on the message of shared duty to the Gospels, and through the Gospels' duty to the entire world, to the "Greeks and non-Greeks, the wise and unwise" – a reference to Romans 1:14.[177] A few years later, the *Jahresbericht* stressed to Hilfsverein supporters the historical commonality between the ancient Germans and contemporary non-Christian communities overseas. Missionaries were Christianizing and civilizing "benefactors" to the ancient Germans, and the descendants of those Germans could now pass on the gift of Christianity to others.[178] The Angermünde leadership reproduced the standard explanation of German Protestant missionary purpose. In 1895 the annual report published a sermon that reminded listeners of the Great Commission, the "fields of the entire world should be prepared and sown with the Gospels." Such work would allow Christianity to bring people around the world to the glory of God's message.[179] In the same sermon, listeners were reminded of their responsibility to their local faith community: "A living church must undertake mission, and a Christian who loves his saviour must take part. We are the light of the world, so we must carry the light of the Gospel everywhere."[180]

The responsibility to mission could also be used as a cudgel to drive German Protestants to do more for the mission society. In 1901, the Belgard chapter of the Berlin Mission celebrated the expansion of the mission and provided its supporters with proof of the breadth of mission in a new age. It recalled how the influence of missionaries, limited for centuries, had now been transformed: 200 missionaries in the field grew to 15,460; 20,000 "native" Christians now numbered over 400,000; the yearly mission collections had gone from 50,000 Marks to 76 million Marks; and the Bible could now be read, "if not in its entirety, certainly in its most important pieces" in 400 languages – making it comprehensible to three-quarters of humanity.[181]

However, the Belgard Hilfsverein pointed out, global mission might be mighty, but Germany's "mission sacrifice" was inadequate – Germans' contribution was only 4 million Marks and 800 mission workers. Even worse, among Germans, Pomeranians contributed only 6.1 Pfennigs per head while Rhinelanders gave 17.3 and Westphalians 17.6 per head.[182] This emphasis on per capita contributions by the Belgard synod was likely convenient shorthand for the necessity of greater devotion. In 1905 the Belgard Hilfsverein leadership pointed out that "Mission is war, a war of conquest." And in this war, the Belgard synod still contributed only 6 Pfennigs per head compared with equivalent contributions of 1.25 Marks per head by the British and 1 Mark per head by the French.[183] In 1898 the *Jahresbericht* for Parchwitz repeated the point that Germany's Protestants continued to lag behind the other mission nations in support: annually, the English mission societies collected 27.5 million Marks, North American mission societies collected 24.5 million Marks, and the sixteen German mission societies collected a "paltry" 4 million Marks.[184] The necessity of undertaking mission work grew out of "grateful love" for Jesus and out of obligation to the heathen. The cultural and material improvement that colonial rule supposedly brought to these people would be "devilish" without the Gospels.[185]

Conclusion

Though this chapter has concentrated on the networks and activities of the Berlin Mission Society, that society was not alone in its methodology and pursuit of its goals. The missionaries from Herrnhut sought support through their networks of Moravian faithful and in the communities surrounding their group's centre in Saxony; the Leipzig Mission operated in communities of Old Lutherans across the Protestant world; and the Bethel Mission sought donors wherever it could across Germany. The support networks for these groups overlapped. For example, the Angermünde Hilfsverein supported multiple mission organizations – its annual reports indicate support to the Berlin Mission, the Gossner Mission (Berlin II), "Berlin III" (the Bethel Mission), the Armenian Mission, the Lepsius Mission, the Rhenish Mission, the Afrika-Verein, the Syrian Orphanage in Jerusalem, the "Orient-Mission," and the Morgenländischen Frauenverein.[186] And the Mützenow Hilfsverein divided its donations broadly among the Berlin Mission, Gossner Mission, Bethel Mission (Berlin III), and other beneficiaries.[187] Many of the Hilfsvereine affiliated with the Berlin Mission made noteworthy contributions to other mission societies as well, indicative of the shared values of the German Protestant mission movement.

The Berlin Mission Society, just one of the many mission societies operating in Germany, developed the infrastructure and the programmatic models for an extensive curriculum of mission education. Using local collaborators, the mission society created Hilfsvereine in communities of all sizes which stimulated local support for the mission's work. Through these organizations the Berlin Mission Society also encouraged the development of Missionsgeist – affiliations with the earthly and spiritual goals of the German Protestant mission movement. Across Germany Hilfsvereine mobilized resources made available to them by the central office of the Berlin Mission Society to put on a robust schedule of mission events for local Protestant congregations and communities. Through these events Protestant mission was brought into local Germans' lives via sermons by missionaries from abroad, magic lantern shows, travelling displays of material culture from the mission field, and visits from "new Christians" of African or East Asian descent. This broad and deep program of mission promotion and education delivered important messages about the world and Christianity's place in it to hundreds of thousands, likely millions, of ordinary Germans.

Germany's Protestant missionaries did not imagine their work as exclusively relevant to the unconverted people of the world. Of course the religious past, present, and future of non-Christian populations on all the globe's continents were of direct concern to the mission societies. But their interest in the religious lives of Protestants in Germany was almost as central to their work. Work in the Heimat was more than just fundraising. Mission societies developed institutional tools for spreading Missionsgeist as far as they could in German parishes. The rewards of a robust "mission spirit" for the individual and a congregation included a deeper religious experience, a greater knowledge of the Christian global community, and direct experience of the universality of God's message. Missionaries worked beyond Germany to expand the flock of Christians. They also worked within Germany to nurture and sustain the flock of Christians in communities small and large, urban and rural, across all of Germany.

Ordinary Germans had access to increasingly diverse sources of information by the outbreak of the First World War. The increasing range and diversity of media and products available for consumption across the country meant an average person's referential framework for understanding colonialism and globalization would be built from a variety of sources. Germany's Protestant mission movement had an outsized influence among religious Germans when it came to the construction of that referential framework. The mission societies and their local supporters delivered a message of multiculturalism to those who were receptive.

6 Iron Sharpens Iron

International Missionary Conferences and Their German Roots

Consider for a moment a 1920 that never was.

During the second week of June 1920, over one thousand missionaries and missionary intellectuals from around the world gathered in the Berlin Cathedral for the opening service of the 1920 World Missionary Conference, the second gathering of its kind. Welcomed by the general superintendent for the Prussian Union Church to Berlin, the delegates from mission societies in the United States, Great Britain, and the rest of Europe looked ahead to a rich ten-day schedule of assemblies and committee hearings on the ongoing work of the global Protestant missionary movement. Participation by non-Europeans had grown as well, with over one-third of delegates coming from "new churches" of colonized people. They represented a restive contingent, agitating for greater local control over their communities. The conference came together under the leadership and guidance of the Continuation Committee, led by the Briton John Oldham and the German Julius Richter, and with the close collaboration of the Ausschuß. The conference's agenda focused on a handful subjects judged to be of international importance. Principal among these were the relationship between the Christian faith and other cultures, religious education, Christian mission and race, "national movements in the colonies," and implications for missionaries of the ongoing economic changes wrought by colonialism.[1] German participants had planned public events at churches across Berlin honouring the memory of the two great advocates of missionary internationalism in Germany, Franz Michael Zahn and Gustav Warneck. Receptions hosted by the three Berlin mission societies and metropolitan Hilfsvereine also demanded attendees' time and devotion. But over and above all else, the gathered delegates anticipated the challenging but promising debates slated for the second half of the conference. They expected that by coming together, as they had several times before, they would once again find the benefits promised in Proverbs: "Iron sharpens iron, and one person sharpens the wits of another."[2] In debate and conversation, the delegates would become wiser and thus better agents of missionary progress.

The highest priority of the 1920 Berlin Conference would be debates discussing the establishment of an International Missionary Council that would act as a permanent representative of the Protestant mission movement in international affairs. The proposed International Missionary Council was to be the final product of a decade's work. The Continuation Committee, formed at the Edinburgh Conference, had become a powerful but informal agent of international missionary collaboration between 1910 and 1920. The Continuation Committee's initial ambit had been to plan the 1920 conference and act as a custodian for "international missionary brotherhood" until the next conference. But through initiatives proposed and especially encouraged by the Ausschuß and many American mission societies, its activities had expanded to include ad hoc policy coordination among mission organizations from both sides of the Atlantic.

The hopes of the gathered missionaries in Berlin were resoundingly fulfilled. In a glorious victory for international cooperation, the conference ended with the formal creation of an international body with official responsibilities to act for the worldwide Protestant mission movement in global affairs. The new International Missionary Council, like other contemporaneous transnational organizations, promised to become a major agent promoting reforms in colonial policy around the world and partnering with colonial governments as their administrations increasingly directed resources to indigenous welfare and economic development.

This story, of course, never happened. No World Missionary Conference was held in 1920, and it most assuredly could not have been held in Berlin. In fact, events in the city tended toward division rather than union. The newly constituted government of the Weimar Republic had only just survived an attempted military coup from the right and a major left-wing workers' revolt in the spring. Furthermore, German mission societies had no capacity to host or even attend a world missionary conference in their capital or anywhere else. In 1920, the Continuation Committee did begin to transform itself into the International Missionary Council, finalizing the process at Lake Mohonk in Upstate New York in 1921. But the German Ausschuß refused to attend on the grounds that Germany's Protestant mission societies would not participate in international gatherings so long as German missions remained barred from Entente-controlled areas in the aftermath of the First World

War.[3] The next official international missionary conference would meet in Jerusalem in 1928 in a geographical and international context vastly different from any imagined Berlin World Missionary Conference.

This vision of international unity among Protestant missionaries captures the hopeful outlook of German missionary internationalists at the beginning of the second decade of the twentieth century. In the summer of 1914, the leadership of the German Protestant mission movement considered with pleasure a future of expanding German influence and participation in global evangelical work. In the first half of 1914, it was not hard for the German missionary elite to begin the planning for a 1920 World Missionary Conference that would finally create the international community of evangelical purpose promised by the age. German goals appeared to have a future at the center of international cooperation in missions.

In fact, as this chapter will show, leaders of Germany's Protestant missions viewed international missionary conferences as opportunities for, and evidence of, the power and potential of a global Protestant movement during the twentieth century. The First World War interrupted this process and, as will be shown, estranged German missionaries from internationalist ideas. But after the First World War, the unities promised in international conferences were renewed and eventually led to the remarkable reconciliations and collaborations of global Christianity that became institutionalized after the First World War. From the first mission conference in the 1860s until the last days before the First World War, German Protestant missionaries argued for international mission conferences to become venues in which a coalition of Protestants from around the world could come together to cement an international alliance. The German Protestant missionaries' focus on achieving their universalist internationalist goals through professional meetings and associations was typical of the time and a definite symptom *and* cause of globalization.[4] While they shared the cultural confidence experienced by the leading lights of Western society in the last decade before the First World War, Protestant missionaries in Germany also shared the nagging doubts that made that confidence so precarious in retrospect. To German missionaries, the universalist future of a wholly (and holy) Protestant humanity was a fact of the future, but the path was fraught with peril. Modernization, secularism, socialism, Islam, and Catholicism all stood in the way of Protestant success. A global alliance of Protestant missionaries and the churches behind them held the greatest promise for defeating those enemies in a limited amount of time.

The expanding sophistication and symbolic prominence of international mission conferences, culminating in the 1910 Edinburgh World

Missionary Conference, encouraged German Protestant missionaries' dreams of Protestant universalism. In Edinburgh, conference attendees set the course for a remarkable century of Christian ecumenical cooperation.[5] And German Protestant mission societies' actions in the last third of the nineteenth century and first decade of the twentieth century laid important groundwork for the advances achieved in that century. Had it taken place, the 1920 Berlin World Missionary Conference would have solidified the power of German missionary internationalist activism.

Inception

Dreams of a Protestant world led by an international coalition of missionaries stretched back to the middle of the nineteenth century. The clearest sign that this dream might become a reality was the Edinburgh World Missionary Conference, a seminal event in missionary history and the history of global Christianity. To German missionaries and many other Protestants, the city of Edinburgh joined Nicaea, Worms, and Augsburg to host one of the great councils of Protestant church history. It was in Edinburgh, missionaries believed, that Protestants entered the twentieth century, united the fractious Protestant sects, and began forming Protestant communities (and eventually Orthodox and Catholic communities) into intersecting networks of faith-based collaboration, most visibly represented in the World Council of Churches, founded in 1948 and eventually including 360 member churches from nearly every country in the world.[6] Today's World Council of Churches has direct origins in attempts in the nineteenth century to coordinate Protestant missionary activity.

In 1910, sixty representatives of the German Protestant mission movement gathered at the Hamburg docks to board a steamer bound for Leith in Scotland. Their departure on 11 June included an enthusiastic send-off by local mission supporters and a delegation from the Hamburg Colonial Institute. After a pleasant forty-hour voyage, the Germans arrived in Edinburgh to be warmly welcomed by their British hosts.[7] Three days later, the University of Edinburgh honoured three German attendees, Julius Richter, Johannes Warneck, and Carl Meinhof, with doctorates of theology in recognition of their service to the Protestant mission movement.[8] By 1910, the global influence of German theological studies made the recognition of German mission academics in this way unsurprising.[9] Their enthusiastic embarkation and celebratory arrival marked an auspicious beginning for German missionary leaders as they prepared to join 1,200 other missionaries for the World Missionary Conference.

Warneck, Meinhof, and the fifty-eight other German luminaries arrived in Scotland bearing with them decades of German hopes for true international collaboration among missionaries. From the beginning, they were nearly rapturous in their praise of the Edinburgh event. Many enthused that the gathering was a meeting on par with the meetings of Protestant church fathers in the decades of the Reformation or the early church councils. Just as the Reformation had loosed a new religious truth in Europe, they dreamed, Edinburgh would finally loose Luther and his fellow Reformers' truths upon the entire world. The twentieth century was going to be the missionary century, and to Protestant Germans the Edinburgh Conference was the authentic realization of that sentiment. Germans' participation at Edinburgh and the presence of over a thousand other missionary leaders legitimated a century of Protestant German missionaries' pursuit of global allies. Together, the attendees would contribute to a glorious transformation of the globe. German Protestant missionaries' decades-long confidence in international Protestant Christianity would be rewarded.

The previous decades had offered a mixture of hope and disappointment for German Protestant missionaries. On the one hand, and to the good, there had been a series of international conferences organized. On the other hand, and to the bad, early international mission conferences in 1866 and 1878 had failed to achieve real significance. Subsequent conferences in 1888 and 1900 did better, but, in the eyes of German missionaries, neither had inspired the creation of a true forum for international collaboration. After these mixed experiences, missionaries from the German Protestant mission societies developed a clear set of expectations for international mission gatherings. To the German missionary leadership, international conferences needed to provide structured opportunities for mission societies from around the world to formulate shared policies and strategies. In the periods between conferences, an organized council of missionary representatives could be formed to guide the mission movement, the Germans suggested. If the world was to become the Protestant community that God intended, German missionaries argued, then Protestant missions needed to support each other across international boundaries.

To the Germans, Protestant internationalism came to life in Edinburgh. It was there that the gathered Protestant missionaries created the first institutions of a truly international mission movement.[10] The exuberance of the German attendees was rapidly transmitted to German audiences. Paul Otto Hennig of the Herrnhut Brotherhood thought the 1910 Edinburgh World Missionary Conference was the "most important gathering since the Reformation."[11] To its gleeful participants, the

Edinburgh Conference belonged among the councils of the old church, councils where Christians had gathered in unity to shape their faith in spiritual and practical ways. At Edinburgh, liturgical and theological differences among Protestants had, according to Walther Trittelvitz of the Bethel Mission Society, been superseded by Protestant devotion to evangelization.[12]

For decades, German Protestant mission leaders had consistently advocated that international mission conferences take a specific form, a form that the Germans believed would unite (Protestant) Christians into a durable and effective coalition that would win the world for Christ. As Protestant missionary leaders in Germany saw it, they and their British and American missionary allies were the natural leaders of a global mission movement. The prevailing interpretation of the conference holds that the Germans' participation was marginal and that the main focus of the conference was on the Anglo-American axis. But the Germans did not see themselves as peripheral. As this chapter will show, many of the key leaders of the international movement were German or drew inspiration from their contact with German Missionswissenschaft. Furthermore, the outcome of the Edinburgh Conference matched German missionary desires.[13] Germany's Protestant mission movement had spent the decades before the First World War organizing itself to protect its interests and autonomy as a collective of internationalist organizations. The tangible commitment to international Protestant missionary unity made at Edinburgh manifested the Germans' vision.

German missionaries, as an evangelizing movement, sought to win hearts and souls. And in their view, there were many competitors for souls across the earth. While pointing out the rising dangers of secularism in their own societies, missionaries also named other threats to their work. Especially in Africa and particularly on the eastern side of the continent, German missionaries sought allies to fight off the perceived threat of a proselytizing Islam.[14] The historical success of Islam in winning converts over the course of the twentieth century validates their concerns.[15]

Other religious rivals inspired the search for allies. The anti-Catholicism of the Protestant mission movement before the First World War ran deep. Beyond the well-documented antagonism within the Protestant mission movement in Germany toward the Roman Church, evidence of the deep well of anti-Catholicism among other missionary nations can be found easily in the records of planning for the Edinburgh Conference. Though it called itself a "world" missionary conference, certain members of the Anglican Church, who considered themselves Anglo-Catholic (because they emphasized the Roman origins of Anglicanism over the church's Protestant origins), were excluded from the gathering despite their official membership in the state church of the hosting nation.[16] The meeting in Edinburgh was to be an alliance of Protestants *against* other faiths, including non-protesting branches of Christendom.

The Edinburgh Conference was a hopeful, exultant gathering whose attendees expected they would be able to transfer their enthusiasm to Protestants wherever they lived. However, it also was a gathering typical of the age. The awareness that missionaries had of the forces globalizing their time and place meant that even when they felt optimistic about the future of mission they also felt deep anxiety.[17] After all, if Protestant people and ideas could travel more easily via locomotives, steamships, and the telegraph, what prevented Catholicism, secularism, Islam, or Buddhism from doing the same? Particularly in the view of the Germans, commerce and modern culture were not always compatible with Protestant evangelism. As a consequence, the Edinburgh Conference was seen as a means of forging defensive alliances as well as planning strategies for global Protestant conversion.

German Protestant Missionaries and Mission Conferences

Before 1860, German mission societies contentedly worked independently and only occasionally joined into highly informal collaborations. However, the state-building project of Otto von Bismarck and his allies in the German territories that began in the early 1860s and continued into the 1880s converted Protestant mission organizations' autonomy into a liability. In the previous era, missionary organizations in the mercantile cities of the north, the industrializing towns and cities of Silesia, and the agricultural villages of southwest Germany dealt with much less imposing state governments. Even during the state-church debates and conflicts of the 1820s and 1830s, missionaries happily avoided getting embroiled in political matters. However, after 1871 and especially after 1884, officials in the imperial government and activists in nationalist and colonialist organizations began to notice the missions and their activities. In 1871, German patriots celebrated the unification of the German states (minus Austria) and, in 1884, German expansionists celebrated the official beginning of Germany's overseas colonial empire. Officials and activists wanted to conscript or enlist the mission societies into their various mercantile and geopolitical colonial projects. Protestant missionary leaders did not overlook outside interventions in what had been an independent mission project. Missionary leaders responded with a robust program of institutional innovation and reorganization. The development of these new institutions mobilized energies for collaboration that, owing to the ideology of the German Protestant missionary movement, soon empowered an internationalist response to the threats and opportunities presented by the newly globalized context of mission work after 1880.

The first of these organizational tools was the Continental Mission Conference, usually referred to as the Bremen Conference, which met first in 1860 and continued meeting into the 1920s. Its main element was a roughly quinquennial meeting of missionary leaders that took place in its eponymous city. It developed into the premier meeting of German missionaries in the nineteenth century. The growth of the Bremen Conference came against the backdrop of intensified state-building in the Germanies. Between 1860 and 1866, Prussia progressively increased its influence across Germany and in 1866 forced Austria's withdrawal from German affairs. In 1867, Prussia joined with other northern German states to form the North German Confederation, the constitutional and institutional forebear of the unified German Empire of 1871. The synchronicity between missionary coalescence and German unification suggests a commonality of causes.

The Bremen Conference began in 1860, when Friedrich Fabri, mission director for the Rhenish Mission Society and subsequent colonialist booster, proposed that the Protestants of the European continent, particularly Germans, should gather for a professional and religious conference to strengthen both the spirit and the activities of missionaries. Although the leadership of the Berlin Mission and the Leipzig Mission, two of the oldest and largest German Protestant societies, declined Fabri's 1860 invitation,[18] the next Bremen Conference in 1866 received a more positive response from the Leipzig Mission because the invitation promised to exclude theological controversies and focus on "practical-technical mission questions."[19] And by 1868, the leaders in Leipzig were promoting conference meetings and connections as important tools of missionary association.[20] Thereafter, it became a key collaborative meeting of missionary minds, encouraged by the practitioners of the new Missionswissenschaft. One irony of these developments is that Fabri sought to bring the mission societies of Germany together to serve Germany's national colonial movement. But his brainchild, the Bremen Conferences, quickly became a key site for the promotion of internationalism among Germany's Protestant mission societies.

The significance of the Bremen Conference for Germany's Protestant mission associations is perhaps most strongly indicated by the foundation of the Ausschuß at the 1884 meeting of the conference. As the midwife of that organization, the Bremen Conference made its strongest contribution to German Protestant internationalist activism.[21] The

Allgemeine Missions-Zeitschrift called the 1884 meeting the most "significant, vital, and practically important" meeting of mission societies. According to the journal, the October founding of the Ausschuß promised to bring order, structure, and unity to the activities of the German Protestant mission societies.[22] The year 1884, which marked the Ausschuß's foundation, coincided with the formal seizure by Germany of overseas colonies in that and the following year.

As before, the German Protestant missionary leadership sought organizational unity in order to resist the nationalizing power of the state and secular colonialism. As an organization, the Ausschuß followed the principles of Warneck and other Missionswissenschaftler. The leading lights of German missionary theology and policy celebrated the movement's long history of independence and internationality. The Ausschuß founding, in 1884, the same year that the "Scramble for Africa" began, was meant to form a bulwark to missionary autonomy. The period between 1860 and 1914 witnessed the emergence and preeminence of the imperialist nation-state. In that same period, the forces of globalization drove the growth of international institutions and movements. Germany's Protestant mission movement considered itself part of the internationalist movement, and thus organized groups like the Ausschuß to preserve and assert its interests against incursions by the nation-state.

German Protestant mission societies' readiness to expand their collaboration beyond the borders of Germany came from the same urge that led to the formation of the Bremen Conference and the Ausschuß. While the missionaries never directly connected their organizational activities with the political situation, mission work was regularly linked with international priorities and anti-statist activities. The Bremen Conference was founded with an avowedly international purpose at a moment of increasing German nationalism, and the Ausschuß was born the same year as Germany's colonial empire. Germany's Protestant missionaries promoted efforts to organize institutionalized international missionary collaboration starting in the 1860s, and with intensifying energy as the decades progressed – not coincidentally as globalization touched more and more communities in Germany, Europe, and beyond.

Shaping the International Conferences

International mission conferences as an idea can be traced back to the earliest days of the modern Protestant mission movement. However, when the first large-scale international mission conferences took place, the German Protestant leadership's response was lukewarm. Before the 1880s, German missionaries had little motivation to formalize their international relationships. Furthermore, the German missionaries disdained the early international conferences. From the beginning, Missionswissenschaftler criticized the practical focus of mission conferences held in England. As time went on, German missionaries took the view that international conferences ought to concentrate on international coordination over such workaday problems as how to integrate industrial education into mission work and how to approach the challenges of biblical translation. By the late 1870s, missionaries in Germany began to engage more directly with international conferences. Though they were more interesting to the Germans, the three conferences in 1878, 1888, and 1900 failed to satisfy the internationalist desires of the Germans. German Protestant missionaries wanted the conferences to be events that encouraged the formation of an international coalition of evangelists.[23]

German ideas about mission conferences grew out of the specific ideology of Missionswissenschaft and Missionswissenschaftler. The mission conferences made sense as part of a series of organizations defined by their geographic boundaries, ascending in size and therefore in aspirations. The more diverse the audience, the more sense it made to adapt the conference's purpose to appeal to broader ideas. As a phenomenon, German missionary conferences merged the traditional councils of church leaders, revivalist meetings of the Awakening movements, and academic conferences to create a multi-layered structure of missionary collaboration. The Bremen Conference and international conferences, of which the Edinburgh Conference was the ultimate example, were at the highest level of organization.

An 1899 description of the various German mission conferences laid out an organized system of missionary collaboration that largely mirrored the real state of that collaboration in Germany. At the most local level, the system of Hilfsvereine engaged local communities in partnership with provincial mission conferences, entities which managed regional networks to serve the fundraising and advocacy needs of the mission societies at the grassroots. As the author of the description, Pastor Richard Döhler, wrote, these provincial conferences were intended "to promote awareness and understanding of mission and to generally nurture … mission life" in the local sphere. On a broader scale, Warneck and his colleagues organized the Saxon Mission Conference in 1878, at the peak of German nationalism and colonialism, for the "awakening and care of mission interests" among members of the politically influential middle classes. The Saxon Conference was, like the Bremen Conference, organized as a national meeting of every

Protestant society. The conference met in Halle, a longtime centre of German and international Pietist activity.

The Bremen and Saxon Conferences, along with the Moravian Brotherhood's Missionswoche (Mission Week) in Herrnhut, promoted cooperation among the Protestant mission societies with discussions of practical mission theology – the tactics of evangelization. Representatives of every German Protestant mission society attended these three gatherings to swap stories and share tactical methods. Still grander were the international mission conferences. According to Döhler, major gatherings like the 1888 London and 1900 New York Conferences dealt with issues of "mission praxis ... important questions" that the whole of international mission needed to collectively consider.[24] Döhler's perception was perhaps grounded more in his idealization of the graduated system of missionary conferencing than in reality.

Döhler's taxonomy of mission conferences clearly laid out the tiered system of mission affiliations and gatherings that helped organize the lives of missionaries, missionary leaders, and mission supporters. The tiers Döhler described began with local and regional mission conferences focused on individual mission societies. Multiple mission societies then collaborated through national conferences, like the Saxon Conference, interested in promoting the shared interests of German mission societies. The whole system culminated in international conferences whose ecumenical task was to address matters of grand strategy and to bring together the Protestant missionary world. It would take time for the international conferences to match the German mission leadership's ideal, but examining the three conferences before 1910 helps illustrate the influence of German missionaries and their role in the World Missionary Conference in Edinburgh.

The 1878 General Missionary Conference in London disappointed nearly everyone. Attendance by the general public was poor and the Basel Mission Society's journal reported that the conference had done little to meet its goal of motivating mission interest. In attendance were German missionaries from the Berlin, Rhenish, and Basel Societies; they included Theodor Wangemann, Karl Plath, Elias Schrenk, and August Schreiber, but there is no record of their impressions. In Germany, the 1878 conference passed with little notice, though the Basel missionaries did not consign the concept to the dustbin. The anonymous author of an article in their journal, *Evangelisches Missions-Magazin, Neue Folge*, concluded that though the conference had made little impact, it should not serve as a mark against the "blessings of Christian community" promised by international cooperation.[25]

In fact, Warneck, the greatest force behind the not-yet-established Ausschuß and intellectual leader of German Protestant mission work, offered his own commentary on the London Conference. Though the conference was not a grand internationalist success, Warneck encouraged readers to hope for another, improved, international conference in the near future. He insisted that the next conference should mostly abandon any overtures to the wider mission public and move away from specific discussions of missionary method. Instead, an international conference focused on a small number of necessarily broad and theoretical topics would be more effective and have the most global impact.[26] Warneck proposed a plan whereby the international conferences would provide valuable contact among missionaries of different countries, promote major questions of missionary interest, and provide a boost to "mission spirit" in the host location without weighing down the program with the distraction of catering to the masses in every session.

The 1878 conference and its German response show that even at an early date, German missionaries, specifically Warneck, had articulated a clear vision for international missionary collaboration. The existing evidence from the Edinburgh Conference planning does not show the direct influence of Warneck, but as we will see, he continued to advocate the same structure over the next thirty years. And the structure of the 1910 World Missionary Conference in Edinburgh closely matches that envisioned by Warneck in 1878.[27] The World Missionary Conference, which has been described by historians of modern Christianity as the cradle of modern ecumenicalism, was built from a German design, one infused with German ideas about international Protestant evangelism.

The next two international missionary conferences received progressively stronger endorsements from the Germans. The 1888 Centenary Mission Conference in London struck German leaders as an improvement on the 1878 conference. Alexander Merensky, whose reputation from his work as a missionary in South Africa made him one of the best-known German missionaries, noted that the 1888 conference (like the 1878 London General Missionary Conference) had been an authentic attempt to organize a "real universal mission conference." Merensky described a three-legged stool of Protestant mission – an international project built on the British, American, and German mission movements.[28] He emphasized that the conference had cut across denominational and national differences to begin the formation of a "coalition for [the] grand global struggle" against heathendom.[29] Merensky, like other missionaries, celebrated the functional beginnings of a truly international collaboration.[30] According to the *Evangelisches Missions-Magazin* of Basel, the organizers had brought missionaries from across the globe together in "brotherly intercourse."[31]

Despite Merensky's positive review of the 1888 conference, it was not judged an unqualified success. On the whole, Germany's Protestant missionaries admired the planners' successful organization, but they criticized the structures and questioned the efficacy of the conference's intellectual goals. Particularly important, one attendee noted, was the success the conference had in bringing American missionaries into contact with their European counterparts. Nevertheless, the conference's program disappointed many German commentators. According to them, its focus on small "practical" issues had engendered disagreement and disrupted friendly intercourse, allowing theological quibbles to cloud sessions. The focus on "practical" matters forced debate to turn on these theological differences and distracted attendees from their shared evangelical purpose.[32] In addition, the programming of "practical" mission topics made the 1888 conference redundant for the German audience. The report of the 1889 Bremen Continental Conference criticized the 1888 conference because the intellectual content had too closely replicated what was offered to attendees at the Bremen Conferences.[33] German missionaries did not want the international conferences to deal with the tactical and practical concerns of missionaries. They hoped the conferences would evolve into an international missionary authority that could shape grand strategies for international mission efforts. German leaders dreamed that cooperation would create allies and advocates in other empires who could appeal to their national governments in the interests of German (and other foreign) missionaries. The Germans wanted to create a unified front to argue for collective action by colonial governments on issues of humanitarian concern; they sought allies in the battle against secularism and other religions, and professional collaborations that could improve the efficacy of Protestant mission work.

In the aftermath of the 1888 conference, Warneck intervened again and tried to shape the future forms of mission conferences. His role as an intellectual leader, the prestige he was progressively building in Germany and abroad, and his editorship of the *Allgemeine Missions-Zeitschrift* meant that his views carried weight and also reflected the state of the conversation among German missionaries and their supporters. In the case of the 1888 Centenary Conference, Warneck approved of the structure. This conference, unlike the 1878 conference, had organized exclusive gatherings of mission experts for the discussion of theoretical and practical mission questions. But when Warneck complained that the session topics were excessively narrow, he suggested alternative topics, such as "the position of mission to contemporary colonial politics, ... the international importance of mission, [and] the challenges of Protestant mission with regard to the growing Roman [Catholic] aggression."[34] As this list indicates, Warneck encouraged international missionary conferences to take on strategic issues that applied to every mission's activities regardless of denominational or national origin. In addition, his words demonstrate the sorts of enemies that Warneck thought the Protestants needed to unite against.

The foremost authority on the Edinburgh Conference, Brian Stanley, identified the 1900 Ecumenical Missionary Conference in New York City as a key precursor of the Edinburgh gathering a decade later.[35] The meeting was celebrated for its size and for the success it had in the capturing attention of the American elite. Former American President Benjamin Harrison and New York Governor Theodore Roosevelt convened the conference at its opening ceremony. Roosevelt welcomed the delegates on behalf of his state and delivered President William McKinley's greetings as well.[36] According to one attendee, Paul Menzel of the German Evangelical Synod of North America,[37] the New York Conference "mark[ed] the new century as a mission century."[38]

The distance and cost of reaching New York meant that attendance by Germans was limited. Those in attendance, however, stressed their feelings of international community. "America, Germany and England," began one celebration of the transatlantic missionary coalition, "are the only Christian lands in possession of the Bible. Upon them rests the great, holy duty to bring God's Word to the rest of the world."[39] This claim captured the strong confessional partisanship of nineteenth-century Protestant missionary internationalism – the Catholic and Orthodox Churches held claim to the text of the Bible, but it would seem from this description that those faiths did not truly "possess" it. This heritage enjoined the Protestant nations to preach the truths of the Reformation to the world so that the world might be saved.[40] To fulfil this obligation, Protestants needed to come together, and the New York Conference had "filed an impressive certificate of authenticity for the unity of Protestantism." Menzel wrote that "the now common phrases of national duty" calling on missionaries to bind their spiritual work to the colonial project were "exceptions" at the New York Conference; instead the missionaries' commitment was to "the Lord whose kingdom is not of this world."[41]

Unsurprisingly, Warneck sought to involve himself in the proceedings in New York even as his own health precluded attendance. This time, instead of waiting until after the conference and restricting his comments to a German-speaking audience, Warneck sent a letter to the conference in New York. The letter, which Menzel reported was read into the record with "personal warmth" by Judson Smith, a prominent American missionary,[42] celebrated the conference as another grand example of missionary cooperation. The New York Conference, Warneck continued, was a "meaningful" step toward truly international collaboration. He argued that if it were followed by deliberate, careful work, the mission movement would continue to expand.[43] According to the German Missionswissenschaftler, Protestant missionaries needed to share their wisdom. And by meeting in international conferences, the leadership of Protestant missions could organize themselves for maximum efficiency and collective action. Warneck's urge to participate in the conference, even from afar, demonstrated the growing utility that Germans saw in these international gatherings and their belief that they had a right to shape their form and purpose.

Anticipating the Edinburgh Conference

The Edinburgh World Missionary Conference was the most anticipated, and ultimately most significant, of all the global meetings of Protestant missionaries. It was also the final international missionary conference before the First World War. German attendees left the conference proud of their place in the international mission movement and filled with positive expectations for the future. Even before the conference met, German missionaries eagerly anticipated the effect the gathering would have upon world mission.[44]

Before the Edinburgh planners began their meetings, Gustav Warneck's son Johannes, himself an accomplished Rhenish Society missionary, proclaimed that Germany's achievements in mission theory and studies promised a special contribution to the ecumenical conference. The union of missionaries from around the world would prove a "treasure trove ... for mission theorists ... an exhilarating afterword for practical [mission] workers, a corrective for doctrinaires, [and] a challenge to deliberate for the over-extended [*Vielgeschäftigen*]."[45] The great intellectual stimulation that would grow out of Edinburgh would propel German and global Protestantism forward. International collaboration would bring together the German, English, and American styles of mission work. Participation by the Germans would allow "the dynamic industry and circumspect energy of our brothers across the Channel and the ocean to ignite our torch. We could learn much from them."[46] A coalition of the major mission nations, Warneck argued, could be created in Edinburgh, one that promised momentous missionary successes.

Eager to demonstrate the worth of their national movement to the rest of the world, and keen to support the international evangelical program, German mission leaders threw themselves into the planning of the Edinburgh Conference. At the Ausschuß's October 1908 meeting, Richter noted that the English and the Americans had shown interest in German assistance "like never before." This good will required a lively participation on the part of Germany, he continued, and Gustav Warneck quickly seconded that notion.[47] It appeared, from the German side, that all three legs of the missionary stool were committed to an international conference oriented to accommodate German interests.

In fact, German missionary leaders had already begun participating in May 1908 by gathering to draft a proposal for the Edinburgh Conference organizers and attendees. They produced a list of issues for the conference to address, with the hope that they could focus the meetings on major issues of mission work with a broad appeal. In their view, the conference should consider concentrating on the "encroachment of Islam in Africa and the defence against the same," and on trade in "alcohol in West Africa and a resolution against opium." The German mission leaders also made suggestions for greater international cooperation – the creation of an international mission library and the standardization of a statistical rubric for recording mission work.[48] German missionaries intended and expected that international conferences be strategic and designed to maximize collaboration on major, international issues, and they conveyed that desire to the organizers of the Edinburgh Conference.

Meanwhile, organizers in Britain and America distributed surveys to mission officials, scholars, and missionaries in the field preparatory to the publication of a massive report on the state of mission around the world. The published report, organized into topical commissions of missionary leaders, theologians, and other dignitaries, would provide the starting point for discussion and debate at the formal meeting in Edinburgh.[49] Among those invited to serve on these commissions were important German mission figures. Richter and Moravian bishop Benjamin La Trobe were members of Commission I, "Carrying the Gospel to All the Non-Christian World," with Richter serving as vice-chairman; Rud Wegner, Missionsinspektor for the Rhenish Mission, joined Commission II, "The Church in the Mission Field." Wilhelm Dilger, Gottfried Simon, and Johannes Warneck, all of whom had worked in Indonesia with the Rhenish Mission, were members of Commission IV, "The Missionary Message in Relation to Non-Christian Religions"; also on that commission was Johannes Lepsius, founder of the *Deutsche Orient-Mission*. The linguist Carl Meinhof was included on

Commission V, "The Preparation of Missionaries"; Commission VI, "The Home Base of Missions," had Friedrich Würz of the Basel Mission as vice-chairman; and, appropriately, Max Berner of the Colonial Office and the Committee of the Berlin Mission was a member of Commission VII, "Missions and Governments." Though he was nearing the end of his life at this point, Gustav Warneck served on the committee for Commission VIII, "Co-Operation and the Promotion of Unity." German and other Continental missionaries were only minimally involved in the writing of the commission reports, and Germans were outnumbered considerably by American, English, and Scottish mission representatives. But the basic concept of the conference, its purpose, and its form clearly correlated with German wishes.[50] German involvement in this conference far exceeded that for any previous conference and the German participants represented an impressive collection of German missionary expertise.

The main activity of each commission was to compose a survey to distribute to missionaries and mission experts around the globe. These surveys asked respondents to answer to the questions to the best of their knowledge in order to provide data for the "state of the mission field" as it related to a respective commission's bailiwick.[51] Then each commission used the surveys to compose a preliminary report for the conference. Though the composition of these surveys did not always match the Germans' "tastes," they would ultimately provide a "sufficient basis" upon which to work, Richter and Johannes Warneck thought.[52] This organizational scheme satisfied the elder Warneck's and other missionaries' hopes that the international mission conferences would focus on major issues of broad concern. From this starting point, conference attendees could then find some consensus around the global state of mission and chart the best course forward for the entirety of the Protestant world.

The conference that took shape between 1908 and 1910 matched in nearly every way Gustav Warneck's 1878 proposal. A key figure in the planning of the conference, its main logistical and organizational leader, John H. Oldham, had a direct connection with Gustav Warneck. From 1904 to 1905, Oldham had studied with him in Halle; there the German theologian's ideas challenged and shaped Oldham's own worldview. Under Oldham's guidance conveners of the conference planned a gathering for the leaders of mission boards, with little intention of organizing a great mass convention of lay people, as Warneck had encouraged thirty years before. The gathered mission leaders would take the work of examining and coordinating international mission work as their main goal.[53]

By the spring of 1910, Germany's missionaries could barely contain their anticipation of an inclusive international conference. Local Hilfsvereine of the Berlin Mission exulted in the coming gathering of "white, yellow, brown, and black Christians" in unity and coalition against the faith's enemies.[54] The Moravians of the Herrnhut Mission hoped the gathering in Scotland would "call together Christians of every nation and church" in devotion to God's missionary message. At that point, every one of the 1,200 delegate tickets had already been taken, proving the wide interest the efforts of the world's missionaries had attracted. The Moravians went on to recount the extensive preparations put into the great meeting. All the preparations, they asserted, strengthened the hope that the result would be a "blessed success" and a new dawning for international Protestantism.[55] Across Germany, Protestant mission societies prepared themselves for Edinburgh and the beginning of a new missionary age.

The 1910 World Missionary Conference

When the Germans reached Edinburgh after their grand journey from Hamburg, they became, by their own accounts, convinced of the holiness of the gathering and the certainty of a future triumph of Protestantism. The Moravian Hennig interpreted his ten days in Edinburgh as proof of the universal power of Christianity; the conference had brought together the "entire Christian world" – at least the Protestant parts.[56] Walther Trittelvitz of the Bethel Society wrote that for ten days Edinburgh was the "spiritual centre of the Earth, the capital city of Christendom."[57] The *Jahrbuch der vereinigten norddeutschen Missionskonferenzen* (Yearbook of the United North German Mission Conferences) called the conference the "most important event" in recent mission history.[58] Hennig evoked the globe-spanning import of the conference by noting that journalists were assigned specially reserved seats, ensuring quick access to express telegraphs and postmen "in order to transmit the latest news of the congress to every corner of the world."[59] The *Jahrbuch* expressed pride in the small but influential presence of German missionary leaders in Edinburgh.[60] And for all attendees, not just the Germans, the Edinburgh Conference was a heady experience; it left most participants feeling they had participated in a profound spiritual event.[61] For years, even decades, the Protestant world had become increasingly fired with evangelical zeal and calls for a final push to "evangelize the world." At Edinburgh, the collective mood created by over 1,200 missionaries, mission society leaders, and mission theologians felt like the fulfilment of God's plan for the world.

The logistics of the conference reinforced German missionaries' confidence in the righteousness of the the attendees and their purpose. This was another way in which the Edinburgh Conference reflected Warneck's 1878 proposal for a carefully curated gathering of international missionary expertise. Conference organizers placed popular and lay gatherings physically and structurally outside the core of the proceedings. Before the first day of the conference, five preliminary gatherings, including a prayer meeting; a grand reception by the Edinburgh lord provost, magistrates, and city councillors; and the conferral by the University of Edinburgh of its honorary degrees created a space for popular devotion without disrupting the deliberations of the missionary experts. After these expressions of popular missionary enthusiasm, the real conference began. Admission to the main gathering in the Assembly Hall of the United Free Church of Scotland was by ticket only. Official delegates sat on the floor while gallery seating was for missionaries on furlough, delegates' wives, and those few members of the public who had acquired one of the scarce tickets.[62] The chairman of the conference, John R. Mott, carefully controlled seating arrangements to facilitate participation by women and non-White delegates in discussions. Debate was carefully controlled by Mott to keep the conference focused and on schedule. Educational and devotional programming was minimized in favour of a gathering that allowed missionary leaders to contemplate and discuss larger issues of policy.[63]

From 15 June to its conclusion on 23 June 1910, the World Missionary Conference followed a carefully managed routine. Sessions began with a fifteen-minute worship service and an equal-length session on conference business. Then that day's scheduled commission report was presented and discussed from 10 a.m. to 12:30 p.m. Attendees then joined in a thirty-minute period of intercessory prayer followed by a light lunch. The afternoon session, from 2:30 to 4:30 p.m., renewed discussion of that day's report. Mott managed debate carefully through a process whereby those who wished to comment submitted their name, mission field of interest, and the topic they wished to address on a notecard. He then sifted and sorted the cards to shape the debate. Each speaker was held to a seven-minute time limit. In this strict time-management regime, each commission report received at least thirty separate commentary speeches, and, according to attendees, the time limit kept the speeches focused and interesting.[64]

Among German attendees, Hennig produced the most articulate and complete narrative of his experience in Edinburgh. His report appeared in the mission journal for the Herrnhut Brotherhood. In it he enthused that the Edinburgh gathering proved that "We stand at the beginning of the mission era of the church, [and] we should expect greatness and will

6.1 The 1910 World Missionary Conference. Assembly Hall, University of Edinburgh.

Source: Wikimedia Commons.

live through greatness!" He described a communion celebrated the final Sunday as one piece of evidence of the international unity spawned at the conference:

> I found myself beside … a cleric of the Scottish state church, ... a Baptist missionary out of distant India, … one or another from the German delegates, … and in the pew opposite me an Indian cleric and his … wife, both in their national dress. Beside him a Japanese woman, in the background the black face of a Negro. We celebrated communion with one another, the repast that the Lord bequeathed to his Church.[65]

For Hennig, the Edinburgh Mission Conference offered a true vision of Protestantism's hopeful future, a gathering of all the communities of the world, and the way toward that vision, a collective international evangelical effort. In similar tones, Trittelvitz, even as a representative of the most nationalist of Germany's mission societies, celebrated the Edinburgh Conference as proof of Protestants' transnational "fighting camaraderie (*Waffenbrüderschaft*)" against heathens and Muslims.[66] The goal of an international missionary alliance as always included an orientation against specific, powerful foes. Trittelvitz, for his part, sought comrades to battle followers of indigenous religions and Islam; before the Edinburgh gathering, the Ausschuß had focused on Islam as well, along with commerce in "immoral" goods like opium and alcohol.

Hennig in particular celebrated the chief legacy of the Edinburgh Conference. Even though planners had promised that there would be no resolutions made to bind attending missionaries to any future course of action, the gathered faithful did in fact commit themselves to a future of greater cooperation. The attendees passed only one resolution in Edinburgh and did so with universal acclaim. In that unanimously supported resolution, the Germans' proposed international consortium of mission societies and a like-minded American initiative came to fruition in the formation of the Continuation Committee of the World Missionary Conference.[67] As agreed in Edinburgh, the Continuation Committee would begin planning for the next World Missionary Conference in 1920. The Germans almost immediately began advocating their country host the conference as part of a general advocacy for expanded international collaboration.

While there is little scholarly literature on the Germans' specific contribution at Edinburgh, and the German attendees themselves do not go into detail of the proceedings, clearly German Protestant missionaries celebrated every element of that gathering and began setting a course for still greater participation. Their joyous anticipation smoothly transitioned into enthusiastic community in Edinburgh and culminated in blissful satisfaction after their return to Germany. In particular, Germans who went to Scotland celebrated the collaborative discussions detailing how Protestants might expand the international community of evangelical Christendom. The diversity of the gathering, the prominent place given German participants, and the intentionally strategic character of the Edinburgh Missionary Conference helped confirm the German vision for international mission conferences. The World Missionary Conference had been a gathering of unlimited optimism and supreme certainty that Christian faith and power would change the world. Though there were instances of competitiveness, discord, and trepidation, the German missionaries who attended returned home thinking only of the glorious potential they had witnessed in Scotland.[68]

Reaction to Edinburgh in Germany

The earliest news of the Edinburgh Conference from German mission sources appeared in the *Allgemeine Missions-Zeitschrift* in July 1910, shortly after the attendees' return. The prevailing German interpretation matched the historical reality: the Edinburgh Conference was perceived as a true international missionary conference with an undeniably transatlantic and arguably global attendance, a gathering that maintained what Germans saw as a necessary focus on issues of shared global concern. And, as the Germans had predicted, the result was an ecclesiastical council that would set the course for a new Protestant future. The British had been won over to create their own national structures of cooperation like those the Americans and Germans had; all three groups had committed to a starting point for international collaboration.[69] The German delegates to the conference addressed a letter to the "Christians of the world," declaring that the next ten years would witness a blessed "turning point in human history."[70]

The experience in Edinburgh, German missionary leaders effused, showed that the work of evangelization was gathering the needed momentum to bring all of humanity over to Christianity. In preparation for this transformation, the World Missionary Conference members had begun organizing for the synchronization and strengthening of mission activities around the world. While global mission advanced closer and closer to its divinely ordained success, the Edinburgh delegates explained, true Christians must still guard against distraction and temptation. According to the conference leaders, the rising demands from the state for "patriotism and sacrifice" threatened to defeat the parallel rise of Christian (meant as international) missionary zeal.[71] Missionary leaders in Germany said that they were prepared for the next phase of international work, and identified one of the movement's enemies – the secular nation-state.

In Germany, the World Missionary Conference had received great attention in the public sphere, and important missionary leaders followed up their attendance in Edinburgh with speaking engagements and cross-country tours. Church communities across Germany eagerly digested presentations about the conference and soon leadership from non-mission sections of the Protestant churches in Germany began speaking of Edinburgh and Protestant unity. At every opportunity, Richter and Hennig prophesied a growth in Protestant enthusiasm and support for missionary work. Many, according to Richter, saw that "through German mission, German prestige [could be] promoted." This, too, Richter hoped would be a sign of a new era, an era of recognition finally given for German missionaries' labours.[72] Hennig reported to an English colleague that he had toured Germany shortly after the conference and found that it had invested a new spirit of mission and cooperation among his listeners.[73] Even four years later, Hennig remained inspired, telling his Moravian colleagues that "Edinburgh showed us duties like never seen by God's Church. [There] [t]he Lord opened the gates of the world wide."[74] Richter declared that German missions had been drawn into a wider world and the conference had been the "greatest, most unforgettable occasion in Protestant mission culture." Every delegate at the conference would remember the "charm and magic" of that "holy day" as one of the most valuable memories of his or her life.[75]

For historians of Christianity, the remarkable transformation of inter-Christian relations from contentious doctrinal disputes to global ecumenicalism had been the most significant religious process of the twentieth century. And much of that history can be traced to the activities of the Continuation Committee and its successors in the period between the world wars. The most significant outcome of the Edinburgh Conference was, therefore, the foundation of the Continuation Committee, and one source of this institutional development was the German Protestant mission movement. In the preliminaries to the Edinburgh Conference, the Berlin Mission proposed that the World Missionary Conference organize an international commission for addressing international mission issues. Beyond discussing a narrow bid to recoup losses from the Boer War, the authors of the proposal noted that if the Edinburgh Conference truly intended to transform Protestant mission into a "world power" then it needed some "central organ" to stand for missionaries in international affairs.[76] The Berliners proposed missionary internationalism take form with representatives to a central mission council from Britain, the Continent, the United States, Canada, South Africa, and Australia.[77]

Richter delivered the German proposal to the British organizers of the World Missionary Conference at a meeting in February 1910 and began winning support for institutionalized international cooperation. The German proposal and the desires behind it were not unique to Germany in the early 1900s. Anticipating the Edinburgh Conference, American missionaries, constituted as the Foreign Mission Conference, produced their own proposal for the formation of an "International Committee." And at the Edinburgh Conference, the resolution to create a body like the Germans and Americans had proposed, called the

Continuation Committee, passed on 21 June by acclamation.[78] Later, looking back, Richter celebrated the cooperative structures formed and launched at Edinburgh. To him, they would reinvigorate the international mission project. The establishment of the Continuation Committee and his naming as vice-chairman of that body had been the "high point" of the Edinburgh Conference.[79]

The official committee had ten members each from Britain, North America, and the European continent. South Africa, Australasia, Japan, China, and India each provided one member. In prologue to the committee's official formation, Richter was appointed to the three-member committee that drafted a constitution for the body.[80] He thought the Continuation Committee could help combine the relative strengths of the German, British, and American Protestant missionary movements. He proposed international ventures to improve cooperation; his suggested initiatives included a unified statistical collection, a global effort to influence public opinion through the daily press, and the creation of an "international mission journal." In 1912, *The International Review of Missions* began under the stewardship of the Continuation Committee. Richter's eventual hope was that the Continuation Committee would either evolve into or lead to the establishment of an international missionary commission that would intercede between mission societies and colonial and national governments, something that did in fact happen, but without German participation after the First World War.[81] This idea was supported by the leaders of the Continental Mission Conference; the key German mission leaders, Theodor Öhler and August Wilhelm Schreiber, backed Richter's proposal in a letter to the members of the Continental Mission Conference.[82] And in 1911, the Ausschuß endorsed Richter's idea for the formation of an international commission for the protection of missionary interests and the pursuit of missionary goals, such as the reduction of the spirit trade; abolition of the opium trade; promotion of international treaties on the protection of indigenous communities; opposition to slavery, the "coolie" trade, and the like; and the "elimination of infringements upon the rights of Christians," and protection of "the interests of mission schools with regards to government policy in the mission territories." In short, the international commission should extend the areas of activity that the Ausschuß itself pursued into the global sphere.[83]

German enthusiasm continued to grow right up to the eve of the First World War. Calls to host the 1920 World Missionary Conference garnered broad support among German mission societies. The Continuation Committee was already entertaining a bid from Toronto as a possible host city. In turn, Öhler and the Ausschuß presented the case for a German host city. They argued with four major suppositions. First, Protestant mission had three wings, American, British, and Continental. The 1900 conference had been in New York and the 1910 conference in Edinburgh; therefore the 1920 meeting should convene somewhere on the Continent. Second, Continental mission had a unique character with special "gifts and strengths": a Continental host city would allow these to reach their fullest potential. Third, were the mission conference held in Toronto, attendance from Continental Europe would be very low, and as a result the conference would be a purely Anglo-Saxon affair. The Edinburgh Conference had shown, by contrast, that a European location was no hindrance to American attendance. Finally, by placing the conference on the Continent, Christian missionaries would place "scientific and practical work" at the centre of the goals of mission by recognizing the importance of the Continental (i.e., German) traditions of mission work.[84] The Protestant mission societies of Germany quickly endorsed Öhler's plan.[85]

Just one month before Germany declared war on France and Russia, and any immediate hopes for international cooperation vanished, Karl Axenfeld authored a German submission to the Continuation Committee for a German conference. This proposal met with such approval from the rest of the Ausschuß that parts of it were reproduced in whole in a memorandum with the same purpose that the Ausschuß submitted to the Continuation Committee. According to Axenfeld, only Germany among the Continental mission nations had a significant missionary presence around the world. He argued that Germany's cultural vitality, as evidenced by its rapid emergence as a political and global power, reinforced the virtues of a German host site. By holding the future 1920 conference in Germany, the international missionary community would recognize the importance of German culture and German mission work to the international community. By implication, this recognition would strengthen the global mission project by making it more than just an Anglo-American enterprise.

Axenfeld described a future mission conference that would expand the international alliance of missionaries. He wrote, "The *goal* of the next world mission conference must be to secure the unity [of international mission] and through that make Christians more willing and more effective for their service to non-Christian humanity." A future German-hosted world mission conference should not be a carbon copy of the Edinburgh Conference; but the "achievements of Edinburgh must constitute the *premise* for the next conference." According to him, in the four years since Edinburgh, significant geopolitical changes had transformed the mission sphere. Missionary leaders had to respond with new strategies devised and implemented by a functioning international missionary leadership committee.[86] The international mission conference of 1920 provided an opportunity, in Axenfeld's mind, for international missionary leaders to go farther than in previous gatherings and to formulate strategic plans for the global evangelical project.[87]

As already mentioned, Axenfeld's ideas carried great weight among German missionaries and the Ausschuß duplicated many of them in its document entitled "Expert Opinion of the German Mission Council on the Next World Mission Conference and Its Meeting in Germany." The Ausschuß directly reproduced Axenfeld's language regarding the necessity of a world mission conference in Germany. While Axenfeld had proposed Berlin, the Ausschuß added Germany's major colonial port Hamburg as a possible site. The leaders of German mission also preserved Axenfeld's argument that the next mission conference should be a strategic meeting. In what had become a German tradition, Axenfeld and the Ausschuß contended that the next international conference should broaden its scope. They argued that some of the topics covered at the Edinburgh Conference – developing indigenous churches, mission school policy, and medical mission to name a few – were important, but threatened to "schematize and flatten mission work." The Ausschuß proposed concentration on broader themes, ones less likely to be distorted by local political and cultural conditions in mission fields: in other words, strategic and broadly theoretical issues of Christian mission which could provide international continuity while preserving mission societies' autonomy.[88] These dreams, like so many others, did not survive the guns of August. By Armistice Day, Germany's Protestant mission movement would be as much a living corpse as the Wilhelmine German Empire, and any notion that German missionaries deserved equal consideration with the British and the Americans had disappeared. Christian ecumenical internationalism would carry on without much German institutional participation.[89]

Shattered Hopes

It is more than just cliché to describe the First World War's effect on the German Protestant mission movement as the end of an era. Missionaries experienced the war like every other German; many served on the front lines of battle; missionary activity abroad in Entente territories was subject to forms of restriction ranging from mild to harsh; and mission houses gave over their space for use as hospitals and convalescence homes for the wounded. Whatever the missionaries' initial reaction to the war, the fighting that dragged into the second and third year became proof that missionary internationalism was dead. Some thought it had been murdered by the British and Americans, while others thought the war proved missionary internationalism had never been more than a phantasm.

The outbreak of the First World War provoked a split in the German Protestant missionary movement; the crack mostly divided the movement along generational lines. Younger leaders like Axenfeld and Richter, educationally and professionally situated within the unified German Empire, tended to give up on internationalism very quickly. In September 1914, Axenfeld proclaimed the war would purify and renew the nation through God's grace, and missionaries must join in the nation's struggles, to "serve and sacrifice [ourselves] with our fighting, bleeding and dying brothers, with our beloved German *Volk*."[90] For Richter, the "awakening and strengthening of the national mind" across Europe was the "strongest and healthiest factor" of Europe's last century.[91] He declared that as German military might could expand German territories, German Christians must channel their pride in their Fatherland into ensuring "a pious, constant *Germania*." Missionaries could not confine themselves to a narrow sphere; they must lead the German *Volk* as the foundation of a Christian worldview for Germany's new global reality.[92]

Nonetheless, others clung to the forms of missionary internationalism through the war. In 1915 Missionsinspektor Detlef Bracker of the Schleswig-Holstein Evangelical Lutheran Mission Society (Schleswig-Holsteinische Evangelisch-Lutherische Missionsgesellschaft), better known as the Breklum Society, objected to the growing and sustained pressure for German mission to have a "national impact." Bracker cited Galatians 3:28[93] as evidence that national difference was meaningless in the practice of Christian faith.[94] As Bracker put it, "Christianity is supranational [*hypernational*] (not international, because spiritual life is not internal, but instead transcendental); it should directly activate in itself the national-ness of natural life, the universal in the particular." He argued that deviation from internationalism filled the world with deadly violence. Furthermore, nationalistic attitudes encouraged non-Christian people's suspicion of missionaries' motives.[95] Bracker's view remained popular among some German Protestants, but Richter and Axenfeld's new view of German national service by the mission soon took over. It seemed to match the contemporary facts far more than the old internationalism.

Shaken by the apparent collapse of internationalism, Axenfeld described how German missionaries had sought at home and abroad a "brotherly community" with foreign mission societies in the past.

Abandoned in the first months of the war, first by the British, according to Axenfeld, this international brotherhood proved nearly impossible to maintain. Axenfeld consoled his countrymen that the brotherhood had been "no illusion." What had gone wrong was that the Germans had "overvalued that which united" the missions of various nationalities and "undervalued that which divided" them. He argued that though the apostle Paul had written in Galatians that faith dissolved nationality, faith could not dissolve racial difference. Christianity could not remove the Christian from his or her family and, in the same way, membership in the kingdom of God could not "dissolve or diminish the relationship between the individual and his national community [*Volksgemeinschaft*]."[96] Having defined the inviolability of national belonging, Axenfeld went on to situate German mission in German national life.

The course of the war and the impact of the war on missionaries' values would bolster the younger generation's nationalism. By the end of the war, though the loss of Germany's colonies made the question largely irrelevant, most German missionaries had abandoned the old internationalism for a new missionary nationalism. To Axenfeld and others, the British and American mission movements were to blame for the death of internationalism. Ernst Dryander, court chaplain, described the certainty of German missionaries returning from Edinburgh that a new "community of the Redeeming Jesus Christ" had been created, only to have that certainty destroyed four years later.[97] Though Dryander may have been one of the first, soon others blamed the war and Britain's entry into it as responsible for the lost "spirit of Edinburgh." In time, membership on the Continuation Committee by Germans Gottlieb Haussleiter, Hennig, and Richter came under severe criticism; to many members of the Ausschuß the Continuation Committee had become a tool of British missionary "aggression" and no German should participate.[98]

A more public break was embedded in a contest between theologians in Germany and those in Britain in the fall of 1914. The "Appeal to Protestants Abroad," penned by Axenfeld and signed by many German theologians,[99] reminded Christians outside Germany of the hopes for cooperation developed at Edinburgh and called for the mission fields of the world to be left out of the fighting to prevent "heathens" from seeing Christians kill one another.[100] The British theological establishment answered with a rebuttal called "To the Christian Scholars of Europe and America: A Reply from Oxford to the German Address to Evangelical Christians," which identified Germany's violation of Belgian neutrality as the moral cause of the war.[101] The British response seemed designed to excite a strong reaction from the Germans. It reminded its readers that the Germans had fought three aggressive wars since the 1860s, that the war reflected a historical plan on Germany's part to expand with total disregard for other Europeans' rights, and declared that "Until the saner elements of German public life can control the baser ... will not the Christian scholars of other lands share our conviction that the contest in which our country has engaged is a contest on behalf of the supremest [*sic*] interests of Christian civilization?"[102] Important missionary publicist August Wilhelm Schreiber's reaction to the "Rebuttal," as the Germans thought of it, was indicative of the document's effect in Germany. Schreiber doubted that words could solve the "sharply embittered" antagonism between England and Germany and noted that the English clergymen had ignored "England's jealousy of Germany's expansion."[103] Axenfeld viewed the response of the forty-two British clergymen as proof that Germany could not expect a fair judgment from that front. He felt he and his colleagues could now only, "as Germans and Christians," hope that experience would teach the British the error of their actions.[104]

Though the will to continue internationalism disappeared between 1914 and 1918, the whole question was largely moot by the end of the war. Richter offered this final verdict: The "world war led directly to a catastrophe of German mission" through British aggression. The Entente powers had abandoned international Christian collaboration for their own national interests.[105] The British government had applied to the conquered German territories a "nationality principle," according to Richter. And yet, even this policy was abused in the interests of a total destruction of German mission activities; even the Basel and Herrnhut Missions, both of which had significant membership from either neutral nations or Entente nations, had been expelled from their mission territories. The British government, filled with "hate for Germany," did not recognize even these missions as international, but instead as German.[106]

The German Protestant mission movement of the nineteenth century did not survive the war. First, almost immediately after the declarations of hostilities, the ability of mission societies to communicate with their workers in the field was terminated by the British blockade. Second, over time missionary manpower disappeared into detention camps in British colonies, and seminarians and trainees in Germany were fed into the military machine. Battlefield casualties in Europe soon transformed missionary facilities into hospitals. The third consequence of the war was a less direct consequence of military matters. The debilitation of the German economy over the course of the war caused a parallel deterioration of missionary finances as well. Since missions' lifeblood was financial support from prosperous (and not-so-prosperous) parishioners in Germany, the collapse of the economy reduced the Protestant mission movement to a desiccated husk. As a result, the German Protestant mission societies had no mission fields in which their missionaries could work, they had no missionaries to work at non-existent mission stations, and they had no money with which to pay for the transport or upkeep of the missionaries and mission stations the societies no longer had. Though African members of the congregations strove to keep their churches open, they could not be called German missions in any way other than a residual sense of the word. The dreams of 1913 made little sense. All hopes for the 1920 Berlin World Missionary Conference had been dashed. As the 1920 report by the German Moravian Church lamented, "[t]he once verdant German mission realm lies desolate," leaving the British and Americans "victorious masters of the world."[107] Even if the Germans had still felt their international commitment in 1918, they would have had no capacity to see their dreams of a World Missionary Conference in Berlin to fruition.

Conclusion

Germany would not host the 1920 World Missionary Conference. In fact, Germany would cease to be a significant figure in international mission by 1920. The First World War destroyed the German Empire and its replacement, the Weimar Republic, was barely stable in 1920 and hardly capable of hosting any international conference. Berlin was briefly held by right-wing putschists in the spring of 1920, and communist insurrection in the Ruhr region led to bitter fighting with right-wing paramilitaries and the German army. Even had the country been peaceful and stable enough to host a gathering of international missionaries, the German mission movement was a shadow of what it had been. German missionaries' commitment to internationalism had largely been lost in the fields of Flanders and northern France. The exciting years between 1910 and 1914 were more epilogue than prologue for the German mission movement's participation in international missionary collaboration.

Nonetheless, the mission conferences clarified the importance and influence of German missionary internationalism at home and abroad. They represented a necessary step in the fulfilment of German Protestant missionaries' internationalist imagination. Though they had success applying the non-statist, internationalist notion of mission purpose and activities to the workings of individual mission societies, missionary leaders in Germany, Warneck and his associates especially, felt profoundly the need for a true global operation. Similarly, the activities of the Ausschuß and the Continental Mission Conference applied missionary internationalism to the interactions among mission societies and between the mission societies and outside groups, but the Ausschuß could not force international cooperation. Germany's Protestant missionaries hoped for and, to a certain degree, pressured international missionary gatherings to conform to their desires. There is clear evidence that Germany's Protestant missionaries had fertilized the soil from which the Edinburgh Conference grew. The meeting in Edinburgh in 1910 was of global significance in the history of Christianity and, as a moment of deep religious inspiration for Protestant missionaries, was fundamental to German Protestant missionaries' aspirational internationalism.

Changes in the composition of German politics and the expanding reach of European power represented by the "new imperialism" and globalization led to the formalization of the German Protestant mission movement. Missionary leaders established the institutions for collective action during the years of German unification and expanded them in the period of colonial fervour after unification. It is possible to interpret the Continental Mission Conferences, or Bremen Conferences, as direct expressions by German missionaries of the new nationalism of the 1860s and 1870s, and some have done so, defining the conventions as narrowly nationalist. And it is similarly possible to see the formation of the Ausschuß der deutschen evangelischen Missionen in 1884 as a tool for integrating German Protestant missionaries into Germany's colonial system of rule.[108] But this is a mistake. These views fail to integrate the conferences and the Ausschuß into the wider context of German Protestant missionary activity. In fact, both institutions were adaptations made by the German Protestant mission movement to changing circumstances. Both were founded with the purpose of safeguarding German Protestant missionary internationalism at a time when pressure for a more nationalist missionary agenda was growing.

The Bremen Conferences and the Ausschuß advocated German internationalism throughout their existence, as shown throughout this book and this chapter. Led by strong internationalists from the "old" Protestant missions of Germany, the programs of the Bremen Conferences regularly featured advocacy for the maintenance of missionary independence and autonomy from the German colonial state. Furthermore, the Ausschuß, as a representative body of Protestant mission societies, regularly represented to the state and the public the cosmopolitan purpose that missionaries had set for themselves. These organizations, though either officially or functionally German in character, were not advocates of a particularist form of mission work and instead gave their loyalties to a universal Christian goal of evangelizing the world.

A number of important German missionary intellectuals, Warneck and Richter at the fore, thought the German internationalist missionary organizations they had founded needed a counterpart that was international in membership and intent. They needed to interact with other missionary movements beyond their borders that would, as the Proverb said, sharpen the wits of Protestants everywhere. It is for that reason that missionaries in Germany regularly called for international mission conferences to expand and modify their compositions to better serve the Germans' globalist vision. For German leaders, the conferences needed to be strategic gatherings with the ability to bring together attendees operating in diverse mission fields and with diverse mission methods. And for these diverse groups, the conferences needed to be able to be more than just consultative; they needed to provide leadership and international advocacy for collective missionary priorities and for individual constituent mission societies. These strategic mission conferences could then, they hoped, incubate a permanent conference, committee, or commission of missionary leaders who would guide, protect, and serve global mission activities.

The experiences and outcomes from Edinburgh that Protestant missionary leaders reported back to Germany represented a fulfilment of German Protestant internationalism. During the second half of the nineteenth century, missionary intellectuals and leaders developed a consensus about the correct relationship between Christian mission and state power and culture. The commitment they made to internationalism was expressed in their relationships with the colonial government in German East Africa and with local parishes in Germany. To them, the Edinburgh Conference and Continuation Committee marked the advent of the next stage – the world was moving beyond preparing for a global Protestant community and toward creating that global Protestant community.

For Germany's Protestant mission movement, the Edinburgh Conference and its main offspring, the Continuation Committee, were an authentic fulfilment of German wishes. The conference validated Germany's membership in a global movement that was increasingly united in its pursuit of a world-spanning Protestant agenda of Christian unity and transformation. The Continuation Committee was seen as (and, in fact proved to be) the first step in global Christian collaboration, and Germany, they hoped, was to be a key participant. Unfortunately, the personal, community, national, and international tragedies of the First World War included the destruction of German missionary internationalism and forestalled any German role in the creation of an international Protestant movement.

Conclusion

When Gustav Warneck launched the *Allgemeine Missions-Zeitschrift* in 1874, he wrote, "One can treat mission with contempt, one can be its enemy, but one can no longer ignore it; it has become a power."[1] Warneck's declaration also explains a major purpose of this work; Germany's Protestant mission movement mattered. Furthermore, the missionaries' internationalism mattered. An adequate history of the German colonial empire, German Protestantism, and colonial culture in Germany cannot ignore the Protestant missionaries and their service to the Great Commission. As modern apostles, the missionaries determined that the end goal of all things was the unification of humanity in Christ's kingdom even as they functioned as agents of empires and subjects of the colonial state. The mission movement is therefore central to understanding the administration of Germany's empire abroad, to appreciating the importance of colonial and global influence in metropolitan Germany, and to describing the global history of Protestantism in the nineteenth and twentieth centuries. The history of German colonialism and racism cannot be told without the history of Germany's missionaries and their mission societies. The historical reality of missionaries' Christian universalism and imagined international community complicates the supposed supremacy of racist, nationalist colonialism in German culture. The majority of missionaries rejected German nationalism for the construction of a heavenly Fatherland.

Germany's Protestant missionaries resolutely sustained a program of Christian universalism into the last days before the First World War. That universalism held that the most important force on Earth came from the Gospel and the most important human project was the evangelization of that good news to all the people of the Earth. Starting from the text of the Bible and then multiplying through texts produced in Europeans' and colonized people's tongues, the German Protestants carried the message of universal inclusion across the ocean and then back to Germany. Their determination to maintain the primacy of mission work overwhelmed any other possible purpose for their work among non-Christians. It also carried a message back to Germany that refused to intentionally denigrate other people for ethnic or racial difference. Missionaries' influence mitigated violent and discriminatory impulses in the formation of a German colonial culture even as they remained chauvinists for Protestant Christianity.

German missionaries proved to be an important constituency shaping global currents before the First World War. But the war ravaged the German mission movement. The mission societies and the Ausschuß found themselves cut off from the mission fields and blockaded from contact with their erstwhile missionary allies in other countries. Eventually most German missionaries in the field found themselves interned by the Entente powers. In the Fatherland, other missionaries soon volunteered for or were conscripted into military service. Mission houses and seminaries became lazarettes. Soon mission societies could not even secure the paper to publish. The highly textual mission movement became illiterate. And this destruction reduced internationalism among the missionaries to little more than an embarrassing memory of their apparent naivete.

Hindsight, in this case, was not 20/20. The missionaries' internationalism was no mirage and its impact was real. The German Protestant missionaries shaped Germany's nineteenth- and twentieth-century history. Between 1860 and 1914, a coterie of Missionswissenschaftler led the mission movement. These theologians crafted a missionary worldview that taught missionaries to navigate politics. They insisted that mission, guided by the Great Commission, must remain independent from secular interference, autonomous from outside control, and international in outlook. The introduction of Missionswissenschaft fostered theological engagement with emergent Christian communities and with the forces and facts of globalization. Its practitioners blended scriptural interpretations of a conservative bent with emerging methodologies and knowledges from the "colonial sciences." The formation of this subdiscipline of theology demonstrated the ease with which missionaries adapted to global interconnectivities.

Missionaries did more than talk, they also walked the walk – applying the ideology promoted by Missionswissenschaftler to their work in the field. As Europeans overseas introducing a Westernized version of Christianity, the missionaries helped colonize the world in the nineteenth and twentieth centuries. Their priorities and inclinations shaped the new forms of culture in Africa, Asia, Oceania, and beyond. The future Christian world that the missionaries thought to build through mission did not, however, fall into line with secular colonial projects. The missionaries' choices of indigenous languages or, failing that, indigenous-language preferences acted as a roadblock to the spread of German national culture. Theologically and methodologically oriented toward the promotion of Volkskirchen, German missionaries became advocates for an indigenous colonial culture that favoured the preservation of many indigenous lifeways. As a result, missionaries stood in the way of a Germanophonic colonial empire by refusing to prioritize German-language instruction. Ironically, it was their German heritage and German traditions of nationalism that led the missionaries to include indigenous communities and culture in their imagined future Christian world.

The missionaries' political influence gave them confidence, and their theology guided them to resist other attempts by secular actors to suborn their work. Economic interests in the colonies – settlers and plantation corporations – produced rhetoric that advocated policies to create an African proletariat. But the social foundation of a Volkskirche, according to the missionaries, needed a core of economically independent families to sustain the churches that would be built. Furthermore, the missionaries' link to German cultural antecedents antipathetic toward capitalism and industrialization reinforced their opposition to maximalist policies of economic transformation and exploitation. Instead, the missionaries supported "native" policies and practices that favoured African economic autonomy, especially agricultural enterprise. As a result, the Protestants provided valuable support to the Rechenberg Reforms in German East Africa and its parallel goals for African agricultural development. The simultaneous compromise on Swahili instruction in the last years before the First World War indicates an accommodation with colonial power. Missionaries' internationalism and their attitude toward the German national colonial project were flexible enough to permit support for colonial policies the missionaries interpreted as likely to support future African Protestant communities.

The creeping accommodation with colonial power and the danger of national feeling proved a real challenge to the Protestant movement. It proved entirely too tempting when the Berlin Mission Society bitterly feuded with the Benedictines of St Ottilien. Though the Protestant missionaries aspired to escape national constraints, they proved incapable of such a break from their history. Indeed, the Protestants brought to German East Africa nearly four centuries of anti-Catholic antagonism. When the events of the Benediktinerstreit aggravated an already stressful situation in the East African colony following the Maji-Maji War, leaders of the Berlin Mission eagerly turned to pro-nationalist and anti-internationalist arguments to condemn the Benedictines. The Protestants' Christian internationalism was narrower than they admitted, precluding any accommodation with Catholics. And the missionaries' undiscarded Germanness made it easy for them to appeal to political allies in this conflict. The extensive networks of German Protestants that became activated in the Benediktinerstreit were an indication of the influence and the extent of the Protestant mission movement in Germany. This colonial conflict was a source of political peril for both Catholic Centre Party delegates and Colonial Department officials, and belongs to a larger pattern of colonial political scandal. The fantasy of German colonialism translated into colonial realities that became expansive issues in the metropole. The Benediktinerstreit came with ready-made connection points for long-running antagonisms in Germany; studying these convergences helps us to recognize the potential impact of missionary politics.

While Germany's Protestant missionaries spent the nineteenth century creating an ideology and theology of mission work, applying that ideology and theology to their work in the colonies, and scrapping with other colonial interest groups, they also embarked on an aggressive program of mission work in the metropole. Mission societies determined that an important part of their work involved ministering to Christian communities. By binding German Protestants to mission work, the missionaries believed they reinforced the Christian spirit of congregations in Germany through service to the Great Commission. In the process, the missionaries became important figures in the creation of Germany's colonial culture before the First World War. The missionaries carried out thousands of events across Protestant Germany that spread the missionaries' universalist and internationalist vision of Christianity. They distilled globalization, its threats and its opportunities, into a manageable message for German consumption. And the message they offered contradicted prevailing notions of racial difference and Africans' (and other cultures') supposed savagery. The mission movement mattered overseas in the colonies, but it also mattered very much in the many communities of Germany where it represented a strong link between ordinary Germans and people around the globe.

The Germans' aspirations did not end at forging links between the colonies and the metropole. Their urge toward universalism meant that as early as the 1860s Protestant mission societies began organizing themselves within the German lands. The foundation of the Ausschuß der deutschen evangelischen Missionen in 1886 created an alliance of mission societies whose purpose was to represent the universalist and internationalist priorities of the German Protestant missions. The Ausschuß spoke for the missions' autonomy, and the same impulses that led to its foundation encouraged the missionaries to seek connections with other mission nations. In this endeavour the missionaries were able to draw upon more than a century of international collaboration and communication; German missionaries had worked with British and other mission societies abroad in the colonies of many empires. International meetings of missionaries became decennial events in the 1870s, and Germany's mission societies eagerly observed and critiqued the events. Gustav Warneck and others pushed for the international conferences to act as strategic, ecumenical gatherings that focused on global collective action by missionaries. And when in 1910 at the World Missionary Conference in Edinburgh the international gathering of church officials voted to create a body, the Continuation Committee, oriented toward developing an international consortium of missionaries, the Germans took the lead as major supporters of the initiative. German missionary theology insisted mission work was an international project and, through networks built between 1860 and 1914, the Germans played a decisive role in a global ecumenical movement, a movement that transformed Christianity in the twentieth century.

The subject of this book is the work of the German Protestants in their mission fields, in Germany, and in international associations. Missionaries and their ideas mattered; they shaped colonialism in the colonies, in the metropole, and beyond. Germany's missionary movement rejected the most extreme elements of racism and imperialism. And as important constituents of Germany's colonial public, the missionaries force a re-evaluation of the history of German racism and its colonial connections. Colonialism was violent, repressive, and brutal whoever the colonial masters were. The Germans committed atrocities against their colonized subjects; the British massacred Xhosa, Indians, and Aborigines; the French slaughtered their subjects on the Upper Volta; and Americans murdered their indigenous populations and Filipinos. The histories converge more than they diverge. And for that reason, the origins of the Holocaust must also be sought beyond Germany's colonial empire.

Although some of this project has been intended to revise interpretations of German racial thought and colonial culture before the First World War, it is not meant to elevate the German missionaries to glorious philanthropic heroes. Too much of the history of missions has been devoted to such hagiographic treatments. The German missionaries, whatever their attitude toward the non-Westerners they missionized and regardless of the benevolence of their intentions, did not journey to

German East Africa and other parts of the world at the invitation of the colonized.[2] Mission was a European project. Missionaries presumed to know what Africans needed and what shape future African communities ought to take. They engaged in ventures that transformed indigenous cultures while insisting on their own moral superiority. When Africans chose to join the missionaries' Christian community, the missionaries were slow to elevate the Africans to full participation – delaying ordinations and the extension of congregational autonomy. Like other missionaries, German missionaries helped colonize the world before and after the First World War. And this study has privileged their views in order to understand German history at the expense of indigenous perspectives and voices. It cannot pretend to be the whole truth of German colonialism. But it does seek to offer some alternatives and fill some gaps, at least from the European side of the story.

Mission Christianity constitutes a major element in cultural imperialism of the modern era. And German colonialism represented a particular form of Western imperial conquest and occupation. The role of German Protestant missionaries in those interrelated projects is complex and, as has been shown, frequently deviated from the standard narrative of cultural destruction and colonial rapacity. Nonetheless, German missionaries' knowledge and activities could only imperfectly remove themselves from these wider narratives of colonial activity. The missionaries might have claimed and tried to divorce their ideas and activities from the worst forms of colonialism, but their intellectual affinities were still compatible with certain forms of discrimination embedded in the national idea. They still had a role in the cultural violence carried out in the name of "civilizing" and "developing" colonized spaces, supposedly for indigenous benefit but actually for the purposes of the colonizer.

Colonial history and Germany's participation in it did not end in 1914 or 1919, but were irreparably altered after the First World War. At that point, the German Protestants could not support a mission movement on the same scale and with the same ambition as they had before the war. The events of the war bankrupted the mission societies, uprooted and diminished the ranks of the missionaries, and exiled the societies from their mission fields. During the war, Britain led an informal reassignment of German mission territories to mission societies from Britain, the United States, and other nations. The Versailles Peace Treaty made the reassignment official. Article 438 of the treaty guaranteed continued mission work in the colonies, but it gave the colonies' new League of Nations mandatory powers the authority to reapportion the mission fields as they wished.[3]

During the interwar years, missionary leaders in Germany faced a number of unpleasant choices. Overcome with the shock of defeat and revolution and caught up in the general condemnation of the peace settlement, they rejected the option of working under the mandatory system.[4] Most opted to join congregations in the Heimat. Their new enemies were secularism and Bolshevism in Germany.[5] According to some missionaries, German Protestants' supposed faithlessness was largely to blame for Germany's defeat. The logic was sound; if trained missionaries could not work among the heathens, instead they could apply their skills to the reconversion of lapsed Protestants in Germany.[6]

During the nineteenth century, Germany's Protestants supported an active and ambitious mission movement. That mission movement operated around the globe through the offices of European missionaries, their families, and indigenous collaborators. Guided by an intellectual class of Missionswissenschaftler, who blended a scriptural understanding of mission work with a globalized universalism born of the mission societies' broad engagement with Protestantism beyond Germany's borders, Germany's Protestant mission movement shaped millions of people's experiences of colonialism. The German missionaries' influence reached well beyond the halls of their seminars and the pages of their journals. Their imperative to preserve the internationalist and ecumenical character of mission work inspired the activities of the missionaries and shaped their interactions with other German colonialists. It directly intervened in the policies of the colonial state in German East Africa. Their work inspired a colonial culture in Germany that differentiated racialist ideas from other sources. Beyond Germany's imperial borders, the German Protestant missionaries' worldview also fed a global movement for Christian unity – inspiring the form and character of the Edinburgh Conference of 1910 and the succession of actions that led to the World Council of Churches after the First World War. The missionaries spurned particularistic nationalism in the name of a Christian internationalism bent on the unification of people into a grand community of Protestant faith. They dreamed that they would build a heavenly Fatherland across the globe. That they failed does not alter the import of their history.

Notes

Introduction

1 On the many and various forms of missionary periodicals in this period, an excellent place to start is Felicity Jensz and Hanna Acke, eds., *Missions and Media: The Politics of Missionary Periodicals in the Long Nineteenth Century* (Stuttgart: Franz Steiner Verlag, 2013).
2 The most significant critical work of mission history is Horst Gründer, *Christliche Mission und deutscher Imperialismus: eine politische Geschichte ihrer Beziehungen während der deutschen Kolonialzeit (1884–1914) unter besonderer Berücksichtigung Afrikas und Chinas* (Paderborn: Ferdinand Schöningh, 1982).
3 David Ciarlo, *Adverising Empire: Race and Visual Culture in Imperial Germany* (Cambridge, MA: Harvard University Press, 2011); Sebastian Conrad, *Globalisierung und Nation im Deutschen Kaiserreich* (Munich: C.H. Beck, 2006); Birthe Kundrus, *Moderne Imperialisten: Das Kaiserreich im Spiegel seiner Kolonien* (Cologne: Böhlau Verlag, 2003); Bradley Naranch and Geoff Eley, eds., *German Colonialism in a Global Age* (Durham, NC: Duke University Press, 2014); Andrew Zimmerman, *Alabama in Africa: Booker T. Washington, the German Empire, and the Globalization of the New South* (Princeton, NJ: Princeton University Press, 2010).
4 Matthew P. Fitzpatrick, *Liberal Imperialism in Germany: Expansionism and Nationalism, 1848–1884* (New York: Berghahn Books, 2008); Suzanne Zantop, *Colonial Fantasies: Conquest, Family, and Nation in Precolonial Germany, 1770–1870* (Durham, NC: Duke University Press, 1997)
5 John Phillip Short, *Magic Lantern Empire: Colonialism and Society in Germany* (Ithaca, NY: Cornell University Press, 2012), 14.
6 Jeff Bowersox, *Raising Germans in the Age of Empire: Youth and Colonial Culture, 1871–1914* (Oxford, UK: Oxford University Press, 2013), 12;

Ciarlo, *Advertising Empire*, 14, 304; Stefanie Wolter, *Die Vermarktung des Fremden: Exotismus und die Anfänge des Massenkonsums* (Frankfurt: Campus Verlag, 2004).

7 Bowersox, *Raising Germans in the Age of Empire*, 5, 12, and 82; Short, *Magic Lantern Empire*, 36.

8 Bowersox, *Raising Germans in the Age of Empire*, 2; Ciarlo, *Advertising Empire*, 14.

9 Ciarlo, *Advertising Empire*, 20.

10 Short, *Magic Lantern Empire*, 27.

11 Short, *Magic Lantern Empire*, 107.

12 Bowersox, *Raising Germans in the Age of Empire*, 214.

13 Wolter, *Die Vermarktung des Fremden*, 22.

14 Ciarlo, *Advertising Empire*, 289 and 304.

15 Short, *Magic Lantern Empire*, 159. Similar hierarchies were communicated through children's toys; see Bowersox, *Raising Germans in the Age of Empire*, 22–4.

16 Jeff Bowersox devotes a short section to missionaries' children's literature and recognizes elements that deviate somewhat from the general narrative of colonial domination, but he does not interrogate the much wider context of German Protestant missionaries in Germany and abroad; see Bowersox, *Raising Germans in the Age of Empire*, 145–52.

17 Isabel V. Hull, *Absolute Destruction: Military Culture and the Practices of War in Imperial Germany* (Ithaca, NY: Cornell University Press, 2006).

18 Jürgen Zimmerer, *Von Windhuk nach Auschwitz? Beiträge zum Verhältnis von Kolonialismus und Holocaust* (Münster: Lit Verlag, 2011), 69; see also Hull, *Absolute Destruction*.

19 Robert Gerwarth and Stephan Malinowski, "Der Holocaust als 'kolonialer Genozid'? Europäische Kolonialgewalt und nationalsozialistischer Vernichtungskrieg," *Geschichte und Gesellschaft* 33(2007): 439–66. See also Jon M. Bridgman, *Revolt of the Hereros* (Berkeley: University of California Press, 1981) and Jakob Zollmann, *Koloniale Herrschaft und ihre Grenzen: Die Kolonialpolizei in Deutsch-Südwestafrika 1894–1915* (Göttingen: Vandenhoeck & Ruprecht, 2010), 350–1.

20 Russell Berman, *Enlightenment or Empire: Colonial Discourse in German Culture* (Lincoln: University of Nebraska Press, 1998); Sara Friedrichsmayer, Sara Lennox, and Susanne Zantop, eds., *The Imperialist Imagination: German Colonialism and Its Legacy* (Ann Arbor: University of Michigan Press, 1998); Catherine Hall, *Civilising Subjects: Colony and Metropole in the English Imagination, 1830–1867* (Chicago: University of Chicago Press, 2002); Mary Louise Pratt, *Imperial Eyes: Travel Writing and Transculturation* (London: Routledge, 1992); Zantop, *Colonial Fantasies*.

21 See John S. Lowry, *Big Swords, Jesuits, and Bondelswarts: Wilhelmine Imperialism, Overseas Resistance, and German Political Catholicism, 1897–1906* (Leiden: Brill, 2015).

22 The preceding chronology of German colonialism draws from Sebastian Conrad, *German Colonialism: A Short History*, tr. Sorcha O'Hagan (Cambridge, UK: Cambridge University Press, 2012), 36–65.

23 Benedict Anderson, *Imagined Communities: Reflections on the Origin and Spread of Nationalism*, rev. ed. (London: Verso, 1991).

24 Hans-Ulrich Wehler and Thomas Nipperdey both postulate German missionary collaboration with the German colonial apparatus. See Hans-Ulrich Wehler, *Deutsche Gesellschaftsgeschichte*, vol. 2, *Von der Reformära bis zur industriellen und politischen "Deutschen Doppelrevolution," 1815–1845/49* (Munich: C.H. Beck, 1987), 469, and Thomas Nipperdey, *Deutsche Geschichte, 1866–1918*, vol. 1, *Arbeitswelt und Bürgergeist* (Munich: C.H. Beck, 1990), 486–90. Wehler's general view is shared in Hajo Holborn, *A History of Modern Germany, 1840–1945* (New York: Alfred A. Knopf, 1969), and somewhat less forcefully in Gordon A. Craig, *Germany, 1866–1945* (Oxford: Oxford University Press, 1978). For a more recent example see Katherine Anne Lerman, "Bismarckian Germany," in *Imperial Germany, 1871–1918*, ed. James Retallack (Oxford: Oxford University Press, 2008), 18–39.

For a discussion of the critiques of Wehler's thesis see the extended discussion in Arne Perras, "Colonial Agitation and the Bismarckian State: The Case of Carl Peters," in *Wilhelminism and Its Legacies: German Modernities, Imperialism, and the Meanings of Reform, 1890–1930*, ed. Geoff Eley and James Retallack (New York: Berghahn Books, 2003), 155–7.

25 Bowersox, *Raising Germans in the Age of Empire*, 6.

26 Conrad, *German Colonialism*, 185. Mark Hewitson has disputed the breadth of Conrad's argument on this subject, arguing that Germans held the wider world at arm's length and injecting a dose of scepticism into the discussion about Germans' "globality." See Mark Hewitson, *Germany and the Modern World, 1880–1914* (Cambridge, UK: Cambridge University Press, 2018), esp. 3–4, 9–16, and 31.

27 Thorsten Altena, *"Ein Häuflein Christen mitten in der Heidenwelt des dunklen Erdteils": Zum Selbst- und Fremdverständnis protestantischer Missionare im kolonialen Afrika 1884-1918* (Münster: Waxmann Verlag, 2003); Sebastian Conrad, *Globalisierung und Nation im Deutschen Kaiserreich* (Munich: C.H. Beck, 2006); Horst Gründer, *Welteroberung und Christentum: Ein Handbuch zur Geschichte der Neuzeit* (Gütersloh: Gütersloher Verlag–Haus Mohn, 1992); Sara Pugach, *Africa in Translation: A History of Colonial Linguistics in Germany and Beyond, 1814–1945* (Ann Arbor: University of Michigan Press, 2012). Beyond Germany, the scholarship on anglophonic missions

takes this representation of missionary colonialism even further. For examples, see Hilary M. Carey, *God's Empire: Religion and Colonialism in the British World, c. 1801–1908* (Cambridge, UK: Cambridge University Press, 2011); Jeffrey Cox, *The British Missionary Enterprise since 1700* (New York: Routledge, 2008); Norman Etherington, ed., *Missions and Empire* (Oxford: Oxford University Press, 2005); Andrew Porter, *Religion versus Empire? British Protestant Missionaries and Overseas Expansion, 1700–1914* (Manchester: Manchester University Press, 2004); and Richard Price, *Making Empire: Colonial Encounters and the Creation of Imperial Rule in Nineteenth-Century Africa* (Cambridge, UK: Cambridge University Press, 2008).

28 Some examples of this perspective: Lara Day and Oliver Haag, Introduction, in *The Persistence of Race: Continuity and Change in Germany from the Wilhelmine Empire to National Socialism*, edited by Day and Haag (New York: Berghahn, 2017), 2; Cristin Ellis, *Antebellum Posthuman: Race and Materiality in the Mid-Nineteenth Century* (New York: Fordham University Press, 2018); A. Dirk Moses, "Conceptual Blockages and Definitional Dilemmas in the 'Racial Century': Genocides of Indigenous Peoples and the Holocaust," *Patterns of Prejudice* 36(2002): 7–36; Bruce Nelson, *Irish Nationalists and the Making of the Irish Race* (Princeton, NJ: Princeton University Press, 2012); Helmut Walser Smith, *The Continuities of German History: Nation, Religion, and Race across the Long Nineteenth Century* (Cambridge, UK: Cambridge University Press, 2008); Heather Streets, *Martial Races: The Military, Race, and Masculinity in British Imperial Culture, 1857–1914* (Manchester, UK: Manchester University Press, 2004); and Eric Weitz, *A Century of Genocide: Utopias of Race and Nation* (Princeton, NJ: Princeton University Press, 2005), esp. 16–52.

29 Wolter, *Die Vermarktung des Fremden*, 21.

30 The racialized German terms *Neger* or *Schwarzer* (Black) were occasionally used by missionaries, but they were far more likely to use the more racially neutral term *Eingeborener* (Native). In the context of this debate, the missionaries conformed to the usages of the economic colonialists and consistently used the racialized *Neger*, though they rarely used it in most other contexts. For more on this issue see chapter 3.

1 Preach the Gospel to All Creation

1 The Great Commission appears in Matthew 28:16–20; Mark 16:14–18; Luke 42:44–9; John 20:19–23; and Acts 1:4–8. All passages from the New Testament and Hebrew Bible are taken from *The New Oxford Annotated Bible: New Revised Standard Version with the Apocrypha*, 5th ed. (Oxford, UK: Oxford University Press, 2018).

2 Introduction, Martin H. Geyer and Johannes Paulmann, eds., *The Mechanics of Internationalism: Culture, Society, and Politics from the 1840s to the First World War* (Oxford, UK: Oxford University Press, 2001), 3.
3 Daniel Gorman, *International Cooperation in the Early Twentieth Century* (London: Bloomsbury Academic, 2017), 35.
4 Catholic Missionswissenschaft was much slower to organize as a professional discipline in Germany. The academic advent of Catholic mission studies in Germany is dated to the launch by Josef Schmidlin of the *Zeitschrift für Missionswissenschaft* in 1913. See Horst Rzepkowski, "Gustav Warneck und die katholische Missionswissenschaft," in *Es began in Halle … Missionswissenschaft von Gustav Warneck bis heute*, ed. Dieter Becker and Andreas Feldtkeller (Erlangen: Verlag der Ev.-Luth. Mission, 1997), 55–86.
5 Hans-Werner Gensichen, "Fabri, Friedrich," in *Biographical Dictionary of Christian Missions*, ed. Gerald H. Anderson (New York: Macmillan Reference USA, 1998), 207.
6 Conrad, *German Colonialism*, 50–3. On the Askari see Michelle R. Moyd, *Violent Intermediaries: African Soldiers, Conquest, and Everyday Colonialism in German East Africa* (Athens: Ohio University Press, 2014).
7 Daniel Jeyaraj, "Mission Reports from South India and Their Impact on the Western Mind: The Tranquebar Mission of the Eighteenth Century," in *Converting Colonialism: Visions and Realities in Mission History, 1706–1914*, ed. Dana Robert (Grand Rapids, MI: William B. Eerdmans Publishing Company, 2008), 22–3.
8 Porter, *Religion versus Empire?*, 29.
9 William Carey, *An Enquiry Into the Obligations of Christians, to Use Means for the Conversion of the Heathens in Which the Religious State of the Different Nations of the World, the Success of Former Undertakings, and the Practicability of Further Undertakings, Are Considered* (Leicester: 1792).
10 Cox, *The British Missionary Enterprise since 1700*, 70; Porter, *Religion versus Empire?*, 40; Bernd Holtwick, "Licht und Schatten: Begründungen und Zielsetzungen des protestantischen missionarischen Aufbruchs im frühen 19. Jahrhundert," in *Weltmission und religiöse Organisationen: Protestantische Missionsgesellschaften im 19. und 20. Jahrhundert*, ed. Artur Bogner, Bernd Holtwick, and Hartmann Tyrell (Würzburg: Ergon Verlag, 2004), 225.
11 Of the fifteen missionaries recruited by the Church Missionary Society between 1804 and 1813, only three were English-speaking. Porter, *Religion versus Empire?*, 56.
12 Two additional mission societies, the Neukirchen and Schleswig-Holstein Mission Societies, began their work very late in the colonial period in German East Africa and never achieved any significance before the First

World War. See Majida Hamilton, *Mission im kolonialen Umfeld: Deutsche protestantische Missionsgesellschaften in Deutsch-Ostafrika* (Göttingen: Universitätsverlag Göttingen, 2009), 14n26.

13 Also known as Lake Malawi. In this work I have adopted the name that is used in Tanzania and that was in use during the period of German colonial activity.

14 John Iliffe, *A Modern History of Tanganyika* (Cambridge, UK: Cambridge University Press, 1979), 217.

15 Marcia Wright, *German Missions in Tanganyika 1891–1941: Lutherans and Moravians in the Southern Highlands* (Oxford: Oxford University Press, 1971), 9–10.

16 Christopher M. Clark, *The Politics of Conversion: Missionary Protestantism and the Jews in Prussia, 1728–1941* (Oxford: Clarendon Press, 1995), 214–15; Gerhard Ruhbach, "Die Religionspolitik Friedrich Wilhelms III. von Preußen," in *Bleibendes im Wandel der Kirchengeschichte: Kirchenhistorische Studien*, ed. Bernd Moeller and Gerhard Ruhbach (Tübingen: J.C.B. Mohr (Paul Siebeck), 1973), 307–30.

17 Wright, *German Missions in Tanganyika, 1891–1941*, 14.

18 Paul Fleisch, *Hundert Jahre lutherischer Mission* (Leipzig: Verlag der Evangelisch-lutherischen Mission, 1936), 3. Initially the mission society was the *Evangelisch-Lutherische Missionsgesellschaft zu Dresden* (Dresden Mission Society, 1832) but it was renamed the *Evangelisch-Lutherische Missionsgesellscafht zu Leipzig* (Leipzig Mission Society) in 1848, when the society relocated to that city.

19 Thorsten Altena, "Grenzüberschreitungen: Zum Beziehungsgeflecht von Innerer und Äußerer Mission in den Anfangsjahren der Bethel-Mission," in Matthias Benad and Vicco von Büllow, eds., *Bethels Mission (3): Mutterhaus, Mission und Pflege* (Bielefeld, Germany: Luther-Verlag, 2003), 151; Thorsten Altena, "Missionare und einheimische Gesellschaft: Zur Kulturbegegnung der Bethel-Mission in Deutsch-Ostafrika 1890–1916," in Matthias Benad, ed., *Bethels Mission (1): Zwischen Epileptischenpflege und Heidenbekehrung* (Bielefeld, Germany: Luther-Verlag, 2001), 7.

20 Artur Bogner, "Zur Entwicklung der Berliner Mission als Bürokratisierungsprozess," in Bogner, Holtwick, and Tyrell, *Weltmission und religiöse Organisationen*, 315.

21 Thorsten Altena, "Missionare und einheimische Gesellschaft: Zur Kulturbegegnung der Bethel-Mission in Deutsch-Ostafrika 1890–1916," in Benad, *Bethels Mission (1)*, 7; Gustav Menzel, *Die Bethel-Mission: Aus 100 Jahren Missionsgeschichte* (Neukirchen-Vluyn, Germany: Neukirchener Verlag des Erziehungsvereins, 1986), 45. For a short biography of Friedrich von Bodelschwingh see Hans-Walter Schmuhl, *Friedrich von Bodelschwingh* (Reinbek bei Hamburg: Rowohlt Verlag, 2005).

22 Thorsten Altena, "'Brüder' und 'Väter im Herrn': Notizen zum inneren Machtgefüge protestantischer deutschsprachiger Missionsgesellschaften 1884–1918," in *Mission und Macht im Wandel politischer Orientierungen: Europäische Missionsgesellschaften in politischen Spannungsfeldern in Afrika und Asien zwischen 1800 und 1945*, ed. Ulrich van der Heyden und Holger Stoecker (Stuttgart: Franz Steiner, 2005), 68.
23 Hans-Joachim Niesel, "Kolonialverwaltung und Missionen in Deutsch-Ostafrika 1890–1914" (PhD. diss., Freie Universität Berlin, 1971), 54.
24 Niesel, "Kolonialverwaltung und Missionen in Deutsch-Ostafrika 1890–1914," 31n9.
25 Fleisch, *Hundert Jahre lutherischer Mission*, 168–9.
26 Wright, *German Missions in Tanganyika 1891–1941*, 15.
27 Wolfgang Gabbert, "Phasen und Grundprobleme protestantischer Mission im kolonialen Afrika – die Brüdergemeine bei den Nyakyusa in Tansania," in Bogner, Holtwick, and Tyrell, *Weltmission und religiöse Organisationen*, 520–1; Altena, "'Brüder' und 'Väter im Herrn'," 61.
28 Wright, *German Missions in Tanganyika, 1891–1941*, 12.
29 Altena, *"Ein Häuflein Christen mitten in der Heidenwelt des dunklen Erdteils,"* 19; Fleisch, *Hundert Jahre lutherischer Mission*, 6.
30 Clark, *The Politics of Conversion*, 227; Verhandlungen über die vom Abgeordnetenhaus gestrichenen 500 Taler (5 January 1870), BMW/bmw1/1134; Kaiser Wilhelm II to Karl Jacobi and Otto Bismarck (21 July 1888), GStAPK, I. HA Rep. 89 Zivilkabinett, Nr. 23572, Bl. 115.
31 Hartmut Pogge von Strandmann, "The Kolonialrat and the Missionary Societies," in van der Heyden and Stoecker, *Mission und Macht im Wandel politischer Orientierungen*, 44.
32 Menzel, *Die Bethel-Mission*, 14–19; Horst Gründer, "Deutsche Missionsgesellschaft auf dem Wege zur Kolonialmission," in *Imperialismus und Kolonialmission: Kaiserliches Deutschland und koloniales Imperium*, 2nd ed., ed. Klaus Bade (Wiesbaden: Steiner, 1984), 76.
33 Altena, *"Ein Häuflein Christen mitten in der Heidenwelt des dunklen Erdteils,"* 55.
34 William Richey Hogg, *Ecumenical Foundations: A History of the International Missionary Council and Its Nineteenth-Century Background* (New York: Harper & Brothers, 1952), 70–3.
35 Gustav Warneck, "Dic cur hic? Unser Programm," *AMZ* 1(1874): 1–4. Warneck's hope to ensnare the educated rode upon a general wave of interest in German scholarship in the non-Western world, one which eventually led to the independence of Religionswissenschaft from theology; see Zachary Purvis, *Theology and the University in Nineteenth-Century Germany* (Oxford, UK: Oxford University Press, 2016), 222.

36 Carine Dujardin, "Mission Research Revised: Missiology as a Project of Modernity and a Contemporary Form of Apologetics," in *Mission and Science: Missiology Revised/Missiologie Revisitée, 1850–1940*, ed. Carine Dujardin and Claude Prudhomme (Leuven: Leuven University Press, 2015), 20–1; Marc Spindler, "The Protestant Mission Study: Emergence and Features," in Dujardin and Prudhomme, *Mission and Science*, 48.

37 Editor's Note to E[rnst] Reichel, "Was haben wir zu thun, damit die deutsche Kolonialpolitik nicht zur Schädigung, sondern zur Förderung der Mission ausschlage?" *AMZ* 13(1886): 39n2.

38 Jeremy Best, "The *Allgemeine Missions-Zeitschrift* and Missionary Nationalism: Science for Mission and Empire," in Jensz and Acke, *Missions and Media*, 57–76.

39 Price, *Making Empire*, 94.

40 This is notably different from contemporary British mission ideology, which, at least in East Africa, argued that commerce and the work of "unofficial empire" were part and parcel of the project of evangelizing indigenous people. See Dana L. Robert, Introduction to *Converting Colonialism*, 11–12.

41 Altena, "*Ein Häuflein Christen mitten in der Heidenwelt des dunklen Erdteils*," 917–18. Gunther Pakendorf, "Berlin in Afrika, oder der historische Ort der deutschen Mission," in *Kolonien und Missionen: Referate des 3. Internationalen Kolonialgeschichtlichen Symposiums 1993 in Bremen*, ed. Wilfried Wagner (Münster: Lit, 1994), 473–5. Werner Ustorf discusses how the old trading houses of the Hanseatic cities of northern Germany joined with mission against the threat of "big capital" during the period of high imperialism, Werner Ustorf, ed., *Mission im Kontext: Beiträge zur Sozialgeschichte der Norddeutschen Missionsgesellschaft im 19. Jahrhundert* (Bremen: Übersee Museum Bremen, 1986), 23.

42 For a brief treatment of German mission periodicals see Peter Scheulen, *Die "Eingeborenen" Deutsch-Südwestafrika: Ihr Bild in deutschen Kolonialzeitschricten von 1884 bis 1918* (Cologne: Rüdiger Köppe Verlag, 1998), 44–5.

43 On the metaphorical bookshelf of all nineteenth-century German missionary published materials, the monthly or quarterly society reports put out by every mission society take up the by far the largest amount of space. These mission society reports usually printed edited and redacted excerpts from the regular reports of their missionaries in the field. The *AMZ* frequently included examples of these reports in its pages. This was similar to the case of British mission periodicals. See Cox, *The British Missionary Enterprise since 1700*, 112 and 114–45; and Terry Barringer, "What Mrs. Jellyby Might Have Read: Missionary Periodicals,

A Neglected Source," *Victorian Periodicals Review* 37, no. 4 (Winter 2004): 46–74.

44 Joachim Kirchner, *Das deutsche Zeitschriftenwesen: Seine Geschichte und seine Probleme*, vol. 2 (Wiesbaden: Otto Harrassowitz, 1962), 278. The 1912 number appears in *Sperlings Zeitschriften-Addressbuch*, 1912, s.v. "Missions-Zeitschrift, Allgemeine."

45 How receptive the intellectual elite of the Kaiserreich was can be inferred from the influence of "cultural diplomacy" when German thinkers sought a way out of Germany's "encirclement" by converting the military and diplomatic contest between the great powers into a cultural contest or by promoting international cooperation. See Rüdiger von Bruch, *Weltpolitik als Kulturmission: Auswärtive Kulturpolitik und Bildungsbürgertum in Deutschland am Vorabend des Ersten Weltkrieges* (Paderborn: Ferdinand Schöningh, 1982).

46 August Hermann Francke, "Die sprachlichen Verhältnisse der Himalayamission der Brüdergemeine," *AMZ* 25(1898): 439–46.

47 [Johann Friedrich] Iken, "Die Missionsthätigkeit des Hamburg-Bremischen Erzbistums im Mittelalter," *AMZ* 19(1892): 145–59, 221–34, 278–89, and 511–29.

48 Matthew Unangst, "Men of Science and Action: The Celebrity of Explorers and German National Identity, 1870–1895," *Central European History* 50(2017), 316.

49 William Richey Hogg, "The Rise of Protestant Missionary Concern, 1517–1914," in *The Theology of the Christian Mission*, ed. Gerald H. Anderson (New York: McGraw-Hill Book Company, 1961), 109. On the quality of missionary knowledge see, for example, Harald Sippel, "Mission und Kodifikation: Der missionarische Beitrag zur Erforschung des afrikanischen Gewohnheitsrechts in der Kolonie Deutsch-Ostafrika," in Wagner, *Kolonien und Missionen*, 493–510.

50 Hans Kasdorf, "Zu Gustav Warnecks Bedeutung für Theologie und Kirche (unter besonderer Berücksichtigung der Missionskonferenzen) in Becker and Feldtkeller, *Es begann in Halle …*, 12.

51 Hans Kasdorf, "The Legacy of Gustav Warneck," *International Bulletin of Mission Research* 4, no. 3 (July 1980): 102–7.

52 Friedrich Fabri, *Bedarf Deutschland der Kolonien? Eine politisch-ökonomische Betrachtung* (Gotha: F.A. Perthes, 1879).

53 Klaus J. Bade, *Friedrich Fabri und der Imperialismus in der Bismarckzeit: Revolution – Depression – Expansion* (Freiburg: Atlantis Verlag, 1975), 314. See also Bade, ed., *Imperialismus und Kolonialmission: Kaiserliche Deutschland und kolonialer Imperium*, 2nd ed. (Wiesbaden: Steiner, 1984). Other notable works on Fabri include Wolfgang R. Schmidt, *Mission, Kirche und Reich Gottes bei Friedrich Fabri* (Wuppertal-Barmen: Verlag der Rheinischen Mission, 1965).

54 Nils Ole Oermann, *Mission, Church, and State Relations in South-West Africa under German Rule, 1884–1915* (Stuttgart: Franz Steiner Verlag, 1999), 35.
55 Bade, *Friedrich Fabri und der Imperialismus in der Bismarckzeit*, 221–31; Heinrich Loth, *Zwischen Gott und Kattun: Der Berliner Konferenz 1884/85 zur Aufteilung Afrikas und die Kolonialismuskritik christlicher Mission* (Berlin: Union Verlag, 1985), 20–1; Menzel, *Die Bethel-Mission*, 11–12.
56 Suzanne Marchand and David Lindenfeld have proposed 1905 as a "turning point" in the cultural history of Germany. In either case, scholars seem to agree that the decades of Wilhelm II's rule were distinct from those of Bismarck's chancellorship. Suzanne Marchand and David Lindenfeld, "Germany at the Fin de Siècle: An Introduction," in *Germany at the Fin de Siècle: Culture, Politics, and Ideas*, ed. Marchand and Lindenfeld (Washington, DC: German Historical Institute and Cambridge University Press, 2009), 16–17. For an argument for 1900 as the "turning point" see the collected essays in Volker Drehsen and Walter Sparn, eds., *Vom Weltbildwandel zur Weltanschauungsanalyse: Krisenwahrnehmung und Krisenbewältigung um 1900* (Berlin: Akademie Verlag, 1996).
57 Mark Hewitson, "Wilhelmine Germany," in Retallack, *Imperial Germany 1871–1918*, 41; Marchand and Lindenfeld, *Germany at the Fin de Siècle*, 3.
58 Matthew Jefferies, *Contesting the German Empire, 1871–1918* (Malden, MA: Blackwell Publishing, 2008), 167.
59 Gustav Warneck, "Missionsmotiv und Missionsaufgabe nach der modernen religionsgeschichtlichen Schule," *AMZ* 34(1907): 3, cited in Ulrich Berner, "Religionsgeschichtliche und Mission: Zur Kontroverse zwischen Ernst Troeltsch und Gustav Warneck," in Drehsen and Sparn, *Vom Weltbildwandel zur Weltanschauungsanalyse*, 109.
60 E[rnst] Reichel, "Was haben wir zu thun, damit die deutsche Kolonialpolitik nicht zur Schädigung, sondern zur Förderung der Mission ausschlage?" *AMZ* 13(1886): 40–2.
61 Reichel, "Was haben wir zu thun, ..." 42–4.
62 [Gustav] Warneck, "Die Aufgabe der Heidenmission und ihre Trübungen in der Gegenwart," *AMZ* 18(1891): 99–111.
63 Warneck, "Die Aufgabe der Heidenmission," 101.
64 F[ranz] M[ichael] Zahn, "Nationalität und Internationalität in der Mission," *AMZ* 23(1896): 62.
65 Zahn, "Nationalität und Internationalität in der Mission," 49–52.
66 Zahn, "Nationalität und Internationalität in der Mission," 54–5.
67 [Gustav] Warneck, "Die christliche Mission und die überseeische Politik," *AMZ* 28(1901): 169.
68 Gustav] Warneck, "Der französische Nationalismus und die Mission," *AMZ* 14(1887): 274.
69 Reichel, "Was haben wir zu thun, ..." 52–3.

70 Warneck, "Die Aufgabe der Heidenmission," 97–9.
71 Warneck, "Die Aufgabe der Heidenmission," 123–4.
72 See chapter 3 of this book.
73 Reichel, "Was haben wir zu thun, ..." 45–9.
74 Reichel, "Was haben wir zu thun, ..." 45.
75 Konrad Canis, *Von Bismarck zur Weltpolitik: Deutsche Außenpolitik 1890 bis 1902* (Berlin: Akademie, 1997), 12, and 223–30.
76 Woodruff D. Smith, *The German Colonial Empire* (Chapel Hill: University of North Carolina Press, 1978), 12–13 and 174–5.
77 Jefferies, *Contesting the German Empire, 1871–1918*, 168.
78 An die evangelischen Christen deutscher Zunge (17 May [1901/02]), BMW/bmw1/2018.
79 The balance of power shifted again after the First World War as German missionaries found themselves weaker than their Chinese congregations; see Albert Monshan Wu, "The Quest for an 'Indigenous Church': German Missionaries, Chinese Christians, and the Indigenization Debates of the 1920s," *American Historical Review* 122(1 Feb. 2017): 85–114.
80 Warneck, *Outline of a History of Protestant Missions*, 299. See also Gustav Warneck, *Die chinesische Mission im Gerichte der deutschen Zeitungspresse*, 3rd ed. (Berlin: Martin Warneck, 1900). With thanks to Albert Wu for the reference.
81 Ute Wielandt and Michael Kaschner, "Die Reichstagdebatten über den deutschen Kriegseinsatz in China: August Bebel und die 'Hunnenbriefe,'" in *Das deutsche Reich und der Boxeraufstand*, ed. Susanne Kuß and Bernd Martin (Munich: Iudicium, 2002), 183.
82 Warneck, "Die christliche Mission und die überseeische Politik," 161–3.
83 Warneck, "Die christliche Mission und die überseeische Politik," 169.
84 Warneck, "Die christliche Mission und die überseeische Politik," 179–80. Colonial administrators at different times shared this same fear; see Andrew Burton, *African Underclass: Urbanisation, Crime and Colonial Order in Dar es Salaam* (Athens: Ohio University Press, 2003), 19.
85 Carl Mirbt, "Die innere Berechtigung und Kraft des Christentums zur Weltmission," *AMZ* 33(1906): 446.
86 Suzanne L. Marchand, *German Orientalism in the Age of Empire: Religion, Race, and Scholarship* (Washington, DC: German Historical Institute and Cambridge University Press, 2009), 270–1, 276–7; Marchand emphasizes how unlikely mass conversion to Buddhism was in Germany.
87 Marchand, *German Orientalism in the Age of Empire*, 375.
88 Mirbt, "Die innere Berechtigung und Kraft," 448–50.
89 Warneck, "Die Mission im Schatten des Weltverkehrs," *AMZ* 35(1908): 9–10.
90 Warneck, "Die Mission im Schatten des Weltverkehrs," 3.

91 Warneck, "Die Mission im Schatten des Weltverkehrs," 4–6.
92 Warneck, "Die Mission im Schatten des Weltverkehrs," 6–8.
93 Warneck, "Die Mission im Schatten des Weltverkehrs," 12–13.
94 Niesel, "Kolonialverwaltung und Missionen in Deutsch-Ostafrika 1890–1914," 289.
95 On Berlin as a colonial, metropolitan city see Ulrich van der Heyden and Joachim Zeller, eds., *Kolonialmetropole Berlin: Eine Spurensuche* (Berlin: Berlin Edition, 2002).
96 Sibylle Benninghoff-Lühl, *Deutsche Kolonialromane 1884–1914 in ihrem Entstehungs- und Wirkungszussammenhang* (Bremen: Übersee-Museum, 1983), 37–8; Bowersox, *Raising Germans in the Age of Empire*, 15 and 140; Ciarlo, *Advertising Empire*, 266–77; Short, *Magic Lantern Empire*, 132–47.
97 Karl Axenfeld, "Weltevangelisation und Ende," *AMZ* 38(1911): 253.
98 Axenfeld, "Weltevangelisation und Ende," 253–4. On the role of technology in the expansion of European imperial capabilities and territorial control, see Daniel R. Headrick, *The Tools of Empire: Technology and European Imperialism in the Nineteenth Century* (Oxford: Oxford University Press, 1981).
99 Axenfeld, "Weltevangelisation und Ende," 259.
100 Julius Richter, "Weltfriede und Weltmission," *AMZ* 41(1914): 4.
101 Richter, "Weltfriede und Weltmission," 5–6.
102 Richter, "Weltfriede und Weltmission," 7.

2 Speaking in Tongues

1 Acts 2:1–12.
2 Mark 16:17; Acts 10: 46; Acts 19:6; 1 Corinthians 12–14; Romans 8:26; Jude 20.
3 To this day, Pentecost remains a holiday for mission donations in many Protestant churches.
4 Genesis 11:1–9.
5 Birgit Meyer, *Translating the Devil: Religion and Modernity among the Ewe in Ghana* (Trenton, NJ: Africa World Press, 1999), 57.
6 See chapter 1.
7 Tuska Benes, *In Babel's Shadow: Language, Philology, and the Nation in Nineteenth-Century Germany* (Detroit: Wayne State University Press, 2008), 21, 294.
8 Gustav Warneck, "Die Bedeutung der Muttersprache für die Mission," from *Der Betrieb der Sendung* cited in *Nachrichten aus der ostafrikanischen Mission* 11(1), 1–2.
9 Pugach, *Africa in Translation*, 29.

10 See Lora Wildenthal, *German Women for Empire, 1884–1945* (Durham, NC: Duke University Press, 2001), and, particularly on German Southwest Africa, Adam A. Blackler, "An Imperial Homeland: Forging German Identity in Southwest Africa" (unpublished manuscript, 29 October 2019), digital file.

11 Johanna Eggert, "The School Policy of the German Protestant Missions in Tanzania before the First World War," in *Missionary Ideologies in the Imperialist Era: 1880–1929*, ed. Torben Christensen and William R. Hutchison (Aarhus: Forlaget Aros, 1982), 201; Edward Graham Norris, *Die Umerziehung des Afrikaners: Togo 1895–1938* (Munich: Trickster Wissenschaft, 1993), 81. See also Johanna Eggert, *Missionsschule und sozialer Wandel in Ostafrika: Der Beitrag der deutschen evangelischen Missionsgesellschaften zur Entwicklung des Schulwesens in Tanganyika 1891–1939* (Bielefed: Bertelsmann Universitätsverlag, 1970).

12 Cox, *The British Missionary Enterprise since 1700*, 14.

13 Alice L. Conklin, *A Mission to Civilize: The Republican Idea of Empire in France and West Africa, 1895–1930* (Stanford, CA: Stanford University Press, 1997).

14 John 1:1. The theological and philosophical interpretations of this line are rich, ranging from discussions of Christian usages of Greek philosophy to theological developments of the Trinitarian theology; Harold W. Attridge, *Oxford Encylopedia of the Bible and Theology*, s.v. "Word (Logos)" (Oxford, UK: Oxford University Press, 2015).

15 Charles W. Forman, "Missions in Papua New Guinea," in Christensen and Hutchison, *Missionary Ideologies in the Imperialist Era*, 26–7.

16 This view developed most strongly among members of the *Allgemeiner Evangelisch-Protestantischer Missionsverein* that was active in China. The prominent theologian Ernst Troeltsch offered one version of this in "Missionsmotiv, Missionsaufgabe und neuzeitliches Humanitätschristentum," *Zeitschrift für Missionswissenschaft und Religionswissenschaft* (1907): 129–39 and 161–6; see Heinrich Balz, "'Überwindung der Religionen' und das Ziel der Mission: Diskussion zwischen G. Warneck und E. Troeltsch 1906–1908," in Becker and Feldtkeller, *Es begann in Halle…*, 109.

17 H. Glenn Penny, *Objects of Culture: Ethnology and Ethnographic Museums in Imperial Germany* (Chapel Hill: University of North Carolina Press, 2002), 23.

18 Wolfgang Hardtwig, "Vom Elitebewußtsein zur Massenbewegung: Frühformen des Nationalismus in Deutschland 1500–1840," in Wolfgang Hardtwig, *Nationalismus und Bürgerkultur in Deutschland 1500–1914: Ausgewählte Aufsätze* (Göttingen: Vandenhoeck & Ruprecht, 1994), 38.

19 Stefan Berger, *Inventing the Nation: Germany* (London: Arnold, 2006), 18–19. Also see chapter 3 of this book.

20 On German state-building projects and their relationship to nationalism as a movement, see Abigail Green, *Fatherlands: State-Building and Nationhood in Nineteenth-Century Germany* (Cambridge, UK: Cambridge University Press, 2001).

21 Berger, *Inventing the Nation*, 26–8. Herder did not necessarily assume that Germany's national identity was strictly Protestant or Christian; see George S. Williamson, *The Longing for Myth in Germany: Religion and Aesthetic Culture from Romanticism to Nietzsche* (Chicago: University of Chicago Press, 2004), esp. 72–120.

22 These conversations proved especially germane with regard to the German-speaking populations of southern Brazil. See Glen S. Goodman, "From German Danger' to German-Brazilian President: Immigration, Ethnicity, and the Making of Brazilian Identities, 1924–1974" (PhD diss., Emory University, 2015), 144–9; and Frederik Schulze, *Auswanderung als nationalistisches Projekt: Deutschtum und Kolonialdiskurse im südlichen Brasilien (1824–1941)* (Cologne: Böhlau Verlag, 2016), 47–8.

23 They did, however, insist that fluency in German was necessary for political participation by linguistic minorities. Brian Vick, *Defining Germany: The 1848 Frankfurt Parliamentarians and National Identity* (Cambridge, MA: Harvard University Press, 2002), 119–28.

24 Benes, *In Babel's Shadow*, 11 and 21.

25 Hans-Werner Gensichen, "German Protestant Missions" in Christensen and Hutchison, *Missionary Ideologies in the Imperialist Era*, 182.

26 Birgit Meyer, "Christianity and the Ewe Nation: German Pietist Missionaries, Ewe Converts and the Politics of Culture," *Journal of Religion in Africa* 32(2): 167–99. Another critique of the Basel Mission's methods can be found in Jonas N. Dah, *Missionary Motivations and Methods: A Critical Examination of the Basel Mission in Cameroon, 1886–1914* (Basel: Basel Mission, 1983).

27 Erin R. Hochman, *Imagining a Greater Germany: Republican Nationalism and the Idea of Anschluss* (Ithaca, NY: Cornell University Press, 2016), 2–4.

28 Stefan Berger, *The Search for Normality: National Identity and Historical Consciousness in Germany since 1800* (Providence, RI: Berghahn Books, 1997), 22.

29 This term was also used by conservative Christian populists like Adolf Stöcker and Reinhold Mumm to refer to an idealized union of church and people in contemporary Germany. See Gangolf Hübinger, *Kulturprotestantismus und Politik*, 301; and Thomas Nipperdey, *Religion im Umbruch*, 90–5, 108.

30 Friedrich Fabri, ever outside the missionary majority, believed the *Volkskirche* concept to be mistaken and argued against it during his time as a leader of the Rhenish Mission Society. See Gerhard Besier, "Mission and Colonialism in Friedrich Fabri's (1824–1891) Thinking," in Christensen and Hutchison, *Missionary Ideologies*, 90.

31 Benes, *In Babel's Shadow*, 294.

32 Karl Rennstich, "The Understanding of Mission, Civilization and Colonialism in the Basel Mission," in Christensen and Hutchison, *Missionary Ideologies in the Imperialist Era*, 97.

33 Arthur J. Knoll, *Togo under Imperial Germany, 1884–1914: A Case Study in Colonial Rule* (Stanford, CA: Hoover Institution Press, 1978), 98–9; Rainer Tetzlaff, "Die Mission im Spannungsfeld zwischen kolonialer Herrschaft und Zivilisierungsanspruch in Deutsch-Ostafrika," in Bade, *Imperialismus und Kolonialmission*, 195.

34 Niesel, "Kolonialverwaltung und Missionen in Deutsch-Ostafrika 1890–1914," 237. Warneck, unsurprisingly, conflated Christianity with cultural superiority. See, Ulrich Berner, "Religionsgeschichte und Mission: Zur Kontroverse zwischen Ernst Troeltsch und Gustav Warneck," in Drehsen and Sparn, *Vom Weltbildwandel zur Weltanschauungsanalyse*, 106 and 110.

35 For one among many examples of African constructions of ethnicity, see Charles H. Ambler, "The Renovation of Custom in Colonial Kenya: The 1932 Generation Succession Ceremonies in Embu," *Journal of African History* 30(1): 139–56.

36 Jean Comaroff and John L. Comaroff, *Of Revelation and Revolution*, 2 vols. (Chicago: University of Chicago Press, 1991–1997).

37 In fact, Edward Graham Norris has argued that the educational project of missionaries was explicitly one of "deculturation." Norris's assessment places the missions completely under the sway of other colonial interests; these colonial interests, however, were far less important to how missionaries formulated their views of Africans and education than Norris suggests. Norris, *Die Umerziehung des Afrikaners*, 86–9.

38 Terence Ranger, "The Invention of Tradition in Colonial Africa," in *The Invention of Tradition*, ed. Eric Hobsbawm and Terence Ranger (Cambridge, UK: Cambridge University Press, 1983), 247–9. On the "tribalization" of Tanzania see Jan-Georg Deutsch, "Vom Bezirksamtmann zum Mehrparteiensystem – Transformationen politischer Herrschaft im kolonialen und nachkolonialen Tanzania," in van der Heyden and von Oppen, *Tanzania: Koloniale Vergangenheit und neuer Aufbruch*, 24.

39 C[arl] Meinhof, "Das missionarische Sprachproblem," *AMZ* 33(1906): 208. Meinhof may have supported the use of African vernacular in some places, but he was also a strong nationalist whose nationalism grew

stronger with time. He also helped shape African linguistic studies into a discipline strongly influenced by racial theory. See Pugach, *Africa in Translation*, 88–9.

40 F[ranz] M[ichael] Zahn, "Die Muttersprache in der Mission," *AMZ* 22(1895): 337–8.

41 Meinhof, "Das missionarische Sprachproblem," 210.

42 Zahn, "Die Muttersprache," 339.

43 Zahn, "Die Muttersprache," 342.

44 Zahn, "Die Muttersprache," 352–3.

45 Zahn, "Die Muttersprache," 356–60.

46 Lamin Sanneh, *West African Christianity: The Religious Impact* (Maryknoll, NY: Orbis Books, 1983), 118.

47 Hermann Petrich, *Allerlei Schulbilder aus der Mission in den deutschen Kolonien*, Neue Missionsschriften Nr. 81 (Berlin: Buchhandlung der Berliner evangelischen Missionsgesellschaft, 1906), 3–4; Sanneh, *West African Christianity*, 118–19.

48 This is a reference by the author of the article, Friedrich Würz, to the Rhenish Mission Society's work among the various peoples of Northern Sumatra with whom German missionaries had been working since 1861. He uses this as an example to support his larger point about the utility of indigenous teachers to missionary work. Of course, this also reflects the role that missionaries played in the creation of ethnicities in colonized areas.

49 Würz, "Die Arbeiterfrage in der Mission," *AMZ* 36(1909): 217.

50 [Alexander] Merensky, "Die Mission der Anwalt der Eingeborenen," *AMZ* 29(1902): 166. For Merensky's intellectual biography see Ulrich van der Heyden, "Alexander Merenskys Beitrag zur ethnographischen und historischen Erforschung der Völkerschaften Südafrikas," *Ethnographisch-Archäologische Zeitschrift* 32(1991): 263–8.

51 Richter, "Mission und Kolonialpolitik," 53.

52 On schools in Prussia and the German Empire before 1918 see Andrew Donson, *Youth in the Fatherless Land: War Pedagogy, Nationalism, and Authority in Germany, 1914–1918* (Cambridge, MA: Harvard University Press, 2010); Ulrich Herrmann, "Pädagogisches Denken und Anfänge der Reformpädogogik," in *Handbuch der deutschen Bildungsgeschichte*, vol. 4, ed. Christa Berg (Munich: Verlag C.H. Beck, 1991); and Marjorie Lamberti, *State, Society, and the Elementary School in Imperial Germany* (Oxford: Oxford University Press, 1989). For specifics of the subjects taught in Prussian and other German primary schools see the tables in Herrmann, "Pädogogisches Denken," 217–27.

53 *Denkschrift des Ausschusses der deutschen evangelischen Missionsgesellschaften, betreffend das Missionschulwesen, insbesondern den Unterricht in fremden*

Sprachen in den Missionsschulen (11 November 1897), BArch R 1001/1.19, Film Nr. 80478, Bd. 6902, pag. 7–9.

54 [Alexander] Merensky, *Deutschlands Pflicht gegenüber den Heiden und dem Heidentum in seinen Kolonien*, Beiträge zur Missionskunde (Berlin: Buchhandlung der Berliner evangelischen Missionsgesellschaft, 1905), 17–18.

55 Minutes of the Deutschen Evangelischen Missionssausschuß (14 October 1904), BMW/bmw1/8186, S. 2. In attendance: Theodor Öhler, Alexander Merensky, Carl Buchner, Paul Schwartz, Gustav Warneck, Gottlob Haussleiter, and August Wilhelm Schreiber.

56 Julius Richter, "Mission und Kolonialpolitik," *Afrika* (1896): 53.

57 Klaus Fiedler, *Christianity and African Culture: Conservative German Protestant Missionaries in Tanzania, 1900–1940* (Leiden, E.J. Brill, 1996), 2–4.

58 Norris, *Die Umerziehung des Afrikaners*, 84.

59 Warneck, "Die Bedeutung der Muttersprache," 1–2. See also Christensen and Hutchison, *Missionary Ideologies in the Imperialist Era*, 6.

60 Th[eodor] Bechler, "Einzug europäischer Kultur am Nyassa," *Evangelisches Missions-Magazin, Neue Folge* 46(1904): 409–10 and 420–2.

61 Julius Richter, "Die Bedeutung der Mission für unsere Kolonien," *Evangelisches Missions-Magazin, Neue Folge* 40(1898): 322.

62 C[arl] Buchner, "Die schwarze Rasse und ihre Zukunft," *AMZ* 31(1904): 393–4.

63 Buchner, "Die schwarze Rasse und ihre Zukunft," *AMZ* 31(1904), 395–6. Buchner shared in German colonists' general approval of economic and social conditions in the US South under Jim Crow laws; see Sven Beckert, "From Tuskegee to Togo: The Problem of Freedom in the Empire of Cotton," *Journal of American History* 92(2): 498–526, and Zimmerman, *Alabama in Africa*.

64 Buchner, "Die schwarze Rasse und ihre Zukunft," *AMZ* 31(1904), 399–405.

65 Merensky, *Deutschlands Pflicht*, 10.

66 Merensky offers *suttee*, the murder of twins, the exile of the elderly, and the drinking of poison as an ordeal as examples. See Merensky, *Deutschlands Pflicht*, 15.

67 [Theodor] Öhler, "Mission und Kultur," *Evangelisches Missions-Magazin, Neue Folge* 50(1908): 49–50.

68 Öhler, "Mission und Kultur," 54.

69 Fitzpatrick, *Liberal Imperialism in Germany*, 9–12.

70 Marchand, *German Orientalism in the Age of Empire*, 337, 342–43; Short, *Magic Lantern Empire*, 27.

71 But the SPD remained resolutely anti-colonialist in the main; see Jens-Uwe Guettel, "The Myth of the Pro-Colonialist SPD: German Social

Democracy and Imperialism before World War I," *Central European History* 45(3) (Sept. 2012): 452–84.

72 German missionaries, who stubbornly adhered to indigenous-language instruction, stood in stark contrast to British missionaries, particularly in India, who were "vernacularists in principle, mission educators [who] became Anglicizers in practice largely in response to student demand for English education." Jeffrey Cox, *Imperial Fault Lines: Christianity and Colonial Power in India, 1818–1914* (Stanford, CA: Stanford University Press, 2002), 190–1. On the conflicts over language in German Togo, see Benjamin Nicholas Lawrance, "Most Obedient Servants: The Politics of Language in German Colonial Togo," *Cahiers d'Études Africaines* 40(159) (2000): 489–524.

73 Hartmut Pogge von Strandmann, *Imperialismus vom Grünen Tisch: Deutsche Kolonialpolitik zwischen wirtschaftlicher Ausbeutung und "zivilisatorischen" Bemühungen* (Berlin: Links, 2009), 15–16. Interestingly, a noteworthy minority of secular imperialists opposed the introduction of German in the colonies because it might undermine German authority. Indigenous people might come to see themselves as the equal of their German rulers if they could understand them in German. See Kundrus, *Moderne Imperialisten*, 188–96.

74 W.D. Smith, *The German Colonial Empire*, 119–21. For a more extensive study of the relationship between imperialism and nationalism in Germany see Kundrus, *Moderne Imperialisten*.

75 von Strandmann, *Imperialismus vom Grünen Tisch*, 11.

76 Thomas Nipperdey, *Gesellschaft, Kultur, Theorie: Gesammelte Aufsätze zur neueren Geschichte* (Munich: Vandenhoeck & Ruprecht, 1998), 174–205.

77 Geoff Eley, *Reshaping the German Right: Radical Nationalism and Political Change after Bismarck* (Ann Arbor: University of Michigan Press, 1991), 10.

78 Marilyn Shevin Coetzee, *The German Army League: Popular Nationalism in Wilhelmine Germany* (Oxford, UK: Oxford University Press, 1990), 8–9.

79 Short, *Magic Lantern Empire*, 25–6; Jake Walton Spidle, "The German Colonial Service: Organization, Selection, and Training" (PhD diss., Stanford University, 1972), 99. See also Elfi Bendikat, *Organisierte Kolonialbewegung in der Bismarck-Ära* (Heidelberg: Kivouvou, 1984); Richard V. Pierard, "The German Colonial Society," in *Germans in the Tropics: Essays in German Colonial History*, ed. Arthur J. Knoll and Lewis H. Gann, 19–38 (New York: Greenwood, 1987).

80 Spidle, "The German Colonial Service," 109.

81 Minutes of the Kolonialrat, IV. Sitzungsperiode 1895/98, Nr. 13 (22 October 1896), BArch R1001/1.22, Film Nr. 80484, Bd. 6968, pag. 8.

82 Minutes of the Kolonialrat, IV. Sitzungsperiode 1895/98, Nr. 3 (26 October 1898), BArch R 1001/1.22, Film Nr. 80485, Bd. 6973, pag. 10.

83 Kenneth J. Orosz, *Religious Conflict and the Evolution of Language Policy in German and French Cameroon, 1885–1939* (New York: Peter Lang, 2008), 21–35.
84 Orosz, *Religious Conflict and the Evolution of Language Policy in German and French Cameroon*, 149.
85 Warneck, "Der deutsche Kolonialbund," 303. See also Norris, *Die Umerziehung des Afrikaners*, 81.
86 Lawrance, "Most Obedient Servants," 506.
87 Lawrance, "Most Obedient Servants," 499. For another example of the role that Africans' educational demands played in the operations of mission schools see Carol Summers, *Colonial Lessons: Africans' Education in Southern Rhodesia, 1918–1940* (Portsmouth, NH: Heinemann, 2002).
88 BArch R 1001/8.25, Film Nr. 79397, Bd. 996, S. 102–21.
89 Minutes of the Kolonialrat, VI. Sitzungsperiod 1901/04, Nr. 9 (1 July 1904), BArch R 1001/1.22, Film Nr. 80487, Bd. 6981, pag. 351–2. These proposed schools should not be confused with the government schools set up in German East Africa during the 1890s and which aggravated missionaries in that colony during this same period.
90 Basel Mission Society to Colonial Secretary Wilhelm Solf (23 April 1913), BMW/bmw1/1701. The Berlin Mission Society also argued in 1911 that "mission must not aspire to a Germanizing or Anglicizing education, but instead an [education] appropriate to the unique qualities of the native." See Report from the Deutschen Evangelischen Missionsausschuß to member societies (16 February 1911), BMW/bmw1/1779.
91 This exact fear was articulated in language battles in Kamerun; see Orosz, *Religious Conflict and the Evolution of Language Policy in German and French Cameroon*, 168.
92 Reinhold Mumm to Theodor Öhler (11 March 1913), BMW/bmw1/8336.
93 What is missing from missionaries' discussions of linguistics is mention of how Africans themselves helped mediate the creation of an idiomatically Christian Swahili. Two works offer good examples of the role played by indigenous linguists in creating the language and literature of mission Christianity. See Isabel Hofmeyr, *The Portable Bunyan: A Transnational History of* The Pilgrim's Progress (Princeton: Princeton University Press, 2004); and Paul S. Landau, *The Realm of the Word: Language, Gender, and Christianity in a Southern African Kingdom* (Portsmouth, NH: Heinemann, 1995).
94 Some of this desire was also fed by the local influence of Askari (soldiers of African background serving in the colonial Schutztruppe) and their use of Swahili. Many of them were also Muslim, adding a level of antagonism between the missionaries and the Askari, even as Askari provided the missionaries with security. See Moyd, *Violent Intermediaries*.

95 Katrin Bromber, "German Colonial Administrators, Swahili Lecturers and the Promotion of Swahili at the *Seminar für Orientalische Sprachen* in Berlin," *Sudanic Africa* 15(2004): 39–54; Ann Brumfit, "The Rise and Development of a Language Policy in German East Africa," *Sprache und Geschichte in Afrika* 2(1980): 219–331.

96 Pugach, *Africa in Translation*, 69.

97 Karl Axenfeld, "Die Sprachenfrage in Ostafrika vom Standpunkt der Mission aus betrachtet," *AMZ* 35(1908): 561–2. Axenfeld's ideas likely grew, in part, out of the work of the mission scholar and linguist Carl Meinhof. In 1906 Meinhof wrote an article advocating the adoption by East African missionaries of a regional communal language because of the economic and political advantages; Meinhof, "Das missionarische Sprachproblem," 205–6, 215–16, and 253–5; see also Eggert, "The School Policy of the German Protestant Missions in Tanzania before the First World War," 205.

98 Axenfeld, "Die Sprachenfrage," 565.

99 For a history of the origins of Swahili in the region see Derek Nurse and Thomas J. Hinnebusch, *Swahili and Sabaki: A Linguistic History*, ed. Thomas J. Hinnebusch (Berkeley: University of California Press, 1993).

100 For a discussion of the relationship between Swahili, mission education policies, and colonial administration in the Belgian Congo, see Johannes Fabian, *Language and Colonial Power: The Appropriation of Swahili in the former Belgian Congo, 1880–1938* (Berkeley: University of California Press, 1986), esp. 70–91. In the Belgian case the colonial administration and Catholic missionaries seemed to have collaborated to help create a Swahili-speaking labour force.

101 Axenfeld, "Die Sprachenfrage," 565.

102 Report of the Deutschen Evangelischen Missionsausschuß to member societies (23 January 1908), BMW/bmw1/1779.

103 Axenfeld, "Die Sprachenfrage," 566.

104 Axenfeld, "Die Sprachenfrage," 567.

105 See chapter 6.

106 Axenfeld, "Die Sprachenfrage," 572–3.

107 Nurse and Hinnebusch, *Swahili and Sabaki*, 32.

108 Lawrance, "Most Obedient Servants," 492–8; see also Meyer, "Christianity and the Ewe Nation."

109 Thoralf Klein, "The Other German Colonialism: Power, Conflict, and Resistance in a German-speaking Mission in China, ca. 1850–1920," *German Colonialism Revisited: African, Asian, and Oceanic Experiences*, ed. Nina Berman, Klaus Mühlhahn, and Patrice Nganang (Ann Arbor: University of Michigan Press, 2014), 161–78.

110 George Steinmetz, *The Devil's Handwriting: Precoloniality and the German Colonial State in Qingdao, Samoa and Southwest Africa* (Chicago: University of Chicago Press, 2007), 45–55. See also Juhani Koponen, "Knowledge, Power and History: German Colonial Studies in Tanzania," in van der Heyden and von Oppen, *Tanzania*, 118–35.
111 For an example of this process see Martin Chanock, *Law, Custom and Social Order: The Colonial Experience in Malawi and Zambia* (Cambridge, UK: Cambridge University Press, 1985).
112 Pugach, *Africa in Translation*, 68.
113 Marchand, *German Orientalism in the Age of Empire*, xxv.
114 Adrian Hastings, "The Clash of Nationalism and Universalism within Twentieth-Century Missionary Christianity," in *Missions, Nationalism, and the End of Empire*, ed. Brian Stanley (Grand Rapids, MI: William B. Eerdmans Publishing Company, 2003), 23.
115 Michael Burleigh and Wolfgang Wippermann, *The Racial State: Germany, 1933–1945* (Cambridge, UK: Cambridge University Press, 1991); George L. Mosse, *Toward the Final Solution: A History of European Racism* (Madison: University of Wisconsin Press, 1985); Fritz Stern, *The Politics of Cultural Despair: A Study in the Rise of the Germanic Ideology* (Berkeley: University of California Press, 1961); Paul Weindling, *Health, Race, and German Politics between National Unification and Nazism* (Cambridge, UK: Cambridge University Press, 1993).
116 Altena, *"Ein Häuflein Christen mitten in der Heidenwelt des dunklen Erdteils,"* 413–14; Landau, *The Realm of the Word*, xvii and 30–52; Price, *Making Empire*, 8; Robert, introduction to *Converting Colonialism*, 4–5.
117 For example, African congregants in German East Africa took over leadership of their own churches after Entente forces deported and interred the German missionaries during the First World War. See Niels-Peter Moritzen, *Werkzeug Gottes in der Welt: Leipziger Mission 1836-1936-1986* (Erlangen: Verlag für Mission und Ökumene, 1986).
118 Richard Elphick, "Missions and Afrikaner Nationalism: Soundings in the Prehistory of Apartheid," in Stanley, *Missions, Nationalism, and the End of Empire*, 54–78; Pugach, *Africa in Translation*, 172–84.

3 Give ... to God the Things That Are God's

1 Matthew 22:21.
2 This perspective is the most widespread in the literature on British missions, a historiography that still dominates the anglophonic (and wider) scholarship on missionaries and imperialism. See Cox, *The British Missionary Enterprise since 1700*; Porter, *Religion versus Empire?*; Price, *Making Empire*; Summers, *From Civilization to Segregation*; and Alison

Twells, *The Civilising Mission and the English Middle Class, 1792–1850: The "Heathen" at Home and Overseas* (New York: Palgrave Macmillan, 2009).

3 The missionaries raised little objection to anti-miscegenation policies pursued in German East Africa, largely because intermarriage among Whites and non-Whites was virtually non-existent. See Wildenthal, *German Women for Empire, 1884–1945*, 88 and 118.

4 John 18:36.

5 Warneck, "Die Aufgabe der Heidenmission," 123–4.

6 Matthew 6:24.

7 Suzanne Miers and Igor Kopytoff, "African 'Slavery' as an Institution of Marginality," in *Slavery in Africa: Historical and Anthropological Perspectives*, ed. Miers and Kopytoff (Madison: University of Wisconsin Press, 1977), 55–6.

8 See Sven Beckert, "From Tuskegee to Togo," 498–526; and Zimmerman, *Alabama in Africa*. On German East Africa see Juhani Koponen, "Knowledge, Power and History," 125.

9 Valentin Amétepé Ahadji, "Mission und Landfrage in Togo, 1884–1914," in van der Heyden and Stoecker, *Mission und Macht im Wandel politischer Orientierungen*, 138; Ustorf, *Mission im Kontext*, 23.

10 At different times there were labour shortages on White-owned plantations. Rainer Tetzlaff suggests the cause was inability to mobilize the available population. Rainer Tetzlaff, *Koloniale Etnwicklung und Ausbeutung: Wirtschafts- und Sozialgeschicte Deutsch-Ostafrika* (Berlin: Duncker & Humblot, 1970), 193.

11 Kuassi Amétowoyopna Akakpo, "Missionspraxis im Lichte der Kritik: kontroverse Debatten über Paul Rohrbachs Thesen zur Missionsarbeit in Afrika," in van der Heyden and Stoecker, *Mission und Macht im Wandel politischer Orientierungen*, 71.

12 Walter Mogk, *Paul Rohrbach und das "Größere Deutschland": Ethischer Imperialismus im Wilhelminischen Zeitalter* (Munich: Wilhelm Goldmann Verlag, 1972), and vom Bruch, *Weltpolitik als Kulturmission*, esp. 69–89.

13 Nipperdey, *Deutsche Geschichte, 1886–1918*, vol. 1, 489–90.

14 Paul Rohrbach, *Die Kolonie* (Frankfurt-am-Main: Rütten & Loening, [1907]).

15 Andrew Porter, *Religion versus Empire?*.

16 Carol Summers, *From Civilization to Segregation*, 81.

17 Terence Ranger, "The Invention of Tradition in Colonial Africa," 213.

18 Brian Stanley, *The Bible and Flag: Protestant Missionaries and British Imperialism in the Nineteenth and Twentieth Centuries* (Leicester: Apollos, 1990), 71–4.

19 Felix Brahm and Eve Rosenhaft, introduction to *Slavery Hinterland: Transatlantic Slavery and Continental Europe, 1680–1850*, ed. Brahm and

Rosenhaft (Woodbridge, UK: Boydell Press, 2016), 21. The link between abolition and mission existed most strongly in Basel; see Peter Haenger, "Basel and the Slave Trade: From Profiteers to Missionaries," in Brahm and Rosenhaft, *Slavery Hinterland*, 83.

20 See chapter 1 of this book. Ranger also acknowledges this distinction between the German and the British case, without noting the cause, by discussing the Basel Mission Society as an exception within a mission movement, an organization he sees as uninterested in addressing Africans' developing status as peasants. Ranger, "The Invention of Tradition in Colonial Africa," 213–14.

21 Deutsch, *Emancipation without Abolition in German East Africa*, 10–11.

22 Loth, *Zwischen Gott und Kattun*, 86; Thaddeus Sunseri, "Slave Ransoming in German East Africa, 1885–1922," *International Journal of African Historical Studies* 26(3): 481–511.

23 Unangst, "Men of Science and Action," 305–6.

24 Deutsch, *Emancipation without Abolition*, 141–2. Overall, this is a largely unresearched area of German history. See also Eugene S. Cassidy, "The Ambivalence of Slavery, the Certainty of Germanness: Representations of Slave-Holding and Its Impact among German Settlers in Brazil, 1820–1889," *German History* 33(3) (Sept. 2015): 367–84; Mischa Honeck, "August Willich, Peter H. Clark, and the Abolitionist Movement in Cincinnati," in *Germans and African Americans: Two Centuries of Exchange*, ed. Larry A. Greene and Anke Ortlepp (Jackson: University Press of Mississippi, 2011), 17–36; Jeannette Eileen Jones, "'On the Brain of the Negro': Race, Abolitionism, and Friedrich Tiedemann's Scientific Discourse on the African Diaspora," in Mischa Honeck, Martin Klimke, and Anne Kuhlmann, *Germany and the Black Diaspora: Points of Contact, 1250–1914* (New York: Berghahn Books, 2013), 133–52; Sarah Lentz, "Abolitionists in the German Hinterland? Therese Huber and the Spread of Anti-Slavery Sentiment in the German Territories in the Early Nineteenth Century," in Brahm and Rosenhaft, *Slavery Hinterland*, 187–211; Edmund Spevack, "Charles Follen's View of Republicanism in Germany and the United States, 1815–1840," in *Republicanism and Liberalism in America and the German States, 1750–1850*, ed. Jürgen Heideking and James A. Henretta (Washington, DC: German Historical Institute and Cambridge University Press, 2002), 235–59.

25 Deutsch, *Emancipation without Abolition in German East Africa*, 2–3 and 122.

26 The most cited example of this position is Paul Rohrbach, *Die Kolonie*. However, Rohrbach's ideas were reflective of a much wider strand of liberal thought on colonialism promoted by, among others, members of the Verein für Sozialpolitik such as Gustav Schmoller and Max Weber. Andrew Zimmerman, "Decolonizing Weber," *Postcolonial Studies* 9(1): 65–8.

27 [Gustav] Warneck, "Der deutsche Kolonialbund als Missions-Gesetzgeber," *AMZ* 31(1904): 302.

28 Oermann, *Mission, Church, and State Relations in South-West Africa under German Rule, 1884–1915*, 106; Richard Pierard, "The Rhenish Mission and the Colonial War in German Southwest Africa," 395. There is some irony that absence of violence against missionaries in German Southwest Africa could be used as pretext for limiting mission societies' autonomy, while deadly violence against missionaries during the Boxer Rebellion also offered evidence that missionaries were hazardous to sensible colonial policy.

29 Warneck, "Der deutsche Kolonialbund," 302–3.

30 Karl Axenfeld to Paul Otto Hennig, Carl Paul, August Wilhelm Schreiber, Julius Richter, and Diedrich Westermann (2 April 1910), BMW/bmw1/2095. For Catholic attitudes toward training for the secular colonial movement, see Bernhard Mirtschink, *Zur Rolle christlicher Mission in kolonialen Gesellschaften: Katholische Missionserziehung in "Deutsch-Ostafrika"* (Frankfurt-am-Main: Haag + Herchen Verlag, 1980), 43 and 78–9.

31 Eggert, "The School Policy of the German Protestant Missions in Tanzania before the First World War," 202; Gensichen, "German Protestant Missions," 186–8; Johannes Christian Hoekendijk, *Kirche und Volk in der deutschen Wissenschaft*, 94; Fiedler, *Christianity and African Culture*, 13–22.

32 There is some evidence that it was not only the Germans who wished to create free-holding agriculturalists. Canadian missionaries working with the indigenous people of the Canadian West shared the ideal of an independent yeomanry developing as a result of their labours. See Jamie S. Scott, "Cultivating Christians in Colonial Canadian Missions," in *Canadian Missionaries, Indigenous Peoples: Representing Religion at Home and Abroad*, ed. Jamie S. Scott and Alvyn Austen (Toronto: University of Toronto Press, 2005), 21–45.

33 Wolfgang Gabbert, "Phasen und Grundprobleme protestantischer Mission im kolonialen Afrika – die Brüdergemeine bei den Nyakyusa in Tansania," in Bogner, Holtwick, and Tyrell, *Weltmission und religiöse Organisationen*, 518; Wright, *German Missions in Tanganyika, 1891–1941*, 20.

34 Oermann, *Mission, Church, and State Relations in South-West Africa under German Rule, 1884–1915*, 177.

35 Altena, *"Ein Häuflein Christen mitten in der Heidenwelt des dunklen Erdteils,"* 416.

36 Rennstich, "The Understanding of Mission, Civilisation and Colonialism in the Basel Mission," 94.

37 [Alexander] Merensky, "Die Mission der Anwalt der Eingeborenen," *AMZ* 29(1902): 166.

38 Christel Adick, "Grundstruktur und Organisation von Missionsschulen in den Etappen der Expansion des modernen Weltsystems," in Bogner, Holtwick, and Tyrell, *Weltmission und religiöse Organisationen*, 459–82.
39 Bernd Arnold, *Steuer und Lohnarbeit im Südwesten von Deutsch-Ostafrika, 1891 bis 1916: Eine historisch-ethnologische Studie* (Münster: Lit Verlag, 1994), 152 and 159.
40 Arnold, *Steuer und Lohnarbeit im Südwesten von Deutsch-Ostafrika*, 203.
41 Roland Oliver, *The Missionary Factor in East Africa* (London: Longmans, Green, 1952), 173; Summers, *From Civilization to Segregation*, 75 and 84.
42 Gerhard Besier, "Mission and Colonialism in Friedrich Fabri's (1824–1891) Thinking," in Christensen and Hutchison, *Missionary Ideologies in the Imperialist Era*, 92.
43 Rennstich, "The Understanding of Mission, Civilization and Colonialism in the Basel Mission," 96–9.
44 Edward Graham Norris makes a similar argument but it is much briefer and situated within an argument about colonialism as a generally "re-educative" institution. Norris, *Die Umerziehung des Afrikaners*, 92–3.
45 Conrad, *Globalisation and the Nation*, 3–5.
46 Conrad, *Globalisation and the Nation*, 24.
47 Bruno W. Nikles, *Soziale Hilfe am Bahnhof: Zur Geschichte der Bahnhofsmission in Deutschland (1894–1960)* (Freiburg: Lambertus, 1994); Alexandra Przyrembel, "The Emotional Bond of Brotherliness: Protestant Masculinity and the Local and Global Networks among Religious in the Nineteenth Century," *German History* 31(2) (2013): 157–80.
48 Nancy R. Reagin, "'A True Woman Can Take Care of Herself': The Debate over Prostitution in Hanover, 1900," *Central European History* 24, no. 4 (Dec. 1991): 356–62.
49 Conrad, *Globalisation and the Nation*, 102–11.
50 Conrad, *Globalisation and the Nation*, 77–9.
51 See Twells, *The Civilising Mission and the English Middle Class*.
52 Ustorf, *Mission im Kontext*.
53 Bodelschwingh served on the Prussian parliament as a conservative member and was a friend of the anti-Semitic politician Adolf Stöcker. However, too many conclusions should not be drawn from this evidence. After the First World War, Bethel missionaries resisted the virulent anti-Semitism and extreme nationalism of the era and opposed accommodations that the larger Bethel Institutes reached with the National Socialists. See Edward Snyder, "Eugenics and Protestant Social Thought in the Weimar Republic: Friedrich von Bodelschwingh and the Bethel Institutions," in *The German Right in the Weimar Republic: Studies*

in the History of German Conservatism, Nationalism, and Antisemitism, ed. Larry Eugene Jones (New York: Berghahn, 2014), 254–60.

54 [Ernst] Johanssen, ""Deutschlands christliche Kulturaufgabe in seinen Kolonien unter besonderer Berücksichtigung von Ostafrika," *Beth-El*(1912): 15–17.

55 Besier, "Mission and Colonialism in Friedrich Fabri's (1824–1891) Thinking," 91.

56 Hans-Werner Gensichen, "German Protestant Missions," in Christensen and Hutchison, *Missionary Ideologies in the Imperialist Era*, 186–7.

57 Forman, "Missions in Papua New Guinea," 26–7.

58 Pugach, *Africa in Translation*, 52.

59 Oliver, *The Missionary Factor in East Africa*, 179–81; Tetzlaff, "Die Mission im Spannungsfeld zwischen kolonialer Herrschaft und Zivilisierungsanspruch in Deutsch-Ostafrika," 190.

60 The lecture also included a comment by Eduard Kratzenstein of the Berlin Mission Society but his remarks were of little relevance to this discussion.

61 Alexander Merensky, "Welches Interesse und welchen Anteil hat die Mission an der Erziehung der Naturvölker zur Arbeit?" *AMZ* 14(1887): 147–8.

62 Merensky, "Welches Interesse und welchen Anteil ...," 149.

63 Bechler, "Einzug europäischer Kultur am Nyassa," 409–10 and 420–2. See also chapter 2.

64 Merensky, "Welches Interesse und welchen Anteil ...," 157–8.

65 Merensky, "Welches Interesse und welchen Anteil ...," 165.

66 Merensky, "Welches Interesse und welchen Anteil ...," 166–7, 171, and 173–4. See also Tetzlaff, *Koloniale Entwicklung und Ausbeutung*, 196.

67 Merensky, "Welches Interesse und welchen Anteil ...," 173–5 and 179.

68 Minutes of the Kolonialrat, IV. Sitzungsperiode 1895/98, Nr. 17 (26 May 1897), BArch R 1001/1.22, Film Nr. 80484, Bd. 6970, pag. 86.

69 Norbert Weber, "Kulturtätigkeit im Süden von Deutsch-Ostafrika," *Gott will es!* 17(7): 195–7.

70 There was some dissent against this view. Carl Gotthilf Büttner, a former Rhenish missionary who had worked in the territories that would become German Southwest Africa, spoke in 1885 of the special opportunity that missionary schoolteachers had to help complete the conquest and civilization of indigenous people. Büttner was atypical of missionary intellectuals; he travelled with Heinrich Göring, German Southwest Africa's first imperial administrator, to help organize the new colony and favoured close missionary-state collaboration. See C[arl] G[otthilf] Büttner, "Mission und Kolonien," *AMZ* 12(1885): 97–112; and Gustav Menzel, *C.G. Büttner: Missionar, Sprachforscher und Politiker*

in der deutschen Kolonialbewegung (Wuppertal: Verlag der Vereinigten Evangelischen Mission, 1992).

71 Warneck, "Die Aufgabe der Heidenmission," 105–7.

72 Warneck, "Die Aufgabe der Heidenmission," 109. There is no discernible connection between Warneck's assertion of Protestantism as a goad to industriousness or other positive economic qualities and Max Weber's *The Protestant Ethic and the Spirit of Capitalism*, published in its first part in 1904.

73 Warneck, deeply involved in German intellectual life, likely would have been familiar with the growing critique of modernity beginning to appear in European culture. For a discussion of this cultural moment and its prevailing currents see Marchand and Lindenfeld, *Germany at the Fin de Siècle*.

74 Warneck, "Die Aufgabe der Heidenmission," 111.

75 Loth, *Zwischen Gott und Kattun*; Niesel, "Kolonialverwaltung und Missionen in Deutsch-Ostafrika 1890–1914," 120; Nils Ole Oermann, "'Hochverehrter Herr Gouverneur' – Zum Verhältnis von Mission und deutschen Kolonialstaat im Zeitalter des Imperialismus," in Bogner, Holtwick, and Tyrell, *Weltmission und religiöse Organisationen*, 610.

76 L.H. Gann and Peter Duignan, *The Rulers of German Africa, 1884–1914* (Palo Alto, CA: Stanford University Press, 1977), 213.

77 Gann and Duignan, *The Rulers of German Africa, 1884–1914*, 35–6.

78 Tetzlaff, "Die Mission im Spannungsfeld zwischen kolonialer Herrschaft und Zivilisierungsanspruch in Deutsch-Ostafrika," 194.

79 Richter, "Mission und Kolonialpolitik," 46 and 52.

80 The literature suggests the generational differences as a source for the changing view of *Kultur* and race over the history of the Kaiserreich. See Andrew D. Evans, *Anthropology at War: World War I and the Science of Race in Germany* (Chicago, University of Chicago Press, 2010). See a similar effect among archaeologists working in the Ottoman Empire before the First World War in Marchand, "Orientalism as *Kulturpolitik*: German Archaeology and Cultural Imperialism in Asia Minor," in George W. Stocking Jr., Volksgeist *as Method and Ethic: Essays on Boasian Ethnography and the German Anthropological Tradition*, History of Anthropology 8 (Madison: University of Wisconsin Press, 1994), 323.

81 H. Glenn Penny, "Bastian's Museum: On the Limits of Empiricism and the Transformation of German Ethnology," in *Worldly Provincialism: German Anthropology in the Age of Empire*, ed. H. Glenn Penny and Matti Bunzl (Chapel Hill: University of North Carolina Press, 2002), 109. See also Andrew Zimmerman, *Anthropology and Antihumanism in Imperial Germany* (Chicago: University of Chicago Press, 2001); and Marchand, "Orientalism as *Kulturpolitik*," 298–300.

82 Evans, *Anthropology at War*, 8–11. Sean McMeekin details similar efforts by German Orientalists during the First World War in the Ottoman, Persian, and Central Asian territories. See Sean McMeekin, *The Berlin-Baghdad Express: The Ottoman Empire and Germany's Bid for World Power* (Cambridge, MA: Belknap Press of Harvard University Press, 2010). Also see chapter 6 of this book.

83 Adam A. Blackler, "From Boondoggle to Settlement Colony: Hendrik Witbooi and the Evolution of Germany's Imperial Project in Southwest Africa, 1884–1894," *Central European History* 50(2017): 470.

84 Lamar Cecil, *The German Diplomatic Service, 1871–1914* (Princeton, NJ: Princeton University Press, 1976), 103.

85 Klaus Epstein, *Matthias Erzberger and the Dilemma of German Democracy* (New York: Howard Fertig, 1971), 56.

86 W.D. Smith, *The German Colonial Empire*, 185–6.

87 W.O. Henderson, *The German Colonial Empire, 1884–1919* (London: Frank Cass, 1993), 99–100.

88 Thaddeus Sunseri, "The *Baumwollfrage*: Cotton Colonialism in German East Africa," *Central European History* 34(1): 46–9.

89 In 1905/6 Africans suffered corporal punishment 6,322 times, in 1908/09 there were 3,746 instances, and between 1909 and 1911 twenty-seven Europeans were convicted for excessive brutality. Tetzlaff, *Koloniale Etnwicklung und Ausbeutung*, 251.

90 Gründer, *Geschichte der deutschen Kolonien*, 161–2. On the construction of the *Zentralbahn* and other railways in German East Africa see Thaddeus Sunseri, "'Dispersing the Fields': Railway Labor and Rural Change in Early Colonial Tanzania," *Canadian Journal of African Studies* 32(3): 558–83.

91 Andrew Zimmerman, "'What Do You Really Want in German East Africa, *Herr Professor*?' Counterinsurgency and the Science Effect in Colonial Tanzania," *Comparative Studies in Society and History* 48(2): 432.

92 Quoted in Tetzlaff, *Koloniale Entwicklung und Ausbeutung*, 200.

93 H. Kurz, "Mission oder Kultur," *Evangelisches Missions-Magazin, Neue Folge* 48(1906): 317.

94 Kurz, "Mission oder Kultur," 317–18. For more on cultural relativism in missionary thought see A[lbert] Hauck, *Evangelische Mission und deutsches Christentum*, Flugschriften der Deutschen Evangelischen Missions-Hilfe 4 (Gütersloh: C. Bertelsmann, 1916); P[aul] O[tto] Hennig, "Die Erziehung des Afrikaners," *Jahrbuch der sächsischen Missionskonferenz* 23(1912): 67–79; and "Die Stellung der evangelischen Mission in Afrika zur Volkssitte," *Evangelisch-Lutherisches Missionsblatt* 46(1893): 291–3.

95 Kurz, "Mission oder Kultur," 320.

96 Kurz, "Mission oder Kultur," 330–1.

97 Öhler, "Mission und Kultur," 55.

98 Tetzlaff, *Koloniale Entwicklung und Ausbeutung*, 260.
99 Gensichen, "German Protestant Missions," 184.

4 Go In and Take Possession of the Land

1 Wildenthal, *German Women for Empire*, 108.
2 There was also a long history of anti-Catholicism built into British and international mission history; see Carey, *God's Empire*, 5.
3 Deuteronomy 1:8.
4 Some elements of collaboration did exist; Josef Schmidlin praised Protestant Missionswissenschaft and attempted to create a complementary Catholic field of study in the decade before the First World War; see Rzepkowski, "Gustav Warneck und die katholische Missionswissenschaft." The Austrian Catholic priest Wilhelm Schmidt included contributions from Protestants in his journal *Anthropos;* see Suzanne Marchand, "Priests among the Pygmies: Wilhelm Schmidt and the Counter-Reformation in Austrian Ethnology," in *Worldly Provincialism*, ed. Penny and Bunzl, 283–316.
5 In general, the Benediktinerstreit has received little attention from scholars. Marcia Wright's work on the topic is the main exception to this; she notes the increasing conflict between Catholics and Protestants in the region; see Wright, *German Missions in Tanganyika, 1891–1941*, 119–21. In general the issue of Protestant-Catholic conflict receives only passing mention in the scholarship that focuses on either the Protestant or the Catholic mission histories. For examples see Gründer, *Christliche Mission und deutscher Imperialismus*, 99; and Ulrich van der Heyden, "Christian Missionary Societies in the German Colonies, 1884/85–1914/15," in *German Colonialism: Race, the Holocaust, and Postwar Germany*, ed. Volker Langbehn and Mohammad Salama (New York: Columbia University Press, 2011), 226. For a discussion of Protestant-Catholic missionary conflict in the German colony of Kamerun see Heinrich Berger, *Mission und Kolonialpolitik: Die katholische Mission in Kamerun während der deutschen Kolonialzeit* (Immensee: Neue Zeitschrift für Missionswissenschaft, 1978), 336–7.
6 By the end, 1800 priests had been imprisoned or exiled, and 16 million Marks of church property taken by the state. Manfred Scholle, *Die Preußische Strafjustiz im Kulturkampf 1873–1880* (Marburg: Elwert, 1974), cited in David Blackbourn, *Marpingen: Apparitions of the Virgin Mary in Bismarckian Germany* (New York: Knopf, 1994), 86.
7 Christopher Clark, "Religion and Confessional Conflict," in Retallack, *Imperial Germany, 1871–1918*, 92; Jonathan Sperber, *Popular Catholicism in Nineteenth-Century Germany* (Princeton, NJ: Princeton University Press, 1984), 277.

8 Blackbourn, *The Long Nineteenth Century*, 286 and 301.
9 Martin Baumeister, *Parität und katholische Inferiorität: Untersuchungen zur Stellung des Katholizismus im Deutschen Kaiserreich* (Paderborn: Ferdinand Schöningh, 1987); David Blackbourn, *Class, Religion and Local Politics in Wilhelmine Germany: The Centre Party in Württemberg before 1914* (New Haven, CT: Yale University Press, 1980), 10; Jefferies, *Contesting the German Empire, 1871–1918*, 96; Ronald J. Ross, *Beleaguered Tower: The Dilemma of Political Catholicism in Wilhelmine Germany* (Notre Dame, IN: University of Notre Dame Press, 1976), xiv, 20–2, and 32.
10 H.W. Smith, *German Nationalism and Religious Conflict*, 42–4.
11 Blackbourn, *Class, Religion and Local Politics in Wilhelmine Germany*, 20; Ronald J. Ross, *The Failure of Bismarck's* Kulturkampf*: Catholicism and State Power in Imperial Germany, 1871–1887* (Washington, DC: Catholic University of America Press, 1998), 122; Sperber, *Popular Catholicism in Nineteenth-Century Germany*, 253–5.
12 Blackbourn, *Class, Religion and Local Politics in Wilhelmine Germany*, 21; Jefferies, *Contesting the German Empire, 1871–1918*, 115; Ross, *Beleaguered Tower*, passim.
13 Blackbourn, *Class, Religion and Local Politics in Wilhelmine Germany*, 23. The Center Party's entente with imperial chancellors had in fact been forged on colonial issues; see Margaret Lavinia Anderson, *Windthorst: A Political Biography* (Oxford: Clarendon Press, 1981), 386–7.
14 Clark, "Religion and Confessional Conflict," 94.
15 See H.W. Smith, *The Continuities of German History*; Helmut Walser Smith, *German Nationalism and Religious Conflict: Culture, Ideology and Religious Conflict, 1870–1914* (Princeton, NJ: Princeton University Press, 1995), 5; Thomas Nipperdey, *Religion im Umbruch: Deutschland 1870–1918* (Munich: C.H. Beck, 1988), 81.
16 Clark, "Religion and Confessional Conflict," 90–3.
17 Michael B. Gross, *The War against Catholicism: Liberalism and Anti-Catholic Imagination in Nineteenth-Century Germany* (Ann Arbor: University of Michigan Press, 2004), 72–3; H.W. Smith, *German Nationalism and Religious Conflict*, 9–10 and 236–7; Olaf Blaschke and Frank-Michael Kuhlemann, eds., *Religion im Kaiserreich: Milieus-Mentalitäten-Krisen* (Gütersloh: Chr. Kaiser/Gütersloher Verlagshaus, 1996), 44; Martin Friedrich, "Das 19. Jahrhundert als 'Zweites Konfessionelles Zeitalter'?: Anmerkungen aus evangelisch-theologischer Sicht," in *Konfessionen im Konflikt: Deutschland zwischen 1800 und 1970: Ein zweites konfessionelles Zeitalter*, ed. Olaf Blaschke (Göttingen: Vandenhoeck & Ruprecht, 2002), 101–2; Ross, *The Failure of Bismarck's* Kulturkampf, 5.
18 Most scholarship on these ideas has focused on the Kulturkampf of the 1870s but the material is applicable to later periods, including

the Benediktinerstreit years. See Wolfgang Altgeld, *Katholizismus, Protestantismus, Judentum: Über religiös begründete Gegensätze und nationalreligiöse Ideen in der Geschichte des deutschen Nationalismus* (Mainz: Matthias-Grünewald-Verlag, 1992), 4–5.

19 Gross, *The War against Catholicism*, 22; Marc Spindler, "The Protestant Mission Study: Emergence and Features," 40; Armin Owzar, "Protestantism, Catholicism and Islam in German East Africa," in Dujardin and Prudhomme, *Mission and Science*, 356.

20 See Gangolf Hübinger, *Kulturprotestantismus und Politik: Zum Verhältnis von Liberalismus und Protestantismus im Wilhelminischen Deutschland* (Tübingen: J.C.B. Mohr (P. Siebeck), 1994).

21 Bade, "Einführung: Imperialismus und Kolonialmission: Das Kaiserliche Deutschland und sein koloniales Imperium," in *Imperialismus und Kolonialmission*, 81; Mirtschink, *Zur Rolle christlicher Mission in kolonialen Gesellschaft*, 33; Spidle, "The German Colonial Civil Service," 22. For one Protestant missionary's view of the Centre Party see [Gustav] Warneck, "Die Mission im deutschen Reichstage," *AMZ* 18(1891): 124–31

22 For examples of the resonance of anti-Catholic attacks in colonial politics, see Johannes Horstmann, ed., *Die Verschränkung von Innen-, Konfessions- und Kolonialpolitik im Deutschen Reich vor 1914* (Paderborn: Katholische Akademie Schwerte, 1987).

23 Blackbourn, *Class, Religion and Local Politics in Wilhelmine Germany*, 24.

24 Epstein, *Matthias Erzberger and the Dilemma of German Democracy*, 56–60; Jefferies, *Contesting the German Empire, 1871–1918*, 177; Lowry, *Big Swords, Jesuits, and Bondelswarts*, 268–9 and 336; Helmut Walser Smith, "The Talk of Genocide, the Rhetoric of Miscegenation: Notes on Debates in the German Reichstag concerning Southwest Africa, 1904–14," in Friedrichsmayer, Lennox, and Zantop, *The Imperialist Imagination*, 107–24.

25 A[lbert] Petri, "Die römisch-katholische Missions-Literatur in ihrem Verhältniß zur evangelischen Mission: Zugleich als ein Blick in die beiderseitige Missions-Methode," *AMZ* 5(1878): 474.

26 Willi Gründler, "Eine Störung unserer Njaßa-Mission durch die Benediktiner," *Berliner Missionsberichte* 90(1 Jan. 1913): 22.

27 F[ranz] M[ichael] Zahn, "Wer gewinnt Afrika?" *AMZ* 17(1890): 475 and 479–80.

28 Carl Mirbt, "Die Missionsmethode der römisch-katholischen Kirche," *AMZ* 28(1901): 264 and 266–7.

29 Pastor Paul, "Die römischen Konkurrenzmissionen, ihre wachsende Gefahr und ihre Abwehr," *Verhandlungen der Kontinentalen Missions-Konferenz* 10(1901): 141–2.

30 Mirbt, "Die Missionsmethode," 267;"Nationale Mission," *Evangelisches Missions-Magazin* 32(1888): 2.

31 Mirbt, "Die Missionsmethode," 258–61. Mirbt's suggestion is, in part, supported by historians' conclusions. See Gross, *The War against Catholicism*, 28, 29–73; and Sperber, *Popular Catholicism in Nineteenth-Century Germany*, 253.
32 [Gustav Warneck], "Ein moderner Kreuzzug," *AMZ* 15(1888): 502.
33 On investment in the colony see Chris M. Peter, "Imperialism and Export of Capital: A Survey of Foreign Private Investments in Tanzania during the German Colonial Period," *Journal of Asian and African Studies* 25(3–4), 197–212.
34 Petri, "Die römisch-katholische Missions-Literatur," 470.
35 [Alexander] Merensky, "Welches Interesse und welchen Anteil hat die Mission an der Erziehung der Naturvölker zur Arbeit?" *AMZ* 14(1887): 162; [Julius] Richter, "Die evangelischen, besonders deutschen Missionen in den deutschen Schutzgebieten," *AMZ* 21(1894): 435.
36 Richter, "Die evangelischen, besonders deutschen Missionen," 435.
37 Niesel, "Kolonialverwaltung und Missionen in Deutsch-Ostafrika 1890 -1914," 153.
38 Lowry, *Big Swords, Jesuits, and Bondelswarts*, 52.
39 H.W. Smith, *Nationalism and Religious Conflict*, 60n47. See also Kasdorf, *Gustav Warnecks missiologisches Erbe*, 45–6 and 276.
40 Clark, "Confessional Conflict," 91.
41 Holtwick, "Licht und Schatten," 230.
42 Paul, "Die römischen Konkurrenzmissionen," 129.
43 [Gustav] Warneck, "'Zur Missionsfrage in unsern Schutzgebieten,'" *AMZ* 19(1892): 442 and 444–5; Carl Paul, *Zwanzig Jahre deutscher Kolonialpolitik in ihrer Bedeutung für die Christianisierung unsrer überseeischen Gebiete* (Berlin: 1904), 110.
44 [Gustav] Warneck, "Zur Lage in Ostafrika," *AMZ* 16(1889): 13–14.
45 Petri, "Die römisch-katholische Missions-Literatur," 470. Mirbt also identified the Jesuits as the core group in Catholic mission activities. See Mirbt, "Die Missionsmethode," 258 and 265.
46 Paul, "Die römischen Konkurrenzmission," 133.
47 "Nationale Mission," 2.
48 Mirbt, "Die Missionsmethode," 268.
49 For a history of Catholic missions in Germany see Hubert Mohr, *Katholische Orden und Deutscher Imperialismus* (Berlin: Akademie-Verlag, 1965).
50 See chapters 2 and 3, respectively.
51 Hartmut Pogge von Strandmann, "The Kolonialrat and the Missionary Societies," in van der Heyden and Stoecker, *Mission und Macht im Wandel politischer Orientierungen*, 37–8; Pogge von Strandmann, *Imperialismus vom Grünen Tisch*.

52 See below. For more detail on Bernhard Dernburg and the genesis and application of his eponymous reforms, see Bradley D. Naranch, "'Colonized Body,' 'Oriental Machine': Debating Race, Railroads, and the Politics of Reconstruction in Germany and East Africa, 1906–1910," *Central European History* 33(3): 299–338.

53 Hans-Joachim Niesel, "Kolonialverwaltung und Missionen in Deutsch-Ostafrika zur Zeit des Maji-Maji-Aufstandes 1905–1907," in *Mit Zauberwasser gegen Gewehrkugeln: Der Maji-Maji-Aufstand in ehemaligen Deutsch-Ostafrika vor 100 Jahren*, ed. Hans-Martin Hinz, Hans-Joachim Niesel, and Almut Nothnagle (Frankfurt-am-Main: Otto Lembeck, 2006), 77–8.

54 Lowry, *Big Swords, Jesuits, and Bondelswarts*, 89; Mirtschink, *Zur Rolle christlicher Mission in kolonialen Gesellschaft*, 78–9.

55 Gabriel K. Nzalayaimisi, "The Berliners and Violence in Eastern and Southern Tanzania, 1887–1919," in van der Heyden and Becher, *Mission und Gewalt*, 474–9. See also Mirtschink, *Zur Rolle christlicher Mission in kolonialen Gesellschaften*, 78–9; and Niesel, "Kolonialverwaltung und Missionen in Duetsch-Ostafrika zur Zeit des Maji-Maji-Aufstandes 1905–1907," 81.

56 Arnold, *Steuer und Lohnarbeit im Südwesten von Deutsch-Ostafrika*, 131–4 and 183–90.

57 Niesel, "Kolonialverwaltung und Missionen in Deutsch-Ostafrika 1890–1914," 143. More broadly, see N. Thomas Håkansson, "Pagan Practices and the Death of Children: German Colonial Missionaries and Child Health Care in South Pare, Tanzania," *World Development* 26(9): 1763–72.

58 Sippel, "Mission und Gewalt in Deutsch-Ostafrika," in van der Heyden and Becher, *Mission und Gewalt*, 530.

59 Karim F. Hirji, "Colonial Ideological Apparatuses in Tanganyika under the Germans," in *Tanzania under Colonial Rule*, ed. M.H.Y. Kaniki (London: Longman Group Limited, 1980), 207–11.

60 Franz Ansprenger, "Schulpolitik in Deutsch-Ostafrika," in *Studien zur Geschichte des deutschen Kolonialismus in Afrika: Festschrift zum 60. Geburtstag von Peter Sebald* (Pfeffenweiler: Centaurus, 1995), 60. For missionaries' own view on the government schools see [Gustav] Warneck, "Eingabe an das Auswärtige Amt betreffend die offizielle Anstellung von mohammedanischen Religionslehrern an deutschen Regierungsschulen," *AMZ* 22(1895): 391–6; *Entwurf einer Eingabe an das Auswärtige Amt, Namen der ev. Mission* ([1894]), BMW/bmw1/2200; Consul Heinke to Berlin Mission Society (23 November 1900), BMW/bmw1/2201; Minutes of the Berlin Mission Society Komitee (2 April 1901), BMW/bmw1/48; and Berlin Mission Society Komitee to Gustav Warneck (25 April 1901), BMW/bmw1/2202, pag. 198.

61 Pogge von Strandmann, *Imperialismus vom Grünen Tisch*, 244.

62 Moyd, *Violent Intermediaries*, 170–4; Michael Pesek, "Kreuz oder Halbmond? Die deutsche Kolonialpolitik zwischen Pragmatismus und Paranoia in Deutsch-Ostafrika 1908–1914," in Heyden and Becher, *Mission und Gewalt*, 109–10; Owzar, "Protestantism, Catholicism and Islam in German East Africa," 355–69. There was a general perception that Islam was on the rise across Africa at the time and there is evidence that Sufistic *tariqa* brotherhoods were growing in the region. For one scholar, Carl Becker, this offered a tool to colonial administrators. See Marchand, *German Orientalism in the Age of Empire*, 365–6. John Iliffe has also argued that imperialism drove the region more fully into the Muslim world; see Iliffe, *A Modern History of Tanganyika*, 215. See also Felicitas Becker, *Becoming Muslim in Mainland Tanzania, 1890–2000* (Oxford, UK: Oxford University Press, 2008); and Oliver, *The Missionary Factor in East Africa*, 202–7.

63 Viera Pawliková-Vilhanová, "Crescent or Cross? Islam and Christian Missions in Nineteenth-Century East and Central Africa," in van der Heyden and Becher, *Mission und Gewalt*, 93; Niesel, "Kolonialverwaltung und Missionen in Deutsch-Ostafrika 1890–1914," 168.

64 Harald Sippel, "Mission und Kodifikation: Der missionarische Beitrag zur Erforschung des afrikanischen Gewohnheitsrechts in der Kolonie Deutsch-Ostafrika," in Wagner, *Kolonien und Missionen*, 502. Missionaries in Germany argued that Islam was a threat to Christian missionaries and to the colonial state because it had a "warlike spirit" and forced itself upon "pagans" while obstructing economic and social development by preventing the political, social, and moral education of Africans. See Holger Weiss, "Islam, Missionaries and Residents: The Attempt of the Basel Missionary Society to Establish a Mission in Yendi (German Togo) before WWI," in van der Heyden and Stoecker, *Mission und Macht im Wandel politischer Orientierungen*, 174.

65 James Giblin and Jamie Monson, introduction to *Maji Maji: Lifting the Fog of War* (Leiden: Brill, 2010), 1.

66 Giblin and Monson, introduction to *Maji Maji*, 1.

67 Iliffe, *A Modern History of Tanganyika*, 191.

68 The name of this large body of water in Africa's Rift Valley is disputed by the Malawian government. In Malawi the lake is known as Lake Malawi. I have chosen to use the name Lake Nyasa primarily because that is the name which German missionaries called it in the late nineteenth century and secondarily because Lake Nyasa prevails in international usage.

69 Giblin and Monson, introduction to *Maji Maji*, 5–8.

70 Iliffe, *A Modern History of Tanganyika*, 193–202.

71 Ahadji, "Mission und Landfrage in Togo, 1884–1914," 138; Andreas Eckert, "Missions, Land Politics and Real Estate in Colonial Douala," in *Land Law and Land Ownership in Africa: Case Studies from Colonial and Contemporary Cameroon and Tanzania*, ed. Robert Debusmann and Stefan Arnold (Bayreuth: Eckhard Breitinger, Bayreuth University, 1996), 189.

72 Nzalayaimisi, "The Berliners and Violence in Eastern and Southern Tanzania, 1887–1919," 478.

73 Harald Sippel, "Aspects of Colonial Land Law in German East Africa: German East Africa Company, Crown Land Ordinance, European Plantations and Reserved Areas for Africans," in Debusmann and Arnold, *Land Law and Land Ownership in Africa*, 17–18 and 25.

74 Niesel, "Kolonialverwaltung und Missionen in Deutsch-Ostafrika 1890–1914," 63 and 208; W.D. Smith, *The German Colonial Empire*, 199–201 and 209–15. See also Heike Schmidt, "(Re)Negotiating Marginality: The Maji Maji War and Its Aftermath in Southwestern Tanzania, ca. 1905–1916," *International Journal of African Historical Studies* 43(1): 27–62; and Karl-Martin Seeberg, *Der Maji-Maji-Krieg gegen die deutsche Kolonialherrschaft* (Berlin: D. Reimer, 1989), 91–2.

75 Pakendorf, "Berlin in Afrika, oder der historische Ort der Deutschen Mission," 481.

76 Aside from dense populations in the kingdoms of Burundi and Rwanda, the average population density of German East Africa was less than four persons per kilometre. Lowry, *Big Swords, Jesuits, and Bondelswarts*, 78.

77 Niesel, "Kolonialverwaltung und Missionen in Deutsch-Ostafrika zur Zeit des Maji-Maji-Aufstandes 1905–1907," 87.

78 Niesel, "Kolonialverwaltung und Missionen in Deutsch-Ostafrika 1890–1914," 211.

79 W.D. Smith, *The German Colonial Empire*, 185–6.

80 Henderson, *The German Colonial Empire, 1884–1919*, 88–91.

81 Short, *Magic Lantern Empire*, 152–3.

82 W.D. Smith, *The German Colonial Empire*, 192–202.

83 Dirk van Laak, *Imperiale Infrastruktur: Deutsche Planungen für eine Erschließung Afrikas 1880 bis 1960* (Paderborn: Ferdinand Schöningh, 2004), 130–46; W. D. Smith, *The German Colonial Empire*, 199–202. The peoples of German East Africa were not practising a purely subsistence economy; they had historically been integrated into larger networks of trade. The German colonial administration's efforts were intended to encourage existing trends within the colonial economy. See Abdul Sheriff, "Economy and Society in East Africa in the Nineteenth and Twentieth Centuries with Special Reference to Tanzania," in van der Heyden and von Oppen, *Tanzania*, 12 and 19.

84 Gründer, *Geschichte der deutschen Kolonien*, 161–2. On the construction of the *Zentralbahn* and other railways in German East Africa see Sunseri, "'Dispersing the Fields,'" 558–3.

85 Walter Rodney, "The Political Economy of Colonial Tanganyika, 1890–1930," in Kaniki, *Tanzania under Colonial Rule*, 134–7.

86 Altena, "*Ein Häuflein Christen mitten in der Heidenwelt des dunklen Erdteils,*" 416–18. The single-family farm, revered by missionaries, was also judged the ideal economic unit by contemporary social scientists. Zimmerman, *Alabama in Africa*, 15.

87 Niesel, "Kolonialverwaltung und Missionen in Deutsch-Ostafrika 1890–1914," 69.

88 Mirtschink, *Zur Rolle christlicher Mission in kolonialen Gesellschaften*, 74–5. Also see chapter 3 of this book.

89 On Protestant missionaries' efforts at conversion see Wolfgang Gabbert, "Social and Cultural Conditions of Religious Conversion in Colonial Southwest Tanzania, 1891–1939," *Ethnology* 40(4): 291–308.

90 Niesel, "Kolonialverwaltung und Missionen in Deutsch-Ostafrika 1890–1914," 56–7.

91 The Basel Mission Society proposed the creation of clear Catholic and Protestant "territories" in Kamerun when the Catholic Pious Society of Missions (known as the Pallotiners) entered that colony in 1880. See Orosz, *Religious Conflict and the Evolution of Language Policy in German and French Cameroon*, 36.

92 Image 4.1 is a reconstruction of Martin Klamroth's map made from a map produced for Wright, *German Missions in Tanganyika, 1891–1941*. The author and cartographer endeavoured to locate the original map by Klamroth in the archives of the Berlin Mission Society but could not. Any limitations in image 4.1 are, at least in part, a result of the commensurate limitations in reproducing a reproduction.

93 [Gustav Warneck], "Die gegenwärtige Lage der deutschen evangelischen Mission," *AMZ* 32(1905): 167.

94 Buchner, "Die römische Aggression," 134.

95 Warneck, "Die gegenwärtige Lage," 168–9.

96 "Warum sollen wir die afrikanischen Missionen unterstützen?" *Gott will es! Monatschrift für alle Förderer u. Freunde d. Bewegung gegen d. afrikanische Sclaverei insbesondere für d. Mitglieder d. Afrika-Vereins Deutscher Katholiken* 5(1893): 225–8.

97 Paul, "Die römischen Konkurrenzmissionen," 125. This news was also reprinted in many German mission sources. For example, see "Etwas über katholische Missionsthätigkeit," *Nachrichten aus der ostafrikanischen Mission* 6(1 Jan. 1892): 29; and Paul, *Zwanzig Jahre*, 110 and 116–17.

98 Buchner, "Die römische Aggression," 134–5 and 138.

99 Warneck, "Die gegenwärtige Lage," 170–1.

100 Though it overemphasizes Merensky's nationalist motivations, a considered discussion of the Berlin Mission leaders', and especially Alexander Merensky's, choice of this region of the colony can be found in Ulrich van der Heyden, "Zu den politischen Hintergründen der Njassa-Expedition von Alexander Merensky," in *Mit Kreuz und deutscher Flagge: 100 Jahre Evangelium im Süden Tanzanias Zum Wirken der Berliner Mission in Ostafrika*, ed. Winfried Brose and Ulrich van der Heyden (Münster: Lit Verlag, 1993), 89–95.

101 Wright, *German Missions in Tanganyika 1891–1941*, 120–1.

102 Thomas Spreiter to Karl Axenfeld (30 September 1912), BMW/bmw1/894.

103 Introduction to *Sechsundsiebzigster Jahresbericht des Missions-Hülfs-Vereins der Berliner Missions-Gesellschaft für die Diöcesen Bunzlau I und II über das Rechnungsjahr 1913/14* (Bunzlau: Druck von J. H. Stoltz, 1914), 3. BMW/bmw1/6842.

104 Max Berner to the Deutschen Evangelischen Missionsausschuß (27 December 1908), BMW/bmw1/8319, 12/27/1908.

105 Deutschen Evangelischen Missionsausschuß to Berner (17 April 1909), BMW/bmw1/894.

106 Berner to the Deutschen Evangelischen Missionsausschuß (27 December 1908), BMW/bmw1/8319. Though it is not referenced directly by Berner, it is very likely that the Colonial Department feared a repeat of the violence which had drawn in missionaries in the kingdom of Buganda in the 1890s. For more on the events in Uganda see Jean-Pierre Chrétien, *The Great Lakes of Africa: Two Thousand Years of History*, trans. Scott Straus (New York: Zone Books, 2003), 207–11 and 224–32; for general background and for a more specific treatment of the issue see Holger Bernt Hansen, *Mission, Church and State in a Colonial Setting: Uganda, 1890–1925* (London: Heinemann, 1984), 3–57; for an interesting treatment of the relationship between Christianity and African notions of honour in the Great Lakes in general and Uganda in particular see John Iliffe, *Honour in African History* (Cambridge, UK: Cambridge University Press, 2005), 161–80.

107 Deutschen Evangelischen Missionsausschuß to Berner (17 April 1909), BMW/bmw1/894.

108 Deutschen Evangelischen Missionsausschuß to Wilhelm Solf (16 January 1913), BArch R1001/8.16, Film Nr. 79832, Bd. 863, pag. 46; Deutschen Evangelischen Missionsausschuß to member mission societies (20 February 1913), BMW/bmw1/1779.

109 Solf to Berner (7 February 1913), BArch R 1001/8.16, Film Nr. 79832, Bd. 863. pag. 50.

110 Solf to the Deutschen Evangelischen Missionsausschuß (7 February 1913), BArch R 1001/8.16, Film Nr. 79832, Bd. 863, pag. 50.
111 Lowry, *Big Swords, Jesuits, and Bondelswarts*, 235.
112 Heinrich Schnee to Axenfeld and Klamroth (11 January 1913), BMW/bmw1/894; see also Berner to the Deutschen Evangelischen Missionsausschuß (3 May 1913), BMW/bmw1/8319.
113 Axenfeld to Berner (29 December 1908), BMW/bmw1/894.
114 Komitee of the Berlin Mission Society to Albert Rechenberg (5 December 1908), BMW/bmw1/1192.
115 G.T. Manley to Axenfeld (25 October 1912), BMW/bmw1/894; Minutes of the Komitee of the Berlin Mission Society (3 December 1912), BMW/bmw1/57. Examples of articles appeared in the *Berliner Neueste Nachrichten*, 18 December 1912; *Volks-Zeitung Berlin*, 17 December 1912; *Deutsch-evangelische Korrespondenz*, 18 December 1912; *Germania*, 18 December 1912.
116 Martin Klamroth, "Denkschrift" ([12 December 1912]), BMW/bmw1/894.
117 Deutschen Evangelischen Missionsausschuß to Wilhelm Solf (16 January 1913), BArch R1001/8.16, Film Nr. 79832, Bd. 863, pag. 45.
118 Bishop Spreiter's protestations to the contrary notwithstanding. See Spreiter to Axenfeld (13 September 1909), BMW/bmw1/894.
119 Berner to Deutschen Evangelischen Missionsausschuß (16 December 1912), BMW/bmw1/8319.
120 Minutes of the Komitee of the Berlin Mission Society (7 January 1913), BMW/bmw1/57.
121 [Karl Axenfeld], "Ist friedliches Nebeneinanderarbeiten mit der römischen Mission möglich?" *AMZ* 41(1913): 26 and 30–1.
122 Gründler, "Eine Störung," 24.
123 Niesel, "Kolonialverwaltung und Missionen in Deutsch-Ostafrika 1890–1914," 256.
124 Gründler to Reinhard Mumm (30 January 1913), BMW/bmw1/894.
125 On the *Evangelischer Bund* (Protestant League), see Olaf Blaschke, *Konfessionen im Konflikt: Deutschland zwischen 1800 und 1970: Ein zweites konfessionelles Zeitalter* (Göttingen: Vandehoeck & Ruprecht, 2002), 56–7; and H.W. Smith, *German Nationalism and Religious Conflict*.
126 Alois Löwenstein to Axenfeld (15 May 1913), BMW/bmw1/895.
127 Berner to the Deutschen Evangelischen Missionsausschuß (3 May 1913), BMW/bmw1/8319.
128 Franz Hespers to Solf (4 May 1913), BArch R1001/8.16, Film Nr. 79832, Bd. 863, pag. 223.
129 Löwenstein to Axenfeld (15 May 1913), BMW/bmw1/895.
130 Axenfeld to Löwenstein (24 May 1913), BMW/bmw1/895.

131 Axenfeld to Christian Schumann (30 May 1913), BMW/bmw1/895. On the ubiquity of militaristic rhetoric in German politics, see Roger Chickering, "Militarism and Radical Nationalism," in Retallack, *Imperial Germany, 1871–1918*, 202–6.
132 Minutes of the Komitee of the Berlin Mission Society (3 June 1913), BMW/bmw1/57 and Solf to Berner (29 May 1913), BMW/bmw1/895.
133 Solf to the Berlin Mission Society (28 December 1913), BMW/bmw1/895; Berner to Axenfeld (1 March 1914), BMW/bmw1/895.
134 Minutes of the Komitee of the Berlin Mission Society (7 April 1914), BMW/bmw1/58.
135 "Bericht über die Entwicklung der Benediktinersache seit Mai 1913" (26 March 1914), BMW/bmw1/895.
136 Berlin Mission Society,"Freunde, die Patrone deutsch-ostafrikaniser Schutz- und Trutzschulen geworden sind" (18 May 1914), BMW/bmw1/901.
137 Minutes of the Komitee of the Berlin Mission Society (3 June 1914), BMW/bmw1/895.
138 Komitee of the Berlin Mission Society to Solf and Berner (3 June 1914), BMW/bmw1/895.
139 On the role of historical "scripts" in German history, see H.W. Smith, *The Continuities of German History*, esp. ch. 4.

5 Tending the Flock

1 1 Peter 5:2.
2 Tertialschreiben LIV (October 1897), BMW/bmw1/2017.
3 The German Colonial Society had 333 local branches at its high point in 1900. Wolfgang Fuhrmann, *Imperial Projections: Screening the German Colonies* (New York: Berghahn, 2015), 33 -4.
4 Przyrembel, "The Emotional Bond of Brotherliness," 166.
5 Conrad, *Globalization and the Nation in Imperial Germany*, 25.
6 Fuhrmann, *Imperial Projections*, 7–8, 9.
7 See Benninghoff-Lühl, *Deutsche Kolonialromane 1884–1914 in ihrem Entstehungs- und Wirkungszusammenhang*; Bowersox, *Raising Germans in the Age of Empire*; Ciarlo, *Advertising Empire*; Short, *Magic Lantern Empire*; and Wolter, *Die Vermarktung des Fremden*.
8 Short, *Magic Lantern Empire*, 49.
9 There was, unsurprisingly, a parallel project on the part of the Catholic mission orders. As shown in chapter 4, part of the Catholic case rested on patriotic loyalty to the German state. See Robbie Aitken, "Selling the Mission: The German Catholic Elite and the Educational Migration of African Youngsters to Europe," *German History* 33(1 Mar. 2015): 30–51.

10 Regionalism, nationalism, and concepts of the Heimat interacted in important ways across Germany during this period. See Celia Applegate, *A Nation of Provincials: The German Idea of Heimat* (Berkeley: University of California Press, 1990); Alon Confino, *The Nation as a Local Metaphor: Württemberg, Imperial Germany, and National Memory, 1871–1918* (Chapel Hill: University of North Carolina Press, 1997); and Matthew Levinger, *Enlightened Nationalism: The Transformation of Prussian Political Culture, 1806–1848* (Oxford, UK: Oxford University Press, 2002).

11 True to its globalist vision, the mission support network in the Heimat could extend beyond the geographical fatherland. In March 1905, Karl Axenfeld contacted William [Wilhelm?] Nordt of Scranton, Pennsylvania, and asked that Nordt distribute fundraising materials to "spiritually related" periodicals in North America. [Karl] Axenfled to [William] Nordt (27 March 1905), BMW/bmw1/2090.

12 "Die Belebung des Missionssinnes," 286.

13 1 Peter 5:4.

14 See, for example, H[ans] Meinhof, "Welchen Gewinn bringt die Arbeit für die Mission Pastoren und Gemeinden?" *AMZ* 37(1910): 239–40.

15 Ustorf, *Mission im Context*, 28–30.

16 [Gustav Warneck], "Die Rückwirkungen der Heidenmission auf das religiöse Leben der Heimat," *AMZ* 8(1881): 147–50.

17 Throughout this chapter and book I refer to locations by their historically contemporaneous names. As Pomerania and Silesia now lie wholly in Poland, the towns in those regions have been renamed or reverted to Polish names. Mützenow is now Możdżanowo and Belgard is now Białogard. For the reader's benefit, I will parenthetically provide the Polish name for cities, towns, and villages at the first in-text mention.

18 For some examples, see Frank Trentmann, ed., *Paradoxes of Civil Society: New Perspectives on Modern German and British History* (New York: Berghahn Books, 2000), and Oded Heilbronner, "The German Bourgeois Club as a Political and Social Structure in the Late Nineteenth and Early Twentieth Centuries," *Continuity and Change* 13, no. 3 (Dec. 1998): 443–73.

19 Total population 2,315 in 1913. *Meyers Orts- und Verkehrs-Lexicon des Deutschen Reichs*, vol. 1: A–K, vol. 2: L–Z, ed. E. Uetrecht (Leipzig: Bibliographisches Institut, 1913). For synodal population in 1907 see *Jahres-Bericht des Synodal-Missions-Hilfsvereins der Synode Ratzebuhr für 1907* (Ratzebuhr i. Pom.: Druck von Ernst Dietrich, [1908]), BMW/bmw1/7288.

20 *Handbuch der Gesellschaften mit beschränkter Haftung im Deutschen Reiche: Ein Hand- und Nachschlagebuch für Bankiers, Kaufleute, Industrielle, Kapitalisten etc.* (Leipzig: A. Schumann's Verlag, 1898), 248.

21 The participation of Arnim drew a personal touch from Karl Axenfeld, who reached out to thank the Count for his donation in 1905. [Karl] Axenfeld to [Dietlof] von Arnim-[Boitzenburg] (20 March 1905), BMW/bmw1/2090.
22 Ulrike Gleixner, "Remapping the World: The Vision of a Protestant Empire in the Eighteenth Century," in *Migration and Religion: Christian Transatlantic Missions, Islamic Migration to Germany*, ed. Barbara Becker-Cantarino (Amsterdam: Rodopi, 2012), 80.
23 *Siebenundzwangzigster Jahres-Bericht des Angermünder Missions-Hülfsvereins für 1900* (Angermünde: Druck von C. Windolff, [1901]), BMW/bmw1/6722.
24 Provinzieller Teil; Schlesische Missionskonferenz (n.d., [1917]), BMW/bmw1/7650.
25 Friedrich Büttner to Martin Gensichen (n.d., [January 1906]), BMW/bmw1/6760.
26 Siegfried Knak to Henriette Werner (11 January 1912), BMW/bmw1/7350; Henriette Werner to Siegfried Knak (n.d., [January 1912]), BMW/bmw1/7350; Siegfried Knak to Henriette Werner (20 January 1912), BMW/bmw1/7350.
27 Wilhelm Papst to Siegfried Knak (25 January 1912), BMW/bmw1/7350.
28 Siegfried Knak to Wilhelm Papst (30 January 1912), BMW/bmw1/7350.
29 Dietmar Neß, *Schlesisches Pfarrerbuch*, Bd. 8: Regierungsbezirk Liegnitz, Teil III (Leipzig: Evangelische Verlagsanstalt, 2016), 384.
30 Another example of the care given to these relationships can be found in Karl Axenfeld to Oberlehrer Baumann (26 September 1906), BMW/bmw1/6842; and Karl Axenfeld to Superintendent and Pastor prim. Straßmann (28 September 1907), BMW/bmw1/6842.
31 Dienstverweisung für den Missions-Sekretär der Provinz Schlesien Herrn Pastor Schmogro in Kunnewitz (Abschrift) (4 March 1902), Archiwum Pánstwowe w Wrocławiu 47/I/2272.
32 Bericht über den Stand der Missionsnähvereine (n.d., [1901]), BMW/bmw1/1562.
33 *33. Jahresbericht des Angermünder Missions-Hilfsvereins für 1906* (Diesdorf bei Gäbersdorf: Buchdruckerei der Schreiberhau-Diesdorfer Rettungsanstalten, [1907]), 4, BMW/bmw1/6722. See also J. Stumpf to Berlin Mission Society (14 April 1891), BMW/bmw1/1550.
34 Superintendent [Namick] to Frau Direktor (9 August 1894), BMW/bmw1/1553.
35 [Ilse Rauch] to [Martin Gensichen] (6 December 1899), BMW/bmw1/1561.
36 [Elise Gensichen] to [Frau Gensichen] (1 December 1896), BMW/bmw1/1554.

37 *Siebenundzwanzigster Jahresbericht des evangelischen Missions-Hilfsvereins im Parchwitzer Kirchenkreise: Nebst Nachweis über Einnahme und Ausgabe im Jahre 1884* (Diesdorf bei Kuhnern: Druck der Schreiberhau-Diesdorfer Rettungs-Anstalten, [1885]), 15–23, Archiwum Pánstwowe w Wrocławiu 47/I/2220.

38 Hermann Johann Karl Friedrich Olshausen to Hermann Theodor Wangemann (27 July 1880), BMW/bmw1/7225.

39 Population statistics taken from *Gemeindelexicon für das Konigreich Preußen. VI. Gemeindelexikon für die Provinz Schlesien* (Berlin: Verlag des Königliches statistisches Bureaus, 1887); *Gemeindelexicon für das Königreich Preußen. VI. Gemeindelexicon für die Provinz Schlesien* (Berlin: Verlag des Königlichen statistischen Bureaus, 1898); and *Meyers Orts- und Verkehrs-Lexicon des Deutschen Reichs.*

40 Fragebogen für die Missionshilfsvereine der Berliner-Missionsgesellschaft: Bunzlau (2 October 1912), BMW/bmw1/6842.

41 Berichterstattung über den Stand der Betheiligung am Werk der äußeren Mission für die Kreissynode des Jahres 1886 (Bunzlau I & II) (30 December 1886), Archiwum Pánstwowe w Wrocławiu 47/I/2281.

42 Fragebogen für die Missionshilfsvereine der Berliner Missionsgesellschaft: Sprottau (15 October 1912), BMW/bmw1/7350; Statistische Nachweisung über den Stand der Äußeren Mission in der Provinz Schlesien für das Jahr 1912 (n.d., [November 1914], Archiwum Pánstwowe w Wrocławiu 47/I/2215.

43 *77. Jahresbericht des Missions-Hilfsvereins zu Mützenow bei Stolp und Umgegend für das Jahr 1906. Synode Stolp-Stadt* (Stolp i. Pom.: Druck der W. Delmanzoschen Buchdruckerei, [1907]), BMW/bmw1/7192.

44 "Provinzial-Nachrichten," *Angermünder Zeitung und Kreisblatt*, Jg. 51, Nr. 127, 14 August 1897.

45 *Jahresbericht des Missions-Hülfs-Vereins der Synode Ratzebuhr für 1899–1900* (Ratzebuhr: Druck von Ed. Zorl's Mw., [1901]); *Jahres-Bericht des Synodal-Missions-Hilfsvereins der Synode Ratzebuhr für 1912* (Diesdorf bei Gäbersdorf: Buchdruckerei der Schreiberhau-Diesdorfer Rettungsanstalten, [1913]), BMW/bmw1/7288.

46 Bericht auf die Zuschrift vom 6. April 1901 (2 May 1901), BMW/bmw1/7350; *Siebenundzwanzigster Jahres-Bericht des Angermünder Missions-Hülfsvereins für 1900* (Angermünde: Druck von C. Windolff, [1900]); *Jahresbericht des Missions-Hilfsvereins der Synode Belgard für das Jahr 1900/1901* (Diesdorf bei Gäbersdorf: Buchdruckerei der Schreiberhau-Diesdorfer Rettungsanstalten, [1901]).

47 *39. Jahresbericht des Angermünder Missions-Hilfsvereins für 1913 (bis Ende Dezember)* (Diesdorf bei Gäbersdorf: Buchdruckerei der Schreiberhau-Diesdorfer Rettungsanstalten, 1914).

48 "Freundliche Einladung zum Missionsfest des Missionshilfs-Vereins vom St. Jakobi am Sonntag, den 20. February 1910" ([Jan/Feb] 1910), BMW/bmw1/6784.
49 Spindler, "The Protestant Mission Study," in Dujardin and Prudhomme, *Mission and Science*, 42.
50 Tertialschreiben LXV (November 1901), BMW/bmw1/2017.
51 *Sechsunddreißigster Jahresbericht des evangelischen Missionshilfsvereins im Parchwitzer Kirchenkreis nebst Nachweis über Einnahme und Ausgabe im Jahre 1893* (Diesdorf bei Gäbersdorf: Buchdruckerei der Schreiberhau-Diesdorfer Rettungsanstalten, [1894]), 5–6, BMW/bmw1/7225.
52 *Achtunddreißigster Jahresbericht des evangelischen Missionshilfsvereins im Parchwitzer Kirchenkreis nebst Nachweis über Einnahme und Ausgabe im Jahre 1895* (Diesdorf bei Gäbersdorf: Buchdruckerei der Schreiberhau-Diesdorfer Rettungsanstalten, [1896]), 5, BMW/bmw1/7225.
53 *Siebenundvierzigster Jahresbericht des evangelischen Missionshilfsvereins im Parchwitzer Kirchenkreis nebst Nachweis über Einnahme und Ausgabe im Jahre 1904* (Diesdorf bei Gäbersdorf: Buchdruckerei der Schreiberhau-Diesdorfer Rettungsanstalten [1905]), BMW/bmw1/7225.
54 Martin Gensichen to Friedrich Büttner (21 April 1908), BMW/bmw1/6760.
55 For example, Otto Ranke to Martin Gensichen (5 January 1905), BMW/bmw1/6785 and Otto Ranke to [Martin Gensichen] (15 January 1906), BMW/bmw1/6785.
56 F. Koehler [Köhler] to [Martin Gensichen] (3 January 1907), BMW/bmw1/6785; F. Koehler [Köhler] to Berlin Mission Society Vorstand (23 June 1908), BMW/bmw1/6785; M[artin] Gensichen to [Otto] von Ranke (8 December 1908), BMW/bmw1/6785; F. Koehler to Berlin Mission Society (23 June 1908), BMW/bmw1/6785 and Martin Wilde to Otto von Ranke (11 September 1908), BMW/bmw1/6785.
57 Abschrift aus dem 6. Bericht des Missionssekretärs Pastor Ernst Moldt in Alt-Werder (pro I. Quartal 1904), BMW/bmw1/6760.
58 "Grosses Volksmissionsfest" (n.d., [June 1910]), BMW/bmw1/2103.
59 "Einladung zum Dampfer-Missions-Fest" (n.d., [June 1911]), BMW/bmw1/2103.
60 "Großes Missionsfest" (n.d., [June 1910]), BMW/bmw1/2103.
61 Mahler's visit to Bunzlau was not the first by an itinerant mission preacher. By 1894 the city was a well-established stop on travelling mission preaching tours. Berthold, *Festschrift zum 25 jährigen Jubiläum des Schlesischen Provinzialvereins für die Berliner Mission ein Beitrag zur Missionsgeschichte Schlesiens* (n.d., [1912]), 30, Archiwum Pánstwowe w Wrocławiu 47/I/2215.

62 *32. Jahresbericht des Angermünder Missions-Hülfsvereins für 1905* (Diesdorf bei Gäbersdorf: Buchdruckerei der Schreiberhau-Diesdorfer Rettungsanstalten, [1906]), 2, BMW/bmw1/6722.

63 "Provinzial-Nachrichten," *Angermünder Zeitung und Kreisblatt* Jg. 48, Nr. 72, 9 May 1894.

64 Abschrift aus dem 6. Bericht des Sekretärs Pastor Hagena in Stolpe (Oder) (pro I. Quartal 1904), BMW/bmw1/6722; Provinzial Nachrichten," *Angermünder Zeitung und Kreisblatt* Jg. 58, Nr. 46, 22 March 1904.

65 Auszugsweise Abschrift aus dem 7. Bericht des Sekretärs P. Hagena-Stolpe (Oder) (April bis September 1904), BMW/bmw1/6722.

66 *31. Jahresbericht des Angermünder Missions-Hülfsvereins für 1904* (Diesdorf bei Gäbersdorf: Buchdruckerei der Schreiberhau-Diesdorfer Rettungsanstalten, [1904]), 2, BMW/bmw1/6722.

67 Otto Hagena to Karl Axenfeld (15 June 1906), BMW/bmw1/6722; *33. Jahresbericht des Angermünder Missions-Hilfsvereins für 1906* (Diesdorf bei Gäbersdorf: Buchdruckerei der Schreiberhau-Diesdorfer Rettungsanstalten, [1907]), 3–4, BMW/bmw1/6722. See Alexander Merensky, "Deutschlands Pflicht gegen seine schwarzen Unterthanen," *Afrika: Monatsschrifte für die sittliche und soziale Entwicklung der deutschen Schutzgebiete* 2 (1895): 77–82; and Alexander Merensky, *Deutschlands Pflicht gegenüber den Heiden und dem Heidentum in seinen Kolonien*, Beiträge zur Missionskunde 13 (Berlin: Buchhandlung der Berliner evangelischen Missionsgesellschaft, 1905).

68 *33. Jahresbericht des Angermünder Missions-Hilfsvereins für 1906* (Diesdorf bei Gäbersdorf: Buchdruckerei der Schreiberhau-Diesdorfer Rettungsanstalten, [1907]), 4, BMW/bmw1/6722.

69 *Reichs-Kino-Addressbuch* (Berlin: LBB, 1920/21). With thanks to Klaus Weber for the citation.

70 [H.] Glüer and [Karl] Axenfeld to Kommittee of the Berlin Mission Society (8 June 1911), BMW/bmw1/2305.

71 At this time, the only significant study of colonial cinema in Germany points out the lack of research on missionary filmmaking. Fuhrmann, *Imperial Projections*, 18.

72 *Fünfundvierzigster Jahresbericht des evangelischen Missionshilfsvereins im Parchwitzer Kirchenkreis nebst Nachweis über Einnahme und Ausgabe im Jahre 1902* (Diesdorf bei Gäbersdorf: Buchdruckerei der Schreiberhau-Diesdorfer Rettungsanstalten, [1903]), 5, BMW/bmw1/7225.

73 *Sechsundvierzigster Jahresbericht des evangelischen Missionshilfsvereins im Parchwitzer Kirchenkreis nebst Nachweis über Einnahme und Ausgabe im Jahre 1903* (Diesdorf bei Gäbersdorf: Buchdruckerei der Schreiberhau-Diesdorfer Rettungsanstalten [1904]), 3–4, BMW/bmw1/7225. Other colonial "entertainments" also included physical objects from

the colonies in their presentations, Carl Müller, one of the earliest colonial film presenters, displayed African game trophies, African handicrafts, and his pith helmet at his screenings. Fuhrmann, *Imperial Projections*, 54.

74 Superintendent Straßmann to Königliche Consistorium der Provinz Schlesien (25 July 1903), Archiwum Pánstwowe w Wrocławiu 47/I/2272. Mahler's extensive work in and around Bunzlau included the writing of a history of the Bunzlau *Missionshilfsverein*. M.W. Mahler, "Geschichte des Missions-Hilfs-Vereins Bunzlau I u. II von Jahr 1832–1903" (unpublished manuscript, n.d.), BMW/bmw1/6842.

75 [Carl] Meinhof to [Hermann Theodor Wangemann] (29 June 29 1893), BMW/bmw1/2033.

76 Ella Mahler to [Martin Gensichen] (24 November 1899), BMW/bmw1/1561.

77 Abschrift aus dem Bericht No. 1 über die Missionstätigkeit des Pfarrer M.W. Mahler vom 1. Januar bis 27. Oktober 1903, BMW/bmw1/6841.

78 Abschrift aus dem 2. Bericht des Missionssekretärs Pfarrer Mahler (November–Dezember 1903), BMW/bmw1/6841.

79 Such large gatherings were not unusual. On 14 May 1905 a children's service gathered over 400 children to hear about the hardships of heathen children and the uplift of converted children in the mission schools. *Achtundsechszigster Jahresbericht des Missions-Hülfs-Vereins der Berliner Missions-Gesellschaft für die Diöcesen Bunzlau I und II über das Rechnungsjahr 1905/06* (Bunzlau: J.H. Stoltz'sche Buchdruckerei, 1906), 4, BMW/bmw1/6842.

80 Abschrift aus dem 2. Bericht des Missionssekretärs Pfarrer Mahler (November–December 1903, BMW/bmw1/6841.

81 Auszugsweise Abschrift aus dem 6. Quartalbericht des Missionssekretärs Pfarrer Mahler-Altjäschwitz (1. Oktober bis 31.12.04), BMW/bmw1/6841.

82 Abschrift aus dem 6. Bericht des Missionssekretärs Pastor Moldt-Alt-Werder (pro I. Quartal 1904) (1904), BMW/bmw1/7192.

83 Tertialschreiben LXX (July 1903), BMW/bmw1/2018.

84 Tertialschreiben LXIX (March 1903), BMW/bmw1/2018.

85 Verhandelt Berliner Missionshaus, den 2. November 1908 (2 November 1908), BMW/bmw1/2035.

86 Bowersox, *Raising Germans in the Age of Empire*, 81–2.

87 Programm für den Missions-Lehrkursus 1895 (n.d., [April 1895]), BMW/bmw1/2033.

88 Siegfried Knak, Ratschläge zur Veranstaltung von Missionspredigtreisen (Spring 1912), 2, BMW/bmw1/2427.

89 Rohr, Orientirende Bemerkungen zu Missions-Predigtreisen (n.d., [1882]), Archiwum Pánstwowe w Wrocławiu (hereafter AP Wrocław) 47/I/2227.

90 Knak, Ratschläge zur Veranstaltung von Missionspredigtreisen, 3–4.
91 *Achtundsechszigster Jahresbericht des Missions-Hülfs-Vereins der Berliner Missions-Gesellschaft für die Diöcesen Bunzlau I und II über das Rechnungsjahr 1905/06* (Bunzlau: J.H. Stoltz'sche Buchdruckerei, 1906), 5, BMW/bmw1/6842; *Vierundsiebzigster Jahresbericht des Missions-Hülfs-Vereins der Berliner Missions-Gesellschaft für die Diöcesen Bunzlau I und II über das Rechnungsjahr 1911/12* (Bunzlau: Druck von J. H. Stoltz, 1912), 4, BMW/bmw1/6842.
92 *78. Jahresbericht des Missions-Hilfsvereins zu Mützenow bei Stolp und Umgegend für das Jahr 1907. Synode Stolp-Stadt* (Stolp i. Pom.: Druck der W. Ddelmanzoschen Buchdruckerei, [1908]), 2, BMW/bmw1/7192.
93 Jens Jaeger, "Colony as *Heimat*? The Formation of Colonial Identity in Germany around 1900," *German History* 27, no. 4 (Oct. 2009): 467–89.
94 *Fünfzigster Jahresbericht des evangelischen Missionshilfsvereins im Parchwitzer Kirchenkreis nebst Nachweis über Einnahme und Ausgabe im Jahre 1907* (Diesdorf bei Gäbersdorf: Buchdruckerei der Schreiberhau-Diesdorfer Rettungsanstalten, [1908]), 3, BMW/bmw1/7225.
95 [Traugott Wilhelm Ludwig] Hanisch to Berlin Mission Society (18 December 1862), BMW/bmw1/6759.
96 Helene Kalliefe to Karl Axenfeld (28 January 1910), BMW/bmw1/6842; Helene Kalliefe to Karl Axenfeld (9 March 1910), BMW/bmw1/6842.
97 Sitzung der Wander-Ausstellungs-Kommission, pg. 1 (20 December 1910), BMW/bmw1/2208.
98 [Karl] Axenfeld to Superintendenten der Berliner Mission in Südafrika, Deutsch-Ostafrika und China (10 June 1911), BMW/bmw1/2208.
99 Sitzung der Wander-Ausstellungs-Kommission, pg. 2 (20 December 1910), BMW/bmw1/2208.
100 [Wilhelm] Gr[ündler] to [Fritz] Reuter (29 August 1912), BMW/bmw1/2208.
101 [Wilhelm] Gründler to Superintenden der Berliner Mission in Südafrika, Deutsch-Ostafrika und China (18 April 1912), BMW/bmw1/2208.
102 Penny and Bunzl, introduction to *Worldly Provincialism*, 2, 17. See also Zimmerman, *Anthropology and Antihumanism in Imperial Germany*.
103 Penny, *Objects of Culture*, 23.
104 [Wilhelm] Gr[ündler] to [Fritz] Reuter (29 August 29 1912), BMW/bmw1/2208.
105 Sitzung der Wander-Ausstellungs-Kommission, pg. 3–4 (20 December 1910), BMW/bmw1/2208; [Paul] Gröschel to Missionaries in German East Africa (28 December 1910), BMW/bmw1/2208.
106 Penny, *Objects of Culture*, 151.
107 Sitzung der Wander-Ausstellungs-Kommission, pg. 5 (20 December 1910), BMW/bmw1/2208.

108 Sitzung der Wander-Ausstellungs-Kommission, pg. 4 (15 March 1912), BMW/bmw1/2208.
109 Betrifft: Missions-Wander-Ausstellung" (25 August 1911), BMW/bmw1/2208.
110 [Wilhelm] Gründler to Chr[istian] Endemann, [Paul] Gröschel, [Richard] Zimmerling, [Wilhelm] Lutschewitz, and [Diedrich] Buck (18 April 1912), BMW/bmw1/2208.
111 S[iegfried] Knak to the Vorstände der Missions-Hilfs und Näh-Vereine, des Lehrer-Missionsbundes, des Laien-Missionsbundes, des Christlichen Vereins jünger Männer, der Stadtmission und an die Herren Geistlichen in Halle a/S. (6 March 1913), BMW/bmw1/2208.
112 S[iegfried] Knak, Herzliche Bitte um Mitarbeit bei der völkerkundlichen Ausstellung aus den Arbeitsgebieten der Berliner Mission (5 March 1913), BMW/bmw1/2208.
113 Einladung zum Besuch der völkerkundlichen Ausstellung aus den Arbeitsfeldern der Berliner Missionsgesellschaft (n.d., [March/April 1913]), BMW/bmw1/2208.
114 Besuch der Wander-Ausstellung in Halle a/S. vom 4. April bis 1. Mai 1913 (n.d., [May 1913]), BMW/bmw1/2209.
115 S[iegfried] Knak to Provincial Mission Secretaries (23 August 1913), BMW/bmw1/2209.
116 Protokoll der Sitzung der Ausstellungskommission (24 February 1914), BMW/bmw1/2209; Einladung zum Besuch der *völkerkundlichen* Ausstellung aus den Arbeitsfeldern der Berliner Missionsgesellschaft (n.d., [June 1914]), BMW/bmw1/2209; Pastor Hasenjäger and Siegfried Knak to Herren Geistlichen der Synoden Kolberg, Köslin, Belgard, Treptow A/R. und Greifenberg (15 June 1914), BMW/bmw1/6760.
117 "Provinzial-Nachrichten," *Angermünder Zeitung und Kreisblatt* Jg. 48, Nr. 82, 29 May 1894.
118 *28. Jahresbericht des Angermünder Missions-Hilfsvereins für 1901* (Diesdorf bei Gäbersdorf: Buchdruckerei der Schreiberhau-Diesdorfer Rettungsanstalten, [1902]), 4, 6, BMW/bmw1/6722.
119 *29. Jahresbericht des Angermünder Missions-Hilfsvereins für 1902* (Diesdorf bei Gäbersdorf: Buchdruckerei der Schreiberhau-Diesdorfer Rettungsanstalten, [1903]), 4, BMW/bmw1/6722. Records of the behind-the-scenes work that went into organizing these visits can be found in the mission archives; see, for example, [Gotthold Wilhelm] Baltzer to Martin Gensichen (30 July 1902), BMW/bmw1/6722.
120 Unangst, "Men of Science and Action," 310–16.
121 Honeck, Klimke, and Kuhlmann, introduction to *Germany and the Black Diaspora*, 6.

122 Robbie Aitken, "Education and Migration: Cameroonian Schoolchildren and Apprentices in Germany, 1884–1914," in Honeck, Klimke, and Kuhlmann, *Germany and the Black Diaspora*, 218–19.

123 *Vierundzwanzigster Jahres-Bericht des Angermünder Missions-Hülfsverein für 1897* (Angermünde: Druck von C. Windolff, [1898]), 3–6, BMW/bmw1/6722.

124 Claudius Torp, "Missionary Education and Musical Communities in Sub-Saharan Colonial Africa," *Itinerario* 41(2): 238–9. Reuter brought the Lobedu to Berlin without the agreement of the Berlin Mission Society's leadership; see Ulrich van der Heyden, "Die Kolonial- und die Transvaal Ausstellung 1896/97," in van der Heyden and Zeller, *Kolonialmetropole Berlin*, 135.

125 Wolter, *Die Vermarktung des Fremden*, 83.

126 Eric Ames, *Carl Hagenbeck's Empire of Entertainments* (Seattle: University of Washington Press, 2008); Nigel Rothfels, *Savages and Beasts: The Birth of the Modern Zoo* (Baltimore, MD: Johns Hopkins University Press, 2002).

127 Short, *Magic Lantern Empire*, 91–3.

128 Torp, "Missionary Education and Musical Communities in Sub-Saharan Colonial Africa," 238.

129 van der Heyden, "Die Kolonial- und die Transvaal Ausstellung 1896/97," 138–9.

130 Torp, "Missionary Education and Musical Communities in Sub-Saharan Colonial Africa," 239.

131 *35. Jahresbericht des Angermünder Missions-Hilfsvereins für 1907* (Diesdorf bei Gäbersdorf: Buckdruckerei der Schreiberhau-Diesdorfer Rettungsanstalten, [1908]), 4, BMW/bmw1/6722. For other examples of Chinese theologians, see Albert Monshan Wu, *From Christ to Confucius: German Missionaries, Chinese Christians, and the Globalization of Christianity, 1860-1950* (New Haven, CT: Yale University Press, 2016), 220-246.

132 *37. Jahresbericht des Angermünder Missions-Hilfsvereins für 1910* (Diesdorf bei Gäbersdorf: Buchdruckerei der Schreiberhau-Diesdorfer Rettungsanstalten, [1911]), BMW/bmw1/6723.

133 *38. Jahresbericht des Angermünder Missionshilfsvereins für 1911–1912* (Diesdorf bei Gäbersdorf: Buchdruckerei der Schreiberhau-Diesdorfer Rettungsanstalten, 1913), BMW/bmw1/6723.

134 *Fünfundfünfzigster Jahresbericht des Missions-Hülfs-Vereins der Berliner Missions-Gesellschaft für die Diöcesen Bunzlau I und II über das Rechnungsjahr 1902/03* (Bunzlau: J.H. Stoltz'sche Buchdruckerei, 1903), 5, BMW/bmw1/6841.

135 Some of these activities date to Pietistic networks in the first half of the eighteenth century. These networks articulated an early modern conception of Protestant empire whose link to late nineteenth-century

German Protestant missionaries is indicated but unproven. Gleixner, "Remapping the World," 85 and 89–90.

136 Karl Axenfeld, "Der Wert einer unmittelbaren festen Verbindung zwischen den Freundeskreisen und den von ihnen unterstützten Missionsgesellschaften" (n.d. [1911]), BMW/bmw1/1538.

137 Reinhold Grundemann, "Beitrag zur Missionsarbeit in der Gemeinde" in *Jahrbüchlein der Missionskonferenz in der Provinz Brandenburg* (1895), 17–19.

138 Missions Homiletische Leitsätze (n.d., ca. 1900–4), BMW/bmw1/2035.

139 Mittel zur Veranschaulichung des beim Lehrerkursus dargebotenen Stoffes (n.d., [1908–10]), BMW/bmw1/2071.

140 Mittel zur Veranschaulichung des beim Lehrerkursus dargebotenen Stoffes (n.d., [1908–10]), 1–4, BMW/bmw1/2071.

141 Mittel zur Veranschaulichung des beim Lehrerkursus dargebotenen Stoffes (n.d., [1908–10]), 3, 15, 17, BMW/bmw1/2071.

142 *Neunundsechszigster Jahresbericht des Missions-Hülfs-Vereins der Berliner Missions-Gesellschaft für die Diöcesen Bunzlau I und II über das Rechnungsjahr 1906/07* (Bunzlau: J.H. Stoltz'sche Buchdruckerei, 1907), 4, BMW/bmw1/6842.

143 *Einundsiebzigster Jahresbericht des Missions-Hülfs-Vereins der Berliner Missions-Gesellschaft für die Diöcesen Bunzlau I und II über das Rechnungsjahr 1908/09* (Bunzlau: J.H. Stoltz'sche Buchdruckerei, 1909), 4.

144 *Neunzehnter Jahres-Bericht des Angermünder Missions-Hülfsvereins für das Jahr vom 1. Juli 1891 bis dahin 1892* (Angermünde: Druck von C. Windolff, [1892]), 6, BMW/bmw1/6722; *Einundzwanzigster Jahres-Bericht des Angermünder Missions-Hülfsvereins für 1894* (Angermünde: Druck von C. Windolff, [1895], 3, BMW/bmw1/6722.

145 *Bericht des Missions-Hülfs-Vereins der Synode Belgard für das Jahr 1890*, BMW/bmw1/6759.

146 *Jahresbericht des Missions-Hilfsvereins der Synode Belgard für das Jahr 1908/09* (Diesdorf bei Gäbersdorf: Buchdruckerei der Schreiberhau-Diesdorfer Rettungsanstalten, [1909]), 4, BMW/bmw1/6760.

147 *Jahresbericht des Missions-Hilfsvereins der Synode Belgard für das Jahr 1906/1907* (Diesdorf bei Gäbersdorf: Buchdruckerei der Schreiberhau-Diesdorfer Rettungsanstalten, [1907]), 2.

148 *Einundsiebzigster Jahresbericht des Missions-Hülfs-Vereins der Berliner Missions-Gesellschaft für die Diöcesen Bunzlau I und II über das Rechnungsjahr 1908/09* (Bunzlau: J.H. Stoltz'sche Buchdruckerei, 1909), 4.

149 *Neunundvierzigster Jahresbericht des Missions-Hülfs-Vereins der Berliner Missions-Gesellschaft für Bunzlau und Umgegend über das Rechnungsjahr 1886/87* (Bunzlau: C.A. Voigt's Buchdruckerei, 1887), 3, BMW/bmw1/6841.

150 *Zweiundzwanzigster Jahresbericht des evangelischen Missions-Hülfs-Vereins im Parchwitzer Kirchenkreise. Nebst Nachweis über Einnahme und Ausgabe im Jahre 1879* (Diesdorf bei Kuhnern: Druck der Schreiberhau-Diesdorfer Rettungs-Anstalten, [1880]), 5, BMW/bmw1/7225.

151 *Siebenundzwanzigster Jahresbericht des evangelischen Missions-Hilfsvereins im Parchwitzer Kirchenkreise. Nebst Nachweis über Einnahme und Ausgabe im Jahre 1884* (Diesdorf bei Kuhnern: Druck der Schreiberhau-Diesdorfer Rettungs-Anstalten, [1885]), 11, Archiwum Pánstwowe w Wrocławiu 47/I/2220.

152 Fragebogen für die Missionshilfsverein der Berliner Misisonsgesellschaft: Ratzebuhr (31 October 1911), BMW/bmw1/7288.

153 [Traugott Wilhelm Ludwig] Hanisch to Berlin Mission Society (14 January 1864), BMW/bmw1/6759; Magdalen Kolbe to Theodor Wangemann (9 March 1867), BMW/bmw1/6759.

154 Meyer to Berlin Mission Society (12 July 1880), BMW/bmw1/6759.

155 *35. Jahresbericht des Angermünder Missions-Hilfsvereins für 1907* (Diesdorf bei Gäbersdorf: Buckdruckerei der Schreiberhau-Diesdorfer Rettungsanstalten, [1908]), 4–5, BMW/bmw1/6722.

156 *36. Jahresbericht des Angermünder Missions-Hilfsvereins für 1909* (Diesdorf bei Gäbersdorf: Buchdruckerei der Schreiberhau-Diesdorfer Rettungsanstalten, [1910]), 3, BMW/bmw1/6722.

157 P. Stange to Martin Gensichen (23 May 1892), BMW/bmw1/6784.

158 Max Sarowy to Berlin Mission Society (13 May 1909), BMW/bmw1/6784; Max Sarowy to Martin Wilde (9 September 1909), BMW/bmw1/6784.

159 Karl Axenfeld to Max Sarowy (16 January 1911), BMW/bmw1/6784.

160 Paul Heese to Karl Axenfeld (20 January 1911), BMW/bmw1/6784; Max Sarowy to Karl Axenfeld (25 January 1911), BMW/bmw1/6784; Karl Axenfeld to Max Sarowy (4 July 1911), BMW/bmw1/6784; Max Sarowy to Karl Axenfeld (9 July 1911), BMW/bmw1/6784.

161 Auszugsweise Abschrift aus dem 8. Bericht des Missionssekretär P. Ernst Moldt in Alt-Werder pro III. Quartal 1904 (26 September 1904), BMW/bmw1/7192.

162 Gottfried Beyer to Martin Gensichen (9 September 1907), BMW/bmw1/6760.

163 F[riedrich] Büttner to Martin Gensichen (24 October 1907), BMW/bmw1/6760.

164 Martin Gensichen to G[ottfried] Beyer (26 October 1907), BMW/bmw1/6760; Martin Gensichen to Friedrich Büttner (26 October 1907), BMW/bmw1/6760.

165 Friedrich Büttner to Martin Gensichen (11 November 1907), BMW/bmw1/6760.

166 G[ottfried] Beyer to Martin Gensichen (7 February 1908), BMW/bmw1/6760.

167 Friedrich Büttner to Martin Gensichen (9 March 1908), BMW/bmw1/6760.

168 Martin Gensichen to Friedrich Büttner (20 March 1908), BMW/bmw1/6760; Friedrich Büttner to Martin Gensichen (27 March 1908), BMW/bmw1/6760; Friedrich Büttner to Martin Gensichen (23 April 1908), BMW/bmw1/6760; Friedrich Büttner to Martin Gensichen (2 April 1909), BMW/bmw1/6760; [H.] Glüer to Friedrich Büttner (13 April 1909), BMW/bmw1/6760.

169 Siegfried Knak to Pastor Haegeholz (13 September 1910), BMW/bmw1/7276.

170 *Jahres-Bericht des Synodal-Missions-Hilfsvereins der Synode Ratzebuhr für 1910* (Ratzebuhr i. Pom.: Druck von Ernst Dietrich, [1911]), BMW/bmw1/7288. On Islam and mission perspectives, see Pawliková-Vilhanová, "Crescent or Cross?," 88; Weiss, "Islam, Missionaries and Residents," 173; Rebekka Habermas, "Islam Debates around 1900: Colonies in Africa, Muslims in Berlin, and the Role of Missionaries and Orientalists," in Becker-Cantarino, *Migration and Religion*, 123–54.

171 Heinrich Julius Oelke, *Als Missionar in Ostafrika: Erinnerungen aus den Jahren 1905-1959*, ed. Ulrich van der Heyden (Bremen: Edition Falkenberg, 2014), 50. Haegeholz had also expanded his knowledge by attending the 1904 Missions-Lehrkursus. See Missions-Lehr-Kursus 1904 (1904), BMW/bmw1/2035.

172 The authors are likely referring to the "Uganda Mutiny" of 1897 and the subsequent reorganization of British rule there between 1897 and 1900.

173 *Jahresbericht des Missions-Hilfsverein der Synode Belgard für das Jahr 1903/1904* (Diesdorf bei Gäbersdorf: Buchdruckerei der Schreiberhau-Diesdorfer Rettungsanstalten, [1904]), 4; *Dreiundsechsziger Jahresbericht des Missions-Hülfs-Vereins der Berliner Missions-Gesellschaft für die Diöcesen Bunzlau I und II über das Rechnungsjahr 1900/01* (Bunzlau: J.H. Stoltz'sche Buchdruckerei, 1901), 3, BMW/bmw1/6841.

174 *81. Jahresbericht des Missions-Hilfsvereins zu Mützenow bei Stolp und Umgegend für das Jahr 1910. Synode Stolp-Stadt* (Stolp i. Pom.: Druck der W. Delmanzoschen Buchdruckerei, [1911]), 4, BMW/bmw1/7192.

175 *Sechsundfünfzigster Jahresbericht des Missions-Hülfs-Vereins der Berliner Missions-Gesellschaft für die Diöcesan Bunzlau I und II über das Rechnungsjahr 1893/94* (Bunzlau: C.A. Voigt's Buchdruckerei, 1894), 3, BMW/bmw1/6841.

176 *Dreiundfünfzigster Jahresbericht des Missions-Hülfs-Vereins der Berliner Missions-Gesellschaft für Bunzlau und Umgegend über das Rechnungsjahr*

1890/91 (Bunzlau: C.A. Voigt's Buchdruckerei, 1891), 2, BMW/bmw1/6841.

177 *Zweiundvierzigster Jahresbericht des Missions-Hülfs-Vereins der Berliner Missions-Gesellschaft für Bunzlau und Umgegend über das Rechnungsjahr 1879/80* (Bunzlau: C.A. Voigt's Buchdruckerei, 1880), 5, BMW/bmw1/6841.

178 The *Jahresbericht* attributes the idea to Gustav Warneck. *Fünfundvierzigster Jahresbericht des Missions-Hülfs-Vereins der Berliner Missions-Gesellschaft für Bunzlau und Umgegend über das Rechnungsjahr 1882/83* (Bunzlau: C.A. Voigt's Buchdruckerei, 1883), BMW/bmw1/6841.

179 *Zweiunzwanzigster Jahres-Bericht des Angermünder Missions-Hülfsvereins für 1895* (Angermünde: Druck von C. Windolff, [1896]), 7, BMW/bmw1/6722.

180 *32. Jahresbericht des Angermünder Missions-Hülfsvereins für 1905* (Diesdorf bei Gäbersdorf: Buchdruckerei der Schreiberhau-Diesdorfer Rettungsanstalten, [1906]), 2, BMW/bmw1/6722.

181 *Jahresbericht des Missions-Hilfsvereins der Synode Belgard für das Jahr 1900/1901* (Diesdorf bei Gäbersdorf: Buchdruckerei der Schreiberhau-Diesdorfer Rettungsanstalten, [1901]), 3, BMW/bmw1/6759.

182 *Jahresbericht des Missions-Hilfsvereins der Synode Belgard für das Jahr 1900/1901* (Diesdorf bei Gäbersdorf: Buchdruckerei der Schreiberhau-Diesdorfer Rettungsanstalten, [1901]), 4, BMW/bmw1/6759.

183 *Jahresbericht des Missions-Hülfsverein der Synode Belgard für das Jahr 1904/1905* (Diesdorf bei Gäbersdorf: Buchdruckerei der Schreiberhau-Diesdorfer Rettungsanstalten, [1905]), 3.

184 *Vierzigster Jahresbericht des evangelischen Missionshilfsvereins im Parchwitzer Kirchenkreis nebst Nachweis über Einnahme und Ausgabe im Jahre 1897* (Diesdorf bei Gäbersdorf: Buchdruckerei der Schreiberhau-Diesdorfer Rettungsanstalten, [1898]), 5, BMW/bmw1/7225.

185 *Zweiundvierigster Jahresbericht des evangelischen Missionshilfsvereins im Parchwitzer Kirchenkreis nebst Nachweis über Einnahme und Ausgabe im Jahre 1899* (Diesdorf bei Gäbersdorf: Buchdruckerei der Schreiberhau-Diesdorfer Rettungsanstalten, [1900]), 4–6, BMW/bmw1/7225.

186 See, for example, *Zwangzister Jahres-Bericht des Angermünder Missions-Hülfsvereins für 1893* (Angermünde: Druck von C. Windolff, [1894], BMW/bmw1/6722; *Zweiundzwanzigster Jahres-Bericht des Angermünder Missions-Hülfsvereins für 1895* (Angermünde: Druck von C. Windolff, [1896]), BMW/bmw1/6722; *Dreiundzwanzigster Jahres-Bericht des Angermünder Missions-Hülfsvereins für 1896* (Angermünde: Druck von C. Windolff, [1897]), BMW/bmw1/6722; *Vierundzwanzigster Jahres-Bericht des Angermünder Missions-Hülfsverein für 1897* (Angermünde: Druck von C. Windolff, [1898]), BMW/bmw1/6722; *Sechsundzwanzigster Jahres-Bericht*

des Angermünder Missions-Hülfsverein für 1899 (Angermünde: Druck von C. Windolff, [1900]), BMW/bmw1/6722; and *38. Jahresbericht des Angermünder Missionshilfsverein für 1911–1912* (Diesdorf bei Gäbersdorf: Buchdruckerei der Schreiberhau-Diesdorfer Rettungsanstalten, 1913), BMW/bmw1/6723.

187 But the Berlin Mission Society received the preponderance of the donations. For example, in 1906 the Berlin Mission Society received 4,137.01 Marks out of 5,710.22 Marks total. See *77. Jahresbericht des Missions-Hilfsverein zu Mützenow bei Stolp und Umgegend für das Jahr 1906. Synode Stolp-Stadt* (Stolp i. Pommern: Druck der W. Delzmanzoschen Buchdruckerei, [1907]), BMW/bmw1/7192.

6 Iron Sharpens Iron

1 Elements of this speculative history are imagined from reports of the second international missionary gathering, the Jerusalem Meeting of the International Missionary Council in 1928. Sources of inspiration included William Paton, "The Jerusalem Meeting – and After," *International Review of Missions* 17, no. 3 (Jul. 1928), 435–44; and Oliver Chase Quick, "The Jerusalem Meeting and the Christian Message," *International Review of Missions* 17, no. 3 (Jul. 1928), 445–54.

2 Proverbs 27:17.

3 Hogg, *Ecumenical Foundations*, 203. In 1920, Julius Richter argued that Germany should be represented at international conferences in "enemy" countries, in spite of their wartime brutality toward Germany and its missions; see Pugach, *Africa in Translation*, 164–5.

4 Geyer and Paulmann, *The Mechanics of Internationalism*, 17–18.

5 Brian Stanley, *The World Missionary Conference, Edinburgh 1910* (Grand Rapids, MI: William B. Eerdmans Publishing Company, 2009), 2.

6 Gorman, *International Cooperation in the Early Twentieth Century*, 121–4.

7 P[aul] O[tto] Hennig, "Der Weltmissionskongreß in Edinburg," *Missionblatt der Brüdergemeine* 74(Aug. 1910): 200–1.

8 "Der Edinburger Missionskongreß," *Jahrbuch der vereinigten norddeutschen Missionskonferenzen* (1911): 9. See also Stanley, *The World Missionary Conference*, 79–80.

9 Purvis, *Theology and the University in Nineteenth-Century Germany*, 218.

10 Stanley, *The World Missionary Conference*, 50.

11 P[aul] O[tto] Hennig, "Der Weltmissionskongreß in Edinburg," *Missionblatt der Brüdergemeine* 74(Aug. 1910): 197.

12 W[alther] Trittelvitz, "Die Tage von Edinburg," *Beth-El* 2(1910): 190.

13 On the marginalization of Germans see Stanley, *The World Missionary Conference*, 31.

14 Equally troubling, they endorsed anti-Jewish views as well. Balz, "Überwindung der Religionen' und das Ziel der Mission," 106–8; Habermas, "Islam Debates around 1900," in Becker-Cantarino, *Migration and Religion*, 137.

15 Becker, *Becoming Muslim in Mainland Tanzania, 1890–2000*, 1.

16 Stanley, *The World Missionary Conference*, 9.

17 Stanley, *The World Missionary Conference*, 16.

18 Minutes of the Komitee of the Berlin Mission Society (4 September 1860), BMW/bmw1/41; Minutes of the Leipzig Mission General Assembly (23 May 1866), AFSt/ALMW-DHM II.2.1.

19 Minutes of the Leipzig Mission General Assembly (23 May 1866), AFSt/ALMW-DHM II.2.1, Item 2.

20 Minutes of the Leipzig Mission General Assembly (3 June 1868), AFSt/ALMW-DHM II.2.1. See also Hogg, *Ecumenical Foundations*, 63.

21 The attendees included Friedrich Fabri, Reinhold Grundemann, Karl Plath, and Ernst Reichel along with other less notable leaders of the Protestant mission movement. Gustav Warneck was unable to attend because of illness. See "Sechste kontinentale Missions-Konferenz in Bremen. 20.-23. Mai 1884," *AMZ* 11(1884): 309.

22 "Eine bedeutsame Missions-Konferenz," 545.

23 Hogg, *Ecumenical Foundations*, 15–16 and 48–50.

24 [Richard] Döhler, "Die deutschen Missionskonferenzen," *AMZ* 26(1899): 493–5.

25 "Die allgemeine Missionskonferenz in London," *Evangelisches Missions-Magazin, Neue Folge* 23(1879): 41–2, 49.

26 [Gustav] Warneck, editorial afterword to "Die allgemeine Missionsconferenz in London vom 21.-26. October 1878," by [August] Schreiber, *AMZ* 5(1878): 579–80.

27 Hogg, *Ecumenical Foundations*, 50. Kenneth Scott Latourette suggests Warneck's ideas had been fully forgotten at that point. Kenneth Scott Latourette, "Ecumenical Bearings of the Missionary Movement and the International Missionary Council," in *A History of the Ecumenical Movement, 1517–1948*, ed. Ruth Rouse and Stephen Charles Neill (Philadelphia, PA: Westminster Press, 1968), 363.

28 A[lexander] Merensky, "Die allgemeine Missionskonferenz in London vom 9.-19. Juni 1888," *AMZ* 15(1888): 401–3.

29 Merensky, "Die allgemeine Missionskonferenz in London," 543–4.

30 Merensky, "Die allgemeine Missionskonferenz in London," 403.

31 "Die allgemeine Missionskonferenz in London," *Evangelisches Missions-Magazin, Neue Folge* 32(1888): 25–8.

32 "Die allgemeine Missionskonferenz in London," *Evangelisches Missions-Magazin, Neue Folge* 32(1888): 25–8.

33 "Bericht über die Verhandlungen der achten kontinentalen Missionskonferenz zu Bremen in der Himmelfahrtswoche 1889," *AMZ* 16(1889): 2.
34 Merensky reported on the various main themes of the London Conference: mission methods, medical mission, instruction and education, women's mission work, organization and leadership of congregations, mission and literature, cooperation with the metropolitan church, missionary comity, and the relationship of trade and diplomacy to mission. Merensky, "Die allgemeine Missionskonferenz in London," 479.
35 Stanley, *The World Missionary Conference*, 26–7.
36 [Paul A. Menzel], "Die allgemeine Missionkonferenz in New York. 21. April bis 2. Mai.," *Evangelisches Missions-Magazin, Neue Folge* 42(1900): 345.
37 The German Evangelical Synod of North America had ties to the Basel and Rhenish Mission Societies.
38 Menzel, "Die allgemeine Missionskonferenz," 344.
39 Menzel, "Die allgemeine Missionskonferenz," 351. Among whom were only two German missionary officials of any note, Alexander Merensky and August Schreiber. This upset Menzel, who called on German missionary circles to strive so that this would not happen in the future. Menzel does report on the letter sent by Warneck and read (in translation) into the record by Judson Smith, Foreign Secretary of the American Board of Commissioners for Foreign Missions.
40 The challenge of defining the Christian world and the mission sphere would nearly condemn the 1910 Edinburgh Conference to a premature death over whether or not to include mission work among Christian, but not Protestant, people. Eventually the conference agreed on a division that placed all Christians on one side of the mission project and all "heathens" on the other. See Stanley, *The World Missionary Conference*, esp. 49–72.
41 Menzel, "Die allgemeine Missionskonferenz," 354–5.
42 Menzel, "Die allgemeine Missionskonferenz," 353.
43 [Gustav] Warneck, "An die Allg. Missions-Konferenz in New York," *AMZ* 27(1900): 201–3. See John R. Mott, *The Evangelization of the World in This Generation* (New York: Student Volunteer Movement for Foreign Missions, 1900).
44 British missionaries felt no less excited. See Stanley, *The World Missionary Conference*, 3.
45 Joh[annes] Warneck, "Zur bevorstehenden Welt-Missions-Konferenz," *AMZ* 37(1910): 3–5.
46 J. Warneck, "Zur bevorstehenden Welt-Missions-Konferenz," 15.

47 Minutes of the Deutschen Evangelischen Missionsausschuß (27 October 1908), AFSt/ALMW-DHM II.27.1.15.I, pag. 3, Item II.

48 Minutes of the Deputierten der deutschen Missionsgesellschaften vor Vorbereitung des Edinburger Missionskongresses (18 May 1909), UA.R.15.A.73.c, S. 25, Item 1 and 2.

49 World Missionary Conference, *Reports of Commissions I to VIII* (Edinburgh: Oliphant, Anderson & Ferrier, [1910]).

50 Stanley, *The World Missionary Conference*, 31.

51 For an example, see the procedure on the compilation of the Report of Commission VII, Missions and Governments. Brian Stanley, "Church, State, and the Hierarchy of 'Civilization': The Making of 'Missions and Governments' Report at the World Missionary Conference, Edinburgh 1910," in *The Imperial Horizons of British Protestant Mission, 1880–1914*, ed. Andrew Porter (Grand Rapids, MI: Wm. B. Eerdmans Publishing Company), 58–84.

52 Richter and Johannes Warneck to Moravian Mission (November 1909), UA.MD 574.

53 Keith Clements, *Faith on the Frontier: A Life of J.H. Oldham* (Edinburgh: T&T Clark, 1999), 77 and 81.

54 *Dreiundziebzigster Jahresbericht des Missions-Hülfs-Vereins der Berliner Missions-Gesellschaft für die Diöcesen Bunzlau I und II über das Rechnungsjahr 1910/11* (Bunzlau: Druck von J. H. Stoltz, 1911), 3, BMW/bmw1/6842. See further examples in *80. Jahresbericht des Missions-Hilfsvereins zu Mützenow bei Stolp und Umgegend für das Jahr 1909. Synode Stolp-Stadt* (Stolp i. Pom.: Druck der W. Delmanzoschen Buchdruckerei, [1910]), 3, BMW/bmw1/7192; and *Jahresbericht des Synodal-Missions-Hilfsvereins der Synode Ratzebuhr für 1909* (Ratzebuhr i. Pom.: Druck von E. Dietrich, [1910]), 3, BMW/bmw1/7276.

55 "Die Weltmissionskonferenz" (n.d., [March 1910]), UA.MD 574.

56 Hennig, "Der Weltmissionskongreß," 1978.

57 Trittelvitz, "Die Tage von Edinburg," 184.

58 "Der Edinburger Missionskongreß," 1.

59 Hennig, "Der Weltmissionskongreß," 202–6.

60 "Der Edinburger Missionskongresß," 2.

61 Stanley, *The World Missionary Conference*, xxi and 88–90.

62 Stanley, *The World Missionary Conference*, 77–83.

63 Stanley, *The World Missionary Conference*, 25–6.

64 Stanley, *The World Missionary Conference*, 84–7.

65 Hennig, "Der Weltmissionskongreß," 212. A profile of one non-White attendee at the conference, the Korean Yun Chi-ho, can be found in Brian Stanley, "Edinburgh and World Christianity," *Studies in World Christianity* 17, no. 1 (2011): 78–82.

66 Trittelvitz, "Die Tage von Edinburg," 188.
67 Hennig, "Der Weltmissionskongreß," 209–11
68 Stanley, *The World Missionary Conference*, 16.
69 Stanley, *The World Missionary Conference*, 278.
70 Minutes of the Komitee of the Berlin Mission Society (5 July 1910), BMW/bmw1/55, Item 1. These feelings were echoed by local missionary organizations. *36. Jahresbericht des Angermünder Missions-Hilfsvereins für 1909* (Diesdorf bei Gäbersdorf: Buchdruckerei der Schreiberhau-Diesdorfer Rettungsanstalten, [1910], 2, BMW/bmw1/6722.
71 "Botschaft der Edinburger Welt-Missions-Konferenz an die Christen der ganzen Welt," *AMZ* 37(1910): 392–3.
72 Richter, "Die Wirkungen der Edinburger Weltmissionskonferenz," 12–13.
73 Hennig to W.J. Oldham (19 January 1911), UA.MD 575.
74 *Mitteilungen aus der General-Synode von Jahre 1914*, vol. 2 (Herrnhut: [Druck von Fr. Lindenbein, 1914]), 41. Martin Gensichen of the Berlin Mission Society also travelled to local parishes to deliver news of the Edinburgh Conference in1911. Einladung zu öffentlichen Vorträgen im Saale der "Reichshalle" zu Angermünde (n.d., [March 1911]), BMW/bmw1/6723. See also Stanley, *The World Missionary Conference, Edinburgh 1910*, 7.
75 Julius Richter, "Die Wirkungen der Edinburger Weltmissionskonferenz auf das kontinentale Missionsleben," *Verhandlungen der Kontinentalen Missions-Konferenz* 13(1913): 9.
76 "Antrag an den Edinburger Missions Kongress 1910, eine international Commission zur Behandlung internationaler Missionsfragen einzusetzen" (14 June 1909), BMW/bmw1/2184, S. 91–4.
77 "Antrag an den Edinburger Missions Kongress 1910, eine international Commission zur Behandlung internationaler Missionsfragen einzusetzen" (14 June 1909), BMW/bmw1/2184, S. 91–4. The proposed composition was six delegates from Britain, six from the United States, four from the Continent, and one representative each from Canada, South Africa, and Australia.
78 Stanley, *The World Missionary Conference*, 277–302.
79 Julius Richter, "Das Continuation Committee," *AMZ* 38(1911): 375.
80 Stanley, *The World Missionary Conference*, 301–2.
81 Richter, "Das Continuation Committee," 376 and 378–81. In May 1911, the same year Richter published his ideas, the Continuation Committee resolved that there would not be a special commission formed to deal with mission societies' relations with foreign governments. It did, however, resolve to serve as best it could to assist in matters which "in the judgment of any national committee, imperatively call for some

international action." See "Resolutions of the Continuation Committee of the World Missionary Conference (22 May 1911), UA.MD 575.

82 Öhler and Schreiber to member societies of the Kontinentale Missions-Konferenz (19 December 1910), UA.MD 573.

83 Deutschen Evangelischen Missionsausschuß to member mission societies (16 February 1911), BMW/bmw1/1779, Item 2.

84 Deutschen Evangelischen Missionsausschuß to member mission societies (1 April 1911), BMW/bmw1/2186, S. 1–2.

85 Minutes of the Komitee of the Berlin Mission Society (2 May 1911), BMW/bmw1/56, Item 2; La Trobe to Deutschen Evangelischen Missionsausschuß (6 May 1911), UA.MD 460; Deutschen Evangelischen Missionsausschuß to member mission societies (14 May 1912), BMW/bmw1/8334;"Gutachten des deutschen Missions-Ausschusses über die nächste Welt-Missionskonferenz und ihre Tagung in Deutschland" (31 July 1914), BMW/bmw1/8334.

86 Axenfeld listed the establishment of the Chinese Republic, the conquest of new Muslim territories by Christians (Morocco, Libya), the Young Turks' revolution in Turkey, and other changes.

87 Karl Axenfeld, "Die nächste Weltmissionskonferenz" (9 July 1914), BMW/bmw1/2186, S. 39–44. Emphasis in the original.

88 "Gutachten des deutschen Missions-Ausschusses über die nächste Welt-Missionskonferenz und ihre Tagung in Deutschland" (31 July 1914), BMW/bmw1/8334.

89 Daniel Gorman, "Ecumenical Internationalism: Willoughby Dickinson, the League of Nations and the World Alliance for Promoting International Friendship through the Churches," *Journal of Contemporary History* 45, no. 1: 51–73.

90 E[rnst] Dryander & K[arl] Axenfeld, *Mission und Vaterland: Deutsch-christliche Reden in schwerer Zeit* (Berlin: Buchhandlung der Berliner Evangel. Missions-Gesellschaft, 1914), 16.

91 Julius Richter, "Ein nationaler Einschlag im Missionsmotiv?" *AMZ* 42(1915): 302.

92 Richter, "Ein nationaler Einschlag im Missionsmotiv?" 303.

93 "There is no longer Jew or Greek, there is no longer slave or free, there is no longer male and female; for all of you are one in Christ Jesus."

94 [Detlef] Bracker, "Ein nationaler Einschlag?" *AMZ* 42(1915): 250 and 254–5.

95 Bracker, "Ein nationaler Einschlag?" 255–7.

96 Karl Axenfeld, "Was verdankt und schuldet die deutsche Mission ihrem Vaterlande?" *AMZ* 24(1915): 417–19.

97 Dryander and Axenfeld, *Mission und Vaterland*, 3.

98 Minutes of the Deutschen Evangelischen Missionsausschuß (15 October 1915), BMW/bmw1/8345.
99 Signatories of the "Appeal" included familiar names from the Protestant mission movement in Germany, including those of several men who had attended the Edinburgh Conference: Karl Axenfeld; Max Berner; Friedrich von Bodelschwingh, the Younger; Gottlieb Haussleiter; Carl Meinhof; Carl Mirbt; Carl Paul; Julius Richter; August Wilhelm Schreiber; Johann Spiecker, Director of the Rhenish Mission; and Johannes Warneck.
100 Charles E. Bailey, "The British Protestant Theologians in the First World War: Germanophobia Unleashed," *Harvard Theological Review* 77(2 Apr. 1984): 201. For the opening efforts to solicit signatories see BMW/bmw1/2250 and AFSt/ALMW-DHM II.27.1.15.II.
101 *To the Christian Scholars of Europe and America: A Reply from Oxford to the German Address to Evangelical Christians* (Oxford, UK: Oxford University Press, 1914); Bailey, "The British Protestant Theologians in the First World War," 202.
102 *To the Christian Scholars of Europe and America*, 4, 6, and 15.
103 Schreiber to Axenfeld, Max Berner, Adolf von Harnack, Friedrich Lahusen, Julius Richter, and Johannes Spiecker (26 October 1914), AFSt/ALMW-DHM II.26.67.
104 Karl Axenfeld, "Zu der Duplik an die Christen des Auslandes" (n.d., [October 20, 1914?]), BMW/bmw1/2251, pag. 76–8.
105 Julius Richter, "Die Veränderung unserer Stellung in der internationalen Missionslage," *AMZ* 45(1918): 11–13.
106 Richter, "Die Veränderung unserer Stellung," 35.
107 *Jahresbericht über das Missionswerk der Brüdergemeine für das Jahr 1919* (Herrnhut: 1920), 3.
108 Stanley, *The World Missionary Conference*, 281.

Conclusion

1 Gustav Warneck, "Dic cur hic? Unser Programm," *AMZ* 1(1874): 5.
2 In some cases indigenous rulers did invite missionaries to their communities but that was by far the exception.
3 "The Treaty of Peace between the Allied and Associated Powers and Germany," 28 June 1919, Article 438.
4 Hartmut Lehmann, "Missionaries without Empire: German Protestant Missionary Efforts in the Interwar Period (1919 -1939)," in Stanley, *Missions, Nationalism, and the End of Empire*, 42–3.
5 For examples of these arguments see [Lars] Dahle, "Die segensreiche Rückwirkung der Heidenmission auf die heimatliche Gemeinde,"

Verhandlungen der Kontinentalen Missions-Konferenz 12(1909): 141–3; R[einhold] Grundemann, "Die Mission auf der Kreissynode: Ein Beitrag zur Theorie des heimatlichen Missionswesens," *AMZ* 26(1899): 365–72; Carl Meinhof, "Gedanken über die Vertiefung unseres Missionsinteresses," *Evangelisches Missions-Magazin* 56(1912): 164–70; Th[eodor] Öhler, "Was kann die heimatliche Kirche von der Mission der Gegenwart lernen?" *AMZ* 35(1908): 217–33; and an internal communication of the Bethel Mission, Walther Trittelvitz, "Grundlinien unserer heimatlichen Missionsarbeit (13 March 1913), HAB 2/51–4.

6 Lehmann, "Missionaries without Empire," 41.

Bibliography

Archives

GERMANY

Berlin

Kirchliches Archivzentrum, Landeskirchliches Archiv der EKBO
  Archiv des Berliner Missionswerks (BMW)
Bundesarchiv (BArch)
  R 1001 Reichskolonialamt
Geheimes Staatsarchiv Preußischer Kulturbesitz (GStAPK)
  GStAPK I. HA Rep. 76 Kultusministerium
  GStAPK I. HA Rep. 89 Zivilkabinett
Staatsbibliothek zu Berlin
  Zeitungsabteilung Westhafen

Bielefeld

Hauptarchiv Bethel
  2/50 Nationalspende
  2/51 Evangelische Missions-Gesellschaft für Deutsch Ostafrika
  2/89 Walther Trittelvitz, "Ein halbes Jahrhundert im Dienste von Bethel"
  B. IX 14 Das Missionswerk

Halle

Studienzentrum August Hermann Francke – Archiv und Bibliothek (AFSt)
  Bestand des Evangelisch-Lutherischen Missionswerks Leipzig

Herrnhut
Unitätsarchiv (UA)
MD 430 Gefallene des Krieges
MD 460 Missionsausschuß
MD 461 DEMA/DEMB
MD 505 Leipzig
MD 517 Deutsche Evang. Missionshilfe
MD 573 Kontinentale Missionskonferenz
MD 574–575 Welt-Missionskonferenz
R 15.A.73.c Weltmissionskonferenz

POLAND

Koszalin
Archiwum Państwowe w Koszalinie
Subgroup 19

Słupsk
Archiwum Państwowe w Koszalinie oddział w Słupsku

Szczecin
Archiwum Państwowe w Szczecinie
Akta Miasta Okonka
Naczelne Prezydium Prowincji Pomorskiej

Wrocław
Archiwum Państwowe w Wrocławiu
Subgroup 47

Zielona Gora
Archiwum Państwowe w Zielonej Górze
955 – Akta miasta Szprotawa

Journals

Afrika
Allgemeine Missions-Nachrichten
Allgemeine Missions-Zeitschrift (AMZ)
Berliner Missionsberichte

Beth-El
Echo aus den Missionen der Väter von Heiligen Geist und unbefleckten Herzen Mariä
Evangelisch-Lutherisches Missionsblatt
Die Evangelischen Missionen Illustriertes Familienblatt
Evangelisches Missions-Magazin
Evangelisches Missions-Magazin, Neue Folge
Gott will es!
Jahrbuch der sächsischen Missionskonferenz
Jahrbuch der vereinigten norddeutschen Missionskonferenzen
Die katholischen Missionen
Missionsblatt der Brüdergemeine
Nachrichten aus der ostafrikanischen Mission
Verhandlungen der Allgemeinen Missionskonferenz
Verhandlungen der Kontinentalen Missions-Konferenz

Published Primary Sources

Axenfeld, Karl, ed. *Missionswissenschaftliche Studien: Festschrift zum 70. Geburtstag des Herrn Prof. D. Dr. Gustav Warneck*. Berlin: Martin Warneck, 1904.

Buchner, Carl. *Unser Missionswerk: Zur Vorbereitung auf die General-Synode im Jahre 1899*. Herrnhut: Kommisionsverlag und Druck von Gustav Winter, 1898.

Carey, William. *An Enquiry Into the Obligations of Christians, to Use Means for the Conversion of the Heathens in Which the Religious State of the Different Nations of the World, the Success of Former Undertakings, and the Practicability of Further Undertakings, Are Considered*. Leicester: 1792.

Dryander, E[rnst], and K[arl] Axenfeld. *Mission und Vaterland: Deutsch-christliche Reden in schwerer Zeit*. Berlin: Buchhandlung der Berliner Evangel. Missions-Gesellschaft, 1914.

Fabri, Friedrich. *Bedarf Deutschland der Kolonien? Eine politisch-ökonomische Betrachtung*. Gotha: F.A. Pertes, 1879.

Handbuch der Gesellschaften mit beschränkter Haftung im Deutschen Reiche: Ein Hand- und Nachschlagebuch für Bankiers, Kaufleute, Kapitalisten etc. Leipzig: A. Schumann's Verlag, 1898.

Hauck, A[lbert]. *Evangelische Mission und deutsches Christentum*. Flugschriften der Deutschen Evangelischen Missions-Hilfe 4. Gütersloh: C. Bertelsmann, 1916.

Ittameier, Matthias. *Die Mission auf dem Allgemeinen deutschen Kongreß: Die evangelisch-lutherische Mission für Ostafrika und ihre Gegner. Eine Schutz- und Verteidigungsschrift*. Rothenburg-ob-der-Tauber: Druck der J. P. Peter'schen Offizin., 1887.

Jahresbericht über das Missionswerk der Brüdergemeine für das Jahr 1916. Herrnhut: Missionsbuchhandlung, 1917.

Jahresbericht über das Missionswerk der Brüdergemeine für das Jahr 1919. Herrnhut: 1920.

Jahresbericht über das Missionswerk der Evangelischen Brüder-Unität (Brüdergemeine) vom Jahre 1908. Herrnhut: Druck von Fr. Lindenbein, 1909.

Jahresbericht über die Entwickelung der Schutzgebiete in Afrika und der Südsee im Jahre 1907/08. Beilage zum Deutschen Kolonialblatt 1909. Berlin: Ernst Siegfried Mittler und Sohn, 1909.

Merensky, [Alexander]. *Deutschlands gegenüber den Heiden und dem Heidentum in seinen Kolonien*. Beiträge zur Missionskunde. Berlin: Buchhandlung der Berliner evangelischen Missionsgesellschaft, 1905.

Mitteilungen aus der General-Synode der Brüder-Unität vom Jahre 1899, No. 3. Herrnhut: Druck von Fr. Lindenbein, [1899?].

Mitteilungen aus der General-Synode von Jahre 1914. Vol. 2. Herrnhut: [Druck von Fr. Lindenbein, 1914?].

Mott, John R. *The Evangelization of the World in This Generation*. New York: Student Volunteer Movement for Foreign Missions, 1900.

The New Oxford Annotated Bible: New Revised Standard Version with the Apocrypha, 5th ed. Oxford, UK: Oxford University Press, 2018.

Paul, Carl. *Zwanzig Jahre deutscher Kolonialpolitik in ihrer Bedeutung für die Christianisierung unsrer überseeischen Gebiete*. Berlin: 1904.

Petrich, Hermann. *Allerlei Schulbilder aus der Mission in den deutschen Kolonien*. Neue Missionsschriften 81. Berlin: Buchhandlung der Berliner evangelischen Missionsgesellschaft, 1906.

Reichs-Kino-Addressbuch. Berlin: LBB, 1920/21.

Richter, Julius. *Die Organisation des heimatlichen Missionswesens*. Beiträge zur Missionskunde 7. Berlin: Buchhandlung der Berliner evangelischen Missionsgesellschaft, 1904.

Rohrbach, Paul. *Die Kolonie*. Frankfurt-am-Main: Literarische Anstalt Rütten & Loening, 1905.

–, ed. *Deutsche Kulturaufgaben in China: Beiträge zur Erkenntnis nationaler Verantwortlichkeit*. Berlin: Buchverlag der "Hilfe," 1910.

To the Christian Scholars of Europe and America: A Reply from Oxford to the German Address to Evangelical Christians. Oxford, UK: Oxford University Press, 1914.

Warneck, Gustav. *Die chinesische Mission im Gerichte der deutschen Zeitungspresse*. 3rd ed. Berlin: Martin Warneck, 1900.

– *Outline of a History of Protestant Missions from the Reformation to the Present*. 7th ed. Translated by George Robson. New York: Fleming H. Revell Company, 1901.

Secondary Sources

Adeleke, Tunde. *Unafrican Americans: Nineteenth-Century Black Nationalists and the Civilizing Mission*. Lexington: University Press of Kentucky, 1998.

Adick, Christel. "Grundstruktur und Organisation von Missionsschulen in den Etappen der Expansion des modernen Weltsystems." In Bogner, Holtwick, and Tyrell, 459–82.

Ahadji, Valentin Amétepé. "Mission und Landfrage in Togo 1884–1914." In van der Heyden and Stoecker, 137–48.

Aitken, Robbie. "Education and Migration: Cameroonian Schoolchildren and Apprentices in Germany, 1884–1914." In Honeck, Klimke, and Kuhlmann, 213–30.

– "Selling the Mission: The German Catholic Elite and the Educational Migration of African Youngsters to Europe." *German History* 33(1): 30–51.

Akakpo, Kuassi Amétowoyopna. "Missionspraxis im Lichte der Kritik: kontroverse Debatten über Paul Rohrbachs Thesen zur Missionsarbeit in Afrika." In van der Heyden and Stoecker, 71–9.

Altena, Thorsten. "'Brüder' und 'Väter im Herrn': Notizen zum inneren Machtgefüge protestantischer deutschsprachiger Missionsgesellschaften 1884–1918." In van der Heyden and Stoecker, 51–70.

– "Missionare und einheimische Gesellschaft: Zur Kulturbegegnung der Bethel-Mission in Deutsch-Ostafrika 1890–1916." In *Bethels Mission(1): Zwischen Epileptischenpflege und Heidenbekehrung*, ed. Matthias Benad, 1–69. Bielefeld: Luther-Verlag, 2001.

– *"Ein Häuflein Christen mitten in der Heidenwelt des dunklen Erdteils": Zum Selbst- und Fremdverständnis protestantischer Missionare im kolonialen Afrika 1884–1918*. Münster: Waxmann Verlag, 2003.

– "Grenzüberschreitungen: Zum Beziehungsgeflecht von Innerer und Äußerer Mission in den Anfangsjahren der Bethel-Mission." In *Bethels Mission (3): Mutterhaus, Mission und Pflege*, edited by Matthias Benad and Vicco von Büllow, 147–70. Bielefeld, Germany: Luther-Verlag, 2003.

Altgeld, Wolfgang. *Katholizismus, Protestantismus, Judentum: Über religiös begründete Gegensätze und nationalreligiöse Ideen in der Geschichte des deutschen Nationalismus*. Mainz: Matthias-Grünewald-Verlag, 1992.

Ambler, Charles H. "The Renovation of Custom in Colonial Kenya: The 1932 Generation Succession Ceremonies in Embu." *Journal of African History* 30(1): 139–56.

Ames, Eric. *Carl Hagenbeck's Empire of Entertainments*. Seattle: University of Washington Press, 2008.

Anderson, Benedict. *Imagined Communities: Reflections on the Origin and Spread of Nationalism*. Rev. ed. London: Verso, 1991.

Anderson, Margaret Lavinia. *Windthorst: A Political Biography*. Oxford, UK: Clarendon Press, 1981.

Ansprenger, Franz. "Schulpolitik in Deutsch-Ostafrika." In *Studien zur Geschichte des deutschen Kolonialismus in Afrika: Festschrift zum 60. Geburtstag von Peter Sebald*. Pfeffenweiler: Centaurus, 1995.

Applegate, Celia. *A Nation of Provincials: The German Idea of Heimat*. Berkeley: University of California Press, 1990.

Arendt, Hannah. *Origins of Totalitarianism*. New York: Harcourt Brace Jovanovich, 1973.

Arnold, Bernd. *Steuer und Lohnarbeit im Südwesten von Deutsch-Ostafrika 1891 bis 1916: Eine historisch-ethnologische Studie*. Münster: Lit, 1994.

Atkin, Nicholas and Frank Tallet. *Priests, Prelates and People: A History of European Catholicism since 1750*. Oxford, UK: Oxford University Press, 2003.

Attridge, Harold W. *Oxford Encyclopedia of the Bible and Theology*. Oxford, UK: Oxford University Press, 2015.

Austen, Ralph. *Northwest Tanzania under German and British Rule: Colonial Policy and Tribal Politics, 1889–1938*. New Haven, CT: Yale University Press, 1968.

Bade, Klaus J. "Einführung: Imperialismus und Kolonialmission: Das Kaiserliche Deutschland und sein koloniales Imperium." In Bade, *Imperialismus und Kolonialmission*, 1–27.

– *Friedrich Fabri und der Imperialismus in der Bismarckzeit: Revolution – Depression – Expansion*. Freiburg: Atlantis Verlag, 1975.

–, ed. *Imperialismus und Kolonialmission: Kaiserliche Deutschland und kolonialer Imperium*. 2nd ed. Wiesbaden: Steiner, 1984.

Bailey, Charles E. "The British Protestant Theologians in the First World War: Germanophobia Unleashed." *Harvard Theological Review* 77(2): 195–221.

Bald, Detlef. *Deutsch-Ostafrika 1900–1914: Eine Studie über Verwaltung, Interessengruppen und wirtschaftliche Erschließung*. Munich: Weltforum Verlag, 1970.

Balz, Heinrich. "'Überwindung der Religionen' und das Ziel der Mission: Die Diskussion zwischen Gustav Warneck and Ernst Troeltsch 1906–1908." In Becker and Feldtkeller, 106–16.

Baranowski, Shelley. *Nazi Empire: German Colonialism and Imperialism from Bismarck to Hitler*. Cambridge, UK: Cambridge University Press, 2011.

Barringer, Terry. "What Mrs. Jellyby Might Have Read: Missionary Periodicals, A Neglected Source." *Victorian Periodicals Review* 37(4): 46–74.

Baumeister, Martin. *Parität und katholische Inferiorität: Untersuchungen zur Stellung des Katholizismus im Deutschen Kaiserreich*. Paderborn: Ferdinand Schöningh, 1987.

Bays, Daniel H., and Grant Wacker, eds. *The Foreign Missionary Enterprise at Home: Explorations in North American Cultural History*. Tuscaloosa: University of Alabama Press, 2003.

Beck, Hartmut. *Brüder in vielen Völkern: 250 Jahre Mission der Brüdergemeine.* Erlangen: Verlag der Ev.-Luth. Mission, 1981.

Becker, Dieter, and Andreas Feldtkeller, eds. *Es begann in Halle … Missionswissenschaft von Gustav Warneck bis heute.* Erlangen: Verlag der Ev.-Luth. Mission, 1997.

Becker, Felicitas. *Becoming Muslim in Mainland Tanzania 1890–2000.* Oxford, UK: Oxford University Press, 2008.

Becker, Felicitas, and Jigal Beez, eds. *Der Maji-Maji-Krieg in Deutsch-Ostafrika, 1905–1907.* Berlin: Ch. Links Verlag, 2005.

Beckert, Sven. "From Tuskegee to Togo: The Problem of Freedom in the Empire of Cotton." *Journal of American History* 92(2): 498–526.

Beidelman, T.O. *Colonial Evangelism: A Socio-historical Study of an East African Mission at the Grassroots.* Bloomington: Indiana University Press, 1982.

Bendikat, Elfi. *Organisierte Kolonialbewegung in der Bismarck-Ära.* Heidelberg: Kivouvou, 1984.

Benes, Tuska. *In Babel's Shadow: Language, Philology, and the Nation in Nineteenth-Century Germany.* Detroit: Wayne State University Press, 2008.

Benninghoff-Lühl, Sibylle. *Deutsche Kolonialromane 1884–1914 in ihrem Entstehungs- und Wirkungszusammenhang.* Bremen: Übersee-Museum, 1983.

Berger, Heinrich. *Mission und Kolonialpolitik: Die katholische Mission in Kamerun während der deutschen Kolonialzeit.* Immensee: Neue Zeitschrift für Missionswissenschaft, 1978.

Berger, Stefan. *The Search for Normality: National Identity and Historical Consciousness in Germany since 1800.* Providence, RI: Berghahn Books, 1997.

– *Inventing the Nation: Germany.* London: Arnold, 2006.

Berghahn, Volker. *Der Tirpitz-Plan: Genesis und Verfall einer innenpolitischen Krisenstrategie unter Wilhelm II.* Düsseldorf: Droste Verlag, 1971.

Berman, Russell. *Enlightenment or Empire: Colonial Discourse in German Culture.* Lincoln: University of Nebraska Press, 1998.

Berner, Ulrich. "Religionsgeschichtliche und Mission: Zur Kontroverse zwischen Ernst Troeltsch und Gustav Warneck." In Drehsen and Sparn, 103–16.

Besier, Gerhard. "Mission and Colonialism in Friedrich Fabri's (1824–1891) Thinking." In Christensen and Hutchison, 85–92.

Best, Jeremy. "The *Allgemeine Missions-Zeitschrift* and Missionary Nationalism: Science for Mission and Empire." In Jensz and Acke, 57–76.

– "Godly, International, and Independent: German Protestant Missionary Loyalties before World War I." *Central European History* 47(3): 585–611.

Blackbourn, David. *Class, Religion and Local Politics in Wilhelmine Germany: The Centre Party in Württemberg before 1914.* New Haven, CT: Yale University Press, 1980.

– *Marpingen: Apparitions of the Virgin Mary in Bismarckian Germany*. New York: Knopf, 1994.

– *The Long Nineteenth Century: A History of Germany, 1870–1918*. Oxford, UK: Oxford University Press, 1998.

Blackbourn, David, and Geoff Eley. *The Peculiarities of German History: Bourgeois Society and Politics in Nineteenth-Century Germany*. Oxford, UK: Oxford University Press, 1984.

Blackler, Adam A. "From Boondoggle to Settlement Colony: Hendrik Witbooi and the Evolution of Germany's Imperial Project in Southwest Africa, 1884–1894." *Central European History* 50(4): 449–70.

– "An Imperial Homeland: Forging German Identity in Southwest Africa." Unpublished manuscript, 29 October 2019.

Blaschke, Olaf, ed. *Konfessionen im Konflikt: Deutschland zwischen 1800 und 1970: Ein zweites konfessionelles Zeitalter*. Göttingen: Vandenhoeck & Ruprecht, 2002.

Blaschke, Olaf, and Frank-Michael Kuhlemann, eds. *Religion im Kaiserreich: Milieus-Mentalitäten-Krisen*. Gütersloh: Chr. Kaiser/Gütersloher Verlagshaus, 1996.

Bley, Helmut. *Kolonialherrschaft und Sozialstruktur in Deutsch-Südwestafrika*. [Hamburg]: Leibnitz-Verlag, 1968.

Block-Schlesier, Andreas von, and Heike Spieker, eds. *900 Jahre Johanniter: Humanitäres Völkerrecht – Humanitäre Hilfe*. Berlin: Berlin Verlag, 1999.

Bogner, Artur. "Zur Entwicklung der Berliner Mission als Bürokratisierungsprozess." In Bogner, Holtwick, and Tyrell, 313–53.

Bogner, Artur, Bernd Holtwick, and Hartmann Tyrell, eds. *Weltmission und religiöse Organisationen: Protestantische Missionsgesellschaften im 19. und 20. Jahrhundert*. Würzburg: Ergon Verlag, 2004.

Boli, John, and George M. Thomas. *Constructing World Culture: International Nongovernmental Organizations since 1875*. Stanford, CA: Stanford University Press, 1999.

Bönker, Dirk. "Global Politics and Germany's Destiny 'from an East Asian Perspective': Alfred von Tirpitz and the Making of Wilhelmine Navalism." *Central European History* 46 (March 2013): 61–96.

Bowersox, Jeff. *Raising Germans in the Age of Empire: Youth and Colonial Culture, 1871–1914*. Oxford, UK: Oxford University Press, 2013.

Brahm, Felix, and Eve Rosenhaft. *Slavery Hinterland: Transatlantic Slavery and Continental Europe, 1680–1850*. Woodbridge, UK: Boydell Press, 2016.

Bridgman, Jon M. *Revolt of the Hereros*. Berkeley: University of California Press, 1981.

Bromber, Katrin. "German Colonial Administrators, Swahili Lecturers and the Promotion of Swahili at the *Seminar für Orientalische Sprachen* in Berlin." *Sudanic Africa* 15(2004): 39–54.

Bruch, Rüdiger von. *Weltpolitik als Kulturmission: Auswärtige Kulturpolitik und Bildungsbürgertum in Deutschland am Vorabend des Ersten Weltkrieges.* Paderborn: Ferdinand Schöningh, 1982.

Brumfit, Ann. "The Rise and Development of a Language Policy in German East Africa." *Sprache und Geschichte in Afrika* 2(1980): 219–331.

Buchheim, Karl. *Ultramontanismus und Demokratie: Der Weg der deutschen Katholiken im 19. Jahrhundert.* Munich: Kösel-Verlag, 1963.

Bunzl, Matti. "Franz Boas and the Humboldtian Tradition: From *Volksgeist* and *Nationalcharakter* to an Anthropological Concept of Culture." In Stocking, 17–78.

Burleigh, Michael, and Wolfgang Wippermann. *The Racial State: Germany, 1933–1945.* Cambridge, UK: Cambridge University, 1991.

Burton, Andrew. *African Underclass: Urbanisation, Crime and Colonial Order in Dar es Salaam.* Athens: Ohio University Press, 2003.

Callahan, Kevin J. *Demonstration Culture: European Socialism and the Second International, 1889–1914.* Leicester, UK: Troubador Publishing, 2010.

Canis, Konrad. *Von Bismarck zur Weltpolitik: Deutsche Außenpolitik 1890 bis 1902.* Berlin: Akademie, 1997.

Carey, Hilary M. *God's Empire: Religion and Colonialism in the British World, c. 1801–1908.* Cambridge, UK: Cambridge University Press, 2011.

Cassidy, Eugene S. "The Ambivalence of Slavery, The Certainty of Germanness: Representations of Slave-Holding and Its Impact among German Settlers in Brazil, 1820–1889." *German History* 33(3): 367–84.

Cecil, Lamar. *The German Diplomatic Service, 1871–1914.* Princeton, NJ: Princeton University Press, 1976.

– *Wilhelm II.* 2 vols. Chapel Hill: University of North Carolina Press, 1996.

Chanock, Martin. *Law, Custom and Social Order: The Colonial Experience in Malawi and Zambia.* Cambridge, UK: Cambridge University Press, 1985.

Chickering, Roger. "Militarism and Radical Nationalism." In Retallack, 196–218.

Chrétien, Jean-Pierre. *The Great Lakes of Africa: Two Thousand Years of History.* Translated by Scott Straus. New York: Zone Books, 2003.

Christensen, Torben, and William R. Hutchison, eds. *Missionary Ideologies in the Imperialist Era: 1880–1929.* Aarhus: Forlaget Aros: 1982.

Ciarlo, David. *Advertising Empire: Race and Visual Culture in Imperial Germany.* Cambridge, MA: Harvard University Press, 2011.

Clark, Christopher M. *The Politics of Conversion: Missionary Protestantism and the Jews in Prussia, 1728–1941.* Oxford, UK: Clarendon Press, 1995.

– "The New Catholicism and the European Culture Wars." In *Culture Wars: Secular-Catholic Conflict in Nineteenth-Century Europe*, edited by Christopher Clark and Wolfram Kaiser, 11–46. Cambridge, UK: Cambridge University Press, 2003.

– "Religion and Confessional Conflict." In Retallack, 83–105.

Clements, Keith. *Faith on the Frontier: A Life of J.H. Oldham*. Edinburgh: T&T Clark, 1999.

Coetzee, Marilyn Shevin. *The German Army League: Popular Nationalism in Wilhelmine Germany*. Oxford, UK: Oxford University Press, 1990.

Comaroff, Jean, and John L. Comaroff. *Of Revelation and Revolution*. 2 vols. Chicago: University of Chicago Press, 1991–7.

Confino, Alon. *The Nation as a Local Metaphor: Württemberg, Imperial Germany, and National Memory, 1871–1918*. Chapel Hill: University of North Carolina Press, 1997.

Conklin, Alice L. *A Mission to Civilize: The Republican Idea of Empire in France and West Africa, 1895–1930*. Stanford, CA: Stanford University Press, 1997.

Conrad, Sebastian. *Globalisierung und Nation im Deutschen Kaiserreich*. Munich: C.H. Beck, 2006.

– *Globalisation and the Nation in Imperial Germany*. Translated by Sorcha O'Hagan. Cambridge, UK: Cambridge University Press, 2010.

– *German Colonialism: A Short History*. Translated by Sorcha O'Hagan. Cambridge, UK: Cambridge University Press, 2012.

Conrad, Sebastian, and Jürgen Osterhammel, eds. *Das Kaiserreich transnational: Deutschland in der Welt 1871–1914*. Göttingen: Vandenhoeck & Ruprecht, 2004.

Cox, Jeffrey. *Imperial Fault Lines: Christianity and Colonial Power in India, 1818–1914*. Stanford, CA: Stanford University Press, 2002.

– *The British Missionary Enterprise since 1700*. New York: Routledge, 2008.

Craig, Gordon A. *Germany, 1866–1945*. Oxford, UK: Oxford University Press, 1978.

Dachs, Anthony J. "Missionary Imperialism – The Case of Bechuanaland." *Journal of African History* 13(4): 647–58.

Dah, Jonas N. *Missionary Motivations and Methods: A Critical Examination of the Basel Mission in Cameroon, 1886–1914*. Basel: 1983.

Day, Lara, and Oliver Haag, eds. *The Persistence of Race: Continuity and Change from the Wilhelmine Empire to National Socialism*. New York: Berghahn, 2017.

Debusmann, Robert, and Stefan Arnold, eds. *Land Law and Land Ownership in Africa: Case Studies from Colonial and Contemporary Cameroon and Tanzania*. Bayreuth: Eckhard Breitinger, Bayreuth University, 1996.

Dedering, Tilman. *Hate the Old and Follow the New: Khoekhoe and Missionaries in Early Nineteenth-Century Namibia*. Stuttgart: Franz Steiner Verlag, 1997.

Deutsch, Jan-Georg. *Emancipation without Abolition in German East Africa, c. 1884–1914*. Athens: Ohio University Press, 2006.

– "Vom Bezirksamtmann zum Mehrparteiensystem – Transformationen politischer Herrschaft im kolonialen und nachkolonialen Tanzania." In van der Heyden and von Oppen, 20–30.

de Vries, Johannes Lucas. *Namibia: Mission und Politik*. Translated by Wolfgang Bunte. Neukirchen-Vluyn: Neukirchener Verlag, 1980.

Dietrich, Stefan. "Katholische Mission und kolonialer Staat: Fragen und Überlegungen." In Wagner, 202–21.

Donald, Moira. "Workers of the World Unite? Exploring the Enigma of the Second International." In *The Mechanics of Internationalism: Culture, Society, and Politics from the 1840s to the First World War*, edited by Martin H. Geyer and Johannes Paulmann, 177–203. London: German Historical Institute, 2001.

Donson, Andrew. *Youth in the Fatherless Land: War Pedagogy, Nationalism, and Authority in Germany, 1914–1918*. Cambridge, MA: Harvard University Press, 2010.

Drechsler, Horst. *Südwestafrika unter deutscher Kolonialherrschaft: Der Kampf der Herero und Nama gegen den deutschen Imperialismus 1884-1915*. Berlin: Akademie-Verlag, 1966.

Drehsen, Volker, and Walter Sparn, eds. *Vom Weltbildwandel zur Weltanschauungsanalyse: Krisenwahrnehmung und Krisenbewältigung um 1900*. Berlin: Akademie Verlag, 1996.

Dujardin, Carine. "Mission Research Revised: Missiology as a Project of Modernity and a Contemporary Form of Apologetics." In *Mission and Science: Missiology Revised/Missiologie Revisitée*, edited by Carine Dujardin and Claude Prudhomme, 9–22. Leuven: Leuven University Press, 2015.

Eckert, Andreas. "Missions, Land Politics and Real Estate in Colonial Douala." In Debusmann and Arnold, 187–99.

Eckert, Andreas, and Michael Pesek. "Bürokratische Ordnung und koloniale Praxis: Herrschaft und Verwaltung in Preußen und Afrika." In Conrad and Osterhammel, 87–106.

Eggert, Johanna. *Missionsschule und sozialer Wandel in Ostafrika: Der Beitrag der deutschen evangelischen Missionsgesellschaften zur Entwicklung des Schulwesens in Tanganyika 1891–1939*. Bielefeld: Bertelsmann Universitätsverlag, 1970.

– "The School Policy of the German Protestant Missions in Tanzania before the First World War." In Christensen and Hutchison, 200–6.

Eley, Geoff. *Reshaping the German Right: Radical Nationalism and Political Change after Bismarck*. Ann Arbor: University of Michigan Press, 1991.

Ellis, Christin. *Antebellum Posthuman: Race and Materiality in the Mid-Nineteenth Century*. New York: Fordham University Press, 2018.

Elphick, Richard. "Missions and Afrikaner Nationalism: Soundings in the Prehistory of Apartheid." In Stanley, *Missions, Nationalism, and the End of Empire*, 54–78.

Epstein, Klaus. *Matthias Erzberger and the Dilemma of German Democracy*. New York: Howard Fertig, 1971.

Etherington, Norman, ed. *Missions and Empire*. Oxford, UK: Oxford University Press, 2005.

Evans, Andrew D. *Anthropology at War: World War I and the Science of Race in Germany*. Chicago: University of Chicago Press, 2010.

Fabian, Johannes. *Language and Colonial Power: The Appropriation of Swahili in the Former Belgian Congo*. Berkeley: University of California Press, 1986.

Fiedler, Klaus. *Christianity and African Culture: Conservative German Protestant Missionaries in Tanzania, 1900–1940*. Leiden: E.J. Brill, 1996.

Fierce, Milfred C. *The Pan-African Idea in the United States: African-American Interest in Africa and Interaction with West Africa*. New York: Garland Publishing, 1993.

Fischer, Fritz. *Griff nach der Weltmacht: Die Kriegszielpolitik des kaiserlichen Deutschland, 1914–18*. Düsseldorf: Droste, 1961.

– *Krieg der Illusionen*. Düsseldorf: Droste, 1969.

Fitzmaurice, Andrew. "Liberalism and Empire in Nineteenth-Century International Law." *American Historical Review* 117(Feb. 2012): 122–40.

Fitzpatrick, Matthew. *Liberal Imperialism in Germany: Expansionism and Nationalism, 1848–1884*. New York: Berghahn Books, 2008.

Fleisch, Paul. *Hundert Jahre lutherischer Mission*. Leipzig: Verlag der Evangelisch-lutherischen Mission, 1936.

Forman, Charles W. "Missions in Papua New Guinea." In Christensen and Hutchison, 23–7.

Forman, Michael. *Nationalism and the International Labor Movement: The Idea of the Nation in Socialist and Anarchist Theory*. University Park: Pennsylvania State University Press, 1998.

Friedrich, Martin. "Das 19. Jahrhundert als 'Zweites Konfessionelles Zeitalter'?" In Blaschke, 95–112.

Friedrichsmayer, Sara, Sara Lennox, and Susanne Zantop. *The Imperialist Imagination: German Colonialism and Its Legacy*. Ann Arbor: University of Michigan Press, 1998.

Fuhrmann, Wolfgang. *Imperial Projections: Screening the German Colonies*. New York: Berghahn, 2015.

Gabbert, Wolfgang. "Phasen und Grundprobleme protestantischer Mission im kolonialen Afrika – die Brüdergemeine bei den Nyakyusa in Tansania." In Bogner, Holtwick, and Tyrell, 517–39.

– "Social and Cultural Conditions of Religious Conversion in Colonial Southwest Tanzania, 1891–1939." *Ethnology* 40(4): 291–308.

Gann, L.H., and Peter Duignan. *The Rulers of German Africa, 1884–1914*. Stanford, CA: Stanford University Press, 1977.

Geiss, Imanuel. *The Pan-African Movement: A History of Pan-Africanism in America, Europe and Africa*. Translated by Ann Keep. New York: Africana Publishing, 1974.

Gemeindelexicon für das Königreich Preußen. VI. Gemeindelexicon für die Provinz Schlesien. Berlin: Verlag des Königliches statistisches Bureaus, 1887.

Gemeindelexicon für das Königreich Preußen. VI. Gemeindelexicon für die Provinz Schlesien. Berlin: Verlag des Königliches statistisches Bureaus, 1898.

Gensichen, Hans-Werner. "German Protestant Missions." In Christensen and Hutchison, 186–7.

Gerwarth, Robert, and Stephan Malinowski. "Der Holocaust als 'kolonialer Genozid'? Europäische Kolonialgewalt und nationalsozialistischer Vernichtungskrieg." *Geschichte und Gesellschaft* 33(2007): 439–66.

Gewald, Jan-Bart. *Herero Heroes: A Socio-Political History of the Herero of Namibia, 1890–1923*. Athens: Ohio University Press, 1999.

Geyer, Martin H., and Johannes Paulmann, eds. *The Mechanics of Internationalism: Culture, Society, and Politics from the 1840s to the First World War*. Oxford, UK: Oxford University Press, 2001.

Giblin, James, and Jamie Monson, eds. *Maji Maji: Lifting the Fog of War*. Leiden: Brill, 2010.

Glassman, Jonathon. *Feasts and Riot: Revelry, Rebellion, and Popular Consciousness on the Swahili Coast, 1856–1888*. London: James Currey Publishers, 1995.

Gleixner, Ulrike. "Remapping the World: The Vision of a Protestant Empire in the Eighteenth Century." In *Migration and Religion: Christian Transatlantic Missions, Islamic Migration to Germany*, edited by Barbara Becker-Cantarino, 77–90. Amsterdam: Rodopi, 2012.

Goodman, Glen S. "From 'German Danger' to German-Brazilian President: Immigration, Ethnicity, and the Making of Brazilian Identities, 1924–1974." PhD diss., Emory University, 2015.

Gorman, Daniel. "Ecumenical Internationalism: Willoughby Dickinson, the League of Nations and the World Alliance for Promoting International Friendship through the Churches." *Journal of Contemporary History* 45(1): 51–73.

– *International Cooperation in the Early Twentieth Century*. London: Bloomsbury Academic, 2017.

Green, Abigail. *Fatherlands: State-Building and Nationhood in Nineteenth-Century Germany*. Cambridge, UK: Cambridge University Press, 2001.

Gross, Michael B. *The War against Catholicism: Liberalism and Anti-Catholic Imagination in Nineteenth-Century Germany*. Ann Arbor: University of Michigan Press, 2004.

Gründer, Horst. *Christliche Mission und deutscher Imperialismus: Eine politische Geschichte ihrer Beziehungen während der deutschen Kolonialzeit (1884–1914) unter besondere Berücksichtigung Afrikas und Chinas*. Paderborn: Ferdinand Schöningh, 1982.

– *Welteroberung und Christentum: Ein handbuch zur Geschichte der Neuzeit*. Gütersloh: Gütersloher Verlag – Haus Mohn, 1992.

– *Geschichte der deutschen Kolonien*. 4th ed. Paderborn: Verlag Ferdinand Schöningh, 2000.

– "Deutsche Missionsgesellschaft auf dem Wege zur Kolonialmission." In Bade, 68–102.

Gründler, W[ilhelm]. *Hundert Jahre Berliner Mission*. Berlin: Buchhandlung der Berliner ev. Missionsgesellschaft, 1923.

Guettel, Jens-Uwe. "The Myth of the Pro-Colonialist SPD: German Social Democracy and Imperialism before World War I." *Central European History* 45(3): 452–84.

Gundermann, Iselin. *Kirchenbau und Diakonie: Kaiserin Auguste Victoria und der Evangelisch-kirchlich Hilfsverein*. Hefte des Evangelischen Kirchenbauvereins. Berlin: Evangelischer Kirchenbauverein, 1991.

Habermas, Rebekka. "Islam Debates around 1900: Colonies in Africa, Muslims in Berlin, and the Role of Missionaries and Orientalists." In Becker-Cantarino, 123–54.

Haenger, Peter. "Basel and the Slave Trade: From Profiteers to Missionaries." In Brahm and Rosenhaft, 65–86.

Håkansson, N. Thomas. "Pagan Practices and the Death of Children: German Colonial Missionaries and Child Health Care in South Pare, Tanzania." *World Development* 26(9): 1763–72.

Hall, Catherine. *Civilising Subjects: Colony and Metropole in the English Imagination, 1830–1867*. Chicago: University of Chicago Press, 2002.

Hamilton, J. Taylor. *A History of the Missions of the Moravian Church during the Eighteenth and Nineteenth Centuries*. Bethlehem, PA: Times, 1901.

Hamilton, Majida. *Mission im kolonialen Umfeld: Deutsche protestantische Missionsgesellschaften in Deutsch-Ostafrika*. Göttingen: Universitätsverlag Göttingen, 2009.

Hansen, Holger Bernt. *Mission, Church and State in a Colonial Setting: Uganda, 1890–1925*. London: Heinemann, 1984.

Hansen, Holger Bernt, and Michael Twaddle, eds. *Christian Missionaries and the State in the Third World*. Oxford, UK: James Currey, 2002.

Hardtwig, Wolfgang. *Nationalismus und Bürgerkultur in Deutschland 1500–1914: Ausgewählte Aufsätze*. Göttingen: Vandenhoeck & Ruprecht, 1994.

Hasing, Per. "German Missionaries and the Maji Maji Rising." *African Historical Studies* 3(2): 373–89.

Hastings, Adrian. *The Construction of Nationhood: Ethnicity, Religion, and Nationalism*. Cambridge, UK: Cambridge University Press, 1997.

– "The Clash of Nationalism and Universalism within Twentieth-Century Missionary Christianity." In *Missions, Nationalism, and the End of Empire*, edited by Brian Stanley, 15–33. Grand Rapids, MI: William B. Eerdmans Publishing Company, 2003.

Headrick, Daniel R. *The Tools of Empire: Technology and European Imperialism in the Nineteenth Century*. Oxford, UK: Oxford University Press, 1981.

Heilbronner, Oded. "The German Bourgeois Club as a Political and Social Structure in the Late Nineteenth and Early Twentieth Centuries." *Continuity and Change* 13(3): 443–73.

Henderson, W.O. *The German Colonial Empire, 1884–1919*. London: Frank Cass, 1993.

Herrmann, Ulrich. "Pädagogisches Denken und Anfänge der Reformpädogogik." In *Handbuch der deutschen Bildungsgeschichte*, vol. 4, edited by Christa Berg, 147–78. Munich: Verlag C.H. Beck, 1991.

Hewitson, Mark. *Germany and the Modern World, 1880–1914*. Cambridge, UK: Cambridge University Press, 2018.

– "Wilhelmine Germany." In Retallack, 40–60.

Hirji, Karim F. "Colonial Ideological Apparatuses in Tanganyika under the Germans." In Kaniki, 207–11.

Hobsbawm, E.J. *Nations and Nationalism since 1780: Programme, Myth, Reality*. Cambridge, UK: Cambridge University Press, 1990.

Hochman, Erin R. *Imagining a Greater Germany: Republican Nationalism and the Idea of Anschluss*. Ithaca, NY: Cornell University Press, 2016.

Hoekendijk, Johannes Christian. *Kirche und Volk in der deutschen Missionswissenschaft*. Translated by Erich-Walter Pollmann. Munich: Chr. Kaiser, 1967.

Hoffmann, Robert. "Die katholische Missionsbewegung in Deutschland vom Anfang des 19. Jahrhunderts bis zum Ende der deutschen Kolonialgeschichte." In Bade, 29–50.

Hofmeyer, Isabel. *The Portable Bunyan: A Transnational History of* The Pilgrim's Progress. Princeton, NJ: Princeton University Press, 2004.

Hogg, William Richey. *Ecumenical Foundations: A History of the International Missionary Council and Its Nineteenth-Century Background*. New York: Harper & Brothers, 1952.

– "The Rise of Protestant Missionary Concern, 1517–1914." In *The Theology of the Christian Mission*, edited by Gerald H. Anderson, 95–111. New York: McGraw-Hill Book Company, 1961.

Holborn. Hajo. *A History of Modern Germany, 1840–1945*. New York: Alfred A. Knopf, 1969.

Holtwick, Bernd. "Licht und Schatten: Begründungen und Zielsetzungen des protestantischen missionarischen Aufbruchs im frühen 19. Jahrhundert." In Bogner, Holtwick, and Tyrell, 225–47.

Honeck, Mischa. "August Willich, Peter H. Clark, and the Abolitionist Movement in Cincinnati." In *Germans and African Americans: Two Centuries of Exchange*, edited by Larry A. Greene and Anke Ortlepp, 17–36. Jackson: University of Mississippi Press, 2011.

Honeck, Mischa, Martin Klimke, and Anne Kuhlmann. *Germany and the Black Diaspora: Points of Contact, 1250–1914*. New York: Berghahn Books, 2013.

Hopkins, A.G., ed. *Globalization in World History*. London: Pimlico, 2002.

Horstmann, Johannes, ed. *Die Verschränkung von Innen-, Konfessions- und Kolonialpolitik im Deutschen Reich vor 1914*. Paderborn: Katholische Akademie Schwerte, 1987.

Houlihan, Patrick J. "Local Catholicism as Transnational War Experience." *Central European History* 45(2): 233–67.

Hübinger, Gangolf. *Kulturprotestantismus und Politik: Zum Verhältnis von Liberalismus und Protestantismus im Wilhelminischen Deutschland*. Tübingen: J.C.B. Mohr (P. Siebeck), 1994.

Hull, Isabel V. *The Entourage of Kaiser Wilhelm II, 1888–1918*. Cambridge, UK: Cambridge University Press, 1982.

– *Absolute Destruction: Military Culture and the Practices of War in Imperial Germany*. Ithaca, NY: Cornell University Press, 2005.

Hutton, J.E. *A History of Moravian Missions*. London: Moravian Publication Office, [1922].

Iliffe, John. *A Modern History of Tanganyika*. Cambridge, UK: Cambridge University Press, 1979.

– *Honour in African History*. Cambridge, UK: Cambridge University Press, 2005.

Iriye, Akira. *Cultural Internationalism and World Order*. Baltimore, MD: Johns Hopkins University Press, 1997.

Ishay, Micheline R. *Internationalism and Its Betrayal*. Minneapolis: University of Minnesota Press, 1995.

Jaeger, Jens. "Colony as *Heimat*? The Formation of Colonial Identity in Germany around 1900." *German History* 27(4): 467–89.

Jandl, Paul. "Vom Nutzen und Nachteil der Schriftsprache für die Einheimischen – Überlegungen zur Funktion und Gestaltung kolonialer und aktueller Schulbücher in Westafrika." In Wagner, 393–9.

Jasper, Gerhard. *Das Werden der Bethel-Mission*. Bethel bei Bielefeld: Anstalt Bethel, 1936.

Jefferies, Matthew. *Contesting the German Empire, 1871–1918*. Malden, MA: Blackwell Publishing, 2008.

Jensz, Felicity, and Hanna Acke, eds. *Missions and Media: The Politics of Missionary Periodicals in the Long Nineteenth Century*. Stuttgart: Franz Steiner Verlag, 2013.

Jeyaraj, Daniel. "Mission Reports from South India and Their Impact on the Western Mind: The Tranquebar Mission of the Eighteenth Century." In Robert, 21–42.

Jobst, Kerstin S. *Zwischen Nationalismus und Internationalismus: Die polnische und ukrainische Sozialdemokratie in Galizien von 1890 bis 1914: Ein Beitrag zur*

Nationalitätenfrage im Habsburgerreich. Hamburg: Dölling und Galitz Verlag, 1996.

Johnston, Anna. *Missionary Writing and Empire, 1800–1860*. Cambridge, UK: Cambridge University Press, 2003.

Jones, Neannette Eileen. "'On the Brain of the Negro': Race, Abolitionism, and Friedrich Tiedemann's Scientific Discourse on the African Diaspora." In Honeck, Klimke, and Kuhlmann, 133–52.

Junge, Peter. *Bibliographie deutscher Kolonialzeitschriften*. Bremen: Übersee-Museum, 1985.

Kaniki, M.H.Y., ed. *Tanzania under Colonial Rule*. London: Longman Group Limited, 1980.

Kasdorf, Hans. *Gustav Warnecks missiologisches Erbe: Eine biographisch-historische Untersuchung*. Giessen, Switzerland: Brunnen Verlag, 1990.

– "The Legacy of Gustav Warneck." *International Bulletin of Mission Research* 4(3): 102–7.

– "Zu Gustav Warnecks Bedeutung für Theologie und Kirche (unter besonderer Berücksichtigung der Missionskonferenzen)." In Becker and Feldtkeller, 23–49.

Kidd, Colin. *The Forging of Races: Race and Scripture in the Protestant Atlantic World, 1600–2000*. Cambridge, UK: Cambridge University Press, 2006.

Kirchner, Joachim. *Das deutsche Zeitschriftenwesen: Seine Geschichte und seine Probleme*, vol. 2. Wiesbaden: Otto Harrassowitz, 1962.

Klein, Thoralf. "The Other German Colonialism: Power, Conflict, and Resistance in a German-Speaking Mission in China, ca. 1850–1920." In *German Colonialism Revisited: African, Asian, and Oceanic Experiences*, edited by Nina Berman, Klaus Mühlhahn, and Patrice Nganang, 161–78. Ann Arbor: University of Michigan Press, 2014.

Knoll, Arthur J. *Togo under Imperial Germany, 1884–1914: A Case Study in Colonial Rule*. Stanford, CA: Hoover Institution Press, 1978.

Kolowa, Sebastian Ignatius. *The Impact of the Christian Church in Tanzania: 1885–1985*. [Arusha, Tanzania?]: Makumira Publications, 1991.

Konrad, Dagmar. *Missionsbräute: Pietistinnen des 19. Jahrhunderts in der Basler Mission*. Münster: Waxmann, 2001.

Koponen, Juhani. "Knowledge, Power and History: German Colonial Studies in Tanzania." In van der Heyden and von Oppen, 118–35.

Koskenniemi, Martti. *The Gentle Civilizer of Nations: The Rise and Fall of International Law, 1870–1960*. Cambridge, UK: Cambridge University Press, 2002.

Kratzenstein, Ed[uard]. *Kurze Geschichte der Berliner Mission*. Berlin: Seblstverhandlung des Missionshauses, 1878.

Krethlow, Carl Alexander. *Der Malteserorden: Wandel, Internationalität und soziale Vernetzung im 19. Jahrhundert*. Bern: Peter Lang, 2001.

Krüger, Gesine. *Kriegsbewältigung und Geschichtsbewußtsein: Realität, Deutung und Verarbeitung des deutschen Kolonialkrieges in Namibia 1904 bis 1907*. Göttingen: Vandenhoeck & Ruprecht, 1999.

Kuklick, Henrika. *The Savage Within: The Social History of British Anthropology, 1885–1945*. Cambridge, UK: Cambridge University Press, 1991.

–, ed. *A New History of Anthropology*. Malden, MA: Blackwell Publishing, 2008.

Kundrus, Birthe. *Moderne Imperialisten: Das Kaiserreich im Spiegel seiner Kolonien*. Cologne: Böhlau Verlag, 2003.

Lamberti, Marjorie. *State, Society, and the Elementary School in Imperial Germany*. Oxford, UK: Oxford University Press, 1989.

Landau, Paul S. "Language." In Etherington, *Missions and Empire*, 194–215.

– *The Realm of the Word: Language, Gender, and Christianity in a Southern African Kingdom*. Portsmouth, NH: Heinemann, 1995.

– *Popular Politics in the History of South Africa, 1400–1948*. Cambridge, UK: Cambridge University Press, 2010.

Latourette, Kenneth Scott. *A History of the Expansion of Christianity*. 7 vols. New York: Harper, 1937–1945.

–. *Christianity in a Revolutionary Age: A History of Christianity in the Nineteenth and Twentieth Centuries*. 5 vols. New York: Harper, 1958–1962.

–. "Ecumenical Bearings of the Missionary Movement and the International Missionary Council." In *A History of the Ecumenical Movement*, edited by Ruth Rouse and Stephen Charles Neill, 353–402. Philadelphia: Westminster Press, 1968.

Lawrance, Benjamin Nicholas. "Most Obedient Servants: The Politics of Language in German Colonial Togo." *Cahiers d'Études Africaines* 40(159): 489–524.

Lehmann, Hartmut. "Missionaries without Empire: German Protestant Missionary Efforts in the Interwar Period (1919–1939)." In Stanley, *Missions, Nationalism, and the End of Empire*, 34–53.

Lentz, Sarah. "Abolitionists in the German Hinterland? Therese Huber and the Spread of Anti-Slavery Sentiment in the German Territories in the Early Nineteenth Century." In Brahm and Rosenhaft, 187–211.

Lermann, Katherine Anne. "Bismarckian Germany." In Retallack, 18–39.

Lester, Alan. *Imperial Networks: Creating Identities in Nineteenth-Century South Africa and Britain*. London: Routledge, 2001.

Leuger-Scherzberg, August Hermann. *Felix Porsch 1853–1930: Politik für katholische Interessen in Kaiserreich und Republik*. Mainz: Matthias-Grünewald-Verlag, 1990.

Levinger, Matthew. *Enlightened Nationalism: The Transformation of Prussian Political Culture, 1806–1848*. Oxford, UK: Oxford University Press, 2002.

Liebersohn, Harry. "Coming of Age in the Pacific: German Ethnography from Chamisso to Krämer." In Penny and Bunzl, 31–46.

Linden, Ian. *Global Catholicism: Diversity and Change since Vatican II*. New York: Columbia University Press, 2009.

Loth, Heinrich. *Kolonialismus unter der Kutte*. Berlin: Dietz Verlag, 1960.

– *Zwischen Gott und Kattun: die Berliner Konferenz 1884/85 zur Aufteilung Afrikas und die Kolonialismuskritik christlicher Mission*. Berlin: Union Verlag, 1985.

Loth, Wilfried. *Katholiken im Kaiserreich: Der politische Katholizismus in der Krise des wilhelminischen Deutschlands*. Düsseldorf: Droste Verlag, 1984.

–, ed. *Deutscher Katholizismus im Umbruch zur Moderne*. Stuttgart: Verlag W. Kohlhammer, 1991.

Lower, Wendy. *Nazi Empire-Building and the Holocaust in Ukraine*. Chapel Hill: University of North Carolina Press, 2005.

Lowry, John S. *Big Swords, Jesuits, and Bondelswarts: Wilhelmine Imperialism, Overseas Resistance, and German Political Catholicism, 1897–1906*. Leiden: Brill, 2015.

Marchand, Suzanne. *German Orientalism in the Age of Empire: Religion, Race, and Scholarship*. Washington, DC: German Historical Institute and Cambridge University Press, 2009.

– "Orientalism as *Kulturpolitik*: German Archaeology and Cultural Imperialism in Asia Minor." In Stocking, 298–336.

Marchand, Suzanne, and David Lindenfeld, eds. *Germany at the Fin de Siècle: Culture, Politics, and Ideas*. Baton Rouge: Louisiana State University Press, 2004.

McMeekin, Sean. *The Berlin-Baghdad Express: The Ottoman Empire and Germany's Bid for World Power*. Cambridge, MA: Belknap Press of Harvard University Press, 2010.

Menzel, Gustav. *Die Bethel-Mission: Aus 100 Jahren Missionsgeschichte*. Neukirchen-Vluyn, Germany: Neukirchener Verlag des Erziehungsvereins, 1986.

– *C.G. Büttner: Missionar, Sprachforscher und Politiker in der deutschen Kolonialbewegung*. Wuppertal: Verlag der Vereinigten Evangelischen Mission, 1992.

Meyer, Birgit. "Christianity and the Ewe Nation: German Pietist Missionaries, Ewe Converts and the Politics of Culture." *Journal of Religion in Africa* 32(2): 167–99.

– *Translating the Devil: Religion and Modernity among the Ewe in Ghana*. Trenton, NJ: Africa World Press, 1999.

Miers, Suzanne, and Igor Kopytoff. "African 'Slavery' as an Institution of Marginality." In *Slavery in Africa: Historical and Anthropological Perspectives*, edited by Miers and Kopytoff, 3–84. Madison: University of Wisconsin Press, 1977.

Milner, Susan. *The Dilemmas of Internationalism: French Syndicalism and the International Labour Movement, 1900–1914*. New York: Berg, 1990.

Mirtschink, Bernhard. *Zur Rolle christlicher Mission in kolonialen Gesellschaften: Katholische Missionserziehung in "Deutsch-Ostafrika."* Frankfurt-am-Main: Haag + Herchen Verlag, 1980.

Mogk, Walter. *Paul Rohrbach und das "Größere Deutschland": Ethischer Imperialismus im Wilhelminischen Zeitalter*. Munich: Wilhelm Goldmann Verlag, 10972.

Mohr, Hubert. *Katholische Orden und Deutscher Imperialismus*. Berlin: Akademie-Verlag, 1965.

Mombauer, Annika. *The Origins of the First World War: Controversies and Consensus*. New York: Longman, 2002.

Moritzen, Niels-Peter. "Koloniale Konzepte der protestantischen Mission." In Bade, 51–67.

– *Werkzeug Gottes in der Welt: Leipziger Mission 1836–1936–1986*. Erlangen: Verlag für Mission und Ökumene, 1986.

Moses, A. Dirk. "Conceptual Blockages and Definitional Dilemmas in the 'Racial Century': Genocides of Indigenous Peoples and the Holocaust." *Patterns of Prejudice* 36(2002): 7–36.

Mosse, George L. *Toward the Final Solution: A History of European Racism*. Madison: University of Wisconsin Press, 1985.

Moyd, Michelle R. *Violent Intermediaries: African Soldiers, Conquest, and Everyday Colonialism in German East Africa*. Athens: Ohio University Press, 2014.

Müller, Karl. *Missionstheologie: Eine Einführung*. Berlin: Dietrich Reimer Verlag, 1985.

Nairn, Tom. *The Break-up of Britain: Crisis and Neo-nationalism*. London: NLB, 1977.

Naranch, Bradley D. "'Colonized Body,' 'Oriental Machine': Debating Race, Railroads, and the Politics of Reconstruction in Germany and East Africa, 1906–1910." *Central European History* 33(3): 299–338.

Naranch, Bradley D., and Geoff Eley, eds. *German Colonialism in a Global Age*. Durham, NC: Duke University Press, 2014.

Neill, Deborah. "Germans and Transnational Activism: The Colonial Anti-Alcoholism Movements, 1885–1914." Paper presented at the annual meeting of the German Studies Association, San Diego, CA, 7 October 2007.

Neill, Stephen. *Colonialism and Christian Missions*. New York: McGraw-Hill, 1966.

Nelson, Bruce. *Irish Nationalists and the Making of the Irish Race*. Princeton, NJ: Princeton University Press, 2012.

Neß, Dietmar. *Schlesisches Pfarrerbuch*, Bd. 8: Regierungsbezirk Liegnitz, Teil III. Lepizig: Evangelische Verlagsanstalt, 2016.

Niesel, Hans-Joachim. "Für Kreuz und Krone: Die deutschen Missionen im Kriegsgebiet." In Becker and Beez, 100–12.

– "Kolonialverwaltung und Missionen in Deutsch-Ostafrika 1890–1914." PhD diss., Freie Universität Berlin, 1971.

– "Kolonialverwaltung und Missionen in Deutsch-Ostafrika zur Zeit des Maji-Maji-Aufstandes 1905–1907." In *Mit Zauberwasser gegen Gewehrkugeln: Der Maji-Maji-Aufstand in ehemaligen Deutsch-Ostafrika vor 100 Jahren*, edited by Hans-Martin Hinz, Hans-Joachim Niesel, and Almut Nothangle, 77–87. Frankfurt-am-Main: Otto Lembeck, 2006.

Nickles, Bruno W. *Soziale Hilfe am Bahnhof: Zur Geschichte der Bahnhofsmission in Deutschland (1894–1960)*. Freiburg: Lambertus, 1994.

Nipperdey, Thomas. *Religion im Umbruch: Deutschland 1870–1918*. Munich: C.H. Beck, 1988.

– *Deutsche Geschichte*. Vol. 1, *Arbeitswelt und Bürgergeist*. Munich: C.H. Beck, 1990–2.

– *Gesellschaft, Kultur, Theorie: Gesammelte Aufsätze zur neueren Geschichte*. Munich: Vandenhoeck & Ruprecht, 1998.

Norris, Edward Graham. *Die Umerziehung des Afrikaners: Togo 1895–1938*. Munich: Trickster Wissenschaft, 1993.

Nuhn, Walter. *Flammen über Deutschost: Der Maji-Maji-Aufstand in Deutsch-Ostafrika, 1905–1906: die erste gemeinsame Erhebung schwarzafrikanischer Völker gegen weisse Kolonialherrschaft: ein Beitrag zur deutschen Kolonialgeschichte*. Bonn: Bernard & Graefe, 1998.

Nurse, Derek, and Thomas J. Hinnebusch. *Swahili and Sabaki: A Linguistic History*. Edited by Thomas J. Hinnebusch. Berkeley: University of California Press, 1993.

Nzalayaimisi, Gabriel K. "The Berliners and Violence in Eastern and Southern Tanzania, 1887–1919." In van der Heyden and Becher, 469–80.

Oelke, Heinrich Julius. *Als Missionar in Ostafrika: Erinnerungen aus den Jahren 1905–1959*. Edited by Ulrich van der Heyden. Bremen: Edition Falkenberg, 2014.

Oermann, Nils Ole. "'Hochverehrter Herr Gouverneur' – Zum Verhältnis von Mission und deutschen Kolonialstaat im Zeitalter des Imperialismus." In Bogner, Holtwick, and Tyrell, 589–611.

– *Mission, Church, and State Relations in South-West Africa under German Rule, 1884–1915*. Stuttgart: Franz Steiner Verlag, 1999.

Öhler, Wilhelm, *Geschichte der deutschen evangelischen Mission*. Baden-Baden: W. Fehrholz, [1949–1951].

Oliver, Roland. *The Missionary Factor in East Africa*. London: Longmans, Green and Co., 1952.

Orosz, Kenneth J. *Religious Conflict and the Evolution of Language Policy in German and French Cameroon, 1885–1939*. New York: Peter Lang, 2008.

Osterhammel, Jürgen. *Die Verwandlung der Welt: Eine Geschichte des 19. Jahrhunderts*. Munich: C.H. Beck, 2009.

Owzar, Armin. "Protestantism, Catholicism and Islam in German East Africa." In Dujardin and Prudhomme, 355–70.

Pakendorf, Gunther. "Berlin in Afrika, oder der historische Ort der deutschen Mission: Ein Beitrag zum Thema Kolonialmission." In Wagner, 472–91.

Paton, William. "The Jerusalem Meeting – and After." *International Review of Missions* 17(3): 435–44.

Pawliková-Vilhanová, Viera. "Crescent or Cross? Islam and Christian Missions in Nineteenth-Century East and Central Africa." In van der Heyden and Becher, 79–96.

Penny, H. Glenn. "Bastian's Museum: On the Limits of Empiricism and the Transformation of German Ethnology." In Penny and Bunzl, 86–126.

– *Objects of Culture: Ethnology and Ethnographic Museums in Imperial Germany*. Chapel Hill: University of North Carolina Press, 2002.

Penny, H. Glenn, and Matti Bunzl, eds. *Worldly Provincialism: German Anthropology in the Age of Empire*. Ann Arbor: University of Michigan Press, 2003.

Perras, Anne. "Colonial Agitation and the Bismarckian State: The Case of Carl Peters." In *Wilhelminism and Its Legacies: German Modernities, Imperialism, and the Meanings of Reform, 1890–1930*, edited by Geoff Eley and James Retallack, 154–70. New York: Berghahn Books, 2003.

Pesek, Michael. *Koloniale Herrschaft in Deutsch-Ostafrika: Expeditionen, Militär und Verwaltung seint 1880*. Frankfurt-am-Main: Campus, 2005.

– "Kreuz oder Halbmond? Die deutsche Kolonialpolitik zwischen Pragmatismus und Paranoia in Deutsch-Ostafrika 1908-1914." In van der Heyden and Becher, 97–112.

Peter, Chris M. "Imperialism and Export of Capital: A Survey of Foreign Private Investments in Tanzania during the German Colonial Period." *Journal of Asian and African Studies* 25(3–4): 197–212.

Pierard, Richard. "The German Colonial Society, 1882–1914." PhD diss., University of Iowa, 1964.

– "The German Colonial Society." In *Germans in the Tropics: Essays in German Colonial History*, edited by Arthur J. Knoll and Lewis H. Gann, 19–38. New York: Greenwood, 1987.

– "The Rhenish Mission and the Colonial War in German Southwest Africa." In van der Heyden and Stoecker, 389–401.

Poewe, Karla. *The Namibian Herero: A History of Their Psychosocial Disintegration and Survival*. Lewiston, NY: Edwin Mellen Press, 1985.

– "The Spell of National Socialism: The Berlin Mission's Opposition to, and Compromise with, the *Völkisch* Movement and National Socialism: Knak, Braun, and Weichert." In van der Heyden and Becher, 268–90.

Pogge von Strandmann, Hartmut. *Imperialismus vom Grünen Tisch: Deutsche Kolonialpolitik zwischen wirtschaftlicher Ausbeutung und "zivilisatorischen" Bemühungen*. Berlin: Links, 2009.

– "The Kolonialrat and the Missionary Societies." In van der Heyden and Stoecker, 37–50.

Porter, Andrew, ed. *The Imperial Horizons of British Protestant Missions, 1880–1914*. Grand Rapids, MI: Wm. B. Eerdmans Publishing Company, 2003.

– *Religion versus Empire? British Protestant Missionaries and Overseas Expansion, 1700–1914*. Manchester: Manchester University Press, 2004.

Pratt, Mary Louise. *Imperial Eyes: Travel Writing and Transculturation*. London: Routledge, 1992.

Price, Richard. *Making Empire: Colonial Encounters and the Creation of Imperial Rule in Nineteenth-Century Africa*. Cambridge, UK: Cambridge University Press, 2008.

Przyrembel, Alexandra. "The Emotional Bond of Brotherliness: Protestant Masculinity and the Local and Global Networks among Religious in the Nineteenth Century." *German History* 31(2): 157–80.

Pugach, Sara. *Africa in Translation: A History of Colonial Linguistics in Germany and Beyond, 1814–1945*. Ann Arbor: University of Michigan Press, 2012.

Purvis, Zachary. *Theology and the University in Nineteenth-Century Germany*. Oxford, UK: Oxford University Press, 2016.

Quick, Oliver Chase. "The Jerusalem Meeting and the Christian Message." *International Review of Missions* 17(3): 445–54.

Raabe, Heribert. "Zur Geschichte und Bedeutung des Schlagwortes "Ultramontan" im 18. und 19. Jahrhundert." *Historisches Jahrbuch* 81(1962): 159–73.

Ranger, Terence. *Dance and Society in Eastern Africa, 1890–1970: The* Beni ngoma. Berkeley: University of California Press, 1975.

– "The Invention of Tradition in Colonial Africa." In *The Invention of Tradition*, edited by Eric Hobsbawm and Terence Ranger, 211–62. Cambridge, UK: Cambridge University Press, 1983.

– "Godly Medicine: The Ambiguities of Medical Mission in Southeastern Tanzania, 1900–1945." In *The Social Basis of Health and Healing in Africa*, edited by Steven Feierman and John M. Janzen, 256–82. Berkeley: University of California Press, 1992.

Ranger, T.O., and Isaria N. Kimambo. *The Historical Study of African Religion*. Berkeley: University of California Press, 1972.

Reagin, Nancy R. "'A True Woman Can Take Care of Herself': The Debate over Prostitution in Hanover, 1900." *Central European History* 24(4): 347–80.

Rennstich, Karl. "The Understanding of Mission, Civilisation and Colonialism in the Basel Mission." In Christensen and Hutchison, 93–101.

Retallack, James, ed. *Imperial Germany, 1871–1918*. Oxford, UK: Oxford University Press, 2008.

Ribbe, Wolfgang. "Zur Entwicklung und Funktion der Pfarrgemeinden in der evangelischen Kirche Berlins bis zum Ende der Monarchie." In *Seelsorge und*

Diakonie in Berlin: Beiträge zum Verhältnis von Kirche und Großstadt im 19. und beginnenden 20. Jahrhundert, edited by Kaspar Elm and Hans-Dietrich Loock, 233–63. Berlin: Walter de Gruyter, 1990.

Richter, J[ulius]. *Geschichte der Berliner Missionsgesellschaft*. Berlin: Berlin ev. Missionsgesellschaft, 1924.

– *Allgemeine evangelische Missionsgeschichte*. 5 vols. Gütersloh: C. Bertelsmann, 1908–1932.

Robert, Dana, ed. *Converting Colonialism: Visions and Realities in Mission History, 1706–1914*. Grand Rapids, MI: William B. Eerdmans Publishing Company, 2008.

Rodgers, Daniel T. *Atlantic Crossings: Social Politics in a Progressive Age*. Cambridge, MA: Belknap Press, 1998.

Rodney, Walter. "The Political Economy of Colonial Tanganyika 1890–1930." In Kaniki, 130–9.

Röhl, John C.G. *The Kaiser and His Court: Wilhelm II and the Government of Germany*. Cambridge, UK: Cambridge University Press, 1994.

– *Wilhelm II: The Kaiser's Personal Monarchy, 1888–1900*. Cambridge, UK: Cambridge University Press, 2004.

Ross, Ronald J. *Beleaguered Tower: The Dilemma of Political Catholicism in Wilhelmine Germany*. Notre Dame, IN: University of Notre Dame Press, 1976.

– *The Failure of Bismarck's* Kulturkampf*: Catholicism and State Power in Imperial Germany, 1871–1887*. Washington, DC: Catholic University of America Press, 1998.

Rothfels, Nigel. *Savages and Beasts: The Birth of the Modern Zoo*. Baltimore, MD: Johns Hopkins University Press, 2002.

Ruhbach, Gerhard. "Die Religionspolitik Friedrich Wilhelms III. von Preußen." In *Bleibendes im Wandel der Kirchengeschichte: Kirchenhistorische Studien*, edited by Bernd Moeller and Gerhard Ruhbach, 307–30. Tübingen: J.C.B. Mohr (Paul Siebeck), 1973.

Rzepkowski, Horst. "Gustav Warneck und die katholische Missionswissenschaft." In Becker and Feltdkeller, 55–86.

Salter, Mark B. *Rights of Passage: The Passport in International Relations*. Boulder, CO: Lynne Rienner Publishers, 2003.

Sanneh, Lamin. *West African Christianity: The Religious Impact*. Maryknoll, NY: Orbis Books, 1983.

Schatz, Klaus. *Zwischen Säkularisation und Zweitem Vatikanum: Der Weg des deutschen Katholizismus im 19. und 20. Jahrhundert*. Frankfurt: Verlag Josef Knecht, 1986.

Scheulen, Peter. *Die "Eingeborenen" Deutsch-Südwestafrika: Ihr Bild in deutschen Kolonialzeitschriften von 1884 bis 1918*. Cologne: Rüdiger Köppe Verlag, 1998.

Schmidt, Heike. "(Re)Negotiating Marginality: The Maji Maji War and Its Aftermath in Southwestern Tanzania, ca. 1905–1916." *International Journal of African Historical Studies* 43(1); 27–62.

Schmidt, Wolfgang. *Mission, Kirche und Reich Gottes bei Friedrich Fabri.* Wuppertal-Barmen: Verlag der Rheinischen Mission, 1965.

Schmuhl, Hans-Walter. *Friedrich von Bodelschwingh.* Reinbek bei Hamburg: Rowohlt Verlag, 2005.

Scholle, Manfred. *Die Preußische Strafjustiz im Kulturkampf 1873–1880.* Marburg: Elwert, 1974.

Schulze, Adolf. *200 Jahre Brüdermission.* 2 vols. Herrnhut: Verlag der Missionsbuchhandlung, 1932.

Schulze, Frederik. *Auswanderung als nationalistisches Projekt: 'Deutschtum' und Kolonialdiskurse im südlichen Brasilien (1824–1941).* Cologne: Böhlau Verlag, 2016.

Scott, Jamie S. "Cultivating Christians in Colonial Canadian Missions." In *Canadian Missionaries, Indigenous Peoples: Representing Religion at Home and Abroad,* edited by Jamie S. Scott and Alvyn Austen, 21–45. Toronto: University of Toronto Press, 2005.

Seeberg, Karl-Martin. *Der Maji-Maji-Krieg gegen die deutsche Kolonialherrschaft.* Berlin: D. Reimer, 1989.

Sheriff, Abdul. "Economy and Society in East Africa in the Nineteenth and Twentieth Centuries with Special Reference to Tanzania." In van der Heyden and von Oppen, 12–19.

Short, John Phillip. *Magic Lantern Empire: Colonialism and Society in Germany.* Ithaca, NY: Cornell University Press, 2012.

Sippel, Harald. "Aspects of Colonial Land Law in German East Africa: German East Africa Company, Crown Land Ordinance, European Plantations and Reserved Areas for Africans." In Debusmann and Arnold, 3–32.

– "Mission und Gewalt in Deutsch-Ostafrika: Das Verhältnis zwischen Mission und Kolonialverwaltung." In van der Heyden and Becher, 525–38.

– "Mission und Kodifikation: Der missionarische Beitrag zur Erforschung des afrikanischen Gewohnheitsrecht in der Kolonie Deutsch-Ostafrika." In Wagner, 493–510.

Smith, Helmut Walser. "An Preußens Rändern oder: Die Welt, die dem Nationalismus verloren ging." In Conrad and Osterhammel, 149–69.

– *German Nationalism and Religious Conflict: Culture, Ideology and Religious Conflict, 1870–1914.* Princeton, NJ: Princeton University Press, 1995.

– *The Continuities of German History: Nation, Religion, and Race across the Long Nineteenth Century.* Cambridge, UK: Cambridge University Press, 2008.

– "The Talk of Genocide, the Rhetoric of Miscegenation: Notes on Debates in the German Reichstag concerning Southwest Africa, 1904–14." In Friedrichsmayer, Lennox, and Zantop, 107–24.

Smith, Woodruff D. *The German Colonial Empire*. Chapel Hill: University of North Carolina Press, 1978.

– *The Ideological Origins of Nazi Imperialism*. Oxford, UK: Oxford University Press, 1986.

Snyder, Edward. "Eugenics and Protestant Social Thought in the Weimar Republic: Friedrich von Bodelschwingh and the Bethel Institutions." In *The German Right in the Weimar Republic: Studies in the History of German Conservatism, Nationalism, and Antisemitism*, edited by Larry Eugene Jones, 244–67. New York: Berghahn Books, 2014.

Sperber, Jonathan. *Popular Catholicism in Nineteenth-century Germany*. Princeton, NJ: Princeton University Press, 1984.

Spevack, Edmund. "Charles Follen's View of Republicanism in Germany and the United States, 1815-1840." In *Republicanism and Liberalism in America and the German States, 1750-1850*, edited by Jürgen Heideking and James A. Henretta, 235-259. Washington, DC: German Historical Institute and Cambridge University Press, 2002.

Spidle, Jake Wilton. "The German Colonial Civil Service: Organization, Selection, and Training." PhD diss., Stanford University, 1972.

Spindler, Marc, "The Protestant Mission Study: Emergence and Features." In Dujardin and Prudhomme, 39-52.

Stanley, Brian. *The Bible and Flag: Protestant Missionaries and British Imperialism in the Nineteenth and Twentieth Centuries*. Leicester: Apollos, 1990.

– "Church, State, and the Hierarchy of 'Civilization': The Making of 'Missions and Governments' Report at the World Missionary Conference, Edinburgh 1910." In Porter, 58–84.

– "Edinburgh and World Christianity." *Studies in World Christianity* 17(1): 72–91.

– *The World Missionary Conference, Edinburgh 1910*. Grand Rapids, MI: William B. Eerdmans Publishing Company, 2009.

Steinmetz, George. *The Devil's Handwriting: Precoloniality and the German Colonial State in Qingdao, Samoa and Southwest Africa*. Chicago: University of Chicago Press, 2007.

Stern, Fritz. *The Politics of Cultural Despair: A Study in the Rise of the Germanic Ideology*. Berkeley: University of California Press, 1961.

Stocking, George W., Jr. *Victorian Anthropology*. New York: The Free Press, 1987.

–, ed. Volksgeist *as Method and Ethic: Essays on Boasian Ethnography and the German Anthropological Tradition*. History of Anthropology 8. Madison: University of Wisconsin Press, 1994.

Streets, Heather. *Martial Races: The Military, Race, and Masculinity in British Imperial Culture, 1857–1914*. Manchester: Manchester University Press, 2004.

Summers, Carol. *From Civilization to Segregation: Social Ideals and Social Control in Southern Rhodesia, 1890–1934*. Athens: Ohio University Press, 1994.

–. *Colonial Lessons: Africans' Education in Southern Rhodesia, 1918–1940*. Portsmouth, NH: Heinemann, 2002.

Sunseri, Thaddeus. "The *Baumwollfrage*: Cotton Colonialism in German East Africa." *Central European History* 34(1): 31–51.

– "'Dispersing the Fields': Railway Labor and Rural Change in Early Colonial Tanzania." *Canadian Journal of African Studies* 32(3): 558–83.

– "Slave Ransoming in German East Africa, 1885–922." *International Journal of African Historical Studies* 26(3): 481–511.

Tetzlaff, Rainer. "Die Mission im Spannungsfeld zwischen kolonialer Herrschaft und Zivilisierungsanspruch in Deutsch-Ostafrika." In Bade, 189–204.

– *Koloniale Entwicklung und Ausbeutung: Wirtschafts- und Sozialgeschichte Deutsch-Ostafrikas 1885-1914*. Berlin: Duncker & Humblot, 1970.

Ther, Philipp. "Deutshe Geschichte als imperial Geschichte: Polen, slawophone Minderheiten und das Kaiserreich als kontinentales Empire." In Conrad and Osterhammel, 129–48.

Thorne, Susan. *Congregational Missions and the Making of an Imperial Culture in Nineteenth-Century England*. Stanford, CA: Stanford University Press, 1999.

Torp, Claudius. "Missionary Education and Musical Communities in Sub-Saharan Colonial Africa." *Itinerario* 41(2): 235–51.

Trentmann, Frank, ed. *Paradoxes of Civil Society: New Perspectives on Modern German and British History*. New York: Berghahn Books, 2000.

Twells, Alison. *The Civilising Mission and the English Middle Class, 1792–1850: The "Heathen" at Home and Oveseas*. New York: Palgrave Macmillan, 2009.

Unangst, Matthew. "Men of Science and Action: The Celebrity of Explorers and German National Identity, 1870–1895." *Central European History* 50(2017): 305–27.

Ustorf, Werner, ed. *Mission im Kontext: Beiträge zur Sozialgeschichte der Norddeutschen Missionsgesellschaft im 19. Jahrhundert*. Bremen: Übersee Museum Bremen, 1986.

Utrecht, E. *Meyers Orts- und Verkehrs-Lexicon des Deutschen Reichs*. Leipzig: Bibliographisces Institut, 1913.

van der Heyden, Ulrich. "Alexander Merenskys Beitrag zur ethnographischen und historischen Erforschung der Völkerschaften Südafrikas." *Ethnographisch-Archäologische Zeitschrift* 32(1991): 263–8.

– "Zu den politischen Hintergründen der Njassa-Expedition von Alexander Merensky." In *Mit Kreuz und deutscher Flagge: 100 Jahre Evangelium im Süden*

Tanzanias Zum Wirken der Berliner Mission in Ostafrika, edited by Winfried Brose and Ulrich van der Heyden, 89–95. Münster: Lit Verlag, 1993.
– "Christian Missionary Societies in the German Colonies, 1884/85–1914/15." In *German Colonialism: Race, the Holocaust, and Postwar Germany*, edited by Volker Langbehn and Mohammad Salama, 215–53. New York: Columbia University Press, 2011.
– "Die Kolonial- und die Transvaal Ausstellung 1896/97." In van der Heyden and Zeller, 135–42.
van der Heyden, Ulrich, and Jürgen Becher, eds. *Mission und Gewalt: Der Umgang christlicher Missionen mit Gewalt und die Ausbreitung des Christentums in Afrika und Asien*. Stuttgart: Franz Steiner Verlag, 2000.
van der Heyden, Ulrich, and Achim von Oppen. *Tanzania: Koloniale Vergangenheit und neuer Aufbruch*. Münster: Lit, 1996.
van der Heyden, Ulrich, and Helmut Stoecker, eds. *Mission und Macht im Wandel politischer Orientierungen: europäische Missionsgesellschaften in politischen Spannungsfeldern in Afrika und Asien zwischen 1800 und 1945*. Stuttgart: Franz Steiner, 2005.
van der Heyden, Ulrich, and Joachim Zeller, eds. *Kolonialmetropole Berlin: Eine Spurensuche*. Berlin: Berlin Edition, 2002.
van Laak, Dirk. *Imperiale Infrastrucktur: Deutsche Planungen für eine Erschließung Afrikas 1880 bis 1960*. Paderborn: Ferdinand Schöningh, 2004.
Vansina, Jan. *Antecedents to Modern Rwanda: The Nyiginya Kingdom*. Madison: University of Wisconsin Press, 2004.
Verhey, Jeffrey. *The Spirit of 1914: Militarism, Myth, and Mobilization in Germany*. Cambridge, UK: Cambridge University Press, 2000.
Vick, Brian. *Defining Germany: The 1848 Frankfurt Parliamentarians and National Identity*. Cambridge, MA: Harvard University Press, 2002.
Wagner, Wilfried, ed. *Kolonien und Missionen: Referate des 3. Internationalen Kolonialgeschichtlichen Symposiums 1993 in Bremen*. Münster: Lit, 1994.
Walkenhorst, Peter. *Nation – Volk – Rasse: Radikaler Nationalismus im Deutschen Kaiserreich*. Göttingen: Vandenhoeck & Ruprecht, 2007.
Wangemann, [Theodor]. *Geschichte der Berliner Missionsgesellschaft*. 4 vols. Berlin: Im Selbstverlag des Ev. Missionshauses in Berlin, 1872–7.
Wehler, Hans-Ulrich. *Bismarck und der Imperialismus*. Berlin: Kiepenheuer u. Witsch, 1969.
– *The German Empire, 1871–1918*. Translated by Kim Traynor. Dover, NH: Berg Publishers, 1985.
– *Deutsche Gesellschaftsgeschichte*. Vol. 2, *Von der Reformära bis zur industriellen und politischen "Deutschen Doppelrevolution," 1815–1845/49*. Munich: C.H. Beck, 1987.
Weindling, Paul. *Health, Race, and German Politics between National Unification and Nazism*. Cambridge, UK: Cambridge University Press, 1993.

Weiss, Holger. "Islam, Missionaries and Residents: The Attempt of the Basel Missionary Society to Establish a Mission in Yendi (German Togo) before WWI." In van der Heyden and Stoecker, 173–86.

Weiss, Otto. "Der Ultramontanismus: Grundlagen – Vorgeschichte – Struktur." *Zeitschrift für bayerische Landesgeschichte* 41: 821–77.

Weitz, Eric. *A Century of Genocide: Utopias of Race and Nation*. Princeton, NJ: Princeton University Press, 2005.

Wielandt, Ute, and Michael Kaschner. "Die Reichstagdebatten über den deutschen Kriegseinsatz in China: August Bebel und die 'Hunnenbriefe.'" In *Das deutsche Reich und der Boxeraufstand*, edited by Susann Kuß and Bernd Martin, 183–202. Munich: Iudicium, 2002.

Wildenthal, Lora. *German Women for Empire, 1884–1945*. Durham, NC: Duke University Press, 2001.

Williamson, George S. *The Longing for Myth in Germany: Religion and Aesthetic Culture from Romanticism to Nietzsche*. Chicago: University of Chicago Press, 2004.

Wolter, Stefanie. *Die Vermarktung des Fremden: Exotisimus und die Anfänge des Massenkonsums*. Frankfurt: Campus Verlag, 2004.

Wright, Marcia. *German Missions in Tanganyika, 1891–1941: Lutherans and Moravians in the Southern Highlands*. Oxford, UK: Oxford University Press, 1971.

Wu, Albert. *From Christ to Confucius: German Missionaries, Chinese Christians, and the Globalization of Christianity, 1860–1950*. New Haven, CT: Yale University Press, 2016.

– "The Quest for an 'Indigenous Church': German Missionaries, Chinese Christians, and the Indigenization Debates of the 1920s." *American Historical Review* 122(1): 85–114.

Zantop, Suzanne. *Colonial Fantasies: Conquest, Family, and Nation in Precolonial Germany, 1770–1870*. Durham, NC: Duke University Press, 1997.

Zimmerer, Jürgen. *Von Windhuk nach Auschwitz? Beiträge zum Verhältnis von Kolonialismus und Holocaust*. Münster: Lit Verlag, 2011.

Zimmerer, Jürgen, and Joachim Zeller. *Völkermord in Deutsch-Südwestafrika: der Kolonialkrieg (1904–1908) in Namibia und seine Folgen*. Berlin: Links, 2003.

Zimmerman, Andrew. *Anthropology and Antihumanism in Imperial Germany*. Chicago: University of Chicago Press, 2001.

– *Alabama in Africa: Booker T. Washington, the German Empire, and the Globalization of the New South*. Princeton, NJ: Princeton University Press, 2010.

– "Decolonizing Weber." *Postcolonial Studies* 9(1): 53–79.

– "'What Do You Really Want in German East Africa, *Herr Professor*?' Counterinsurgency and the Science Effect in Colonial Tanzania." *Comparative Studies in Society and History* 48(2): 419–61.

Zollmann, Jakob. *Koloniale Herrschaft und ihre Grenzen: Die Kolonialpolizei in Deutsch-Südwestafrika 1894–1915*. Göttingen: Vandenhoeck & Ruprecht, 2010.

Index

Note: Page numbers in *italics* indicate illustrative material

GERMAN AND EUROPEAN STUDIES

General Editor: Jennifer L. Jenkins

1 Emanuel Adler, Beverly Crawford, Federica Bicchi, and Rafaella Del Sarto, *The Convergence of Civilizations: Constructing a Mediterranean Region*
2 James Retallack, *The German Right, 1860–1920: Political Limits of the Authoritarian Imagination*
3 Silvija Jestrovic, *Theatre of Estrangement: Theory, Practice, Ideology*
4 Susan Gross Solomon, ed., *Doing Medicine Together: Germany and Russia between the Wars*
5 Laurence McFalls, ed., *Max Weber's "Objectivity" Revisited*
6 Robin Ostow, ed., *(Re)Visualizing National History: Museums and National Identities in Europe in the New Millennium*
7 David Blackbourn and James Retallack, eds., *Localism, Landscape, and the Ambiguities of Place: German-Speaking Central Europe, 1860–1930*
8 John Zilcosky, ed., *Writing Travel: The Poetics and Politics of the Modern Journey*
9 Angelica Fenner, *Race under Reconstruction in German Cinema: Robert Stemmle's Toxi*
10 Martina Kessel and Patrick Merziger, eds., *The Politics of Humour: Laughter, Inclusion, and Exclusion in the Twentieth Century*
11 Jeffrey K. Wilson, *The German Forest: Nature, Identity, and the Contestation of a National Symbol, 1871–1914*
12 David G. John, *Bennewitz, Goethe,* Faust: *German and Intercultural Stagings*
13 Jennifer Ruth Hosek, *Sun, Sex, and Socialism: Cuba in the German Imaginary*
14 Steven M. Schroeder, *To Forget It All and Begin Again: Reconciliation in Occupied Germany, 1944–1954*
15 Kenneth S. Calhoon, *Affecting Grace: Theatre, Subject, and the Shakespearean Paradox in German Literature from Lessing to Kleist*
16 Martina Kolb, *Nietzsche, Freud, Benn, and the Azure Spell of Liguria*
17 Hoi-eun Kim, *Doctors of Empire: Medical and Cultural Encounters between Imperial Germany and Meiji Japan*
18 J. Laurence Hare, *Excavating Nations: Archeology, Museums, and the German-Danish Borderlands*
19 Jacques Kornberg, *The Pope's Dilemma: Pius XII Faces Atrocities and Genocide in the Second World War*
20 Patrick O'Neill, *Transforming Kafka: Translation Effects*

21 John K. Noyes, *Herder: Aesthetics against Imperialism*
22 James Retallack, *Germany's Second Reich: Portraits and Pathways*
23 Laurie Marhoefer, *Sex and the Weimar Republic: German Homosexual Emancipation and the Rise of the Nazis*
24 Bettina Brandt and Daniel L. Purdy, eds., *China in the German Enlightenment*
25 Michael Hau, *Performance Anxiety: Sport and Work in Germany from the Empire to Nazism*
26 Celia Applegate, *The Necessity of Music: Variations on a German Theme*
27 Richard J. Golsan and Sarah M. Misemer, eds., *The Trial That Never Ends: Hannah Arendt's* Eichmann in Jerusalem *in Retrospect*
28 Lynne Taylor, *In the Children's Best Interests: Unaccompanied Children in American-Occupied Germany, 1945–1952*
29 Jennifer A. Miller, *Turkish Guest Workers in Germany: Hidden Lives and Contested Borders, 1960s to 1980s*
30 Amy Carney, *Marriage and Fatherhood in the Nazi SS*
31 Michael E. O'Sullivan, *Disruptive Power: Catholic Women, Miracles, and Politics in Modern Germany, 1918–1965*
32 Gabriel N. Finder and Alexander V. Prusin, *Justice behind the Iron Curtain: Nazis on Trial in Communist Poland*
33 Parker Daly Everett, *Urban Transformations: From Liberalism to Corporatism in Greater Berlin, 1871–1933*
34 Melissa Kravetz, *Women Doctors in Weimar and Nazi Germany: Maternalism, Eugenics, and Professional Identity*
35 Javier Samper Vendrell, *Seduction of Youth: Print Culture and Homosexual Rights in the Weimar Republic*
36 Sebastian Voigt, ed., *Since the Boom: Continuity and Change in the Western Industrialized World after 1970*
37 Olivia Landry, *Theatre of Anger: Radical Transnational Performance in Contemporary Berlin*
38 Jeremy Best, *Heavenly Fatherland: German Missionary Culture and Globalization in the Age of Empire*

www.ingramcontent.com/pod-product-compliance
Lightning Source LLC
LaVergne TN
LVHW040152080826
844660LV00014B/933/J

* 9 7 8 1 4 8 7 5 0 5 6 3 9 *